SCRIPTURE POLITICS

SCRIPTURE POLITICS

*Ulster Presbyterians
and Irish Radicalism in the
Late Eighteenth Century*

I. R. McBRIDE

CLARENDON PRESS · OXFORD

1998

Oxford University Press, Great Clarendon Street, Oxford OX2 6DP
Oxford New York
Athens Auckland Bangkok Bogota Bombay Buenos Aires
Calcutta Cape Town Dar es Salaam Delhi Florence Hong Kong Istanbul
Karachi Kuala Lumpur Madras Madrid Melbourne Mexico City
Nairobi Paris Singapore Taipei Tokyo Toronto Warsaw
and associated companies in
Berlin Ibadan

Oxford is a registered trade mark of Oxford University Press

Published in the United States
by Oxford University Press Inc., New York

British Library Cataloguing in Publication Data
Data available

Library of Congress Cataloging in Publication Data
McBride, Ian.
Scripture politics : Ulster Presbyterians and Irish radicalism in
the late eighteenth century / I. R. McBride.
p.   cm.
Includes bibliographical references and index.
1. Ireland—Politics and government—18th century.
2. Presbyterians—Ulster (Northern Ireland and Ireland)—
History—18th century. 3. Ulster (Northern Ireland and Ireland)—
Politics and government. 4. Christianity and politics—Ireland—
History—18th century. 5. Radicalism—Ireland—History—18th
century. 6. Ireland—History—1760–1820. I. Title.
DA948.5.M38   1998
941.607—dc21   98–3202

ISBN 0–19–820642–9

1 3 5 7 9 10 8 6 4 2

Typeset by Graphicraft Typesetters Ltd, Hong Kong
Printed in Great Britain
on acid-free paper by
Bookcraft Ltd, Midsomer Norton
Nr. Bath, Somerset

[T]he great body of the Bible is almost entirely *political*. Of this, the prophetic writings, from beginning to end, are one continued testimony. They scarcely contain a single exhortation, precept, promise, or threat, addressed to man as individuals, or members of a family; but as *states* or *nations*. And whenever they descend to particulars, it is to denounce the tyranny of kings, the corruption of governments, and the *unprincipled* connivance and rapacity of Priests and Prophets.

William Steel Dickson, *Three Sermons on Scripture Politics* (1793)

ACKNOWLEDGEMENTS

THIS book has its origins in a University of London Ph.D. thesis. My doctoral research was funded by a grant from the Department of Education for Northern Ireland and later by a Scoloudi Research Fellowship at the Institute of Historical Research, London. Between 1993 and 1996, as a research fellow at Corpus Christi College, Cambridge, I was able to revise the text for publication. I am glad finally to have the opportunity to express my thanks to all these bodies. In particular I would like to thank the Master and Fellows of Corpus Christi College for enabling me to live and work in such a congenial environment.

There is not enough room here to mention all the friends and colleagues who have supplied me with ideas, information, and references, as well as more general guidance on the direction of my research. My greatest debts are to Roy Foster and Marianne Elliott, who have been unfailingly generous with their time, advice, and encouragement, and who have read and commented on parts of the text. I am grateful also to A. T. Q. Stewart, who offered assistance when I first began to think about postgraduate research, and to Stephen Conway of University College London, who supervised my thesis with patience and care. I have learned much from conversations with Toby Barnard, James Bradley, and Colin Kidd, while Greg Claeys, Nancy Curtin, Allan Blackstock, David Hayton, Finlay Holmes, James Kelly, John McBratney, Alison McBride, Jim Smyth, John Walsh, Tim Wales, and Kevin Whelan have all helped in different ways. Not all of them, of course, may agree with everything said in this book.

I am also indebted to the staffs of the various libraries in which I have worked, and, in particular, the Linenhall Library, the Presbyterian Historical Society, the Public Record Office of Northern Ireland, and the Union Theological College. For permission to quote from manuscript collections I would like to thank the British Library, the Director, National Archives of Ireland, the Deputy Keeper of the Records, Public Record Office of Northern Ireland, C. M. Duffin, Vice Admiral A. Hezlett, and Lady Mairi Bury.

Finally, on a more personal level, there are those who have had to live with my work quite literally. Dave Anderson, Amy Edwards, Susie McNaughton, Simon Tuttle, and Kate Wolstenholme all deserve thanks for their friendship and forbearance. Above all, my parents have remained supportive throughout my years in Oxford, London, and Cambridge. This book is dedicated to them.

CONTENTS

ABBREVIATIONS

BL	British Library
BNL	*Belfast News-Letter*
Charlemont MSS	*Manuscripts and Correspondence of James, First Earl of Charlemont*, 2 vols., HMC, 12th report, app. pt. 10 (1891), 13th report, app. pt. 8 (1894)
DNB	*Dictionary of National Biography*
Drennan Letters	D. A. Chart (ed.), *The Drennan Letters, 1776–1819* (Belfast, 1931)
HMC	Historical Manuscripts Commission
IESH	*Irish Economic and Social History*
IHS	*Irish Historical Studies*
MCD	Magee College Derry (University of Ulster)
NAI	National Archives of Ireland
NHI	*A New History of Ireland*
NLS	National Library of Scotland
NS	*Northern Star*
PHSI	Presbyterian Historical Society of Ireland
PRIA	*Proceedings of the Royal Irish Academy*
PRONI	Public Record Office of Northern Ireland
QUB	The Queen's University of Belfast
RGSU	*Records of the General Synod of Ulster from 1691 to 1820*, 3 vols. (Belfast, 1890–9)
SVEC	*Studies in Voltaire and the Eighteenth Century*
TCD	Trinity College, Dublin
UCD	University College, Dublin
WMQ	*William and Mary Quarterly*

INTRODUCTION

The dissenters of the north, and more especially of the town of Belfast, are, from the genius of their religion, and from the superior diffusion of political information among them, sincere and enlightened republicans.

(Wolfe Tone, *The Life of Theobald Wolfe Tone*)[1]

FEW periods in Irish history occupy such a powerful place in the nationalist imagination as the revolutionary decade of the 1790s. The United Irishmen's attempt to overthrow British rule, first by constitutional agitation and later by armed rebellion, supplies a central chapter in the story of Ireland's struggle for national liberation. Nationalists of every stripe have worshipped at the shrine of 1798, from the rebels of Easter 1916 to the present-day supporters of the Provisional IRA. The southern state traces its ancestry back to the republican vision of the 1790s, and each year the *taoiseach* visits Wolfe Tone's grave at Bodenstown to make a 'state of the nation' address. Indeed, all the major parties in the south have at some time sought to appropriate various aspects of the United Irish legacy to legitimate their political programmes. Meanwhile, for the nationalist community in the six northern counties, the relevance of the moment 'when Ulster joined Ireland' has increased as the partition of the island has endured.[2]

Modern Irish nationalism has become irreversibly associated with Roman Catholicism. As a political movement, it has expressed the social and economic aspirations of the Catholic population; as an ideology, it has fed on the values and imagery of the Catholic Church. There is also a cultural dimension to Irish national identity, rooted in the language, literature, and customs of the Gaelic past. The nineteenth century introduced the conception of nationality as a supernatural, organic force which was necessary to sustain intellectual and spiritual life; theories of language and race would later reinforce the picture of a native Gaelic culture which had to be purified from the corrupting process of anglicization. Thus the study of the Irish past, promoted (often by marginalized Protestants) as a means of transcending sectarian divisions, had the opposite effect. By 1920, when an independent state was finally established, Young Ireland romanticism, resurgent Catholicism, and Gaelic chauvinism had all but smothered the original republican impulse of the 1790s.

In retrospect, it seems ironic that republicanism should have originated not with the dispossessed Catholic population, but with the Presbyterians of Ulster, and, in particular, of the town of Belfast. It was there, on 18 October 1791, that the Society of United Irishmen first met to condemn 'English influence' in the government

---

[1] *Life of Theobald Wolfe Tone*, ed. W. T. W. Tone, 2 vols. (Washington, 1826), i. 48.

[2] This well-known phrase seems to have originated in J. W. Good's *Ulster and Ireland* (Dublin, 1919), ch. 3.

of their country, and to call for 'a cordial union among ALL THE PEOPLE OF IRELAND'.[3] Throughout the revolutionary decade, Belfast supplied the ideological leadership of the movement and the north-east remained the stronghold of organized republicanism. Although military action had effectively broken the northern movement by 1797, tens of thousands still turned out to participate in the abortive rebellion of 1798. Viewed backwards across the last two centuries, the spectacular rise and sudden collapse of Presbyterian radicalism clearly poses special problems for the historian.

In the heyday of nationalist historiography in Ireland it sometimes seemed as if the United Irishmen had sprung supernaturally from an engagement with the divine force of nationality. For the triumphant generation which witnessed the creation of an independent state, it seemed as if the United Irishmen were merely the instruments of an eternal 'underground nation . . . the spirit of Ireland'.[4] The conversion of Ulster Presbyterians to nationalism was seen as just one example of the assimilative powers of the Gael: like previous waves of settlers they had abandoned their colonial attitudes to embrace their true interest and identity. In de Valera's Ireland the events and personalities of the eighteenth century were easily arranged according to twentieth-century priorities. Historians of the 1790s like Rosamund Jacob thus took as their main themes the progress of Catholic emancipation, the evolution of the separatist idea, and the revival of interest in the Gaelic world.[5]

There was an in-built tendency in nationalist historiography to deny legitimacy to alternative identities on the island of Ireland, and especially to Protestant Ulster's sense of separateness. The planter culture of the north was seen as an artificial product of British imperialism, and the distinctive values and traditions of Ulster Protestants reduced to a series of negative stereotypes. Needless to say, nationalist historians had little time for such subjects as the polemical theology of the Ulster Presbyterians or the intellectual influences of the Scottish Enlightenment and English Dissent. Before the 1960s, Wolfe Tone's contempt for the Roman Catholic Church and his indifference to Gaelic culture tended to be ignored or excused by his biographers.[6] Only the eccentric Leo McCabe, in his clerical polemic *Wolfe Tone and the United Irishmen: For or Against Christ?* (1937), saw the republicanism of the 1790s for what it was: Protestant, heretical, and anti-Catholic.[7]

If later generations of Catholic nationalists have appropriated the United Irish legacy for their own purposes, Ulster Protestants usually have disowned it altogether. In the nineteenth century a number of Presbyterian historians—often Liberal in affiliation—wrote sympathetically of the United Irishmen, while carefully distancing

---

[3] Quoted in Marianne Elliott, *Wolfe Tone: Prophet of Irish Independence* (New Haven, 1989), 140.

[4] P. S. O'Hegarty, quoted ibid. 418.

[5] It was said that the United Irishmen 'derived its life from the historic Irish nation': Rosamund Jacob, *The Rise of the United Irishmen 1791–94* (London, 1937), 79.

[6] There were early exceptions such as Frank MacDermot's *Theobald Wolfe Tone: A Biographical Study* (London, 1939), but the turning point did not come until Maureen Wall's 'The United Irish Movement', *Historical Studies*, 5 (1965), 122–40.

[7] Leo McCabe, *Wolfe Tone and the United Irishmen: For or Against Christ?* (London, 1937). This remarkable book denounced Presbyterian radicalism as 'the child of Lucifer's proud and evil spirit' (p. 70).

them from later nationalists.[8] As Irish politics became polarized during the home rule crisis, however, the Dissenting voice within Ulster Protestantism all but disappeared, and the memories of '98 along with it. Although Protestant Ulster has produced a disproportionate number of Irish historians, there have been few attempts to construct a distinctively northern interpretation of the Irish past. The major exception is A. T. Q. Stewart, who first sought to restore the United Irishmen to their eighteenth-century Presbyterian setting.[9] Although Stewart has had a profound, often unacknowledged, influence on historians of the 1790s, there has so far been no comprehensive study of Presbyterian radicalism.

Irish nationalists and Ulster unionists have thus conspired to detach the United Irishmen from their proper historical context. As academic research has mushroomed over the last twenty-five years, however, historians have begun to correct this failure. In addition to the general political narratives compiled by R. B. McDowell and the path-breaking scholarship of Marianne Elliott, several monographs, essay collection, and articles have been devoted to the subject.[10] Many aspects of United Irish politics have been subjected to detailed research for the first time, and, in the process our understanding of republican ideology and aims, Franco-Irish connections, Defenderism, and popular politicization have been transformed. One consequence of this historiographical revolution has been a heightened appreciation of the distinctive contribution of Presbyterian Ulster to early Irish republicanism. It is surely time that this topic, whose importance has long been recognized by scholars, was subjected to systematic investigation.

Scripture Politics builds upon recent historiography, while seeking to modify and refine it, in an attempt to uncover the ideological and organizational dynamics of Presbyterian radicalism. Following the directions laid down by Wolfe Tone, it locates the origins of Ireland's first republican movement in the distinctive cultural formation

[8] An example is W. T. Latimer's *Ulster Biographies, Relating Chiefly to the Rebellion of 1798* (Belfast, 1897).

[9] Stewart pioneered the study of this subject in his influential MA thesis 'The Transformation of Presbyterian Radicalism in the North of Ireland, 1792–1825' (QUB, 1956). Some of the insights were published in ' "A Stable Unseen Power": Dr William Drennan and the Origins of the United Irishmen', in John Bossy and Peter Jupp (eds.), *Essays Presented to Michael Roberts* (Belfast, 1976), 80–92; *The Narrow Ground: Aspects of Ulster 1609–1969* (Belfast, 1977 edn.), 96–110; and more recently *A Deeper Silence: The Hidden Origins of the United Irishmen* (London, 1993).

[10] R. B. McDowell, *Ireland in the Age of Imperialism and Revolution, 1760–1801* (Oxford, 1979); Marianne Elliott, *Partners in Revolution: The United Irishmen and France* (New Haven, 1982); ead., *Wolfe Tone*; J. S. Donnelly, 'Propagating the Cause of the United Irishmen', *Studies*, 69 (1980), 5–23; N. J. Curtin, 'The Transformation of the Society of United Irishmen into a Mass-Based Revolutionary Organization, 1794–6', *IHS* 24/96 (1985), 463–92; Jim Smyth, *The Men of No Property: Irish Radicals and Popular Politics in the Late Eighteenth Century* (Dublin, 1992); David Dickson and Hugh Gough (eds.), *Ireland and the French Revolution* (Dublin, 1990); David Dickson, Dáire Keogh and Kevin Whelan (eds.), *The United Irishmen: Republicanism, Radicalism and Rebellion* (Dublin, 1993); Dáire Keogh, *'The French Disease': The Catholic Church and Radicalism in Ireland 1790–1800* (Dublin, 1993). Since I first began my own research four more studies have appeared: N. J. Curtin, *The United Irishmen: Popular Politics in Ulster and Dublin 1791–98* (Oxford, 1994); M. H. Thuente, *The Harp Restrung: The United Irishmen and the Rise of Irish Literary Nationalism* (Syracuse, 1994); E. W. McFarland, *Ireland and Scotland in the Age of Revolution: Planting the Green Bough* (Edinburgh, 1994); and Kevin Whelan, *The Tree of Liberty: Radicalism, Catholicism and the Construction of Irish Identity 1760–1830* (Cork, 1996).

of the Dissenting north. My own account of the 1790s is thus less concerned with
the development of national consciousness, the political resurgence of Catholicism,
or the rediscovery of the Gaelic past, than with those subjects excluded from the
old nationalist agenda: the political theologies of different Presbyterian factions, the
political culture of volunteering, and the denominational and ethnic affiliations which
fed into the 1798 insurrections. It is based on a study of Presbyterian church records,
sermons, treatises, and pamphlets, as well as the more familiar manuscript collections and newspapers. These sources reveal that, in addition to the revolutionary
ideas imported from America and France, the United Irishmen were able to draw
on an older, indigenous tradition of radicalism, nurtured by decades of theological
disputation. The rhetoric of Presbyterian radicalism was suffused with theological
learning, biblical imagery, and religious conviction.

At the close of the eighteenth century, religion and politics were not the separate and discrete categories of thought and activity that they constitute for most people
in the western world today. A growing body of historical scholarship in Britain and
North America has been devoted to the recovery of the theological dimensions of
eighteenth-century experience. In one extreme case, it has been claimed that all the
political allegiances which characterized the period were ultimately determined by
conflicting forms of religious belief. According to Jonathan Clark's *ancien régime* thesis,
first set out in his iconoclastic *English Society* (1985), Hanoverian Britain remained
a confessional state; radicalism was simply the political expression of Protestant
Dissent—more specifically, the 'rational' variety of Dissent which rejected or modified
the orthodox formulation of the Trinity.[11] The connection between religious faith,
political discourse, and social antagonisms was certainly more complicated than Clark
suggests. It is impossible to make sense of the development of radicalism, in Britain
or Ireland, without taking into consideration a whole range of popular demands concerning the lack of accountability in national government and oligarchic rule as well
as the closed nature of the ecclesiastical system. In other words, denominational
identities interacted with social identities to produce oppositional ways of thinking
about the established order. But if Clark's more provocative claims have attracted
little sympathy, few of his critics would now deny the key role of theological arguments in the generation of eighteenth-century ideologies.[12]

---

[11] J. C. D. Clark, *English Society 1688–1832: Ideology, Social Structure and Political Practice During
the Ancien Regime* (Cambridge, 1985), 1, 277–8; id., 'On Hitting the Buffers: The Historiography of
England's Ancien Regime: A Response', *Past & Present*, 117 (Nov. 1987), 199; id., *The Language of
Liberty 1660–1832: Political Discourse and Social Dynamics in the Anglo-American World* (Cambridge,
1994). For some reactions to Clark see Joanna Innes, 'Review Article: Jonathan Clark, Social History
and England's "Ancien Regime"', *Past & Present*, 115 (1987), 165–200; 'Symposium: Revolution
and Rebellion', *Parliamentary History*, 7 (1988), 329–38, esp. the contribution by H. T. Dickinson;
J. G. A. Pocock, 'Within the Margins: The Definitions of Orthodoxy', in Roger D. Lund (ed.), *The
Margins of Orthodoxy: Heterodox Writing and Cultural Response, 1660–1750* (Cambridge, 1995), 33–53;
Knud Haakonssen, *Enlightenment and Religion: Rational Dissent in Eighteenth-Century Britain* (Cambridge,
1996), esp. the essays by Seed, Waterman, and Gascoigne.

[12] See Martin Fitzpatrick, 'Toleration and Truth', *Enlightenment and Dissent*, 1 (1982), 3–31; id.,
'Heretical Religion and Radical Political Ideas in Late Eighteenth-Century England', in Eckhart
Hellmuth (ed.), *The Transformation of Political Culture: England and Germany in the Late Eighteenth
Century* (Oxford, 1990), 338–72; Mark Philp, 'Rational Religion and Political Radicalism in the 1790s',

In a constitutional system where Church and State were still interlinked, the survival of alternative theologies inevitably posed a political threat. Research on late eighteenth-century Britain has demonstrated that the clergy of the established church formed the chief bulwark in the ideological fortifications of the Hanoverian order. The necessity of submission to the civil authority, the dangers of popular tumult, the superiority of Britain's constitution, the benefits of the rule of law, and the connection between religious uniformity and social stability were all recurrent themes in the Anglican sermons preached on official thanksgiving and fast-days.[13] The divine right theory of kingship, gradually driven underground in the decades after 1688, was reincarnated in the 1770s as the divine right of the king-in-Parliament. In Ireland, too, historians are beginning to uncover the contributions of churchmen to the intellectual defence of the Irish elite, from its emergence in the decade after the Boyne to the vindication of Protestant Ascendancy mounted in the 1780s and 1790s. As long as allegiance to the civil magistrate retained this theological component, the rejection of establishment Anglicanism naturally carried subversive implications.

Like other Dissenter communities in the British state-system, then, Irish Presbyterians were compelled to define their own theoretical positions on questions such as the nature and rights of the established church and its connection with the civil power. This highly contested territory was the subject of a series of radical sermons published by the Revd William Steel Dickson in 1793, from which I have borrowed the title of this book. Taking the well-known text 'My kingdom is not of this world', Dickson elaborated a powerful defence of religious freedom against the claims of those corrupt priests and politicians who had polluted pure, scriptural religion with human traditions and laws, and usurped the spiritual authority of Jesus Christ over his church. These ecclesiological matters were intimately connected with broader political and constitutional topics such as the origins of civil society, the limits of political obligation, and the right of resistance against tyrannical governments, topics which eighteenth-century preachers felt free to address. The science of government, as Dickson defined it, was merely one branch of Christian teaching, the only sure guide to the happiness of mankind; on the level of abstract theory, it was therefore natural that he should attempt to establish the United Irish case upon theological foundations.[14]

Enlightenment and Dissent, 4 (1985), 35–46; J. E. Bradley, *Religion, Revolution, and English Radicalism: Nonconformity in Eighteenth-Century Politics and Society* (Cambridge, 1990). For America see Patricia Bonomi, *Under the Cope of Heaven: Religion, Society and Politics in Colonial America* (Oxford, 1986); N. O. Hatch, *The Sacred Cause of Liberty: Republican Thought and the Millennium in Revolutionary New England* (New Haven, 1977); R. H. Bloch, *Visionary Republic: Millennial Themes in American Thought, 1756–1800* (Cambridge, 1985); Clark, *Language of Liberty*.

[13] Recent work has emphasized the centrality of the Church as an ideological force, as a pillar of the constitutional system, and as a guarantor of social hierarchy. See J. E. Bradley, 'The Anglican Pulpit, the Social Order, and the Resurgence of Toryism during the American Revolution', *Albion*, 21 (1989), 361–88; Robert Hole, *Pulpits, Politics and Public Order in England, 1760–1832* (Cambridge, 1989); Paul Langford, 'The English Clergy and the American Revolution', in Hellmuth (ed.), *Transformation of Political Culture*, 338–72; Emma Vincent, 'The Responses of Scottish Churchmen to the French Revolution, 1789–1802', *Scottish Historical Review*, 73 (1994), 191–215.

[14] William Steel Dickson, *Three Sermons on the Subject of Scripture Politics* (Belfast, 1793).

The sermon, it should be remembered, was still the most effective means of relaying information and ideas to a wide audience, and the meeting-house remained vital to the social life of local communities. Throughout this study I have brought to the foreground the services of the Presbyterian clergy to the cause of reform and the use of the Presbyterian pulpit as a vehicle for the dissemination of radical propaganda. Ministers saw themselves not only as spiritual leaders, but as tribunes of the people.[15] In the course of this book they appear in many guises: as political orators and agitators, elections agents, chaplains and officers of Volunteer companies, journalists, pamphleteers, and rebel soldiers. Reflecting upon the origins of the '98 rebellions, Alexander Knox, secretary to Viscount Castlereagh, observed that Ulster possessed 'a distinct moral existence' which placed it outside the dominion of the British crown. The lynchpin of this autonomy was the clerical order, free from state control and bound to its people through the representative structures of the church.[16]

The weight attached here to religious modes of thought may seem at odds with the popular image of the United Irishmen as the progenitors of the enlightened, secular republic. The real issue, however, was not between sectarianism and secularism, but between competing varieties of Christian faith. Those who desired a pluralist republic were neither hostile nor indifferent to revealed religion: on the contrary, they believed that the abolition of traditional confessional divisions was essential if divine truth was to flourish. There was no contradiction in the political stance of radicals like William Steel Dickson who called for the complete separation of Church and State while treating political science as a kind of applied theology. The same point is borne out by considering the somewhat ambiguous position occupied by Thomas Paine within this tradition. While Presbyterians admired *Common Sense* and *Rights of Man*, many were alarmed by the anti-Christian tendencies of his *Age of Reason*; if Paine was 'an able politician', noted one clergyman, he made 'a most miserable divine'.[17] Although a few of the Ulster radicals dabbled with Deism, the vast majority saw no incompatibility between the republic of virtue and the kingdom of God.

The literature on the religious thought of eighteenth-century Ireland is comparatively thin, but in this field, as elsewhere, I am indebted to the work of earlier scholars. In his pioneering study of Belfast politics, A. T. Q. Stewart related the rise and fall of Presbyterian radicalism to the changing doctrinal complexion of the Ulster synod. The subscription controversy of the 1720s, he suggested, was the

---

[15] For a defence of political preaching see Dickson, *Three Sermons*, 47–57; Thomas Ledlie Birch, *The Obligations upon Christians and Especially Ministers to be Exemplary in their Lives . . . A Sermon Preached before the Very Reverend, The General Synod of Ulster, at Lurgan, June 26th 1793* (Belfast, 1794), 16–19.

[16] Alexander Knox to Castlereagh, 15 July 1803, *Memoirs and Correspondence of Viscount Castlereagh*, ed. Charles Vane, 12 vols. (London, 1848–54), iv. 287.

[17] John Abernethy [of Templepatrick], *Philalethes, or, Revelation Consistent with Reason: An Attempt to Answer the Objections and Arguments against it in Mr Paine's Book, Entitled, Age of Reason* (Belfast, 1795), 5. See also A Citizen of the World, *Paine's Age of Reason, with Remarks, Containing a Vindication of the Doctrine of Christianity from the Aspersions of that Author* (Belfast, 1794); William Stavely, *Appeal to Light; or, The Tenets of Deists Examined and Disapproved; and the Authority of the Holy Scriptures Asserted and Vindicated* (Belfast, 1796); letter from 'T', *Northern Star*, 7 Mar. 1796.

eighteenth-century manifestation of an inherent tension within Presbyterianism between fundamentalism and the right of private judgement. The repudiation of the Westminster Confession of Faith was thus the necessary prelude to the United Irish project.[18] Marianne Elliott has also highlighted the importance of the non-subscribers as carriers of classical republican ideas; she suggests that the theories of religious toleration devised by the New Light or latitudinarian ministers may go some way to explain the emergence of a non-sectarian reform programme in Belfast.[19] Like Stewart, she too views New Light divinity as an expression of a perennial radicalism, derived from the democracy and discipline of the Presbyterian polity.

Much of the literature on the 1790s thus equates radical politics with the 'rational' wing of Dissent, although it is fair to say that no one has attempted a close examination of this relationship. Of late, however, some historians have turned to the alternative thesis put forward by D. W. Miller, which plays down the enlightenment philosophy of the non-subscribers in favour of the 'prophetic' strain of divinity found in orthodox Calvinism.[20] My own account strives to pay due attention to all shades of radical opinion from the rational republicanism of the non-subscribers to the theological irredentism of the Seceders and Covenanters. The New Light camp, with its openness to innovatory currents of thought and its faith in the perfectibility of mankind, undoubtedly provided Presbyterian radicalism with its most articulate spokesmen. Their fundamental conviction that religious truth could not be furthered by compulsion, but only by persuasion and argument, made them the earliest and most fervent converts to Catholic emancipation. The Old Lights could not match the non-subscribers for intellectual vigour or social respectability, but their more populist brand of Dissent was probably more important in mobilizing rank-and-file reformers. Throughout the book I have tried to clarify the lines of divergence between these various groupings, while not losing sight of the common ground that still united them.

It may be helpful, in the remainder of this introduction, to sketch out in greater detail the ground covered by the book. Following an introductory survey of eighteenth-century political and social structures, I make use of sermons, pamphlets, and church records in Part I to reconstruct the fissiparous culture of controversy which was so central to eighteenth-century Presbyterianism. We shall examine the differences which separated New Lights from Old Lights and Seceders from Covenanters; decode the broader social and cultural meanings of these fissures; and identify their political repercussions. If the protagonists of these doctrinal battles seem pedantic and self-absorbed, we should recall that the questions which they tackled were being debated throughout Europe in an age of vehement religious controversy. To what extent was biblical revelation consistent with the rational, scientific methods of an enlightened epoch? Were Christians to be judged by their fidelity to the traditional codes of the church or by the sincerity of their beliefs? Above all, how was

---

[18] Stewart, *Narrow Ground*, 96–110.

[19] Elliott, *Partners in Revolution*, pp. xiii, 20, 27–9; ead., *Wolfe Tone*, 103–4, 116–17; ead., *Watchmen in Sion: The Protestant Idea of Liberty* (Derry, 1985), esp. 6–12.

[20] D. W. Miller, 'Presbyterianism and "Modernisation" in Ulster', *Past & Present*, 80 (1978), 66–90.

the kingdom of Christ to be governed, and in what relation did it stand to the kingdoms of this world?

In Chapter 2, I chart the rise of the New Light party which dominated the General Synod of Ulster for most of the eighteenth century. The intellectual case against compulsory subscription to the Westminster Confession of Faith is summarized, and I contend that the subscription controversy should be understood as a clash of broad social and cultural values rather than well-defined doctrinal positions. In their rejection of all creeds and confessions, the New Light ministers employed arguments which could be applied to dissolve the ideological bonds of the church–state partnership. The New Light, however, was a social as well as an intellectual phenomenon. All the evidence suggests that the non-subscribers were dependent upon the middle-class circles of Belfast and the towns, and that traditional orthodox views persisted throughout the countryside; the rational, polite sermons of New Light preachers had no appeal for the majority of the population. Any investigation of their role as the vanguard of Presbyterian radicalism must also take into account their conservative social attitudes.

From the learned world of the polite Presbyterians, we move on in Chapter 3 to the Seceders and Covenanters who took up the defence of traditional Calvinism after the Old Lights lost control of the Synod. Both groups won support in rural Ulster for their rigid adherence to the principles of Scotland's 'second reformation' of 1638–49. The difficulties of reconciling the obligations of the Solemn League and Covenant with the constitutional order established by the Revolution settlement generated a tortuous literature. On the one hand, the Covenanters remained true to the seventeenth-century vision of a covenanted kingdom where church and state would join in a Presbyterian partnership. Their alienation from the episcopalian regime of the Hanoverians, combined with the popular contract theory of militant Calvinism, made them unusually receptive to the radical propaganda of the United Irishmen. Many of the Seceding ministers, on the other hand, were moving away from inherited notions of the Presbyterian polity towards an 'inward religion' which prefigured the evangelical tone of nineteenth-century Ulster. A gradual retreat from the political theology of the Covenanting tradition was accompanied by a growing acceptance of the Hanoverian monarchy: the Seceding clergy (though not always the laity) would play a conspicuous role in opposing Irish Jacobinism.

I attempt in Chapter 4 to tease out some of the connections between theological disputation and radical political discourse in the late eighteenth century. I begin by reviewing the various modes of political criticism available, from constitutional mythologies to natural jurisprudence to classical republicanism. In the white heat of the 1790s these diverse strands were welded together into a more democratic vocabulary under the tutelage of Thomas Paine. My focus, however, is on the theological and ecclesiastical allegiances which often supplied the context within which these more 'secular' discourses established their meaning. At the extreme edge of the theological spectrum the Covenanters insisted that all government, temporal and spiritual, must be based on those patterns allegedly found in the scriptures. For mainstream Presbyterians, who took the view that no particular form of government could claim biblical sanction, the case for democratic politics was phrased predominantly in the language of constitutional precedent and natural rights; but these arguments retained associations with various dissident theological positions. The binary oppositions around which so much political discussion turned—such as liberty/slavery or virtue/corruption—were historically, and often conceptually, linked to the master opposition of Protestantism and popery.

There was a tendency, moreover, for conflicts within Church and State to become fused together with explosive results. As Joanna Innes observes, it is impossible to account for the violence of the reform debate 'unless it is understood that contention over political and over religious subjects frequently had the appearance of being the same conflict carried on at two different levels'.[21] To contemporaries, as well as historians, 'radicalism' was the direct translation of alternative theologies into the political sphere. Just as their detractors insisted that religious uniformity and social stability were indissolubly linked, Ulster Presbyterians subscribed to a providential vision of historical development in which civil and religious liberty rose and fell together. Religious convictions shaped and stiffened radical theory, giving coherence and force to the constitutional arguments of the Ulster radicals, while denominational loyalties provided a firm basis for political activism.

In Part II, I shall aim to describe how this refractory subculture was transformed into a powerful political bloc. The decisive turning point in this process was the outbreak of war with the American colonies, which were connected to Ulster by trade networks, family links, and by cultural ties. The imperial crisis which came to a head after 1775 reopened old debates concerning allegiance and sovereignty; by focusing attention on political representation it also called into question the oligarchic nature of the British and Irish constitutional system. Moreover, the war impinged directly on the Presbyterian community, as the economy was disrupted, troops were recruited, and ministers were called upon to observe fast-days in support of British arms. This apparently unjust war, and the conflict of loyalties which it forced, interacted with a host of domestic grievances associated with Britain's control over Irish government, parliamentary corruption, and the impositions of the Anglican church to detach the Presbyterians from their inherited allegiance to the Hanoverian regime.

The American repudiation of the British constitution not only created a defining issue for the disaffected: it also provided a novel opportunity for political organization in the shape of the Irish Volunteers. In Chapters 5 and 6, I suggest that the unprecedented mobilization which took place between 1778 and 1785, and its dramatic impact upon political attitudes and social relationships, have not been fully appreciated by historians. The massive scale of volunteering drew a large proportion of the adult male population into the public sphere for the first time. The Ulster Convention of 1783, attended by delegates from 272 companies, claimed to represent at least 18,000 Volunteers, the great majority of whom were Presbyterians.[22]

[21] Innes, 'Jonathan Clark', 189.
[22] *History of the Proceedings and Debates of the Volunteer Delegates of Ireland on the Subject of a Parliamentary Reform* (Dublin, 1784), 9.

As they elected officers, attended political meetings, discussed resolutions, collected petitions, and drew up instructions for MPs, thousands of Ulstermen acquired their first taste of active citizenship. The Volunteer movement introduced 'the people' into the politics of eighteenth-century Ireland; Francis Dobbs anticipated a common complaint of the 1790s when he remarked that 'The doctrine, of every man being fit to legislate, is pretty industriously propagated.'[23]

The intensive extra-parliamentary activity of 1778–85—culminating in the provincial conventions held at Dungannon—fostered the development of an alternative political culture outside the formal structures of the state. Its very existence posed an implicit challenge to an increasingly corrupt Irish House of Commons, and the demand for Parliamentary reform was the natural outgrowth of political ideas and practices which may be described as republican in the eighteenth-century sense of the word. In Chapter 5 I have tried to approach volunteering from a new angle, exploring the rhetorical and symbolic expressions of the movement, and describing how the Irish Volunteer was depicted as the reincarnation of the classical citizen-soldier. The self-image of the Volunteers, the delegatory conception of political authority embodied in their reviews and conventions, and the practice of issuing constituency instructions to MPs, all suggested a model of continuous participation in the political process which was radically out of step with the Anglo-Saxon parliamentary tradition. By 1783 it was clear to the ministry that Parliament and the Volunteers were joined in a conflict for the effective control of the kingdom. Unless the citizen army could be dissolved, urged Charles James Fox, 'government and even the name of it must be at an end'.[24]

Armed service, perhaps inevitably, also produced a temporary breakdown in traditional social patterns. The radical pamphleteer William Drennan described how 'the levelling of all civil distinctions of rank and fortune, necessary in martial evolution and manoeuvre' had helped to give 'the lower ranks of the community an independence and republicanism of spirit'.[25] Sir Richard Musgrave, Orange historian of the '98 rebellion, argued that volunteering had eroded social boundaries and created fertile ground for 'levelling principles'.[26] The mid-1780s saw schisms develop in a number of companies, as reformers broke away from officers who had voted with the government in parliamentary debates or who had attempted to use 'unconstitutional influence' over their tenants during elections.[27] A brief look at electoral organization and propaganda during this period allows us to glimpse a primitive ideology of 'independence' which envisaged both local and national parliamentary politics as a contest between aristocratic influence and the independent (or popular) interest. The radical rejection of oligarchic rule in the 1790s must be set against this older tradition of hostility to the political dominance of the landed elite.

[23] Francis Dobbs, A History of Irish Affairs (Dublin, 1782), 152.
[24] Charles James Fox to Northington, 1 Nov. 1783, BL, Add. MS 38716, fo. 133.
[25] [William Drennan], A Letter to Edmund Burke (Dublin, 1780), 15.
[26] Richard Musgrave, Memoirs of the Different Rebellions in Ireland (Dublin, 1801), 51.
[27] Minutes of the Newry Volunteers, 13 Apr. 1784, PRONI, T3202/1A; An Historical Account of the Late Election of Knights of the Shire for the County of Down (n.p., 1784), 109–10, 117.

Volunteering was only the most startling expression of a rich associational culture which included Masonic lodges, constitutional clubs in Lisburn, Belfast, and Newtownards, and the lively democracy of the Belfast town meeting. The period of the American secession thus saw a denominational group recast as a civic community, and its aspirations reformulated in the wider currency of patriotism. Yet in Chapters 5 and 6 we can see the continuing importance of the clergy in providing the reform movement with ideological direction, the interaction of new political demands with traditional ecclesiastical and theological principles, and the use of the sermon as a vehicle for political argument. It is not surprising, therefore, to find that politicians, landlords, and magistrates frequently pinpointed the Presbyterian pulpit as the driving force behind popular disaffection. The Earl of Hillsborough, the great County Down magnate, acquired an enduring jealousy of the 'Dissenting parsons' who fomented sedition and rebellion within his sphere of influence. Here was the source of republican doctrines, he informed the government in 1784, describing how, at Volunteer reviews 'the poor ignorant people are taught by their Ministers to believe they are slaves'.[28] When the Duke of Rutland, who took up the Lord Lieutenancy in the same year, visited the north, he also found that 'The dissenting ministers are for the most part very seditious, and have great sway over their flocks.'[29] That these claims were not without foundation is demonstrated in Chapter 5, where I explain the role of the clergy in the creation of public opinion. United by the provincial organization of their Synod, by a common education, and often by family ties, the Ulster clergy were vital agents in that 'diffusion of political information' which Wolfe Tone believed characterized the northern province.

Thus in Part II I suggest that the launch of the United Irish society, once viewed as a sudden aberration in conventional alignments, should be seen as the culmination of a series of radical initiatives which emerged from late eighteenth-century Belfast. Ulster's extraordinary receptivity to the rhetoric of the French Revolution can only be understood in the light of the extensive politicization of the Presbyterian community which took place after 1775. In personnel, propaganda, and extra-parliamentary organization, the Volunteers had already anticipated much of the content and style of subsequent radical protest. In 1783, however, attempts to mobilize public opinion behind the banner of Parliamentary reform had run up against the obstacle of the Catholic question. The revival and extension of radicalism in the 1790s, and the conversion of the Presbyterian radicals to the Catholic cause, form the subject of the third and final part of the book.

The ignominious collapse of the reform movement made it plain that Presbyterian radicalism still operated within the limits set by the Protestant confrontation with Rome. After 1789, however, this fundamental polarity, which had structured collective consciousness in the English-speaking world for centuries, was rapidly dissolved. As the French *ancien régime* crumbled, the parameters of Irish politics were suddenly expanded. In Chapter 7, we review the disagreements over the nature

---

[28] Hillsborough to [Rutland], 15 July 1784, in *The Manuscripts of His Grace the Duke of Rutland, K.G. Preserved at Belvoir Castle*, iii, HMC, 14th report, app. pt. 1 (1894), 124.
[29] 'Journal of the Duke of Rutland's tour of the North of Ireland', ibid. 421.

of the French Revolution, the readmission of Catholics to political rights, and Britain's participation in the war against the revolutionary republic. We trace the emergence of the Society of United Irishmen from the Belfast Volunteers, and the subsequent transition from constitutional pressure group to militant, insurrectionary movement. It is argued that the responses of the various Presbyterian groups to the French Revolution were conditioned by theological differences. The significance of the revolution lay in the dismantling of the Roman Catholic Church in France, which Presbyterians interpreted, either literally or figuratively, as a vital step towards the destruction of the Roman Antichrist. With the collapse of papal power apparently imminent, the moral regeneration of the native Irish became a possibility. Presbyterian support for emancipation was thus conditional on the belief that organized Catholicism was a spent force.

It is regrettable that we still lack a detailed, regional study of the United Irish movement, based on a comprehensive investigation of the various social relationships in the north, the politics and personalities of the great county families, and the individual ambitions and aspirations of radical activists.[30] The north of Ireland, as John Whyte has noted in a different context, encompasses a number of distinct subregions, and the degrees of political, social, and economic division differ markedly as we pass from one to another.[31] In Chapter 8, I suggest that the political choices made in the 1790s must be viewed from a more parochial perspective which attends to territorial loyalties, local social structures, and the ethnic frontiers that defined zones of settlement in Ulster. Ironically, perhaps, the United Irishmen were strongest where Presbyterians lived in relative isolation from their Catholic countrymen, and weaker in those areas where the two groups existed in close physical proximity. 'The extent to which each of the northern counties was involved in the insurrection', as A. T. Q. Stewart has observed, 'appears to be in inverse proportion to its Catholic population.'[32]

In my account of the popular mobilization which led to the '98 rebellions, I have again highlighted the importance of religious habits of thought, using political sermons, tracts, and magistrates' reports to reconstruct the millenarian current within Presbyterianism which had been activated in the 1790s by the fall of the Bourbon monarchy. I do not wish to suggest that the religious themes explored here can provide an explanation for the launching of the United Irish societies, much less for the '98; the origins of the battles of Antrim and Ballynahinch lie in the social grievances of the Presbyterian population, and in the political upheavals which destabilized

---

[30] Within the limits of this book it is only possible to hint at local variations in United Irish politics. Cf. the excellent studies now available for the southern counties: L. M. Cullen, 'The 1798 Rebellion in Wexford: United Irishman Organization, Membership, Leadership', in Kevin Whelan (ed.), *Wexford: History and Society* (Dublin, 1987) 248–95; Kevin Whelan, 'Politicisation in County Wexford and the Origins of the 1798 Rebellion', in Dickson and Gough (eds.), *Ireland and the French Revolution*, 156–78; L. M. Cullen, 'Politics and Rebellion: Wicklow in the 1790s', in Ken Hannigan and William Nolan (eds.), *Wicklow History and Society: Interdisciplinary Essays on the History of an Irish County* (Dublin, 1994), 411–501; Ruan O'Donnell, 'The Rebellion of 1798 in County Wicklow', ibid. 341–78.

[31] John Whyte, *Interpreting Northern Ireland* (Oxford, 1991), 93, 111.

[32] Stewart, 'Transformation of Presbyterian Radicalism', 72.

the established order throughout Europe. What I do hope to show is that these material forces were often perceived in essentially religious terms. The '98 was a rebellion of New Lights against the priestcraft and superstition perpetuated by Church and State, of Old Lights against an erastian, idolatrous, and unscriptural establishment, and of all Presbyterians against a government which had allied itself with the forces of civil and religious tyranny. To some extent, then, Presbyterian radicalism represented the continuation of the war against popery by other means.

It is impossible for historians of Ireland (or of any country) to step outside their own social and cultural formations on to some pure, unworldly level of scholarly inquiry, particularly when the subject matter is so deeply embedded in national consciousness. If the recent controversy over historiographical revisionism has taught us anything, it has made us more aware of the active role of ideology and imagination in shaping historical narratives.[33] But to draw the conclusion, as some have, that we should return to the polemical and partisan perspectives of more innocent times is surely misguided. It has been suggested that the 'received version of Irish history', organized around the concepts of nationality and liberty, constitutes 'a beneficent legacy—its wrongness notwithstanding'.[34] Such attitudes betray a dangerous disregard for the ways in which the language of nationalism has been structured according to the imperatives of religion and ethnicity (not to mention class and gender). The latest generation of Irish historians has exploded the idea that 'Irishness' is merely a fixed essence passed down through the centuries. Like all nations, the Irish nation is the product of a particular configuration of intellectual and social forces, and its meaning continues to be contested and redefined as those forces shift. Part of the historian's task is to uncover the ways in which concepts of nationality and liberty were discovered, popularized, appropriated, and revised. This book is intended as a contribution to that process.

[33] For the debate on revisionism see Ciaran Brady (ed.), *Interpreting Irish History: The Debate on Historical Revisionism, 1938–1994* (Dublin, 1994); D. G. Boyce and Alan O'Day (eds.), *The Making of Modern Irish History: Revisionism and the Revisionist Controversy* (London, 1996).

[34] Brendan Bradshaw, 'Nationalism and Historical Scholarship in Modern Ireland', *IHS* 26/104 (1989), 347–8, repr. in Brady, *Interpreting Irish History*, 191–216.

I

EIGHTEENTH-CENTURY IRELAND

> O what a happy country we had before men turned their thoughts to thinking!
> Catholics thought of nothing but just getting leave to live, and working for their
> meat; Presbyterians thought of nothing but wrangling about religion and
> grumbling about tythes; and Protestants thought of nothing but doing and
> saying what their betters bid them. . . . O how times are changed, and all for
> the worse!
>
> ('Billy Bluff and Squire Firebrand', *Northern Star*, 1796[1])

In the eighteenth century all Irishmen claimed to be oppressed, but some were clearly
more oppressed than others.[2] At various junctures Protestants, Catholics, and Dissenters would all take up the cause of Ireland, erecting their own sectional discontents
into national grievances. The consequent variety of nationalisms—Williamite,
Jacobite, and Jacobin—would be hammered into a rich, versatile, and unstable republican tradition by the United Irishmen in the 1790s. The first of these strands, the
patriotic voice of the Anglican elite, has never lacked historians, and the 'hidden'
Ireland of the Catholic population is at last beginning to receive the attention it
deserves. The subject of this book is the third tributary which fed into Irish republicanism, the rebellious culture of Ulster Presbyterianism. The purpose of this
preliminary chapter is to provide a background sketch both of the Presbyterian
population and of the wider political and social structures of eighteenth-century
Ireland.

Protestants

The established Church of Ireland, an offshoot of the Church of England,
accounted for about an eighth of all Irish souls. Outside Dublin and the plantation
settlements of the north, Anglicans were thinly spread. Nevertheless, they enjoyed
a monopoly of landed wealth, social prestige, and political power. From their ranks
were drawn not only the 300 members of the Irish House of Commons, but also
the grand juries and magistrates in the counties and the corporations in the towns.
But although conformity to the Anglican communion was essential for membership
of the ruling classes, it was not sufficient. The 'Protestant Ascendancy'—the term
used by historians to describe the Irish elite—was confined to the top drawer of

---

[1] [James Porter], 'Billy Bluff and Squire Firebrand', *Northern Star*, 18 July 1796.

[2] For the historiography see S. J. Connolly, 'Eighteenth-Century Ireland: Colony or *Ancien Régime?*',
in D. G. Boyce and Alan O'Day (eds.), *The Making of Modern Irish History: Revisionism and the Revisionist
Controversy* (London, 1996), 15–33.

the Anglican community, the narrow band which influenced government at local or national level. Recent descriptions of the governing class have therefore given less weight to the confessional divisions peculiar to Ireland than to differences of wealth and status which determined the social structure throughout *ancien régime* Europe.[3] The important point is that political power, in Ireland as elsewhere, was based upon landed property. There was, of course, another political world existing outside College Green, inhabited by freeholders, pamphleteers, and journalists, but the term 'Protestant Ascendancy' is best reserved for the propertied class which influenced the selection of the House of Commons.[4]

The dominance of the Irish elite thus rested on a combination of religion, ethnicity, and social status. Each of these components permitted a small degree of upward mobility. An impressive number of the best-known parliamentarians were self-made men: Foster, Flood, Grattan, Curran, and Fitzgibbon all came from professional backgrounds. The meteoric rise of Fitzgibbon, the talented son of a convert lawyer, reminds us too that Catholic families had been successfully integrated into the Protestant elite. Finally, the Ascendancy had absorbed some old Gaelic families: one example was the O'Neills of Shane's Castle, County Antrim, who used their descent from Ulster's old kings to boost their patriotic credentials. While these exceptions should be noted, the close connection between the ownership of land, Anglicanism, and English ancestry must be central to any depiction of the governing elite. Moreover, Ireland was distinguished from other European societies of the *ancien régime*, in that the landed class was marked out as foreign by most of the population. Protestant power rested upon conquest, confiscation, and colonization, and the continuing awareness of this fact was reflected not just in the popular culture of the native inhabitants but in the sense of insecurity so evident in Protestant consciousness.

The Ascendancy mind had been moulded by the upheavals of the seventeenth century and by two events in particular: the Irish rebellion which broke out on 23 October 1641, and the Jacobite war of 1688–91. The atrocities committed by the native rebels in 1641 had been graphically and gruesomely exaggerated in Sir John Temple's *The Irish Rebellion*, first published in 1646 and regularly reprinted throughout the eighteenth century. Temple's grisly catalogue of drownings and disembowellings hammered home the lesson that the native race was irredeemably treacherous, vicious, and debauched. Fired by ancestral hatreds, it seemed that the Irish would never rest until they had recovered their lands and re-established their religion.[5] These perceptions were reinforced by another popular work, William King's *The State of the Protestants in Ireland* (1691), which dwelt upon the wicked designs of the Catholics in the reign of James II to reverse the land settlement and destroy

---

[3] Notably S. J. Connolly, *Religion, Law and Power: The Making of Protestant Ireland 1660–1760* (Oxford, 1992).

[4] A. P. W. Malcomson, *John Foster: The Politics of the Anglo-Irish Ascendancy* (Oxford, 1978), pp. xviii–xix. For the origins of the term see James Kelly, 'The Genesis of "Protestant Ascendancy": The Rightboy Disturbances of the 1780s and their Impact upon Protestant Opinion', in Gerard O'Brien (ed.), *Parliament, Politics and People: Essays in Eighteenth-Century Irish History* (Dublin, 1989), 93–127.

[5] Thomas Bartlett, *The Fall and Rise of the Irish Nation: The Catholic Question 1690–1830* (Dublin, 1992), 7–8.

Protestantism.[6] Throughout the next century the anniversaries of these two conflicts were marked by commemorative sermons which hailed each miraculous deliverance of Protestant Ireland as a providential intervention on behalf of a divinely favoured people.[7]

There was nothing peculiarly Irish about the eighteenth-century obsession with popery, as a whole series of recent studies has demonstrated. In popular memory the Reformation did duty for England's war of independence: her public rituals, her folklore, filled with examples of Catholic perfidy and cruelty, and her sense of providential destiny were all rooted in a history of confrontation with the Catholic continental powers. In eighteenth-century sermons, pamphlets, and cartoons, in popular celebrations and 'pope-burnings', the perceived unity of Catholicism, slavery, and poverty continued to underline the unique blessings of the freeborn Englishman. Colin Haydon has drawn attention to nationwide concern about 'the growth of popery' in the mid-1730s and mid-1760s, and mass anti-Catholic hysteria in 1745, which resemble the better-known *peurs* of 1641–2 and 1688. Such fears, he suggests, were given greater plausibility by the cases of religious persecution in France, Spain, Austria, and Poland reported in the British press.[8] In the quasi-colonial conditions of eighteenth-century Ireland these anxieties naturally acquired an added urgency.

Anti-popery was a remarkably elastic ideology, capable of taking disruptive as well as cohesive forms, depending on the political and economic context.[9] It was a favourite trick of Anglican polemicists to portray the Presbyterian as a species of papist: each was obliged by his fanatical creed to extirpate rival faiths; each kept his congregation in a state of slavery; and each claimed an absolute ecclesiastical jurisdiction which threatened to dissolve the bonds of civil society. Dissenters, of course, countered that episcopalianism, which retained the basic structure of the Roman Church, was simply popery without the Pope. Nevertheless, Protestantism united the majority of British subjects in a common sense of identity that sustained them through a series of massive wars with France between 1689 and 1815.[10] As we shall see, it was only the retreat of institutional Catholicism in the wake of the French Revolution that weakened this basic polarity, allowing Dissenters the freedom to mount a full-scale assault on establishment Anglicanism.

At the centre of the Ascendancy world was the Irish Parliament, founded in the Middle Ages on the English model and jealous of its ancient privileges. For most

[6] Thomas Bartlett, *The Fall and Rise of the Irish Nation: The Catholic Question 1690–1830* (Dublin, 1992), 13–16.

[7] T. C. Barnard, 'The Uses of 23 October and Irish Protestant Celebrations', *English Historical Review*, 106 (1991), 889–920.

[8] Colin Haydon, *Anti-Catholicism in Eighteenth-Century England, c.1714–80: A Political and Social Study* (Manchester, 1993).

[9] Much is to be learned about this subject from two highly original and very different articles: Mark Goldie, 'The Civil Religion of James Harrington', in Anthony Pagden (ed.), *The Languages of Political Theory in Early-Modern Europe* (Cambridge, 1987), 197–222; Peter Lake, 'Anti-Popery: The Structure of a Prejudice', in Richard Cust and Ann Hughes (eds.), *Conflict in Early Stuart England: Studies in Religion and Politics* (London, 1989), 72–106.

[10] Linda Colley, *Britons: Forging the Nation 1707–1837* (London, 1992).

of the seventeenth century the legislature had been summoned at infrequent and irregular intervals, but in the 1690s it became an indispensable part of the governance of Ireland. From then onwards it met once every two years, and, after 1785, annually. To a large extent the rise of Parliament was a product of the revolutionary wars of 1689–91, which had completed the transference of land from the old Catholic ruling class to the Protestant settlers. The total defeat of Catholic power had made Protestant Ascendancy inevitable, but it was the Irish Parliament rather than the English government which determined what form that ascendancy would take. Convinced that the Treaty of Limerick—which had concluded hostilities— had not sufficiently punished the Catholic elite, the Protestants determined to secure a settlement that would guarantee their supremacy. The English government, which placed Ireland second to wider imperial considerations, was often indifferent or even hostile to their predicament, and the Protestants quickly realized the usefulness of their Parliament in forcing through their demands. Between 1695 and 1728 a series of acts were passed designed to destroy the landed base of Catholic society, to dismantle the structure of the Roman Catholic Church, to deprive Catholics of public office and eventually of the franchise. This penal code was modelled upon English legislation, but it is important to remember that it originated not in London but in Dublin. In the 1690s the Irish Parliament thus came to acquire special significance as the guarantor of Protestant security, just as the Stormont assembly became identified with the survival of Ulster Unionism after 1922. In both cases the Protestant ruling classes quickly recognized the value of local institutions as a defence against the Catholic threat, a threat which always seemed more real to Irish Protestants than to their London overlords.[11]

A second reason for the enhanced role of Parliament was the increasing dependence of the monarch on taxation for the revenue needed to finance a series of continental wars. In 1692 the commons exploited this situation by claiming the 'sole right' to control Irish taxation, an issue which would flare up again in the eighteenth century.[12] It was in economic affairs, however, that Ireland's subordination to English interests was most painfully demonstrated. The restrictions imposed on Irish exports by the Westminster Parliament, most notoriously by the Woollen Act of 1699, were identified as the source of Ireland's poverty. Although historians have now established that these measures had less impact upon the Irish economy than was once supposed, the mercantilist policy pursued in London contributed more than any other factor to the development of a sense of separate, corporate identity in the Dublin legislature. From the 1690s onwards the governing classes campaigned for greater equality within the Empire. Initially this offensive emphasized the rights of Irish Protestants to

[11] For Protestant fears of a British sell-out, see Connolly, *Religion, Law and Power*, 264–6; D. W. Hayton, 'The Williamite Revolution in Ireland, 1688–91', in Jonathan Israel (ed.), *The Anglo-Dutch Moment: Essays on the Glorious Revolution and its World Impact* (Cambridge, 1991), 185–213; Patrick Kelly, 'Ireland and the Glorious Revolution: From Kingdom to Colony', in Robert Beddard (ed.), *The Revolutions of 1688* (Oxford, 1991), 163–90.

[12] J. I. McGuire, 'The Irish Parliament of 1692', in Thomas Bartlett and D. W. Hayton (eds.), *Penal Era and Golden Age: Essays in Irish History, 1690–1800* (Belfast, 1979), 1–31.

commercial and constitutional independence on the grounds that they were British subjects, an argument which led many of them to advocate a union with Great Britain. At the same time, Irish Protestants were driven to revive the claims, previously made by the Catholic elite which they had dispossessed, for the historic rights of Irish parliamentary institutions. It was this argument, often labelled by historians as 'colonial nationalism', that came to dominate patriot thinking in the eighteenth century.

The definitive statement of Irish patriotism was William Molyneux's *The Case of Ireland's Being Bound by Acts of Parliament in England, Stated*, first published in 1698 and reprinted many times in the next hundred years. Although scholarly attention has often centred on Molyneux's deployment of natural rights arguments (borrowed from his correspondent John Locke), this was in fact a minor current in his thinking. Irish patriots typically relied upon legal and historical arguments to demonstrate that Ireland was a not a subordinate colony like Virginia, New England, or Maryland, but 'a complete kingdom within itself' linked to England only by its allegiance to the Crown.[13] Their demand was not for separation but for equal status within the British imperial system. Although the British Parliament confirmed its right to legislate for Ireland in the Declaratory Act of 1720, Westminster's authority to interfere in Irish affairs was used sparingly, and a *modus operandi* was worked out between the administration and the parliamentary chiefs (the 'undertakers') who controlled the Commons.[14] At moments of constitutional crisis, however, such as the Wood's halfpence controversy in the 1720s and the Money Bill Dispute of 1753, the claim for equal status with Westminster inevitably resurfaced. Finally, in 1782, Ireland's legislative autonomy was successfully asserted by Grattan and Flood against the backdrop of American independence.

Ascendancy patriotism was fuelled by other concrete grievances, such as the reservation of many administrative, ecclesiastical, and judicial posts for English appointees. Equally vital, but more difficult to chart, was the growing Protestant identification with the history and topography of the island of Ireland.[15] In part, this was a natural reaction to English condescension; it might also be seen as an example of the legendary assimilative processes which had always made foreign settlers *Hiberniciores ipsis Hibernicis*. During the long peace inaugurated by the Hanoverian succession the Ascendancy class developed an attachment to the Irish landscape, and many of its members demonstrated a keen interest in the antiquities and language of Gaelic Ireland. The lighter side of this phenomenon was captured by one pamphleteer in 1762 who explained to the incoming Lord Lieutenant that the Irish Protestants were as 'warmly attached and bigotted' to their island as the English were to theirs: 'our bilberries and our potatoes are in our mouths as delicious and

---

[13] Quoted in Connolly, *Religion, Law, and Power*, 105.

[14] D. W. Hayton, 'The Beginnings of the "Undertaker System"', in Bartlett and Hayton, *Penal Era and Golden Age*, 32–54.

[15] See R. F. Foster, *Modern Ireland 1600–1972* (London, 1988), ch. 8; Connolly, *Religion, Law and Power*, 120–4; D. W. Hayton, 'Anglo-Irish Attitudes: Changing Perceptions of National Identity Among the Protestant Ascendancy in Ireland, *c*.1690–1750', *Studies in Eighteenth-Century Culture*, 17 (1987), 145–57.

high-flavoured as the best grapes and melons in the mouth of an Italian or Frenchman nor should we endure the man who would propose an exchange.'[16]

What exactly was the constitutional status of the kingdom of Ireland? The patriots adhered to the fiction that Ireland and Britain were separate and coequal kingdoms existing under the dual monarchy of the Hanoverians. It was the proud boast of Irish Protestants that they enjoyed the benefits of the unique British constitution. The Irish government was held up as an example of a mixed or balanced constitution combining the three pure types of polity: monarchy, aristocracy, and democracy. The reality of course was very different. Under Poynings' Law (1494), legislative measures initiated by the Irish Parliament had to be submitted to the English Privy Council where they could be rejected or amended. As we have seen, the legislative powers of the Irish Parliament were further curtailed by the Declaratory Act. But these statutes comprised just the formal mechanisms of English control. Even after 1782, when 'Grattan's Parliament' claimed the sole right to pass laws for Ireland, the reality of subordination remained. The fundamental problem was that the executive at Dublin Castle was not accountable to the legislature at College Green. The Lord Lieutenant and the chief secretary who headed the Castle administration were Englishmen appointed by the British ministry, and were thus subject not to public opinion in Ireland but to the vicissitudes of party politics in London. The government could secure a majority in the Commons only by buying off the great aristocratic interests. One result was that the Irish political system was even more dependent on patronage than the English; another was that opposition politics in Ireland was often more rhetorical than real.[17]

If Parliament represented one pillar of the Protestant Ascendancy, the Established Church could claim to be another. In Ireland, as throughout Europe, Church and State were held to be two expressions of the same national community. To the Established Church was entrusted the spiritual life of the nation; in return it demanded the active protection of the civil authority and the financial support of the people. The practice, of course, fell miserably short of the theory. In its pastoral role the Church was undermined by the fact that it commanded the allegiance of only a small minority of the population. Even Edmund Burke, the great theorist of established religion, found it difficult to defend the Anglican position in Ireland. 'It is not the religion of the people of Ireland,' he lamented. 'No church, in no Country in the world is so circumstanced.'[18] In addition, it has generally been assumed that the Church of Ireland suffered from all the defects of its English prototype— absenteeism, pluralism, corruption, an archaic structure, and spiritual decline— problems greatly multiplied by the adherence of the vast majority of Irish families

---

[16] Thomas Bartlett, ' "A People Made Rather for Copies than for Originals": The Anglo-Irish, 1760–1800', *International History Review*, 12/1 (1990), 12.

[17] The Irish administration is dealt with in E. M. Johnston, *Great Britain and Ireland 1760–1800: A Study in Political Administration* (Edinburgh, 1963) and James Kelly, *Prelude to Union: Anglo-Irish Politics in the 1780s* (Cork, 1992), ch. 1.

[18] Burke to Fitzwilliam, 21 Oct. 1794, *The Correspondence of Edmund Burke*, ed. T. W. Copeland *et al.*, 10 vols. (Cambridge, 1958–78), viii. 55.

to Roman Catholicism.[19] The traditional picture of the English Church has been modified, however, and there is mounting evidence to suggest that Irish Anglicanism too exhibited more vitality than historians once suspected.[20]

As we have seen, 'colonial nationalism'—the campaign to free the Irish Parliament from external interference—was bound up in its origins with the internal struggle for Anglican supremacy. Initially, this meant the subjection of Catholicism, but increasingly it involved also the negation of the threat posed by the Presbyterian population in the north. One of the major flashpoints in Anglo-Irish relations was created by the desire of Whig ministries in London to ameliorate the position of Irish Dissenters by removing the sacramental test which excluded them from public office. The sectarian character of early patriotism was demonstrated in the person of Jonathan Swift, whose well-known support for Irish autonomy was clearly subordinated to his defence of Anglican privilege.[21] Even Molyneux's *Case* was linked to the contest between Anglican and Presbyterian interests, since one of the complicated constitutional controversies of the 1690s originated with a legal dispute in which the Presbyterian majority on the Londonderry corporation had opposed Bishop William King.[22]

A new appreciation of the centrality of Anglicanism to the Hanoverian regime has led some historians to describe eighteenth-century Ireland as a 'confessional state'.[23] The usefulness of this term is questionable; it should certainly not be taken to imply a complete symmetry between the ecclesiastical and civil spheres. The enforcement of religious uniformity with the aid of the civil power had been abandoned long before the Toleration Act of 1719 offered protection to Protestant Dissent and ended the legal monopoly of the Church of Ireland over the religious life of the nation. Since the death of Queen Anne the power of the Established Church had waned in other ways too. After 1714 convocation was not summoned, and the Church was deprived of its independent voice; in the decades that followed, the ecclesiastical courts had gone into irreversible decline. On both the national and local levels, the established clergy were henceforth subordinated to lay elites, and Anglican privilege depended upon parliamentary support, not always forthcoming if the interests of landlords and bishops clashed. If the Church was part of an Irish

---

[19] David Hempton, 'Religion in British Society 1740–1790', in Jeremy Black (ed.), *British Politics and Society from Walpole to Pitt 1742–1789* (London, 1990), 201–21.

[20] For the reforming impulse in the Church of Ireland see T. C. Barnard, 'Protestants and the Irish Language, c.1675–1725', *Journal of Ecclesiastical History*, 44 (1993), 243–72; id., 'Reforming Irish Manners: the Religious Societies in Dublin during the 1690s', *Historical Journal*, 35 (1992), 805–38; and the essays by Barnard, Connolly, and Hayton in Alan Ford, James McGuire, and Kenneth Milne (eds.), *As by Law Established: The Church of Ireland since the Reformation* (Dublin, 1995).

[21] J. C. Beckett, 'Swift: The Priest in Politics', in id., *Confrontations: Studies in Irish History* (London, 1972), 111–22.

[22] J. C. Beckett, 'William King's Administration of the Diocese of Derry, 1691–1703', *IHS* 4 (1944), 164–80.

[23] The term was popularized by J. C. D. Clark: see his *English Society 1688–1832: Ideology, Social Structure and Political Practice During the Ancien Regime* (Cambridge, 1985); id., 'England's Ancien Regime as a Confessional State', *Albion*, 21 (1989), 450–74. For its adoption by Irish historians see Connolly, *Religion, Law and Power*, and C. D. A. Leighton, *Catholics in a Protestant Kingdom: A Study of the Irish Ancien Régime* (Basingstoke, 1994).

ancien régime, it was certainly the weakest part, and the monarchy and aristocracy demonstrated a disconcerting readiness to sacrifice its interests in favour of their own.

Similarly, we should be careful when describing the ideological functions of established religion. There are obvious difficulties in casting the Anglican clergy as the intellectual guardians of the sort of hierarchical social order found throughout *ancien régime* Europe. Although many clergymen regarded the penal code as a mechanism for compelling the Catholics to come into the church, there were also many pessimists who viewed anti-Catholic legislation as a defensive shield designed to insulate them from the majority of the population. The political theology and public ritual of the Anglican Church, which were such powerful integrating factors in English society, carried very different implications across the Irish Sea. Robert Eccleshall and Toby Barnard have produced a nuanced picture of Anglican civil religion in which the sanctification of the social order interacted with assertions of ethnic and linguistic superiority to produce a distinctive mentality that had no exact parallel in either *ancien régime* Europe or its overseas colonies.[24]

In the last quarter of the eighteenth century the equation of political stability with Anglican hegemony was forcefully reasserted by Richard Woodward, Bishop of Cloyne, in *The Present State of the Church of Ireland* (1786). Although primarily concerned with anti-tithe protests in Munster, which some saw as evidence of a popish conspiracy, the bishop did not hesitate to extend his attack to the republican and levelling principles of the Presbyterians.[25] It is worth pointing out, however, that Woodward chose to take his stand upon utilitarian grounds: Anglicanism was to be upheld because it underpinned the social hierarchy and complemented limited monarchy, rather than because it was doctrinally pure or laid claim to apostolic foundations.[26] It is a telling sign of government priorities, moreover, that when the archbishopric of Armagh fell vacant in 1783, Woodward was rejected by Dublin Castle because of his known antipathy to Roman Catholicism.[27] Nevertheless, the intellectual prominence of Woodward, and other Anglican apologists such as Arthur Browne, Thomas Elrington, John Giffard, and Patrick Duigenan, ensured that the Established Church would become interlinked with the British connection and the land settlement as a bulwark of Protestant Ascendancy.

The concept of the 'confessional state' must therefore be used with care. In conclusion, however, it is vital to stress that the Church was a not just a department of State, an adjunct of old corruption, but an integral part of the political system. Although Anglicans were unable to prevent concessions to Presbyterians and Catholics, the establishment principle itself remained sacrosanct, and, in return,

---

[24] Barnard, 'Irish Protestant Celebrations'; Robert Eccleshall, 'Anglican Political Thought in the Century after the Revolution of 1688', in D. G. Boyce, R. Eccleshall, and V. Geoghegan (eds.), *Political Thought in Ireland since the Seventeenth Century* (London, 1993), esp. 60–4.

[25] Richard Woodward, *The Present State of the Church of Ireland* (Dublin, 1787), 10. For the background see James Kelly, 'Inter-Denominational Relations and Religious Toleration in Late Eighteenth-Century Ireland: The "Paper War" of 1786–88', *Eighteenth-Century Ireland*, 3 (1988), 39–67; id., 'Genesis of Protestant Ascendancy'; id., 'Eighteenth-Century Ascendancy: A Commentary', *Eighteenth-Century Ireland*, 5 (1990), 173–87.　　　　　　　　　　　　[26] Woodward, *Present State*, 5–19.

[27] Bartlett, *Catholic Question*, 110.

the clergy offered divine sanction to the political and social order. The religious celebrations held on royal and patriotic anniversaries, the dominance of the clergy in intellectual life, and the local role of the Church in welfare and education all re-inforced the link between confessional identity and political allegiance. In theory, the Church of Ireland remained an essential part of national and local administration, and in practice the clergy played a prominent part in the maintenance of public order: at the end of the eighteenth century just over 10 per cent of JPs were in holy orders.[28] Anglicanism coloured all expressions of political authority, uniting the clergy, the landowners, and the local administration. As long as this union of Church and State remained solid, it was inevitable that disputes over theological matters would have important political implications.

Catholics

The Georgian glamour of the Ascendancy is routinely contrasted with the 'hidden Ireland' of the Catholic masses. For historians of the latter, the eighteenth century is dominated by the penal code or 'popery laws'. This string of statutes has vari-ously been seen as a series of precautionary measures taken in self-defence, a sys-tematic attempt to subjugate, degrade, or even obliterate an entire culture, an essentially political measure designed to deprive the Catholic elite of property and influence, or a zealous drive aimed at the conformity and conversion of the popu-lation. The first point to be made about the penal code is that, whatever the logic behind it, its authors lacked both the will and the resources to implement it. By the late 1730s the local authorities had abandoned any attempt to enforce the penal laws against the Church, along with any serious hopes of converting the Irish. The limited impact of anti-Catholic legislation can be measured by looking at three dis-tinct areas: religion, property, and politics.

The assault on the ecclesiastical organization of the Roman Catholic Church was the least effective part of the penal code. In addition to the oath of abjuration, by which all priests were required to renounce Jacobite loyalties, the activities of the priesthood were restricted by the Registry Act, Catholic schools were prohibited, and pilgrimages and visits to holy wells were outlawed. Most importantly, by an act of 1697 all bishops and religious orders were to be expelled from the country. Since new priests could not be ordained without bishops, this act must be taken as a serious attempt to dismantle the church structure. The execution of these meas-ures was in the hands of the unpaid magistrates, however, who were often reluct-ant to provoke local conflicts. Even in the early decades of the century, when the penal code was more rigorously enforced, the Church was able to survive as an under-ground organization. In much of the country mass was said in thatched cabins, in private houses, in sheds, or in the open air, although Dublin and other towns boasted more impressive buildings. By the late 1730s the Church had weathered the storm. An official inquiry of 1731 revealed that Ireland contained 1,700 priests including

---

[28] R. B. McDowell, *Ireland in the Age of Imperialism and Revolution 1760–1801* (Oxford, 1979), 66.

254 friars, 892 mass-houses, and 549 schools.[29] Even in Ulster, where the Church infrastructure was weakest, Catholic worship was becoming more visible.[30]

The second aspect of the Protestant offensive was economic. Beginning in 1695, a series of laws were enacted aimed at the destruction of the Catholic landowning class. The Catholic share of land, already reduced to 22 per cent in 1688, had fallen to 14 per cent by 1704, and declined further under the penal laws as landowners conformed to the Established Church to secure their property.[31] This does not present an accurate picture of the amount of wealth in Catholic hands, however. Historians have begun to investigate the strategies employed by landed Catholics to circumvent the law. In particular they have discovered a 'convert interest' made up of conformed Catholics who straddled the worlds of the Protestant elite and the old Catholic gentry.[32] Secondly, by concentrating on the distribution of land held in fee simple, older accounts have overlooked the increasing wealth of Catholic middlemen and tenant farmers.[33] In Ulster the Catholic landed interest had been completely wiped out by the plantation, but in many southern counties networks of Catholic families managed to protect their property.[34] Finally, and most importantly, trade remained open to all denominations; there is now general agreement that one of the central developments of the penal era was the appearance of a large merchant class in the towns, and particularly in the ports.[35] By the 1750s, indeed, the argument that the penal laws were depriving the national economy of the large fortunes amassed by Catholic traders had become a standard plank in the emancipationist platform.

While restrictions on economic activity and religious worship could sometimes be evaded, the exclusion of Catholics from the public world of Irish politics was complete. The two Houses of Parliament, the municipal corporations, the magistracy, and the legal profession were all closed. Finally, in 1728 the Catholics, most of whom were already unable to vote because of their objections to the oath of abjuration, were formally disenfranchised. Although individual propertied Catholics could still influence the votes of their Protestant tenants,[36] Catholic Ireland had effectively been eliminated from the political process. It is arguable that, given the oligarchic nature of the eighteenth-century political system, this may not have mattered much. Indeed, admission to the franchise did not figure among early Catholic aims. It is important to note, though, that any reform of the electoral system would further disadvantage

[29] J. L. McCracken, 'The Ecclesiastical Structure, 1714–60', in T. W. Moody and W. E. Vaughan (eds.), *A New History of Ireland*, iv, *Eighteenth-Century Ireland 1690–1800* (Oxford, 1986), 92, 94; Connolly, *Religion, Law and Power*, 151. Since the Roman Catholic Church was naturally anxious to avoid publicity at this time, these figures must be taken as underestimates.

[30] Patrick Rogers, *The Irish Volunteers and Catholic Emancipation (1778–1793)* (London, 1934), 5. See also P. J. Corish, *The Catholic Community in the Seventeenth and Eighteenth Centuries* (Dublin, 1981); Kevin Whelan, 'The Regional Impact of Irish Catholicism 1700–1850', in W. J. Smyth and Kevin Whelan (eds.), *Common Ground: Essays on the Historical Geography of Ireland* (Cork, 1988), 253–77.

[31] Connolly, *Religion, Law and Power*, 147.

[32] L. M. Cullen, 'Catholics Under the Penal Laws', *Eighteenth-Century Ireland*, 1 (1986), 27–8.

[33] Connolly, *Religion, Law and Power*, 148.   [34] Cullen, 'Penal Laws', 24, 33–4.

[35] But see also David Dickson, 'Catholics and Trade in Eighteenth-Century Ireland: An Old Debate Revisited', in T. P. Power and Kevin Whelan (eds.), *Endurance and Emergence: Catholics in Ireland in the Eighteenth Century* (Dublin, 1990), 85–100.   [36] Cullen, 'Penal Laws', 26–7.

middle-class Catholics by making Parliament more responsive to popular Protestantism. It is no accident that Catholic agitation accelerated when parliamentary reform became a burning issue in the 1780s.

Between 1691 and 1798 there was no Catholic insurrection against the Protestant regime in Ireland. During the Jacobite rebellion of 1745 the hierarchy had issued declarations of loyalty to allay Protestant fears. The sporadic outbursts of agrarian trouble which were a regular feature of eighteenth-century Ireland should not be attributed to political disaffection, as the nervous Ascendancy thought, or affected to think. Organized agrarian resistance in Ireland was often given the generic label of 'whiteboyism', following the widespread agitation in Munster in the 1760s masterminded by the 'Whiteboys'. In fact, rural disturbances usually arose from specific, localized situations: the protests of the Whiteboys were initially provoked by the enclosure of common land, though they came to focus on tithes, while the 'Rightboys' of the 1780s added to customary grievances the financial claims of the Catholic priesthood.[37]

Although the secret societies of rural Ireland were conservative in nature, appealing to traditional economic practices in the face of commercialization, their organized, conspiratorial character fuelled Protestant fears of Catholic revanchism. Ascendancy suspicions were not entirely unjustified. Observers of eighteenth-century Ireland found a sense of dispossession running through the popular myths and memories of the countryside. 'However it might be disguised or suppressed', wrote Wolfe Tone, 'there existed in the breast of every Irish Catholic, an inextirpable abhorrence of the English name and power.'[38] This disaffection was most pronounced among the overtly sectarian Defenders, who emerged in the Ulster borderlands in the 1780s. Defenderism was markedly more 'modern' in character than its southern predecessors; it spanned a wider social constituency, reflecting the extent of industrialization in the linen triangle of south Ulster. In the 1790s the parochial meetings organized by the Catholic Committee, the slogans and images of the French Revolution, and the democratic propaganda disseminated by the United Irishmen would bridge the gap between the economic grievances of the Defenders and national politics.[39]

The political behaviour of the Catholic hierarchy, meanwhile, was generally docile and passive. Of all the groups who were disadvantaged by the Revolution Settlement the Catholics found it most difficult to adapt to the politics of the excluded. Their intellectual heritage, maintained by training in *ancien régime* France, did not facilitate the adoption of a dissenting mentality, nor did it equip them with languages of political opposition or resistance theories. Disaffection under the Hanoverians

---

[37] J. S. Donnelly, jun., 'The Rightboy Movement 1785–8', *Studia Hibernica*, 17–18 (1977–8), 120–202; id., 'The Whiteboy Movement 1761–5', *IHS* 21 (1978), 20–54; id., 'Irish Agrarian Rebellion: The Whiteboys of 1769–76', *PRIA* 83C, no. 12 (1983); M. J. Bric, 'Priests, Parsons and Politics: The Rightboy Protest in County Cork, 1785–1788', in C. H. E. Philpin (ed.), *Nationalism and Popular Protest in Ireland* (Cambridge, 1987), 163–90; S. J. Connolly, 'Violence and Order in the Eighteenth Century', in T. P. O'Flanagan, P. Ferguson, and Kevin Whelan (eds.), *Rural Ireland: Modernisation and Change* (Cork, 1987), 42–61. For a contrasting view see Luke Gibbons, 'Identity without a Centre: Allegory, History and Irish Nationalism', in *Transformations in Irish Culture* (Cork, 1996), 134–47.

[38] *The Life of Theobald Wolfe Tone*, ed. W. T. W. Tone, 2 vols. (Washington, 1826), ii. 52.

[39] For the development of Catholic agrarian radicalism see Jim Smyth, *The Men of No Property: Irish Radicals and Popular Politics in the Late Eighteenth Century* (London, 1992), esp. chs. 2–3.

was thus limited to a residual Jacobitism which, until recently at least, historians have regarded as a literary rather than a political phenomenon.[40] Although the priesthood reflected a cross-section of society, and was maintained by the people without state aid, Irish Catholicism remained hierarchical in its structure and fearful of popular initiatives. The bishops took a tough line against agrarian rebels and instilled the virtues of loyalty on such occasions as the '45.[41]

Political leadership eventually came not from the Church but from the gentry and the urban middle classes. A Catholic Committee was established in Dublin in 1759 by medical men such as John Curry and impoverished gentlemen such as Charles O'Conor and Thomas Wyse. It issued the first of many addresses stressing the attachment of the Catholics of Ireland to the Hanoverians. For the next thirty years, the main work of the Committee was designed to confront the mythology which had grown up around the horrors of 1641 and to disassociate Irish Catholics from the Jacobite cause. An important turning point came in 1766 when the Old Pretender, James III, died, and the Pope abandoned his support for the Stuart dynasty, leaving Irish Catholics free to swear allegiance to George III.

One by-product of this propaganda effort was the adoption of a revisionist view of Irish history which accepted the 1688 settlement as a permanent feature of the Irish landscape. A series of Catholic apologetics, some of them actually written by Protestants such as Edmund Burke and Henry Brooke, injected into Catholic political discourse the vocabulary of whig constitutionalism.[42] Catholic writers began to stress the role of their ancestors in the evolution of the British constitution (this would later be a major theme of United Irish propaganda). By 1786 Charles O'Conor was able to remark, albeit with some irony, that 'we are all become *good Protestants in politics*'.[43] The process by which Catholics learned to couch their demands in the terms of English whiggery remains a mystery, but it was the necessary precondition to their participation in Irish radicalism in the 1790s. William Drennan, a founding member of the United Irishmen, found that while the Catholic masses still followed 'the political doctrine of priests and the old tory nobility' the mercantile class had adopted 'somewhat of the language of liberty'.[44]

Eventually, the collapse of the Jacobite cause, the decline of papal authority in Europe, and the latitudinarian breezes of the Enlightenment would combine to produce a feeling that the penal code was unjust, anachronistic, and counter-productive. But the liberalization of the penal restrictions which began in 1778 owed less to the changing situation in Ireland than to the strategic requirements of imperial Britain. It was during the Seven Years' War that Irish Catholics were first enlisted in the British army, though their recruitment was legally forbidden. In 1778 and 1782, in order to secure the co-operation of Irish Catholics during the American war, two

---

[40] See the pioneering studies of Breandán Ó Buachalla, e.g. 'Irish Jacobitism and Irish Nationalism: the Literary Evidence', in Michael O'Dea and Kevin Whelan (eds.), *Nations and Nationalisms: France, Britain, Ireland and the Eighteenth-Century Context* (Oxford, 1995), 103–16. A more sceptical view can be found in Connolly, *Religion, Law and Power*, 233–49.   [41] Ibid. 158.

[42] J. R. Hill, 'Popery and Protestantism, Civil and Religious Liberty: The Disputed Lessons of Irish History', *Past and Present*, 118 (1988), 104–6.   [43] Quoted in Foster, *Modern Ireland*, 207.

[44] Drennan to Samuel McTier, 3 Feb. 1792, PRONI, Drennan Papers, T765/298.

relief acts removed the most severe restrictions on Catholics holding and leasing land.[45] Imperial considerations were also uppermost in the passage of the Catholic Relief Acts of 1792 and 1793, which granted the vote, the right to bear arms, and admission to the legal profession, grand juries, guilds, and corporations. This time the essential backdrop was the international threat posed by revolutionary France; the Roman Catholic Church could now be seen as a valuable ally against Jacobinism.

In effect, the British had now declared their neutrality in Ireland's religious politics. The internal ramifications of this adjustment in the balance of power cannot be underestimated. On the one hand, the relief bills provoked a backlash throughout the country as corporations and grand juries rallied to the standard of 'Protestant Ascendancy'.[46] At the same time these concessions contributed to the radicalization of the Catholic Committee. 'Emancipation'—now defined precisely as the right to sit in Parliament—had become all the more desirable. While the Catholic leaders studiously courted the Castle administration, they also flirted with first the Volunteers and then the United Irishmen in the hope that any reform package would include substantial benefits for the Catholic population. In 1791 the secession of Archbishop Troy and Lord Kenmare from the Committee marked the triumph of the 'democrats', led by John Keogh. The following year Catholic opinion was mobilized on an unprecedented scale, culminating in the meeting of a democratically elected convention in Dublin. The Catholics, as Drennan remarked, had attained a 'self-sufficiency'; political alignments were increasingly determined by the single overriding issue of emancipation.[47]

Presbyterians

In eighteenth-century Ireland the terms 'Protestant Dissenter' and 'Presbyterian' were often used interchangeably.[48] Unlike the other nonconformist minorities which survived in Britain and Ireland, the Ulster Presbyterians formed a disciplined, organized body, concentrated into one region. They were united by their Scottish origins and maintained close links with their mother country, where Presbyterianism was now the established religion. Most importantly, in their north-eastern stronghold they constituted the majority of the population.

Ulster Presbyterianism is a product of seventeenth-century settlement. Its strength and distribution cannot, however, be explained by reference to the official 'Ulster Plantation' which was concentrated into the years between 1609 and 1625. This government-sponsored scheme provided for the colonization of the six confiscated counties of Armagh, Cavan, Coleraine, Donegal, Fermanagh, and Tyrone by settlers

---

[45] J. R. Hill, 'Religious Toleration and the Relaxation of the Penal Laws: An Imperial Perspective', *Archivium Hibernicum*, 44 (1989), 90–110. [46] Smyth, *Men of No Property*, 20.

[47] Drennan to the McTiers, 10 Dec. [1792], in D. A. Chart (ed.), *The Drennan Letters, 1776–1819* (Belfast, 1931), 107.

[48] A number of nonconforming sects had survived from the Civil War period, but these were declining in numbers, and possessed no political influence.

from England and Scotland. By 1622 the main influx of planters was over, and British strongholds had emerged in several parts of Ulster. To the west and south of Lough Neagh, parts of Armagh and Tyrone had been intensively colonized; there was concentrated settlement also in the Foyle basin in north-west Ulster, where the towns of Londonderry and Strabane acted as focal points. The plantation had taken hold to a lesser extent around the Erne basin, the lower Bann valley, and north-east Londonderry.[49] Ironically, however, the most successful British penetration took place in Antrim and Down, two counties not included in the original scheme. Settlement in this area took place over a much longer period and can only partly be attributed to the policy of British colonization; it must also be seen in the context of a centuries-old tradition of migration between Scotland and Ulster.

Philip Robinson has identified four core areas of Scottish settlement within the British plantation: north Down, south Antrim, the 'Route' area of north Antrim and north-east Londonderry, and the area of the Foyle basin in north-east Donegal and north-west Tyrone known as the 'Laggan'.[50] It was precisely in these areas that the first four Irish presbyteries were established. This was by no means an inevitable development: although the early Scots settlers were predisposed towards the Presbyterian form of church government, they were initially comprehended within the Church of Ireland at a time when the distinction between episcopacy and presbytery was somewhat blurred. When Ulster Presbyterianism became a distinct Church after the Restoration it seems likely that many isolated Scots remained within the Established Church under its new dispensation. By this stage, however, a new phase of colonization was beginning. Between 1660 and 1690, according to one contemporary, 30,000 Scottish immigrants had arrived in Ulster. After a series of bad harvests in the early 1690s immigration rocketed: in 1692 it was said that 10,000 Scots had come in the previous year alone.[51] It was this final influx which ensured that east Ulster would remain not just Scottish, but also Presbyterian in character.

Broadly speaking, then, the English settled in the middle and south of the province, while the Scots were concentrated in the north and the east. By the last quarter of the eighteenth century there were as many as half a million Presbyterians in Ulster, despite the exodus to North America which had begun before 1720. There is no way of measuring the Presbyterian population at this time with any accuracy, but a rough idea can be obtained from the computations of William Campbell, agent of the Synod of Ulster in the 1780s. At that time, 180 congregations belonged to the Synod, which, Campbell reckoned, contained an average of 400 families each. Taking six persons as the typical family size, he calculated that the Synod catered

[49] P. S. Robinson, *The Plantation of Ulster: British Settlement in an Irish Landscape, 1600–1670* (Dublin, 1984), 94–5.   [50] Ibid. 112.

[51] R. G. Gillespie (ed.), *Settlement and Survival on an Ulster Estate: The Brownlow Leasebook 1667–1711* (Belfast, 1988), p. xviii. The most recent estimates of Scottish migration to Ulster put the figure for 1650 to 1700 at somewhere between 60,000 and 100,000 people, with the 1690s perhaps accounting for between 40,000 to 70,000 of these: T. C. Smout, N. C. Landsman, and T. M. Devine, 'Scottish Emigration in the Seventeenth and Eighteenth Centuries', in Nicholas Canny (ed.), *Europeans on the Move: Studies on European Migration, 1500–1800* (Oxford, 1994), esp. 88.

for a total of 432,000 souls. In addition there were 46 Seceding congregations, which Campbell put at 300 families each, making 82,800. Omitting the small Reformed Presbytery and the eighteen congregations of the Southern Association, the Presbyterian population could therefore be estimated at 514,800.[52]

In the last quarter of the eighteenth century there was not one Presbyterian church in Ireland but six. The main ecclesiastical body was the General Synod of Ulster, founded in 1690 shortly after the arrival in Ireland of William of Orange. Its establishment marked the culmination of a long and unsteady process of construction and consolidation which went back to the early decades of the century. During the plantation Presbyterianism had grown up within the Church of Ireland, then Calvinist in theology. Although Episcopalians and Presbyterians agreed on the need to purge the Christian Church of the superstitious and corrupt practices of Rome, they were divided by numerous disputes over theology and liturgy; it was the imposition of the English Prayer Book, after all, which had provoked the Scottish revolt against Charles I, and sparked off the civil war. The central difference, of course, focused on church government, the Presbyterians opting for a more democratic model of ecclesiastical polity. Within the recently planted Church of Ireland, however, a number of bishops were prepared to make the necessary compromises in order to ordain Scottish ministers.[53]

The history of the Presbyterian Church in Ireland really begins with the arrival of Robert Monroe's Scottish army in 1642. It was this force, dispatched to put down the rebellion, that established the first presbytery in Ireland in June of that year. Presbyterianism was transformed from a tendency within the Church of Ireland into a rival structure outside the establishment. A year later, militant Presbyterianism received a further boost with the introduction of the Solemn League and Covenant. This oath pledged assistance to the English Parliament in return for the establishment of the Kirk throughout the three kingdoms; its signatories were therefore bound to extirpate prelacy and popery throughout the British Isles. The Covenant was administered not only to the Scottish army, but to the settler population at large, for whom this ritual possessed symbolic significance as an expression of their communal solidarity against the Catholic rebels.[54] By 1661, when nonconforming ministers were ejected from their livings, Presbyterianism was sufficiently rooted in Ulster to ensure that most of the Scottish population adhered to its pastors. Over the next thirty years their ministers were subject to intermittent persecution by the Church of Ireland, but the episcopal authorities were helpless to prevent the steady progress of Presbyterianism. In 1690, with a Calvinist king battling against their popish enemies, and with the Scottish Kirk entering into its inheritance, the Ulster Presbyterians took the first opportunity to summon a Synod.

The essential distinction between Presbyterianism and Episcopacy turned on the office of bishop: whereas the Church of England retained the hierarchical structure

[52] William Campbell, journal, pp. 3–4, PHSI, Campbell MSS.

[53] The origins of Ulster Presbyterianism are briefly and lucidly recounted in Peter Brooke, *Ulster Presbyterianism: The Historical Perspective 1610–1970* (Dublin, 1987), ch. 2.

[54] D. W. Miller, *Queen's Rebels: Ulster Loyalism in Historical Perspective* (Dublin, 1978), 11–15.

of Rome, the ministers of the Scottish Kirk were equals, whose authority derived from popular consent. The system of courts or committees which governed the Presbyterian Church was therefore democratic, at least in theory. The basic unit of this structure was the kirk session, consisting of the minister and his elders. It was the role of the session to exercise moral and spiritual discipline within the congregation. The elders, who were laymen nominated by the session and then approved by the congregation, were each appointed a district or 'quarter' within the bounds of the congregation. Anglican clergymen frequently commented on the tight discipline and organization of the Kirk: William King claimed that Ulster Presbyterians were 'under an absolute slavery' to their ministers and elders.[55] Those minute-books which still survive certainly attest to their vigour: hundreds of sabbath-breakers, adulterers, fornicators, bigamists, drunks, thieves, dishonest businessmen, and slanderers were forced to repent their ways. In addition, the session managed the financial affairs of the congregation, maintained a school if it was able, and dispensed charity to the poor.[56]

Each minister, following his university training in the arts and in divinity, was received into the Church as a licentiate or probationer. It was then necessary to undergo a series of theological examinations or 'trials', during which time he might preach for vacant congregations or find work as a schoolmaster. The probationer might then receive a 'call' from one or more of these congregations and, following the approval of the local presbytery, would then be ordained. Throughout his ministry each clergyman was supported by a fixed stipend from the congregation and a share of the *regium donum*, the small grant which the Synod of Ulster received from the government. In addition, he was often supplied with a farm which was worked by members of the congregation.

At the close of the seventeenth century, with the machinery of Presbyterian government firmly in place, the Ulster Synod decided to regularize its proceedings, adopting many of the rules enacted by the General Assembly of the Church of Scotland. One result was the introduction of subscription to the Westminster Confession of Faith as a requirement for all students entering the ministry. It was this obligation which produced a violent schism among the Ulster Presbyterians, provoking a string of controversies over the next 150 years. In 1725 the Presbytery of Antrim, whose members tended towards a more liberal or 'New Light' interpretation of Presbyterian doctrine, was separated from the Synod. Although these ministers refused to subscribe to the Westminster Confession, they maintained friendly relations with their former colleagues. The other Presbyterian bodies, the Seceders and the Covenanters, had their origins in Scottish controversies which will be fully described in Chapter 3. To complicate matters further, the Seceders were themselves divided into two branches, the burghers and antiburghers, following a quarrel over the burgess oath in Scotland.

---

[55] Connolly, *Religion, Law and Power*, 167.
[56] Much useful information has been extracted from session minute-books by J. M. Barkley in *The Eldership in Irish Presbyterianism* (Belfast, 1963), ch. 2.

The final category of Presbyterians in Ireland embraces the congregations outside Ulster, most of which were affiliated to the 'Southern Association'.[57] Dublin and, to a lesser extent, Cork possessed considerable Presbyterian communities, and each of the three southern provinces had a sprinkling of congregations. Most important was the Dissenting presence in the capital, where Scottish influences were mingled with a strong English Puritan tradition. As the seat of government and the cultural and commercial centre of the kingdom, Dublin boasted many of the most talented and influential Dissenting ministers, and in the late seventeenth and early eighteenth centuries they included the chief Presbyterian spokesman, Joseph Boyse. In later decades, however, the capital's six Presbyterian congregations began to dwindle. The star of Belfast, meanwhile, was in the ascendant. When the Revd William Bruce of Dublin considered a call to the Belfast First Congregation in 1789, his close friend Dr William Drennan advised him that the north was the 'Dissenting Station' and Belfast its 'metropolis'; as pastor of First Belfast, Bruce would be 'Primate of the Presbyterians, Primus inter pares'.[58] In the last quarter of the century the Dublin meeting-houses retained some influence over intellectual trends in Irish Presbyterianism, and their social prestige made them attractive to upwardly mobile Dissenters who were looking for a halfway house on the road to conformity. It was only in Ulster, however, that Presbyterianism existed as a powerful political force.

According to Wolfe Tone, the Ulster Presbyterians had few 'overgrown landed proprietors' among them, being mostly engaged in manufacturing and trade; this social base, he believed, accounted for their lack of dependence on the English connection.[59] It is certainly true that most Presbyterian landed families had conformed along with their Catholic counterparts. In 1732 Archbishop Boulter wrote that the Dissenters were 'not proprietors of much land or wealth', estimating that there were only twenty gentlemen among them who would qualify to be Justices of the Peace if the Test Act was removed.[60] The Ulster middle class, on the other hand, was solidly Presbyterian. The travel writer John Gamble divided the Ulster population into three classes: the gentry, whom he called the 'English Irish'; the merchants, shopkeepers, and manufacturers, who were the 'Scotch Irish'; and the servants and labourers, mostly composed of the native Irish. 'The second class', he continued, 'is by far the most rational, the most enlightened, and the most industrious body.'[61] Edward Wakefield also found that those engaged in commercial pursuits were almost all Dissenters of Scottish extraction.[62]

From the middle of the eighteenth century, visitors to Ulster regularly commented on the increasing prosperity of the province, reflected in its rapidly rising population.

---

[57] There is no modern history of southern Presbyterianism, but J. Armstrong, *History of the Presbyterian Churches in the City of Dublin* (Dublin, 1829) and C. H. Irwin, *History of Presbyterianism in Dublin and the South and West of Ireland* (London, 1890) contain some useful information; J. S. Reid, *History of the Presbyterian Church in Ireland*, ed. W. D. Killen, 3rd edn., 3 vols. (Belfast, 1867), is essential as always. [58] Drennan to Bruce, [*c*.Oct. 1789], PRONI, Drennan/Bruce Papers, D553/67.
[59] *Life of Tone*, i. 45. [60] Quoted in Connolly, *Religion, Law and Power*, 163.
[61] John Gamble, *Sketches of History, Politics and Manners, Taken in Dublin, and the North of Ireland in the Autumn of 1810* (London, 1811), 285.
[62] Edward Wakefield, *An Account of Ireland, Statistical and Political*, 2 vols. (London, 1812), ii. 730.

New wealth derived partly from the growing demand across the water for Ulster livestock and partly from the retailing of the manufactured products of industrial Britain. Its core, however, was the expanding linen industry in the triangle formed by Dungannon, Lisburn, and Newry.[63] Before the 1780s, Ulster cloth had been exported to England via the White Linenhall in Dublin. The northern linendrapers bitterly resented the dominance of Dublin over the industry, however, and in August 1782 they assembled at Dungannon to protest against an act of Parliament recently introduced by the Dublin Linen Board. At this meeting, which was compared with the Volunteer convention of the same year, it was decided to erect a white linenhall in Ulster, and Newry and Belfast emerged as the two obvious contenders for the site. In the end both towns constructed linenhalls, but the greater diversification of the Belfast economy meant that it soon emerged as undisputed capital. By the turn of the century Belfast's booming wholesale trade had made it 'the warehouse of the North' and its traders were importing manufactured goods and exporting farm products to Britain, while the cotton industry, pioneered in the late 1770s, now employed 13,500 persons within a ten-mile radius of the town.[64]

At the apex of the Belfast middle class stood the general merchants who, in addition to their trading activities, offered a number of more general services such as banking and insurance. They also provided the capital for many of the manufacturing concerns in the town—ropeworks, iron foundries, glassworks, pottery, and shipbuilding.[65] In 1783, fifty-nine of these merchants, led by Waddell Cunningham, came together to establish a chamber of commerce. Their early achievements included the passage of an act in 1785 setting up 'the Corporation for Preserving and Improving the Port and Harbour of Belfast'; this body, better known as the Ballast Board, laid the foundations of the shipbuilding industry which later came to dominate the town. Since Belfast was a corporation borough under the control of the Earl of Donegall, however, the growing commercial and industrial power of its citizens was not matched by political influence.

For the most part, Ulster's textile industries were still organized on a domestic basis. Farming families had supplemented their earnings from land by spinning and weaving for decades, and in many areas, notably Armagh, linen production had become the primary economic activity. This mixed economy incurred the censure of Arthur Young, who believed that constant shifting from the shuttle to the spade impaired the worker's hands, but it pleased the classical republican William Drennan, who countered that the combination of agriculture and industry gave northerners a certain independence which, reinforced by their Dissenting principles, made them

---

[63] The work of W. H. Crawford is indispensable: 'Change in Ulster in the Late Eighteenth Century', in Bartlett and Hayton, *Penal Era and Golden Age*, 186–203; 'Ulster Economy and Society in the Eighteenth Century', Ph.D. thesis (QUB, 1983). See also Graeme Kirkham's introduction to R. J. Dickson, *Ulster Emigration to Colonial America 1718–1775*, 2nd edn. (Belfast, 1988).

[64] W. H. Crawford, 'The Belfast Middle Classes in the Late Eighteenth Century', in David Dickson, Dáire Keogh, and Kevin Whelan (eds.), *The United Irishmen: Republicanism, Radicalism and Rebellion* (Dublin, 1993), 66–8; id., 'Change in Ulster', 192–8.

[65] N. E. Gamble, 'The Business Community and Trade of Belfast 1767–1800', Ph.D. thesis (University of Dublin, 1978).

natural whigs.[66] Without entering into the eighteenth-century debate about the implications of the division of labour for the civic personality, one can easily accept Drennan's point that the market towns where the independent weavers sold their webs of cloth were also sources of political news. The growth of the linen manufacture had another, more immediate, effect. As an increasing number of families took up weaving they were able to subdivide their farms, allowing population density in industrial areas to soar. Since rents had kept pace with industrial growth, these tenant-weavers were extremely vulnerable in times of recession. Particularly exposed were the lower ranks of tenants, the small occupiers who were often removed from the landowner by several degrees.

Ulster had its own variation on the whiteboy theme, demonstrated in two spectacular eruptions of popular protest organized by the 'Oakboys' and 'Steelboys'.[67] The Hearts of Oak or Oakboys, who seem to have embraced all denominations, terrorized landowners and Anglican clergy in the summer of 1763, beginning in Armagh and then spreading into Tyrone, Derry, Fermanagh, Monaghan, and Cavan. The insurrection of the predominantly Presbyterian Hearts of Steel, a much more serious threat lasting from the summer of 1770 to the end of 1772, was concentrated in Antrim and Down, though disturbances also spread into Armagh, Tyrone, and Londonderry. The Oakboy agitation was provoked by an increase in local taxation in Armagh caused by the approval of presentments for roads, bridges, and buildings by the grand jury of Armagh. The rebellion of the Hearts of Steel, on the other hand, had its origin in the renewal of leases on the Upton and Donegall estates in south Antrim; their hostility was directed against their landlords, who had taken the opportunity to raise rents and impose renewal fines, and against the 'middlemen', a number of wealthy Belfast merchants who had leased large areas of land and then sublet them to undertenants at a profit.

In each case the sources of discontent lay in immediate, localized circumstances, but agrarian agitation was able to spread quickly, tapping into a wide range of rural grievances focused on county cess, tithes, and high rents. In some areas the rebels mimicked the operations of the official courts, even erecting gallows on occasion.[68] The Steelboys attempted to regulate rents and tithes and even food prices. Their authority was enforced primarily by intimidation: magistrates and clergymen were forced to swear oaths upholding popular definitions of fair conduct. The Hearts of Steel also employed more violent tactics, destroying crops, maiming cattle, burning houses, and even murdering their opponents. On some occasions, bands of Steelboys clashed with troops, and in 1772 they were bold enough to invade Belfast to rescue an imprisoned leader. In their tactics and in their oath-bound organization they clearly prefigured the United Irish cells which spread through east Ulster in the 1790s. Their proclamations, in which criticisms of the land structure were often

    [66] Drennan, *A Letter to the Right Honourable Charles James Fox*, 2nd edn. (Dublin, 1806), 5–9.
    [67] W. A. Maguire, 'Lord Donegall and the Hearts of Steel', *IHS* 21/84 (1979), 351–76; James S. Donnelly, jun., 'Hearts of Oak, Hearts of Steel', *Studia Hibernica*, 21 (1981), 7–73; Anthony Canavan, 'The Hearts of Steel: Agrarian Protest in Ulster 1769–1773', MA thesis (QUB, 1982).
    [68] Donnelly, 'Hearts of Oak, Hearts of Steel', 41.

blended with religious perceptions of the Anglican state, contributed towards the development of a powerful language of grievance.

Like their Catholic counterparts, the agrarian rebels of the north provide evidence of a 'moral economy' operating in eighteenth-century Ireland. But the traditional social order imagined by Protestant tenant farmers and weavers was skewed by their contractual understanding of the Ulster plantation.[69] When the Steelboys aimed to restore the customary relationship between landlord and tenant they were also calling for a reaffirmation of their privileged status as Protestants. One Steelboy declaration asserted 'That we are all Protestants and Protestant Dissenters and bear unfeigned loyalty to his present majesty and the Hanoverian Succession', and went on to complain that Catholics were outbidding them for land. As always, liberty was closely bound up with loyalty.[70]

This peculiarly Ulster version of the moral economy can be seen most clearly in the alternative pattern of rural violence which emerged in County Armagh in the late eighteenth century. In this densely populated county a bitter sectarian war had erupted in the mid-1780s between Protestant 'Peep O' Day Boys'—so called because of their daybreak raids on Catholic homes—and the Catholic Defenders. Here, resentment against the commercialization of agriculture, which had been directed against middlemen in the east, was focused on Catholics who competed for land. Fluctuations in the local economy thus led to a resurgence of ethnic and religious tensions. One account of the Armagh troubles described how this gang warfare could take on a millenarian colouring which anticipated the troubles of the late 1790s:

The next plan our heros [*sic*] set out on, is to prophesy; one day they tell the credulous peasant, that the Scotch are to rise on a certain night, and massacre all the Papists. Watches are stationed in different places to give the alarm: the night passes away, and no Scotch appears, the prophet gets an *anim a duel* from the drowsy weaver, the next day when nodding on his loom.

The Papists are next to rise on a certain night, and destroy the Scotch. The Scotch take the same precautions, as the Irish did, but contrary to their expectations find that all their prophets are a damned lying set of rogues.[71]

Explanations of the 'Armagh Outrages' have generally focused on the economic competition between Protestants and Catholics in both farming and weaving. There was also a political dimension to the conflict from the beginning, however—a reaction against the Catholic Relief Acts of 1778 and 1782, and against the arming of some Catholics by the Volunteers.[72] As Defenderism became linked with the revolutionary programme of the United Irishmen in the 1790s, the Protestants, who founded the Orange Order in 1795, provided the backbone of the loyalist forces in the north.

[69] D. W. Miller, *Queen's Rebels: Ulster Loyalism in Historical Perspective* (Dublin, 1978), 49–54.

[70] Hereward Senior, *Orangeism in Ireland and Britain, 1795–1836* (London, 1966), 5.

[71] J. Byrne, *An Impartial Account of the Late Disturbances in the County of Armagh. . . . By an Inhabitant of the Town of Armagh*, originally published in Dublin, 1791, reprinted in D. W. Miller (ed.), *Peep O'Day Boys and Defenders: Selected Documents on the County Armagh Disturbances 1784–96* (Belfast, 1990), 54. The Gaelic phrase may be roughly translated as 'go to hell'.

[72] For recent debates on the origins of Orangeism see D. W. Miller, 'Politicisation in Revolutionary Ireland: The Case of the Armagh Troubles', in *IESH* 23 (1996), 1–17; L. M. Cullen, 'The Political Troubles of County Armagh: A Comment', in *IESH* 23 (1996), 18–23.

Although the Orange Order, seen by many Presbyterians as a church-and-king mob, is usually associated with the Established Church, there is evidence to suggest that the Peep O' Day Boys were largely Presbyterian, if only in a nominal sense.[73]

Ulster in the Late Eighteenth Century

English travellers in Ireland were generally comforted by the familiar landscape they found in the northern province. On his first Irish tour in 1756, John Wesley was relieved to cross into Ulster where 'the ground was cultivated just as in England, and the cottages not only neat, but with doors, chimney and windows'.[74] Three years later, Chief Baron Willes, travelling on the north-eastern circuit, recorded that from Monaghan to Carrickfergus was 'beautiful country'—well cultivated, prosperous, full of neat cabins with orchards and gardens, manufacturers' houses and gentlemen's seats, dotted with bleach greens.[75] Those who journeyed as far as Belfast were generally impressed by the prosperity and energy of the inhabitants, and it was frequently remarked that the town had 'an English look' about it.[76] Others, with more reason perhaps, compared east Ulster to the Scottish lowlands. In 1796 de Latocnaye observed that

Belfast has almost entirely the look of a Scotch town, and the character of the inhabitants has considerable resemblance to that of the people of Glasgow. If you start a conversation with them about the Emperor or General Fairfax, they will possibly talk about the prices of sugar or linen, according as they are trading in one or other, or may remark that if peace is not made promptly they do not know how they are going to get rid of their muslin or how they are to buy wine.[77]

As we have seen, Belfast was now recognized as the capital of the north. Around the middle of the century it had replaced Dublin as the centre of Protestant Dissent, and it was now extending its economic hegemony beyond Antrim and Down into mid-Ulster.[78] Its growing commercial importance was reflected in several spates of civic activity. The first hesitant steps were taken in the 1750s, when the town, according to the first census ever taken, had a tiny population of 8,549 persons.[79] Bishop Pococke, who visited Belfast around this time found that it consisted of 'one long broad Street, and of several lanes in which the inferior people live'. He noted that of 400 households, only 60 belonged to the established church, the rest being New Lights (including 'the richer people'), Old Lights, and papists. The New Lights, he found, were regarded as Arians, and 'these two lights have a greater aversion to

---

[73] Miller (ed.), *Peep O'Day Boys and Defenders*, 49, 65.

[74] Quoted in David Hempton and Myrtle Hill, *Evangelical Protestantism in Ulster Society 1740–1890* (London, 1992), 9.　　　　　　　　　　　　　　　　[75] *Letters of Chief Baron Willes*, 31.

[76] Quoted in McDowell, *Ireland*, 36.

[77] Chevalier de Latocnaye, *A Frenchman's Walk through Ireland*, trans. John Stevenson (Belfast, 1917), 222.

[78] For eighteenth-century Belfast see George Benn, *A History of the Town of Belfast from the Earliest Times to the Close of the Eighteenth Century* (London, 1877); Mary McNeill, *The Life and Times of Mary Ann McCracken 1770–1866: A Belfast Panorama*, 2nd edn. (Belfast, 1988).　　　[79] Benn, *Belfast*, 598.

each other than they have to the church'.[80] The New Lights played a prominent part in the formation of the Belfast Charitable Society in 1752 and the establishment of a Poor Law system five years later. Although the society had a shaky existence until 1768, it later took upon itself many of the functions of the corporation, assuming responsibility for the town water supply as well as building a poorhouse and opening a dispensary. Belfast's first short-lived bank was also established in 1752, and in the same year a stagecoach began operating from Belfast to Dublin. Three years later a private school was opened in Clugston's Entry by Daniel Manson, who would become renowned for his innovative teaching methods.

The 1770s saw a number of new buildings added to the town—a Brown linenhall, a new parish church, and a poorhouse. But it was in the following decade that the prosperity of the professional and commercial classes really found expression. As we have already seen, 1783 saw the establishment of a Belfast Chamber of Commerce, and the 'Ballast Board' followed two years later. A Discount Office was opened in 1785, and soon two more banks were established. The greatest monument to Belfast's commercial success, the White Linen Hall, was also completed in 1785. Meanwhile the religious and cultural life of the town was enhanced. In 1783 the First Congregation erected an elegant new meeting-house at the cost of £2,300.[81] From 1786 the sons of the Belfast merchants could receive their secondary education at Belfast Academy, although students of the arts, divinity, and medicine still had to take their degrees in Scotland. The townsfolk acquired a literary society in 1782 in the shape of the Adelphi Club, and in 1788 a group of 'worthy plebeians' formed a reading society, the first step in the creation of the Linenhall Library.[82] By this time Belfast also boasted two theatres, supplying the usual diet of Shakespeare and Sheridan. In addition they laid on special performances of patriotic plays like Addison's *Cato* for the Volunteers, and occasionally featured local talent in the form of Francis Dobbs's 'The Patriot King; or Irish Chief' and the improbably titled 'Love in a Bog', written by a local physician.[83]

By the last quarter of the eighteenth century the large northern towns had circulating libraries and there were book clubs in villages like Doagh, Portaferry, Newtownards, Ballynahinch, Banbridge, Dromore, and Hillsborough.[84] Presbyterian Ulster was already a highly literate society, and the expansion of the middling ranks supplied a new readership for books and newspapers. Most towns had at least one bookseller, and there were printing firms in Belfast, Newry, Londonderry, Strabane, and Armagh.[85] Early printing in Belfast was stimulated by the dispute over subscription to the Westminster Confession of Faith: James Blow published the works of the non-subscribers while Robert Gordon set up business on behalf

---

[80] Richard Pococke, 1752, quoted in R. W. M. Strain, *Belfast and its Charitable Society* (London, 1961), 10–11. [81] Benn, *Belfast*, 391.

[82] Martha McTier to Drennan, 28 Oct. 1792, *Drennan Letters*, 92; John Killen, *A History of the Linenhall Library 1788–1988* (Belfast, 1990), ch. 1.

[83] W. S. Clark, *The Irish Stage in the County Towns 1720–1800* (Oxford, 1965), 232–5, 241–3, 248, 251.

[84] J. R. R. Adams, *The Printed Word and the Common Man: Popular Culture in Ulster 1700–1900* (Belfast, 1987), 37–9. [85] Ibid. 24–7.

of the orthodox. Later in the century the names of Belfast's printers' shops still
bore testimony to their religious origins: James Magee at 'The Bible and Crown',
John Hay at 'The Two Bibles', Robert Smith at 'The Sign of the Gilt Bible'.[86] There
were local papers in Londonderry, Strabane, and Newry, but the most influential
was the *Belfast News-Letter*, first produced in 1737. As Ulster politics radicalized
after the American war the editor, Henry Joy, was challenged by the *Belfast Mercury*
(1783–7) and the *Northern Star* (1792–7). In 1795 the *News-Letter* claimed that it had
a circulation of 3,000, each read by six people; two years later the more democratic
Star boasted sales of 4,000.[87]

There is plenty of evidence here to support Tone's claim that political information was widely diffused in the north. But what exactly did the members of this
literate society read? An impressionistic view can be found in Gamble:

In general they are great readers of the Bible.—It is the first book that is put into their hands,
and all their ideas take a tinge from it; and often their phrases—they are accustomed to reflect,
and to talk on the doctrines it contains, and are, therefore, great reasoners on theological as
well as other subjects.[88]

At an inn in Ballygawley, County Tyrone, Gamble found that the Presbyterian
landlord's library was limited to the Bible, the Psalms, and two devotional works
by Richard Baxter and John Willison, although the maid, who had taken him for
an army officer, later presented him with a copy of Richardson's epistolary novel
Clarissa.[89] On a later trip he came across a bleacher who had collected the *Encyc-
lopaedia Britannica*, various treatises on agriculture and bleaching, Smith's *Wealth
of Nations*, and a few works of fiction. Another Presbyterian household, he noted
with dismay, possessed copies of old Covenanting and Seceding works like *A Hind
Let Loose* and *The Marrow of Modern Divinity*, and (even worse) Sir John Temple's
The Irish Rebellion.[90]

J. R. R. Adams has conducted an exhaustive study of Ulster publications
between 1700 and 1900. A high proportion of the eighteenth-century material he
has discovered consists of Bibles, catechisms, devotional works such as *The Pilgrim's
Progress*, and the tracts of the Scottish Seceders Ralph and Ebenezer Erskine. Also
prominent were popular fables and romances like *Valentine and Orson* and *The Most
Pleasing and Delightful History of Reynard the Fox*.[91] Adams found remarkably little
material of native origin, the main exception being the controversial sermons and
pamphlets upon which this book is partly based. There was one other specifically
Ulster genre, however, which has only rarely found its way into anthologies of Irish
literature. This was the poetry of the 'rhyming weavers', who flourished between
1750 and 1850 and whose chosen medium was Ulster Scots dialect. As the name
suggests, these rural bards came from artisan communities, and the genre rose and
fell with the domestic linen industry. The weaver poets were a local phenomenon,

---

[86] Benn, *Belfast*, 428–9.   [87] Adams, *Printed Word*, 34–6.
[88] Gamble, *Sketches of History, Politics and Manners*, 286.   [89] Ibid. 214–15.
[90] John Gamble, *A View of Society and Manners in the North of Ireland in the Summer and Autumn of
1812* (London, 1813), 123, 264.   [91] Adams, *Printed Word*, chs. 3–5.

drawing on the experience of the rural communities of Antrim and Down. Their small volumes, funded by subscription, contained conventional pastorals and topographical poems composed in standard English, but they are better known for the vernacular verse which recorded something of the humour and social conditions of Ulster life. Their poetry thus bore witness to the hybrid culture of Presbyterian Ulster:

> I love my native land, no doubt,
> Attach'd to her thro' thick and thin,
> Yet tho' I'm Irish all without,
> I'm every item Scotch within.[92]

Conclusion

By 1775 the traditional political and social structure of Ulster society was under threat from two distinct directions. The most obvious was the spasmodic resistance offered by the tenant-weavers to the collection of rents and tithes. As we have seen, however, agrarian discontent assumed traditional, conservative forms, and had not yet been channelled towards political ends. The second potentially disruptive force in Ulster society was the resentment of the Presbyterian professional and commercial classes at their exclusion from county and borough politics. The wealth of the middling Presbyterians, combined with the intellectual leadership supplied by their ministers, made them a formidable force. During the Money Bill dispute of 1753 they had enthusiastically joined Patriot Clubs, finding in 'colonial nationalism' a useful vehicle for their own grievances.[93] Presbyterian sermons from this period expressed support for the Hanoverian regime and for imperial expansion, while reiterating the case against the Test Act. With the passage of the Octennial Act in 1768, which for the first time provided for regular general elections, Dissenting freeholders could hope to exercise more influence over their representatives. Before 1775, however, they could find neither major issues to mobilize around, nor an organizational structure to express their opinions. This situation was transformed by the outbreak of war with the American colonies. The response of Ulster Presbyterians to the disintegration of the British Atlantic community will be analysed in detail in the second part of this book. But first it is necessary to come to grips with the theological categories and frames of reference which shaped their own critique of the established order in Church and State.

---

[92] Samuel Thompson, 'To Captain M'Dougall, Castle-Upton', quoted in Ivan Herbison, 'Oor Ain Native Tung', in *Talking Scots*, a supplement published with *Fortnight: An Independent Review of Politics and the Arts*, 318 (June 1993).

[93] See *A Layman's Sermon, Preached at the Patriot Club of the County of Armagh, which Met at Armagh, the 3rd of Sept. 1755* (Dublin, 1755); *Advice to the Patriot Club of County Antrim* (Dublin, 1756); *Remarks on a Late Pamphlet Entitled, Advice to the Patriot Club of County Antrim* (Dublin, 1756). This dispute saw Patriot politics move beyond Dublin for the first time. In addition to counties Antrim and Armagh, there were Patriot Clubs in County Down and Newry.

PART I

The Genius of Their Religion

2

THE REIGN OF THE NEW LIGHT

THAT the Presbyterian Church in Ireland has always been vulnerable to schism is well known. The involvement of the laity in the government of the Church, and the elevation of scriptural precept above human authority, has ensured that the General Synod (now the General Assembly) has been harassed by a fringe of splinter groups ranging from the Seceders and Covenanters of the eighteenth century to today's Free Presbyterians. But two controversies, both concerning the status of the Westminster Confession of Faith, tower above the rest. During the 1720s the machinery of the Church was paralysed for seven years as a handful of ministers—the 'New Lights'—argued that the practice of subscription to the Confession had no scriptural foundation and infringed upon the fundamental right of private judgement. The resulting fissure, which cut through the Synod, the sub-synods, the presbyteries, and even individual congregations, led eventually to the expulsion of those ministers and elders who had openly espoused the cause of the New Light. Ulster Presbyterianism thus suffered its first schism as the non-subscribing Presbytery of Antrim went its own way.

It was, however, an odd sort of schism. Links with the expelled presbyters were not entirely severed. Above all, there was never any suggestion that the non-subscribers would be deprived of their share of the *regium donum*. Although the dissident clergymen were no longer permitted to sit in the Synod, Christian communion was maintained and the adherents of the two bodies often exchanged pulpits. By the mid-century the Antrim Presbytery was sending commissioners to synodical meetings, and the two bodies happily co-operated on financial matters. Moreover, a growing minority within the Synod sympathized with the New Light men and looked forward to a reunion, though they themselves were not prepared to go to the lengths of open opposition to the Westminster Confession. Here was the germ of a New Light party within the Synod itself, and by the middle decades of the century ministers were able to preach heterodox doctrines before its annual assemblies with impunity. There were no more dramatic confrontations, but the presbyteries one by one stopped subscribing until, in 1783, the requirement was effectively dropped.

In the last quarter of the eighteenth century, a time described by one ecclesiastical historian as 'the reign of the New Light',[1] subscribers and non-subscribers were able to coexist peaceably within the Synod of Ulster. The Westminster Confession was never officially abandoned, but a consensus developed as a series of compromises prevented theological disputes from surfacing at the annual gatherings of the Synod. In true eighteenth-century fashion, the penalties for heresy remained

---

[1] W. T. Latimer, *A History of the Irish Presbyterians* (Belfast, [1893]), ch. 28.

on the statute book but were never implemented. The spread of the New Light thus lacked an institutional foundation and relied on an atmosphere of toleration and forbearance in the church organization. When the mood changed in the 1820s, and Henry Cooke began his crusade against the 'infidels', the New Light tendency learned how insecure its position really was. Cooke's novelty lay not so much in his doctrinal position—there was no abrupt theological shift in the Church—but in his style and manner. His assault on the easy-going, consensual arrangements of the previous fifty years eventually succeeded in reducing a complex spectrum of opinions to one black-and-white issue.[2]

It is an important coincidence that the first historians of Irish Presbyterianism had lived through and participated in this second great subscription controversy. The events of the 1820s inevitably coloured their perceptions of the contest which had begun a hundred years before. Whereas Cooke and his enemies joined battle on the specific question of the Trinity, the doctrinal issues in the previous century were, I shall argue, confused and somewhat obscure. Inevitably, historians of both parties tended to view the first subscription controversy simplistically as a straightforward collision of Arians and Trinitarians. The pioneering scholar James Seaton Reid, for example, served as moderator in 1828; his work reflects the polarized environment of the 1820s and 1830s, and conceals the fact that he himself had earlier belonged to the large moderate party which proposed a compromise with Montgomery and the Arians.[3] On the other side, both William Bruce and Henry Montgomery now publicly declared their conversion to Unitarianism and looked to their non-subscribing forebears for historical legitimacy.

These mistakes have often been duplicated by ecclesiastical historians, whose interests are primarily theological and whose investigations do not usually extend to the social and cultural context within which the Church operated.[4] A wider view has been offered in Peter Brooke's *Ulster Presbyterianism* (1987), an analysis of the theological controversies of the eighteenth century which benefits greatly from his understanding of the sociological functions of religion and nationality. Nevertheless, Brooke's fascinating survey remains an exercise in intellectual history based on the usual sources: the pamphlet literature of New Lights, Old Lights, Seceders, and Covenanters. There is little awareness of the wider framework—the cultural values,

---

[2] See Peter Brooke, *Ulster Presbyterianism: The Historical Perspective, 1610–1970* (Dublin, 1987), ch. 7. See also below, Ch. 9.

[3] Robert Allen, *James Seaton Reid: A Centenary Biography* (Belfast, 1951), 47–8; James Seaton Reid, *The History of the Presbyterian Church in Ireland, Briefly Reviewed and Practically Improved* (Belfast, 1828), 41–2.

[4] Several theses by theology students can now be added to the standard works of Reid *et al.*; e.g. William McMillan, 'The Subscription Controversy in Irish Presbyterianism from the Plantation of Ulster to the Present Day: With Special Reference to Political Implications in the Late Eighteenth Century', MA thesis (University of Manchester, 1959); A. W. G. Brown, 'Irish Presbyterian Theology in the Early Eighteenth Century', Ph.D. thesis (QUB, 1977). Some of Brown's work is summarized in 'A Theological Interpretation of the First Subscription Controversy (1719–1728)', in J. L. M. Haire (ed.), *Challenge and Conflict: Essays in Irish Presbyterian History and Doctrine* (Antrim, 1981), 28–43. For a new perspective on non-subscription see M. A. Stewart, 'Rational Dissent in Early Eighteenth-Century Ireland', in Knud Haakonssen (ed.), *Enlightenment and Religion: Rational Dissent in Eighteenth-Century Britain* (Cambridge, 1996), 42–63.

social activities, aspirations, and so on—within which these texts must be located. For the non-subscription controversy had a wider cultural dimension which ranged from pulpit delivery to clerical dress. This is not to say that theological beliefs can be dismissed as froth whipped up by the great waves of social and economic change. On the contrary, historians are learning to grant a generous measure of autonomy to religious belief. Nevertheless, it is possible to demonstrate that the doctrinal debates of the eighteenth century intersected with wider cultural and social differences concerning the nature of knowledge and the place of religion in society.

The following chapter sets out to recover this wider context. In the first two sections we examine the progress of New Light Presbyterianism from its origins in the 1720s to its triumph in the late eighteenth century. It will be argued that the preoccupation of many historians with the Trinitarian debate has obscured a diverse and often confused range of beliefs. A number of questions then emerge. What exactly were the theological issues at stake and what underlying differences did they reflect? What relation did they bear to developments in Irish society? How was the Synod of Ulster able to comprehend such diverse viewpoints? And, perhaps most difficult of all, how can the impact of the New Light be assessed? While there is no clear-cut relationship between theology and social status, it will be suggested that the distribution of New Light sentiment corresponded loosely to economic and geographical divisions within the north of Ireland, and that its rise is best seen as a response to the new intellectual trends of the Enlightenment and, not least, the need for Presbyterians to relaunch their product in the new market of polite society.

The subscription controversy

It was not until 1698, when the newly established Synod began to regularize its proceedings, that subscription was made compulsory in Ulster, and even then it seems that little importance was attached to the matter. The Synod was merely following the practice of the General Assembly of the Church of Scotland, whose acts it had recently examined. The situation was transformed, however, by the imprisonment in 1705 of Thomas Emlyn, a Dublin Dissenting minister who had published a refutation of the doctrine of the Trinity. In the meeting-houses of the capital the clergy maintained their opposition to the use of creeds and confessions, but in the north the Emlyn scandal produced an immediate reaction, and a second act requiring candidates for the ministry to subscribe to the Westminster Confession was passed, apparently without opposition.[5]

Ironically, this year also saw the formation of the Belfast Society, a coterie of clergymen, theological students, and laymen, led by John Abernethy, and dedicated to the advancement of religious knowledge.[6] It was through their inquiries that a new theological vocabulary was made available to Ulster Presbyterians, a vocabulary which

---

[5] J. M. Barkley, *The Westminster Formularies in Irish Presbyterianism* (Belfast, 1956[?]), 8–14.
[6] On Abernethy see R. B. Barlow, 'The Career of John Abernethy (1680–1740), Father of Non-subscription in Ireland and Defender of Religious Liberty', *Harvard Theological Review*, 78 (1985), 399–419.

was soon dubbed the 'New Light'. At their meetings sermons were preached on such subjects as 'the nature, and Scriptural Terms, of the unity of the Christian Church; the nature, and mischief of Schism; the Rights of conscience, and of private judgement; the sole dominion of Christ in his own kingdom; the nature, power, and effects of excommunication'. Problematic passages of the Scriptures were read and various interpretations discussed. Recent publications were swapped and their merits debated. Members delivered dissertations demonstrating the excellence of the Christian religion, attacking superstition and enthusiasm, and carefully avoiding all 'curious and Unscriptural Speculations'. The objections of infidels of all kinds were considered, as were the customs of the different Christian denominations.[7] It is hardly surprising, then, that over the next few years these clergymen exhibited a profound interest in debates taking place elsewhere on the nature of Christian liberty.

The deliberations of the Belfast Society must be set against the background of a series of incidents which caused much anxiety in the Calvinist churches of Europe. Closest to home was the trial of John Simson, professor of divinity at Glasgow, on a charge of Arminianism between 1714 and 1717. Unfortunately, the current boom in Scottish intellectual history has so far overlooked Simson, and the exact nature of his teachings is far from clear. Nevertheless, there can be no doubt that the general tendency of his work was to emphasize the extent to which the doctrines of Christianity were in accord with the conclusions of rational inquiry, and to elevate reason at the expense of revelation. Leading non-subscribers like Abernethy and Kirkpatrick had been contemporaries of Simson at Glasgow, while most of the younger New Lights had studied under his supervision.[8]

In England, too, the Presbyterian clergy had been shaken by the appearance of Samuel Clarke's *The Scripture-Doctrine of the Trinity* (1712). Though its heretical tendencies were much exaggerated, the controversy surrounding Clarke's book led directly to the great Salter's Hall debates, when a proposal for subscription to the doctrine of the Trinity was narrowly defeated. Attention then turned to the relationship between temporal and spiritual authority, following the defence of the rights of conscience against both Church and State made by Benjamin Hoadly, the Bishop of Bangor. Two Ulster ministers, Samuel Haliday and Samuel Dunlop, had been in London during the Salter's Hall debates, and it was Dunlop's suspicion that his companion sympathized with the Arians which triggered the discord in Ireland. In 1718, Francis Hutcheson, who had just returned from his studies in Scotland, found 'a perfect Hoadly mania' among the younger ministers in the north, but suspected that underneath the opposition to creeds and confessions lay the spread of Clarke's views on the Trinity.[9] Letters from members of the Belfast Society were said to be in circulation in which the New Light ministers acknowledged their doubts

---

[7] See James Kirkpatrick's 'Conclusion', in James Duchal's *A Sermon on Occasion of the Much Lamented Death of the Late Reverend Mr John Abernethy* (Belfast, 1741), 48–62; also the Belfast Society circular, dated 7 Dec. 1720, in the Presbytery of Antrim, *A Narrative of the Proceedings of Seven Synods of the Northern Presbyterians in Ireland* (Belfast, 1727), 18–33.

[8] J. S. Reid, *History of the Presbyterian Church in Ireland*, ed. W. D. Killen, 3rd edn. (Belfast, 1867), iii. 114.   [9] Quoted ibid. 115–16.

regarding the Saviour's deity, and it was alleged that the theories of Whiston and Clarke were a common topic of conversation in Antrim and Down.[10]

These accusations eventually acquired some substance with the appearance of John Abernethy's *Religious Obedience Founded on Personal Persuasion* in 1719, a sermon preached on the text, 'Let every man be persuaded in his own mind'. In that year a Toleration Act had been passed, protecting Dissenters from the penalties of the Acts of Uniformity. Archbishop William King of Dublin perceptively remarked that 'the act seems not designed to gratify the generality of the Dissenters, for they desired no act of such latitude, but to screen those that are resolved to trouble themselves with no religion'.[11] By restricting its operations to constitutional principles alone, the 1719 act may have unintentionally emboldened the Belfast Society. In any case, *Personal Persuasion* was the first attack on the doctrines of the Westminster Confession. The sermon was brazenly Arminian in tone, laying great stress on the individual's capacity for moral improvement, and placing sincerity of belief rather than the redemptive work of Christ at the centre of his theology.[12] Calvin, not Athanasius, was to be the main victim of the New Light.

Largely as a result of this publication, the annual meeting of the Synod of Ulster in 1720 was preoccupied with rumours that some ministers had adopted new 'schemes' of both doctrine and church government. In an effort to contain dissensions a 'Pacific Act' was passed, confirming subscription according to the 1705 rule, with the qualification that any minister who objected to certain phrases in the Confession might replace them with his own wording, provided that the presbytery was satisfied. Non-subscribers later claimed that this meant assent to the vital doctrines of the Confession, not strict agreement with every word.[13]

What scuppered this compromise was the refusal of Samuel Haliday, at his installation in the First Belfast congregation, to subscribe in any shape or form. By June 1721, when the next synod met to discuss Haliday's case, it was again asserted that the heretical views current in England were spreading to Ireland. Already some ministers had subscribed voluntarily to satisfy jealous congregations, and the Synod received eighteen petitions requesting all ministers to sign the Confession.[14] When a voluntary declaration concerning the eternal deity of the Son of God was proposed, the Belfast Society refused; although they did not contest the doctrine, they objected to the circumstances, which they fancifully compared with the Spanish Inquisition.[15] The next day the vast majority of ministers at the Synod subscribed to the Westminster Confession of Faith according to the terms of the Pacific Act. Those who refused—twelve ministers led by Abernethy, Kirkpatrick,

---

[10] Ibid. 120; Gilbert Kennedy, *A Defence of the Principles and Conduct of the Reverend General Synod of Ulster* (Belfast, 1724), p. iv. William Whiston, who suceeded Isaac Newton as Lucasian professor of mathematics at Cambridge, was also an Arian.

[11] King to the Archbishop of Canterbury, 1 Dec. 1719, quoted in Richard Mant, *History of the Church of Ireland*, 2 vols. (London, 1840), ii. 340.

[12] In addition to *Religious Obedience*, see Samuel Haliday, *Reasons Against the Imposition of Subscription to the Westminster Confession of Faith* (Belfast, 1724). For a full account of the subscription controversy see Reid, *Presbyterian Church in Ireland*, iii. 110–211.

[13] Presbytery of Antrim, *Seven Synods*, 1–4.   [14] Ibid. 35.   [15] Ibid. 36.

Haliday, Thomas Nevin, and Michael Bruce, and four elders—were henceforth
known as 'non-subscribers'.[16]

After this meeting, relations between the parties rapidly deteriorated. Discontented elements in the laity began to desert ministers who had been branded as New
Light men. Congregations refused to join together at the vast gatherings where the
sacrament of the Lord's Supper was customarily observed. A pamphlet war began,
which would chalk up more than fifty publications over the next five years, some
of them running into hundreds of pages. Above all, the smear campaign against the
non-subscribers gathered pace. News of their supposedly heretical opinions spread,
particularly on the vexed question of 'the FUNDAMENTALITY (as it was call'd)
of the orthodox Doctrine of Christ's Divinity'.[17]

At the 1722 Synod, a breach with the non-subscribers was openly floated for the
first time. Twenty-three subscribers opposed this motion, however, and the final
outcome was a series of resolutions stressing the need for Christian forbearance.[18]
The following year an appeal from the Sub-Synod of Belfast, alleging that non-
subscribing principles opened the door to 'Errors and Heresys', was granted, but
still an open schism was averted.[19] In an effort to dampen the conflict the ministers
in the Sub-Synod of Belfast were reshuffled in 1725, so that all the non-subscribers
were now gathered together in the Presbytery of Antrim, and strict penalties were
proposed for anyone who refused to subscribe or to respect the authority of the
Synod.[20] But this regrouping of clergymen proved to be the prelude to an open
rupture, which finally occurred in the following year. The details of the vote to expel
the Presbytery of Antrim are worth noting. The motion was carried by thirty-six
ministers to thirty-four, while eight others declined voting, and two opponents of
the breach were unable to attend. It was the orthodox zeal of the elders, therefore,
that carried the day for the Westminster Confession.[21]

It has been necessary to deal with these debates in detail because they shed some
light on the balance of power within Presbyterian Ulster, and particularly on the
role of the laity, which forms the central theme of this chapter. The New Light
ministers found themselves in a tiny minority, but their position was not quite so
isolated as a bald outline of events might suggest. To begin with, there was some
middle ground between the two parties, represented by a number of 'moderates'
who worked persistently to restore calm—men like Robert Higinbotham and John
Elder who wanted to maintain fellowship with their New Light friends. Thus a
sizeable contingent of 'false brethren' (as Reid called them) remained within the
Synod after the split.[22] Also sympathetic to the non-subscribers were the Dublin
Dissenters, whose commissioners consistently pressed for the matter to be dropped
and recommended more charitable attitudes year after year.[23] Throughout the controversy the strength of the subscribing party was found among the lay elders who
possessed the right to vote; it was they who had forced through the original motion
for voluntary subscription in 1721.[24] These years had seen a remarkably high turnout

---

[16] Presbytery of Antrim, *Seven Synods*, 42–8.   [17] Ibid. 59.   [18] Ibid. 66–7.
[19] Ibid. 74–7.   [20] Reid, *Presbyterian Church in Ireland*, iii. 196, 201.   [21] Ibid. 209.
[22] Ibid. 210.   [23] Presbytery of Antrim, *Seven Synods*, 59, 69.   [24] Ibid. 45–6.

of elders, averaging 90 between 1720 and 1726 and then dropping to a more normal level of 59. The 1724 debates witnessed the highest attendance of the eighteenth century—123 ministers and 106 elders.[25] The letters of the distinguished Dublin pastor Joseph Boyse reveal the hopes of the southern representatives that the 'moderate subscribers' might succeed in averting an open rift, provided they were not outnumbered by the 'dead weight of the Ruling Elders'.[26]

As we turn from the synodical debates to local events the significance of lay conservatism becomes even more apparent, for it was the social tensions at this level which kept the issue of subscription alive. The trouble had been triggered by the objections of the Belfast presbytery to Haliday's installation, and it was sustained by the trial of Thomas Nevin of Downpatrick for heresy, and the rebellious behaviour of Alexander Colville, a licentiate who travelled to London for ordination when his own presbytery refused to perform the service.[27] The subordinate courts of the Church—especially the Presbytery of Down and the Sub-Synod of Belfast—were also thrown into confusion. Above all, the popular pressure exerted on individual preachers by their congregations fuelled the bitterness which characterized these debates. A year after the exclusion of the Antrim presbyters the Scottish chronicler Robert Wodrow was informed that Michael Bruce's congregation had abandoned him, complaining that his sermons skipped over the doctrine of the Trinity, with the result that Bruce now depended for his income on fortnightly lectures given in Belfast. Abernethy and Nevin, he learned, were also 'much deserted', and even the town-based congregations of Haliday and Kirkpatrick were growing thinner.[28]

For those historians who have sung the praises of the Church's much-vaunted democratic procedures, the events of the 1720s will make salutary reading. Non-subscribing ministers, whose learning had once commanded universal admiration, now watched as their parishioners defected to neighbouring congregations; the same fate befell those orthodox ministers who had advocated a conciliatory approach.[29] Early in 1724 passions reached new heights as the people of Connor prevented a non-subscribing minister from preaching in their meeting-house, an unprecedented example of insubordination which appalled many clergymen.[30] Connor set a pattern which was repeated throughout Antrim and Down. A typical example is the case of John Orr, ordained at Comber in January 1724. Although he had subscribed 'after some sort', Orr had sympathized with the non-subscribers.[31] The greater portion of his congregation (100 out of 120 families) consequently applied to be detached from their pastor. When the Presbytery of Down, which considered the affair in

---

[25] Reid, *Presbyterian Church in Ireland*, iii. 179.

[26] Joseph Boyse to Thomas Steward, n.d. [*c.*1725], 7 May 1726, Magee College Derry, Steward Correspondence, MS 46, fos. 148, 152.

[27] Reid, *Presbyterian Church in Ireland*, iii. 132–6, 176–82, 191–4.

[28] Robert Wodrow, *Analecta: or Materials for a History of Remarkable Providences; Mostly Relating to Scotch Ministers and Christians*, ed. Matthew Leishman for the Maitland Club, 3 vols. (Edinburgh, 1842–3), iii. 466–8.

[29] Ibid. 202–3; J. W. Kernohan, *The County of Londonderry in Three Centuries* (Belfast, 1921), 71.

[30] Reid, *Presbyterian Church in Ireland*, iii. 174.

[31] Samuel Smith to Robert Wodrow, 15 Sept. 1724, NLS, Wodrow MSS, XXI.

August 1725, refused to sanction the move, and Orr joined the ranks of the Presbytery of Antrim, the bulk of the congregation took possession of the meeting-house and prevented him from officiating in it.[32]

When the conflict over subscription is examined at congregational level the social tensions which kindled the antagonism between New Light and Old can most clearly be seen. James Kirkpatrick, the non-subscribing minister of Second Belfast, complained:

Nothing is more common amongst poor Country-People, and amongst all who are ignorant of the state of the controversy, than to vent their jealousies against the *Non-subscribers*, and to say plainly that *there must be something at the bottom of their Non-subscribing more than what has come to light*; and by this means, all the ministers who have subscribed are teaz'd for their charity and Christian Forbearance toward their dear Brethren.[33]

Joseph Boyse accused some of the subscribers of deliberately encouraging a factious spirit among 'the most ignorant and injudicious of their people'.[34] On the other hand, there was an obvious connection between latitudinarianism and the well-to-do merchants and professional classes of Belfast. Wodrow noted that Haliday and Kirkpatrick, 'being in a toun, and in a collegiat life', possessed a strong base, and that the non-subscribers could count on the contributions of the 'gentry and the rich people'.[35] His Irish correspondent, the minister of the breakaway Third Congregation, agreed that the non-subscribers had the 'chief men' in the town.[36] Missionaries from the Scottish Secession would later exploit popular resentment against the wealthy oligarchies who were able to run ecclesiastical affairs in an increasing number of congregations.

How seriously should we treat the cries of heresy which were raised by the Old Light camp? Professor John Barkley has taken the non-subscribers at their word, insisting that they were essentially orthodox.[37] On the other hand, Henry Montgomery, leader of the Arians in the first half of the nineteenth century, refused to believe that Abernethy and his colleagues were either Calvinists or Trinitarians.[38] It seems unlikely that the gossip surrounding the deviation of the non-subscribers was wholly without foundation. It must be conceded that the doctrine of the Trinity was never explicitly attacked, and that the names Arian and Socinian, which were at this period pejorative terms, were not openly avowed. Haliday, the most stubborn non-subscriber of all, declared his belief in the Trinity and in the supreme deity of the Saviour in convincing terms, as did many of his colleagues.[39] Even the

[32] Reid, *Presbyterian Church in Ireland*, iii. 185.
[33] [James Kirkpatrick], *A Vindication of the Presbyterians in the North of Ireland* (Belfast, 1724), 22. This pamphlet was published under the name of Dr Victor Ferguson, an elder in the Second Belfast Congregation.
[34] Boyse to Thomas Steward, 1 Nov. 1726, MCD, Steward Correspondence, MS 46, fo. 156.
[35] Wodrow, *Analecta*, iii. 467–8.
[36] Charles Masterton to Robert Wodrow, 16 Sept. 1724, NLS, Wodrow MSS, XXI.
[37] J. M. Barkley, *A Short History of the Presbyterian Church in Ireland* (Belfast, 1959), 28.
[38] Henry Montgomery, 'Outlines of the History of Presbyterianism in Ireland', *Irish Unitarian and Bible Christian*, 2 (1847), 205.
[39] Samuel Haliday, *A Letter to the Reverend Gilbert Kennedy* (Belfast, 1725), 48.

reckless Thomas Nevin was said to have preached a sermon against Arianism in Dublin.[40] In 1721, according to the records of the Synod, the New Lights had expressed their belief in the deity of Christ in the strongest language, although the accuracy of these minutes was later questioned by the Sub-Synod of Derry.[41]

On the other hand, accusations that the non-subscribers simply skipped over these doctrines in their sermons were commonplace. The charges made against them typically concerned sins of omission. Wodrow was told that when Michael Bruce of Holywood came to preach on 1 John 5: 8, a text which dealt with the Trinity, he informed his hearers that there were conflicting views on the subject and declined entering into the debate.[42] Some years later he learned from Dublin that Abernethy was avoiding the subject of the divinity of Christ.[43] When challenged on doctrinal questions, the non-subscribers typically resorted to evasion and obscurantism. The explanation for this behaviour, however, lies in the absence of a well-defined New Light position, rather than wilful deception. A neat illustration can be taken from the turbulent career of Glasgow professor John Simson, who in 1727 was again brought to trial, this time for denying the necessary existence of the Son and the numerical oneness of the Trinity.[44] In a somewhat farcical attempt to ascertain his teachings, the notebooks of Simson's students were examined, but, as his lectures were delivered in Latin, it proved impossible to obtain an exact statement of his actual words. Simson's offence was not that he introduced heretical notions of the Trinity, but that he advocated a general spirit of inquiry; it was said that he had mastered 'the art of teaching heresy orthodoxly'.[45]

So how exactly are we to describe New Light thought? The starting point must be the rationale behind non-subscription. First, it was argued that the executive, legislative, and judicial authority of the Church was lodged in Jesus Christ, its sole king, and that he had laid down all the terms of Christian communion. To alter or add to these was to usurp his authority, to sit in the throne of God. Next to the sovereignty of Christ stood the sufficiency of the Scriptures: 'The WHOLE *Discipline* of the Church of Christ as well as its Doctrine, and Worship is *perfectly* and *fully* described in the BIBLE.'[46] All the rules for the government of the Church by kirk sessions, presbyteries, and synods were to be found in the New Testament. This much was accepted by all Presbyterian ministers; the difficulty arose when it came to safeguarding the Church against the intrusion of heresy and impiety. At this point the majority in the General Synod defended the Westminster Confession as a useful summary of Christian doctrine. The non-subscribers, conversely, maintained that the introduction of human creeds and confessions amounted to the corruption of the pure Christian doctrines found in the Bible.

The strengths of the non-subscribing case thus lay in its appeal to fundamental principles of the Protestant tradition; these were the same arguments which had

---

[40] Reid, *Presbyterian Church in Ireland*, iii. 182.   [41] Ibid. 175.
[42] Wodrow, *Analecta*, iii. 466.   [43] Ibid. iv. 162.
[44] James Coutts, *A History of the University of Glasgow* (Glasgow, 1909), 28.   [45] Ibid. 221.
[46] [John Abernethy], *A Letter from the Presbytery of Antrim, to the Congregations under their Care* (Belfast, 1726), 20.

been used to explain the rise of papal power and to justify the continuing reformation of the Christian Church. Its weakness lay in the inability or reluctance of the non-subscribers to provide their brethren with a convincing account of their own beliefs. To say that one's religion was that of the Scriptures was not enough. Thus the orthodox clergy understandably refused to join in communion with those whose principles they could not ascertain. The Belfast Society was repeatedly challenged to state its own creed. Matthew Clerk complained that

this way of Writing and Speaking you Use, is Nothing but Quibbling and Wheedling like Judgements with their hard Words, *Hocus Pocus, Maccahelum Macahinglum,* Which Words are as Intelligible to a People, as *Essential* and *Extra-essential* Points in our *Confession* of *Faith*.[47]

Most of the ministers of the Synod would have agreed with Clerk that the campaign against subscription was really a smokescreen generated by the non-subscribers to disguise their drift towards heresy. An anonymous piece of doggerel verse preserved in a collection of Dublin broadsides in the British Library complained that their principles admitted to Christian communion Turks, Jews, Quakers, Free-Thinkers, and Anabaptists:

> Yet by the *New Light*
> They are all in the Right,
> And can prove it on any Occasion,
> If the Doctrine be true
> That Obedience is due
> To a Man's own immediate Perswasion [*sic*].

Inevitably the allegation of heterodoxy followed:

> Ne'er listen or hark
> To *Whiston* or *Clarke*,
> Mistake not your Favourite *Hoadly*,
> And let nothing incline us
> To join with Sosinus [*sic*],
> Such Principles suit not the Godly.[48]

In their defence the non-subscribers retorted that the only difference between the two parties related to Church power, and that matters of doctrine were not in dispute. From the very beginning, however, they demonstrated a fundamentally different approach to Church teaching. In the case against subscription, much play was made of the crucial distinction between essential and non- or extra-essential doctrines. Attesting to the influence of Locke's epistemology, Abernethy insisted that human knowledge of the Creator was necessarily limited and an infinite diversity of opinion on theological subjects was inescapable. The terms of Christian communion should therefore be limited to those fundamental principles which were

---

[47] Matthew Clerk, *A Letter from the Belfast Society . . . with an Answer to the Society's Remarks on a Pamphlet lately Publish'd, Entitled, A Letter from the Country, to a Friend in Belfast* (Belfast[?], 1723), 23–4.   [48] *New Light* [Dublin, 1725].

plainly laid down in the Scriptures and which united all Protestants. The problem with the Westminster Confession of Faith was that it contained not only these essential articles, but also 'a great many judicious Decisions, concerning some of the most arduous and knotty Controversies of School-Divinity'.[49] For the majority of the Synod's members the idea that many of the Confession's articles were not necessary for salvation was news indeed.

The desire to strip Protestant Christianity down to essentials, a reflection of the latitudinarian breezes which were blowing through Calvinist churches everywhere, represented a considerable break with the traditional theology of Ulster Presbyterianism, but more fundamental still was the radical deployment by the non-subscribers of the right of private judgement. According to Abernethy, matters of conscience were exempt from human jurisdiction. The moral autonomy of the individual was central to Abernethy's understanding of the relationship between God and mankind: salvation lay not in conformity to articles of faith, but in the scrutiny of the Scriptures, and in rational persuasion, that is, 'Assent formed upon Evidence and Attentive Reasoning'.[50] But if sincerity was the test of human obedience to God's will, less room was left for the doctrine of Atonement. There was thus some truth in the charge that Abernethy had substituted a doctrine of works for one of grace. Rejecting the primacy of personal persuasion, one Old Light apologist asserted that 'when a doctrine appears to be from God, we must acquiesce in it, and, though it be above our comprehension, we must believe it, because our reason finds in it the Word, which carries in it all the reasons of believing'.[51]

Finally, the New Lights demonstrated a marked hostility towards ecclesiastical authority throughout the years of the subscription controversy. In denying the right of the Synod to inquire into the beliefs of its members, the non-subscribers were challenging the very basis of the Presbyterian system. Their own model of church government resembled a sort of Independency, in which each pastor was accountable only to his congregation. Hutcheson, who was courted by several Irish bishops and seriously considered conforming to the establishment, adopted a typically utilitarian attitude to matters of church polity:

I do not imagine that either the government or the externals of worship are so determined in the gospel, as to oblige men to one particular way in either; [but rather think] that all societies may, according to their own prudence, choose a form of government in the church, and agree upon such external order of worship, as they think will do most good, to promote the true end of all, real piety and virtue, but without any right of forcing others into it.[52]

Separation from an established church could only be justified if it would do more good than conformity. Hutcheson seems to have regarded the Church as analogous to civil society, divine in its origin but owing its form to a human contract. From

---

[49] Haliday, *Letter to Revd Kennedy*, 6–7.

[50] John Abernethy, *Religious Obedience Founded on Personal Persuasion* (Belfast, 1720), 12.

[51] Robert McMaster, quoted in Thomas Witherow (ed.), *Historical and Literary Memorials of Presbyterianism in Ireland*, 2 vols. (Belfast, 1879–80), ii. 12.

[52] Francis to John Hutcheson, 4 Aug. 1726, quoted in William Bruce, 'Progress of Non-Subscription to Creeds', *Christian Moderator* (1827), ii. 351.

the middle of the century a more belligerent attitude towards the Church of Ireland became conspicuous, targeted at the idea of an establishment, rather than episcopacy itself; but a glance at the careers of upwardly mobile Dissenters confirms that membership of a New Light congregation, particularly in Dublin, often served as a stepping stone to conformity.

The triumph of the New Light, 1726–1780

The purge of 1726, far from rooting out heresy in the Synod, proved to be just the first battle in the conflict between New Light and Old. The ministers of the independent Presbytery of Antrim initially paid the price of further secessions from their congregations, but they could now afford to be less inhibited in their preaching. As the leading subscriber, William Livingston, recognized, the breach actually worked to the New Lights' advantage: 'They have now none in their meetings to contradict them, and they may plot and contrive what they will without opposition under the cover of a regular Presbytery.'[53] More surprising, perhaps, was the continuing vulnerability of the Synod itself to the New Light contagion. To begin with, a minority of ministers remaining under its jurisdiction sympathized with the non-subscribers: by the 1740s they would be known as 'moderate men'.[54] Ministers and congregations could move from the jurisdiction of the Presbytery of Antrim to the General Synod and back again without comment, suggesting that doctrinal differences between the two bodies had become blurred. Already in 1734–5 it was thought necessary to frame new rules in order to prevent the formula of subscription from being expressed in ambiguous phraseology, and in 1749 it was noted that several formulae appeared to be in force.[55]

By 1747 the moderates felt confident enough to propose a reconciliation for the first time. An important link was established four years later by the creation of the Widows Fund. This scheme, which provided for the relief of families of deceased clergymen, was suggested by the Dublin bookseller William Bruce, and the Presbytery of Antrim sent a commission to sit in on the Synod's discussions on the matter.[56] In 1759, elders were somewhat surprised when another deputation presented itself to the Synod, led by Alexander Colville, who had been thrown out at the height of the subscription controversy.[57] After the accession of George III, however, when the two bodies issued a joint address as 'The Presbyterian Ministers of the Northern Association in Ireland', such consultations became common.

The pattern of disputed settlements in the congregations continued unabated. Henry Montgomery noted that 'on the occurrence of every vacancy, Candidates were subjected to the severest doctrinal scrutiny—especially by the humbler classes of the people, who viewed with great jealousy the influence and opinions of their more affluent fellow-worshippers.'[58] The rejection of Gilbert Kennedy, jun., by Lisburn in 1730 and the withdrawal of a large part of George Ferguson's flock at Markethill

---

[53] William Livingston to Robert Wodrow, 3 Sept. 1725, NLS, Wodrow MSS, XX.
[54] Reid, *Presbyterian Church in Ireland*, iii. 263 n. 41.   [55] *RGSU*, ii. 346.
[56] Ibid. 292.   [57] Ibid. 320–1.   [58] Montgomery, 'Outlines', 228.

in 1741 are just two examples of continuing pressure from below.[59] Throughout the century this tension between an increasingly heterodox clergy and a mainly orthodox laity continued. But the Old Lights were gradually losing the ability or the inclination to resist. One indication of this decline was the replacement of the orthodox John Stirling at Ballykelly with John Nelson. When on trial, the members of the congregation had found the new candidate sound in doctrine, but once settled, they perceived a change in his views and complained to the Presbytery of Derry. Though there was much evidence of his heterodoxy, he was acquitted by the Synod, and it was only the enduring hostility of the congregation which forced him to resign.[60]

One way to chart the progress of heterodoxy in Ulster is to examine the sermons preached before the Synod's annual assembly. Each meeting was opened with a discourse by the outgoing moderator, which was often published, and on the second day another minister, frequently someone who was tipped to be the next moderator, would be asked to preach. After the subscription controversy died down these sermons seem to have been conspicuously sound; in 1730, for example, William Boyd's *A Good Conscience* attacked Abernethy's *Personal Persuasion*.[61] But six years later George Cherry caused a stir by preaching that 'unanimity amongst Christians in matters of faith is never to be expected', recommending moderation and forbearance and advising that where there were conflicting views on non-essential doctrines, ministers should present both interpretations.[62] In 1745 John Carlisle went much further in his *The Nature of Religious Zeal*, a bold strike against the use of subscription. The main thrust of the sermon was to distinguish true Christian zeal, described as 'impartial enquiry after truth, or the knowledge of the will of God, and the practice of virtue and piety', from mistaken zeal, which judged truth according to the writings of men instead of the 'infallible standard of right reason and the word of God', and by its obsession with trifling points led to the fragmentation of Christianity.[63] Turning to the contentions of the previous twenty years he then condemned 'fury and fierceness in smaller matters', and advised elders not to meddle in affairs which they did not understand.[64] Complaints from the Old Light benches were heard over the following decades as New Light sermons were preached by John Maxwell, Gilbert Kennedy, James Hull, Andrew Alexander, and Moses Neilson.

It would be misleading to suggest that the New Lights had it all their own way during these years. In 1747, when four congregations from the Presbytery of Dromore complained of errors creeping into the Church, the Synod responded by drawing up 'A Serious Warning' to be read from the pulpits, condemning Arminian and Arian errors, and declaring adherence to the Westminster Confession of Faith.[65] But this apparent burst of Calvinist zeal amongst the Presbyterian clergy can be explained by the threat now posed by Seceding missionaries from Scotland who had formed their first Irish congregation at Lylehill in 1745, and were now well positioned to catch the discontented congregations of the Synod of Ulster. Even

---

[59] Reid, *Presbyterian Church in Ireland*, iii. 253–4.   [60] Ibid. 327–9.
[61] Witherow, *Memorials*, ii. 3–4.   [62] Reid, *Presbyterian Church in Ireland*, iii. 244.
[63] John Carlisle, *The Nature of Religious Zeal. A Sermon on Phil. 3: 6* (Belfast, 1745), 9, 17–18, 22.
[64] Ibid. 29–30.   [65] Printed in full by Reid, *Presbyterian Church in Ireland*, iii. 264–5.

this episode adds to the impression that subscription was becoming increasingly nominal—a matter of keeping up appearances.

Contrasted with the flurry of pamphlets which stimulated the Belfast printing industry in the 1720s and 1730s, the second half of the eighteenth century produced remarkably little in the way of controversial literature. The tranquillity of ecclesiastical affairs was threatened only once, by the refusal of Samuel Martin Stephenson to sign the Confession of Faith after a call to the congregation of Greyabbey, which belonged to the Presbytery of Bangor. When asked to subscribe, Stephenson had declined and published a vindication of his conduct, to the satisfaction of the congregation. Bangor Presbytery finally agreed to ordain him when he threatened to lead his parishioners into the rival Presbytery of Antrim, but a minority of orthodox presbyters objected and, after an unsuccessful appeal to the Synod to have the ordination overturned, they seceded to form the Presbytery of Belfast. Both groups remained within the Synod.

The subdivision of this presbytery provides an interesting contrast with the drastic measures of the 1720s, demonstrating that disagreements over subscription, which had once rent the Church organization, could now be contained at a local level. The enforcement of orthodox standards from the centre was no longer possible, and the Synod had come to resemble a loose association of autonomous presbyteries, some requiring subscription, others not. Secondly, the dispute shows how far the Old Light had lost ground. The orthodox members had been willing to go some distance to accommodate Stephenson. According to John King of Holywood, they had for several years permitted their New Light brethren to subscribe to a meaningless formula stating merely that 'all the important doctrines of the Christian religion are contained in the Westminster Confession of Faith'.[66] Moreover, King insists that if Stephenson had drawn up a sufficient test in his own words when first given the chance to do so, the presbytery would have accepted it.[67]

Nothing demonstrates the capitulation of the Synod to this more tolerant, consensual mood better than the final, farcical, settlement of this contentious issue. At each synod the various presbyteries presented their 'returns', including a list of newly licensed and newly ordained ministers. It was customary for these reports to state that the candidate had signed the Westminster Confession. In 1781, the Presbytery of Armagh reported the licensing of one Joseph Denham 'according to synodical regulations', a phrase which had often been used. When asked whether Denham had signed the confession, the Armagh presbyters admitted that he had not. In fact, some confusion seems to have existed for decades, with some presbyteries installing their ministers in the manner of Armagh, others specifically mentioning that candidates had subscribed, or had subscribed 'according to the Pacific Act', and still others keeping silent on the subject. A proposal that the Synod should vote on the question of subscription was deferred by a great majority until the next meeting.

---

[66] John King, *Remarks on the Reverend S. M. Stephenson's Declaration of Faith* (Belfast, 1774), 9–10.
[67] Ibid. 11.

The following year the Synod resolved that 'if no one moves for a repeal of the rule respecting subscription, then the rule remains in its full force—and as no one moved for its repeal the rule continued'. It was plausibly argued by Henry Montgomery that this motion had been prompted by the encroachment of the Seceders within the bounds of the Synod, and was carried 'through the acquiescence of fear, and with a view to throw dust into the eyes of the people'.[68] A year later, a calmer assembly unanimously agreed that 'as usual' should be inserted in the place of 'full force'.[69] Thereafter, the authority of the Church to regulate the theological opinions of its members was devolved to the various presbyteries, and ministers were licensed and ordained according to local custom. A few years later only four of the fourteen presbyteries kept up even a nominal subscription.[70]

The central features of the New Light creed—the right of private judgement, the principled opposition to creeds and confessions, the emphasis on sincerity—all combined to form a powerful reading of history in which the struggle to pursue the pure, simple truths of the gospel in the face of the tyranny, corruption, and superstition of ecclesiastical power supplied the central dynamic. As mentioned above, the linchpin of Abernethy's theology was a 'self determining power' or a 'power of choosing or refuting', the correct exercise of which constituted virtue and brought happiness.[71] Any constraint placed on the right of private judgement thus impeded man's ability to imitate his maker. The New Light understanding of religious liberty, moulded during the subscription controversy, gave rise to a powerful critique of all creeds and confessions, which ultimately challenged the alliance of Church and State. As the theological bonds of Presbyterianism were progressively loosened, Dissenting ministers increasingly derived their character and cohesion from a passionate commitment to civil and religious liberty, and 'popery' became redefined to include any form of religious persecution.

This was Rational Dissent at its most radical—a complete spiritual libertarianism which was sometimes, but not necessarily, carried into the political sphere. For the most part, however, New Light preaching confined itself to the propagation of the sort of practical morality which was taught at the Scottish universities. Christianity was no longer to be enforced by the rewards or punishments of the next life, but was justified according to its practical benefits and utility; it was the most powerful bond which united mankind, and it offered the strongest incentives to the practice of virtue.[72] In the words of Abernethy, 'its principle view is to form men's tempers and direct their behaviour towards each other, as well as towards Almighty God; particularly to inspire them with the strongest sentiments of mutual benevolence and teach them offices of the tenderest sympathy and compassion'. Religion was valued for its role in the gradual civilization and refinement of human society.[73]

---

[68] Montgomery, 'Outlines', 290.   [69] *RGSU*, iii. 35, 41–3.

[70] Montgomery, 'Outlines', 291.

[71] John Abernethy, *Sermons on Various Subjects*, 4 vols. (London, 1748–51), iv. 54.

[72] See e.g. William Crawford, *Remarks on the Late Earl of Chesterfield's Letters to his Son* (London, 1776), 21.   [73] John Abernethy, *Persecution Contrary to Christianity* (Dublin, 1735), 25.

It was exactly this sort of philosophical teaching which provoked John Witherspoon's biting satire *Ecclesiastical Characteristics* (1753). A staunch defender of orthodoxy in Scotland, and later a president of Princeton, Witherspoon had in his sights the 'moderate men' of the Scottish Kirk, but his strictures might easily be applied to Moderatism's close relative across the water. Indeed, the target of his attack was Glasgow University—where most of the Ulster clergy received its education—and in particular the disciples of the Scots-Irish professor Francis Hutcheson. Witherspoon's main charges were that the Moderates had shunned the Scriptures in favour of heathen writers, and that they valued learning and politeness above soundness. They cultivated an air of gentility and accommodated their worship to the tastes of the fashionable gentry; hence their consistent unpopularity with the common people. Their sermons, he protested, were restricted to social duties, recommended to their hearers on rational, practical grounds. Recently Ian Clark has sought to revise the received picture of Moderatism as a superficial, complacent, and corrupt creed.[74] Polite Presbyterianism, while easily satirized, represented an honest attempt to reconcile Christianity with the rational spirit of the Enlightenment. Nevertheless, it is undeniable that Moderate teaching witnessed a shift away from doctrine towards conduct. One Scottish lady remembered that the lectures and sermons of William Hamilton and the Wisharts at Edinburgh, and of Hutcheson and his protégé Leechman at Glasgow, set standards of taste for the young people of fashion. They learned that 'whoever would please God must resemble him in goodness and benevolence, and those that had it not must affect it by politeness and good manners'.[75] The radicalism of the New Light pulpit, then, was tempered by a more conservative emphasis on propriety and practical morality.

Once separated from the Synod of Ulster the Antrim presbyters felt less need to placate popular suspicions concerning their views, and increasingly they dwelt on the human pursuit of virtue whilst paying lip service to Christian revelation. After Abernethy's death, his successor at Wood Street, Dublin, discovered some 'pretty amazing' passages in his diary, but, in keeping with New Light discretion, these were never made public.[76] There can be no doubt, however, that a few non-subscribers moved along the slippery slope to full-blown Unitarianism. The doctrine of the Trinity was one main casualty of the increasing elevation of scientific reasoning. Once original sin was gone, Christ's role in the redemption of humankind became increasingly irrelevant, and the Son of God was logically demoted to the human teacher of a pure system of morality. The interdependent doctrines of Adam's transgression, imputed sin, the unity of the Trinity and the divinity of Christ, and the doctrine of Atonement were subject to a domino effect which must be traced

---

[74] I. D. L. Clark, 'From Protest to Reaction: The Moderate Regime in the Church of Scotland, 1752–1805', in N. T. Phillipson and Rosalind Mitchell (eds.), *Scotland in the Age of Improvement* (Edinburgh, 1970), 200–24.

[75] Elizabeth Mure, 'Some Remarks on the Change of Manners in My Own Time', in *Selections from the Family Papers Preserved at Caldwell*, ed. and presented to the Maitland Club by William Mure, 3 vols. (Glasgow, 1854–5), i. 267–8.

[76] T. D. Hincks, 'Notices of William Bruce, and of his Contemporaries and Friends, Hutcheson, Abernethy, Duchal, and Others', *Christian Teacher*, NS 5 (1843), 79.

all the way back to Abernethy's assertion that 'personal persuasion' was the regulating principle of religious belief. William Drennan, who travelled farther than most down this path, greeted the progress of Paine's deism in the 1790s with cheerful indifference. 'Trust like a papist', he advised his sister, 'for, if you doubt like a dissenter, the same restless faculty that rejects the Athanasian creed . . . will begin to nibble at the Incarnation, the Miraculous Conception, etc., and thus Priestley lifts the hatch for Paine to enter.'[77] But it must be stressed that Drennan was the son of one of the pastors of First Belfast, and his views cannot be taken as representative of the Dissenters of the Presbytery of Antrim, nor even of its most advanced congregation.

The theological anatomy of the Synod in the late eighteenth century

It is extremely difficult to measure the impact of New Light divinity. In Belfast and in parts of Antrim and Down, party distinctions were probably clear due to the Presbytery of Antrim's own corporate identity, but in much of Ulster the lines between Old Light and New must have been blurred. The task of getting at the clergy's beliefs is of course easiest when dealing with those ministers who left pamphlets and printed sermons behind them, especially where these publications are disputatious. Thomas Witherow, the evangelical clergyman who published *Historical and Literary Memorials of Presbyterianism in Ireland* in 1879–80, counted eighty-six ministers who published sermons during the eighteenth century, forty-one of whom can be classified as New Light without stretching the definition too far. Unfortunately, this calculation merely confirms that the non-subscribers were disproportionately represented among the intellectual elite, a fact bemoaned by Witherow and other Victorian historians who wondered why the devil always had the best tunes.

Nor do church records offer much help. We know that by the 1770s there were only four presbyteries which continued to require subscription from their clergy. Further information might emerge from a series of detailed studies at the most local level, based on the records of presbyteries and even of individual congregations. As I have suggested above, however, the act of subscription cannot be used as a test of theological opinion. The Commissioners of the Irish Education Inquiry found in 1824 that some of the presbyteries which had dispensed with the practice were staunchly Calvinist.[78] They also learnt from Henry Cooke that only thirty-four or thirty-five of the 200 ministers in the Synod of Ulster were suspected Arians. In Cooke's opinion the heresy had been strongest in the 1720s, had declined, revived again in the 1770s and 1780s, and was now on the wane once more.[79] Cooke seems to have selected these decades merely because they saw open opposition to the Westminster Confession, however; he well knew that few clergymen had openly taught Arian views until the nineteenth century. Significantly, he attributed the revival of the Old Light to a more vigorous leadership and to the organizational structure

---

[77] Drennan to Martha McTier, [Feb. 1796], [Oct. 1799], *Drennan Letters*, 232, 293.
[78] *First Report of the Commissioners of Education in Ireland*, HC (1825), xii. 823.   [79] Ibid.

supplied by Bible and missionary societies, rather than a sea change in doctrinal views.[80] In the absence of more information on individual ministers, therefore, we can only presume that a majority of Presbyterian ministers had never strayed from the orthodox path.

What can be said with some certainty is that the New Light had its base in the wealthier meeting-houses. A complete list of congregations drawn up at the end of the century by the agent for the *regium donum* reveals the distribution of wealth in Presbyterian Ulster. The first category contained eleven congregations which could afford a stipend of £100 or more. Five of these—Derry, Newry, First Belfast, and the two Dublin congregations which were affiliated to the Synod—actually exceeded £200; the others were Second, Third, and Fourth Belfast, Armagh, Strabane, and Dromore. Only two were orthodox. In the second class (between £70 and £100) were twenty towns, which can be divided roughly between the two parties. Of the remaining 150, only a handful had known New Light connections.[81]

How, then, can we explain the remarkable hegemony exercised by this minority? According to Reid, a favourite maxim of the New Light party was 'think with the wise and speak with the vulgar'.[82] On the whole, they seem to have followed this advice. In one of the more tortured passages in his diary, Abernethy wrote of the temptation to conform to conventional views to salvage his popularity, but eventually resolved never 'to practice the arts of dissimulation, and make such base compliances as even *seem* to be inconsistent with the prerogative of Jesus Christ, as king of his church, or the sacred rights of his subjects'.[83] But others did not put up such a struggle. Francis Hutcheson, for example, subscribed twice, once on his admission to the Presbytery of Armagh as a licentiate in 1719, and again when he took up the moral philosophy chair at Glasgow, yet there can be no doubt that privately he questioned many of the tenets contained in the Confession. Perhaps this behaviour, like his movements towards conforming to the Established Church, was due to what his friend William Bruce termed 'your superior latitude with respect to compliances of this sort'.[84] In any case, there can be little doubt that many ministers followed Hutcheson's example and subscribed with their fingers crossed behind their backs.

It is hard to avoid the impression that New Light influence was based partly on discretion, perhaps even deception. The papers of John Caldwell, an Antrim Presbyterian who later became a United Irishman, provide a fascinating insight into the ways in which the relationships between rational and orthodox Presbyterians were worked out in practice. According to Caldwell the Ballyclare congregation was composed predominantly of Calvinists, yet there were 'a few,' he recalled, 'an enlightened few, who had the temerity to presume to think for themselves'.[85] He had often heard his father, in private conversation with the minister, express doubts about some

---

[80] *First Report of the Commissioners of Education in Ireland*, HC (1825), 824.

[81] List of congregations of the Synod of Ulster and their stipends, PRONI, Castlereagh Papers, D3030/1009.   [82] Reid, *Presbyterian Church in Ireland*, iii. 329.

[83] Abernethy, *Sermons*, vol. i, p. lxxiv.

[84] Bruce to Hutcheson, 6 Oct. 1738, NLS, Dunlop Papers, MS 9252, fo. 128.

[85] John Caldwell, 'Particulars of a North County Irish Family', PRONI, Caldwell Papers, T3541/5/3, p. 80.

of the doctrines contained in the Westminster Confession, and as he grew older he himself joined in these discussions. 'The result was that after faithfully and attentively reading the book of life, I felt persuaded that many of the opinions and dogmas imposed on us as divine truths were merely the offspring of priestcraft, kingcraft and moneycraft.'[86] In some towns, then, the New Lights may have formed an inner circle within the congregation, reminiscent of the Puritan 'gathered church' movement of the previous century.

Clearly, the New Light ascendancy cannot be explained solely as a fraud; we must look also at what happened to the subscribers. Although the orthodox apologists had never been a match for the big guns of the opposite camp, their intellectual profile in the second half of the century was particularly poor. The only heavy-weight they could muster was Benjamin McDowell, minister of Ballykelly and then of Dublin, and McDowell, born in America of Covenanting parents and educated at Princeton, is the exception that proves the rule. The controversial writings of McDowell's lesser colleagues are chiefly interesting for the amount of ground which they concede to the New Light persuasion. The contamination of the Calvinists with some of the moderate spirit advocated by their opponents opened the way for the exercise of toleration, and the creation of a real consensus in parts of Ulster. Thus Caldwell, mentioned above, goes on to explain that at communion services Dissenters of different opinions would gather together in crowds of up to seven hundred and would receive communion from the minister of their choice. This arrangement, he says, was 'understood but not commented on'.[87]

Finally, some clues to the New Light supremacy lie in the workings of the Church organization. There was no equivalent of the Scottish Patronage Act in Ireland, but a rule passed in 1733 stipulated that the election of ministers was no longer to be determined by a simple majority but by the 'synodical majority' in which greater weight was conferred on the votes of those laymen who contributed most to the minister's stipend, that is, the 'respectable' members of the congregation.[88] The government of the Synod of Ulster in the eighteenth century was therefore not a democracy, but an oligarchy. The non-subscribers may also have been better organized, and their concentration in the towns enabled them to attend the annual synods more regularly than the orthodox backwoodsmen.[89] By and large, however, their ascendancy reflected their superior eloquence and literary accomplishments and, consequently, the higher social profile of their congregations and their influence with the ruling classes. It is significant that in all official dealings with the government, the Synod of Ulster was represented by Arians like William Campbell and Robert Black, who had friends in high places, or by members of the small Presbytery of Antrim.

Conclusion

By searching for the cultural and social meanings of the theological questions which were agitated in the Synod of Ulster, and by focusing on relations between the clergy and the laity, the subscription controversy can be made to yield new conclusions

[86] Ibid. 80.   [87] Ibid. 80–1.   [88] Reid, *Presbyterian Church in Ireland*, iii. 242.
[89] Ibid. 317.

about the development of Dissent in eighteenth-century Ireland. First, the infection of Irish Presbyterianism with the Arian heresy has often been exaggerated. Inroads were made into Calvinist theology, the most important break being the rejection of original sin in favour of a more optimistic emphasis on the capacity of mankind for moral improvement. But the overriding message in the New Light gospel centred on the need to peel away the layers of human superstition that had obscured the divine word, and to restore Christianity to its pristine condition. The implications of this enterprise for the central doctrines of traditional Presbyterianism were not fully worked out until almost a century later. It was the news of heterodoxy in other churches and the trial of Thomas Emlyn which concentrated the popular mind on the question of the Trinity, and which produced an obsession with Arianism and Socinianism during the 1720s. For most of the eighteenth century these labels were used loosely by orthodox ministers as umbrella terms for all kinds of deviations from traditional Presbyterian teaching. The situation remained fluid until the 1820s, when two developments served to polarize Presbyterian Ulster. The first, of course, was the revitalization of the orthodox camp by the injection of new evangelical energies into the General Synod. The second was the appearance of a more dogmatic tone among some of the New Lights. The legalization of Unitarianism in Britain in 1813 and in Ireland four years later contributed to the emergence of a more aggressive Arian party.

Secondly, the brand of enlightenment rationality espoused by New Light Presbyterians challenged existing political and ecclesiastical structures by calling for the reordering of society on an essentially republican basis, giving each citizen the opportunity of moral fulfilment through self-government. In practical terms, this could mean the abolition of the Established Church, and the removal of aristocratic corruptions in the political system. But the sort of transformation envisaged here was moral rather than material, and it is at this point that the social bias of moderation and politeness becomes obvious. For the Rational Dissenters Christianity was above all a civilizing force which had 'descended from heaven to enlighten and enlarge the human mind, to melt down the ruggedness of barbarism into the unsuspicious intercourse, the sweet amaenity of civil life'. Until the final triumph of pure Christianity, the powerful religious antipathies of the lower orders would have to be tempered by the tolerance of the 'middle and superior ranks'.[90] The correlation between heterodoxy and radical politics was not a straightforward one.

The natural social constituency for polite Presbyterianism, as Francis Hutcheson argued, was to be found among the virtuous gentry.[91] In Scotland, backed by the patronage of the landed classes, the Moderates had seized control of both the General Assembly and the universities by the middle of the century, and enjoyed remarkable prestige and authority for their services in the legitimation of the social and political order constructed after the Union. In Ireland, of course, the Presbyterians were excluded from the institutions of the Ascendancy, but they were not wholly

---

[90] [William Drennan], *Letters of Orellana* (Dublin, 1785), 34, 37.
[91] [Francis Hutcheson], *Considerations on Patronage. Addressed to the Gentlemen of Scotland* (London, 1735), 16.

alienated from landed society, as the many connections between the New Light clergy and the Ulster gentry show. Moreover, the emergence of a new, closely knit mercantile and professional elite in Belfast and its hinterland compensated for the defection of landed families to the Established Church which had weakened the Synod of Ulster earlier in the century. New Light clergymen dominated the committees of the various philanthropic and educational bodies so conspicuous in Georgian Belfast, and they acted as arbiters of taste and fashion for the townspeople.

But the final, and perhaps most important, conclusion is that the New Light was in some ways merely skin deep. The ideological cleavage in the Church reflected social and cultural differences. Opposition to subscription began with the Belfast Society, and drew its strength chiefly from Dublin, Belfast, and other northern towns, whilst in remoter parts of Ulster orthodoxy remained unchallenged. And Ulster was still an overwhelmingly rural society: it has been estimated that by 1800 only fourteen northern towns could claim a population of more than 2,000, and only a tenth of the population lived in settlements of more than 1,000 people.[92] The ideals of moderation and tolerance won acceptance in the General Synod, and latitudinarian sentiment and language was widely diffused. Nevertheless, the rapid expansion of the Seceders, who could claim sixty congregations by the end of the century, testifies to the suspicion with which New Light doctrines were regarded by the population at large.

In the early decades of the nineteenth century, industrialization brought not only increased prosperity, but also social fragmentation to Belfast. Even before the massive population shift during the famine, it contained 75,000 inhabitants. Polite Presbyterianism was swamped by an influx of rural immigrants, not just the thousands of Roman Catholics who settled in pockets on the outskirts of the town, but also the Protestants of the Ulster countryside who brought with them the sectarian politics of the Orange Order. This latter group was untouched by the moral philosophy and scholarship of New Light sermons and provided a ready audience for the more evangelical strain making headway in the Synod of Ulster. After all, even the great Abernethy, whose elegant discourses were widely admired, found it 'extremely difficult to speak down to the understandings of all' despite the pleas of his friends.[93] If 'the reign of the New Light', as I have suggested, rested on such precarious foundations, then its sudden eclipse in the nineteenth century can be more easily explained.

[92] W. H. Crawford, 'Ulster Economy and Society in the Eighteenth Century', Ph.D. thesis (QUB, 1983), 135. [93] Duchal, *Sermon on Death of Abernethy*, 22.

3
'THE RATTLING OF DRY BONES': SECEDERS AND COVENANTERS

IN opposition to the New Light ideals of politeness and moderation stood the menace of 'enthusiasm'. The dangers of the fanaticism which had disfigured religion in the seventeenth century furnished a stock theme of New Light polemic. There was nothing peculiarly Presbyterian about this preoccupation; fear of enthusiasm was deeply embedded in the political culture of Hanoverian Britain. In his classic pronouncement on the subject, the Scottish philosopher and historian David Hume had depicted the 'matchless' constitution of Great Britain being pulled in contrary directions by two corruptions of true religion. The first, of course, was popery, the source of ignorance, superstition, and passive obedience; but just as alarming was the furious and violent zeal which stemmed from hope, pride, and a 'warm Imagination'. Behind the polite façade of Augustan politics loomed the enthusiasm of the civil war period. Writing with first-hand experience of Presbyterian extremism, Hume ranked the Scottish Covenanters along with the Levellers among the forces of darkness and disorder. There was abundant evidence to show that those who claimed privileged access to the divine plan threatened the very fabric of civil society. 'In a little Time,' warned Hume, 'the inspir'd Person comes to regard himself as the chief Favourite of the Divinity; and when this Frenzy takes Place, which is the Summit of Enthusiasm, every Whimsy is consecrated: Human Reason, and even Morality are rejected as fallacious Guides.'[1]

For Presbyterians, increasingly embarrassed by the excesses of their seventeenth-century forefathers, the civil wars raised the spectre of the Solemn League and Covenant.[2] Agreed by the Scots and the English Parliament in 1643, this treaty was the climax of Scotland's Calvinist reformation. Whereas its predecessor, the National Covenant of 1638, had merely denounced the Arminian innovations imposed on the Scottish Church by Archbishop Laud, this second pact had pledged the two parties to extirpate prelacy and popery in Scotland and to extend the Presbyterian revolution to England and Ireland as well. In return for Scottish intervention in the civil war, the English Parliament had agreed to bring the Churches of the three kingdoms into conformity with the true religion. The re-establishment of episcopacy at the Restoration, and its confirmation in England by the Revolution Settlement, removed this crusade from the realm of practical politics. The Covenant was broken by the King, disowned by the English, and quietly dropped by chastened Presbyterians

---

[1] David Hume, 'Of Superstition and Enthusiasm', in id., *Essays Moral, Political and Literary*, ed. E. F. Miller, rev. edn. (Indianapolis, 1987), 74.

[2] See e.g. Alexander Colville, *The Persecuting, Disloyal and Absurd Tenets of those Who Affect to Call themselves Seceders* (Belfast, 1749), 6–12.

with various degrees of relief. But not all Scots agreed that their oath to presbyterianize the three kingdoms was no longer binding. The Church of Scotland would be troubled throughout the eighteenth century by parties of ultra-Presbyterians who claimed to be the true heirs of the seventeenth-century reformation. The two most important expressions of this tendency were the Associate Synod, or Secession, and the Reformed Presbytery, commonly known as the Covenanters. In their zeal to recall the Kirk to its past glories, both would look across the sea to the Scots colony in the north of Ireland.

While the Synod of Ulster's liberal vanguard has been the subject of much historical comment, its conservative offshoots have received comparatively little attention. Lecky dismissed the adherents of the Secession as 'merely simple-minded and well-meaning fanatics', drawn from the poorer classes, who 'exercised no political influence on the country'.[3] The Seceders and Covenanters have recently begun to generate more interest, a development which can be attributed to the appearance of David Miller's 1978 article 'Presbyterianism and "Modernization" in Ulster'.[4] In the first serious treatment of the subject, Miller challenged the assumption that religious latitudinarianism and political liberalism went hand in hand by demonstrating that the ministers implicated in the '98 rebellion can be divided more or less evenly into subscribers and non-subscribers. Moreover, he argued that the ideology of the United Irishmen in Ulster owed as much to the millennial drive of orthodox Calvinism as it did to the enlightenment prescriptions of the Belfast radicals. My own study of clerical involvement in seditious activity, while differing in several respects from Miller's, supports his general conclusion.[5]

To eighteenth-century historians, religious enthusiasm calls to mind the rise of Methodism and the quickening of evangelical energies within the Protestant churches generally. As such, the spread of 'vital religion' has been associated primarily with political and social conservatism: the *locus classicus* is E. P. Thompson's attack on 'the chiliasm of despair'.[6] It is important to establish at the outset of this chapter that evangelicalism was not indigenous to the Ulster Scots settlement. A distinction must be made between what David Miller has referred to as the 'conversionist' and 'prophetic' strains within the Protestant heritage. The first, embracing Methodism and the Calvinism of New England, is characterized above all by the centrality of the 'new birth', and was sometimes called 'experiential' or 'experimental' religion. The latter, which predominated in Scotland and its Ulster colony, was preoccupied with the system of ecclesiastical discipline required to govern the elect.[7] While the first revolves around the salvation of the individual, the second is more concerned with the spiritual health of the whole community. Although Miller offers a sociological explanation for this difference by reference to the uneven

---

[3] W. E. H. Lecky, *A History of Ireland in the Eighteenth Century*, 5 vols. (London, 1913; first pub. 1892), v. 439.　　　　　　　　　　　　　[4] *Past & Present*, 80 (1978), 66–90.

[5] Ch. 8 below and app.

[6] E. P. Thompson, *The Making of the English Working Class*, 3rd edn. (London, 1988; first pub. 1963), 385–440.

[7] D. W. Miller, 'Presbyterianism and "Modernization" in Ulster', *Past & Present*, 80 (1978), 67, 72.

modernization of the Ulster economy, he also notes that the distinction is partly a cultural one, between Anglo-American and Ulster-Scottish styles which would eventually confront each other in the American colonies during the Great Awakening.

In fact, popular revivalism in Ulster was not without precedent. Recently, Marilyn Westerkamp has drawn attention to a strain of Scots-Irish religiosity which originated in the Sixmilewater revival of the 1620s and culminated ultimately in the Great Awakening.[8] Yet Miller's distinction holds: Presbyterian revivals focused on the ritual purification of the community rather than personal redemption. It may be partly because they already had their own devotional forms and ritualistic expressions that Scotland and Ulster proved to be stony ground for the evangelicals. The great revivalist George Whitefield thus met with a chilly response when he visited Scotland in the 1740s. The Covenanters warned their people against the 'vagrant prelatic priest' who inspired the famous 'Cambuslang wark'; the Seceders, initially hopeful that Whitefield might help them in their battle against the Church of Scotland, turned against him when he refused to endorse the Presbyterian form of church government.[9]

Ulster was to prove equally resistant to the good news of the itinerant preachers. Irish Methodist numbers rose from 4,237 in 1775 to 19,292 in 1800, but they were concentrated in the linen country of north Armagh and the district around Lough Erne, both areas of low Scottish settlement.[10] Visiting Belfast in 1756, Wesley complained that 'between Seceders, old self-centred Presbyterians, New-Light men, Moravians, Cameronians, and formal "Churchmen", it is a miracle if any here bring forth fruit to perfection'.[11] This impression can be backed up with letters from Scots-Irish emigrants in North America, recording their astonishment at the hysteria of frontier religion.[12] While the colonies awakened, then, Ulster continued to slumber.

The distinction between the conversionist and prophetic varieties of Protestantism, long familiar to historians of the Great Awakening, can by illustrated by a brief examination of the troubles experienced by Thomas Ledlie Birch in the American backcountry. Birch had been minister of the orthodox congregation of Saintfield, County Down, for over twenty years before his arrest and deportation following the Battle of Ballynahinch, yet when 'called' by the people of Washington, Pennsylvania,

[8] M. J. Westerkamp, *Triumph of the Laity: Scots-Irish Piety and the Great Awakening 1625–1760* (Oxford, 1988).

[9] Adam Gib, *A Warning against Countenancing the Ministrations of Mr. George Whitefield* (Edinburgh, 1742); Matthew Hutchison, *The Reformed Presbyterian Church in Scotland: Its Origin and History 1680–1876* (Paisley, 1893), 179; Ned Landsman, 'Evangelists and their Hearers: Popular Interpretation of Revivalist Preaching in Eighteenth-Century Scotland', *Journal of British Studies*, 28 (1989), 147.

[10] David Hempton and Myrtle Hill, *Evangelical Protestantism in Ulster Society 1740–1890* (London, 1992), 38; see also 33–5.   [11] Quoted ibid. 9.

[12] John Nevin to James Nevin, 10 Apr. 1804, PRONI, McClelland Papers, D2966/57/1; Jane Smith to John Weir, n.d. [1775], PRONI, Weir Papers, D1140/3. See also James Horner's remarks on Methodism in Philadelphia, PRONI, T1592/17. When the colonial church split in 1741 over the issues thrown up by the revival, Irish Presbyterians were to be found in both camps, but the majority took the anti-evangelical 'Old Side', which was sometimes labelled the Scotch-Irish party: Patricia Bonomi, *Under the Cope of Heaven: Religion, Society, and Politics in Colonial America* (New York, 1986), 137; Ned Landsman, *Scotland and its First American Colony, 1683–1765* (Princeton, 1985), 243.

he found the Presbytery of Ohio unwilling to install him. Admittedly, his involvement in the Irish rebellion and rumours of his drunken behaviour had done little for his reputation. The Presbytery's main objection, however, was a theological one, namely, that Birch did not possess an 'experimental' acquaintance with religion. In Scotland and Ireland presbyteries were primarily concerned to establish that new ministers were sound on the fundamental doctrines of the Westminster Confession and possessed of the requisite academic qualifications. At his examination by the Ohio presbyters Birch naturally tried to demonstrate his solid grasp of scripture, only to discover that 'What would have pleased the Presbytery (as I have frequently learned since) was, if I had told them of a certain time and place when I became assured of eternal happiness, or to use their own words, knowing myself once blind, now I see.'[13]

Birch's mocking tone was typical of a widely shared scepticism about the 'new birth'. Presbyterian misgivings usually fell into one of three categories. To begin with, Calvinism, even in its most rigid forms, was essentially a cerebral creed, and the Presbyterian suspicion of emotional religion died hard. The physical manifestations of evangelical fervour would always arouse scorn and distaste, even during the celebrated revival of 1859. Secondly, Presbyterian ecclesiology entailed a lofty conception of the ministerial office, whereas revivalism tended to stress the autonomy of lay men and women. Evangelical ministers rarely possessed the formal qualifications prized by the Synod of Ulster and its offshoots, and their itinerant preaching circuits conflicted with the high premium placed on order and regularity by Presbyterian churches. Needless to say, those who trespassed on the territorial boundaries of older congregations met with the opposition of resident ministers who feared for their stipends. Finally, and most importantly, evangelical movements were by their very nature inter-denominational, and so cast doubt on the unique claims made for the Presbyterian polity. The laity was constantly warned against 'promiscuous' communion with other sects. For these reasons Ulster Presbyterianism remained impervious to 'vital' religion until the foundation of the Evangelical Society of Ulster in the aftermath of the '98 rebellion.

In this chapter, I shall be concerned predominantly with the history of the Seceding and Covenanting sects—their distinctive teachings, their organizational development, and their success in detaching communicants from the Synod of Ulster. By 1792 the Secession contained forty-six ministers, compared to the 185 attached to the General Synod and the Presbytery of Antrim, while the Reformed Presbytery could claim only six.[14] The significance of these breakaway groups cannot be understood in institutional terms alone, however. It is more helpful to think of the polite Presbyterianism professed by the New Light elite and the enthusiasm of the Seceders and Covenanters as conflicting tendencies within a broad Ulster Presbyterian tradition. Although these sects attracted relatively few ministers, each one might serve

---

[13] Thomas Ledlie Birch, *Seemingly Experimental Religion* (Washington, Pa., 1806), 36–8. The Washington congregation included many Irish immigrants.

[14] J. S. Reid, *History of the Presbyterian Church in Ireland*, ed. W. D. Killen, 3rd edn., 3 vols. (Belfast, 1867), iii. 368 n. 78.

several congregations. Orthodox families within the Synod who disliked New Light tendencies but stopped short of schism sometimes attended a Secession meeting as well as their own. In Scotland it was said that such 'occasional hearers' sometimes outnumbered the congregation.[15] Furthermore, this extreme wing of Ulster Presbyterianism was its most dynamic element. The Secession was expanding rapidly, and it was intellectually robust. In the absence of Old Light leadership within the Synod the defence of orthodoxy fell to these fundamentalists; they should not, therefore, be dismissed as a lunatic fringe.

The third section also contains the first detailed investigation of the politics of the two bodies. As we shall see in the next two chapters, the Covenanting heritage in Ireland became deeply divided, with the Seceding clergy supporting the loyalists, almost to a man, while the Reformed Presbyterians were conspicuous for their role in the insurrection. The divergence of the two groups can be explained by locating the late eighteenth century within a long transformation from a 'prophetic' to a 'conversionist' style of Protestantism, from religion as public testimony to religion as private spirituality. At this extreme edge of Presbyterianism we can find both the last adherents of the Covenanting cause and the first ministers to rally to the new evangelical standard.

The origins of the Covenanting tradition

The Solemn League and Covenant of 1643 was designed to protect the gains made by the Calvinist reformation in Scotland and to export the Presbyterian model of church government to England and Ireland. Scotland's progress from reformation to revolution is best understood within the context of what seventeenth-century historians have begun to call the British problem, that is, the troubled interaction of the three kingdoms (and churches) which comprised the Stuart inheritance. Taking their bearings from Calvin rather than Luther, the Scottish reformers had always insisted on a more thoroughgoing opposition to Rome, and looked upon the Genevan model of church government with greater favour. The liturgical innovations imposed by Charles I, his elevated conception of the episcopal office, and the imposition of his policies by royal prerogative, all contributed to the polarization of ecclesiastical politics north of the border. Yet presbyters and bishops coexisted in the Scottish Church until a surprisingly late stage. It was Charles I's repeated failure to consider Scottish susceptibilities which finally convinced the nobles, barons, burgesses, and clergy of Scotland that the Reformation was under threat, thus ensuring the victory of the Presbyterian party.[16]

The Solemn League and Covenant and the Westminster Confession which followed it constituted a radical programme for the reordering of society on a Calvinist basis. The distinctive features of this programme lay not so much in its theology as in its ecclesiology, or its idea of the Kirk. Covenanting theories of the relationship

---

[15] Hutchison, *Reformed Presbyterian Church*, 252.
[16] See David Stevenson, *The Scottish Revolution, 1637–44: The Triumph of the Covenanters* (Newton Abbot, 1973).

between *sacerdotium* and *magisterium* were highly problematic, for reasons that lie both within Calvinist doctrine itself, with its mixture of repression and radicalism, and within the historical development of the Scottish Kirk. On the one hand, Presbyterian purists advocated the strict separation of Church and State, the 'doctrine of the two kingdoms' identified with Andrew Melville. According to this doctrine, the civil magistrate had been granted the power of the sword, but this authority was restricted to secular affairs; in spiritual matters the king was simply a member of the Church like any other, subject to the clergy who had been entrusted with the keys of the kingdom of heaven. The interference of the civil power in the ecclesiastical government of the Church, like that of popes and prelates, was seen as an invasion of the prerogatives of Christ, the only head and king of the Church. Hence the profound offence caused by the Patronage Act and by state-appointed fast days in eighteenth-century Scotland.

These theoretical objections to government interference were reinforced by practical experience. Scotland had been reformed largely in defiance of royal authority, while the Presbyterian colony in Ulster occupied an anomalous and insecure position within the British state-system. A tradition of independence from the civil magistrate was thus encouraged which clashed with the erastian regime developed in England after 1689 and with the establishment whig conception of parliamentary sovereignty. To make matters worse, the Scots had a disconcerting habit of deposing monarchs who differed from them on points of religion. During their struggles with the House of Stuart, the theories of popular sovereignty, contract, and resistance associated with George Buchanan had been absorbed into Presbyterian discourse with the result that Scottish whigs were able to justify armed resistance to James II with few of the doubts and inhibitions that deeply troubled their English counterparts.[17]

While Covenanters incessantly denounced the supremacy of the civil magistrate over Christ's kingdom, however, they showed little compunction in blurring the distinction between secular and spiritual jurisdiction when it came to clerical interference in the political sphere. The key point to remember is that, unlike New Light divinity, orthodox Presbyterianism was thoroughly hospitable to the conception of a national Church; it had never, after all, been noted for its toleration of diversity and difference. The Kirk was a visible community, a self-governing corporation, distinct from civil society, yet fully entitled to the aid of the magistrate whose duty it was to back up ecclesiastical sanctions with secular punishments in the suppression of idolatry, blasphemy, and heresy. Calvin himself had recognized the need for state assistance in the effective policing of the true religion, and the Westminster Confession accordingly bestowed upon the civil magistrate the authority to enforce doctrinal standards in the Church, creating an ambiguity that was to perplex many eighteenth-century theologians.[18] The Seceders and the Covenanters were caught between the high-flying ideal of church establishment and the dismal reality of their position as minority sects.

[17] Quentin Skinner, *The Foundations of Modern Political Thought*, 2 vols. (Cambridge, 1978), vol. ii, ch. 7; R. M. Kingdon, 'Calvinism and Resistance Theory, 1550–1580', in J. H. Burns and Mark Goldie (eds.), *The Cambridge History of Political Thought 1450–1700* (Cambridge, 1991), 193–218.

[18] John McKerrow, *History of the Secession Church*, rev. and enlarged edn. (Glasgow, 1841), 378–475.

If the two-kingdoms ecclesiology made little sense in a Scotland which was forced to share a king and later full sovereignty with its stronger episcopalian neighbour, it made even less sense in the dependent kingdom of Ireland. Nevertheless, the Presbyterians of the plantation had conceived of themselves as 'ye church off Ireland', entitled to public support in the form of tithes, and responsible not only for the private spirituality, but the public morality of those people who fell within their jurisdiction. As a strong, centralized institution, the Synod resembled not so much a nonconformist group petitioning for toleration as a national Church (or part of one) demanding legal recognition. When one Presbyterian preacher was interrogated on the subject of Church–State relations by the Privy Council in 1681, he therefore acknowledged the authority of the king to establish ecclesiastical government, but only within scriptural limits: 'I do not believe that the king has power to set up what government he pleases in the Church; but that he has power to set up the due and true government of the Church.'[19] It was assumed, then, that magistrates and ministers, although supervising separate spheres, would be brought into close harmony. Under the Covenanters, indeed, it seemed that the state might be used as an instrument for reformation; the idea of a covenanted king was the equivalent of the godly prince of the English puritans, and proved just as elusive.

Robert Monroe's Scottish army was responsible both for the foundation of the first presbytery in Ireland and for the introduction of the Solemn League and Covenant to the Ulster Scots population; it was natural that the two should be closely associated in the popular mind. By the late seventeenth century the Covenants had acquired an almost talismanic force. Evidence unearthed by Raymond Gillespie suggests that in parts of east Ulster admission to the Solemn League and Covenant had even been incorporated into the sacrament of baptism.[20] The Presbyterian programme had become the focal point for an apocalyptic view of history which conferred upon the Scots a unique role in the battle against Antichrist. Unlike the millenarianism of the Anabaptists in sixteenth-century Germany or the English sectaries of the 1640s, this sense of mission was closely bound up with feelings of national identity. The Covenant thus symbolized Scotland's leadership in the establishment of Christ's kingdom, and signified a unique relationship between the Scottish people and their God.[21] In the heightened religious excitement of the 1790s the keepers of the Covenanting flame would be reminded of their historic task.

The Covenanting movement did not survive the return of the House of Stuart in 1660. Presbyterian sympathy for the new monarch was not reciprocated, and episcopacy was restored in all three kingdoms. The defenders of the second reformation refused to conform and were ejected, and the thirty years of episcopacy that followed meant that the Kirk would never attain Presbyterian purity again. Meanwhile the Presbyterians became dissenters, protesting against the restoration

[19] Reid, *Presbyterian Church in Ireland*, ii. 580.
[20] Raymond Gillespie, 'The Presbyterian Revolution in Ulster, 1660–1690', in W. J. Sheils and Diana Wood (eds.), *Studies in Church History*, xxv, *The Churches, Ireland, and the Irish* (Oxford, 1989), 166.
[21] S. A. Burrell, 'The Apocalyptic Vision of the Early Covenanters', *Scottish Historical Review*, 43 (1964), 1–24.

of episcopacy. In June 1680 one Covenanting leader, James Cameron, went further in the famous Sanquhar declaration, proclaiming that Charles II had forfeited his right to the throne by breach of covenant. It was this renunciation of allegiance to the king which marked the emergence of the Covenanters as a separate, distinct sect.[22]

The history of embattled Presbyterianism in the Restoration period has often been told in heroic terms.[23] Preachers with prices on their heads led their people out of the parish churches into barns and fields. Outlawed ministers travelled through Ulster and the west of Scotland, attracting large audiences to their outdoor meetings. Attempts to put down these 'conventicles' led to futile insurrections like the Pentland rising of 1666 and the battle of Bothwell Bridge in 1679. It was during this period that the persecution of Presbyterian extremists reached its height, and the Covenanters were gradually reduced to a handful of individual charismatic preachers who had managed to maintain personal followings. These were men like Alexander Peden, the eponymous James Cameron, James Renwick, David Houston, and Alexander Shields, author of the radical treatise *A Hind Let Loose* (1687). Their sufferings would later be immortalized in *A Cloud of Witnesses*, the Covenanting Book of Martyrs, which went through many editions in the eighteenth century.[24]

In 1690 the Scottish Presbyterians who had been catapulted back into power by the Glorious Revolution found their freedom of manoeuvre curtailed both externally, by the victory of a whiggish episcopacy in England, and internally, by the large number of clergymen it had inherited from the previous regime. Inevitably, the Revolution church was built upon compromise. Thus, while the Presbyterian form of church government was restored to national status, no mention of the Covenants was made. The architects of the new settlement chose to look back to 1592 rather than the 'second reformation' of 1638. Furthermore, an oath of allegiance to the Crown was imposed on the Kirk, the first of a series of oaths which were construed as implying support for the Church of England, whose episcopal government and royal supremacy the Covenanters were pledged to overthrow.

Those who remained committed to the Covenanting ideal were profoundly disappointed with a national Church which submitted to the erastian control of an uncovenanted king and settled for Presbyterianism in one country. The Church of Scotland was seen as sinfully subservient to the civil authority and an accomplice of the idolatrous Church of England, a view which could only be strengthened by the parliamentary union of 1707. In 1692 the self-styled 'Remnant' published a declaration disowning William III as it would later disown Anne and, with more moderate language, the Hanoverians. The Cameronians would accept neither a popish nor a prelatic pretender. After the Hanoverian succession they repeated their belief that the assumption of the royal supremacy was a blasphemous usurpation of Christ's sovereignty, and argued that George I's alliance with popish states abroad made

---

[22] Hutchison, *Reformed Presbyterian Church*, 42–3.
[23] I. B. Cowan, *The Scottish Covenanters 1660–1688* (London, 1976).
[24] *A Cloud of Witnesses, for the Royal Prerogatives of Jesus Christ or, the Last Speeches and Testimonies of those who have Suffered for the Truth in Scotland since the Year 1680*, 5th edn. (Glasgow, 1751).

him a supporter of the kingdom of Antichrist.[25] Without a regular ministry, the remnant survived as a network of 'societies', co-ordinated by a 'General Meeting', and maintaining a correspondence with Irish and Dutch allies.[26] It was not until 1743, when John McMillan established the Reformed Presbytery, that they acquired some institutional substance. McMillan, who had been deposed by the Church of Scotland in 1704 for refusing to abjure 'anti-government principles', became the recognized leader of the recalcitrant Presbyterians, now referred to variously as Cameronians, McMillanites, Society-men, or simply the 'anti-government party'.

The scarcity of documentary material on Irish Presbyterianism at this time makes it difficult to gauge the extent to which the Covenanter mentality still survived in Ulster. Evidence of Presbyterian aggression can be culled from one highly unreliable source, the polemical pamphlets of Anglican apologists. According to William Tisdall, the vicar of Belfast, the Presbyterians continued to claim direct jurisdiction over the civil magistrate and circulated copies of the Solemn League and Covenant and Shields's *A Hind Let Loose* at the end of Anne's reign.[27] But Tisdall was willing to use any weapon that came to hand, as his allegations that Presbyterians toasted Cromwell and propagated Milton's republican doctrines show. James Kirkpatrick of Belfast denied that disloyal books were printed in Ulster or that Presbyterian principles demanded the extirpation of episcopacy.[28] In fact, the official Presbyterian line was one of quietism. The Synod's aim was to keep a low profile while it consolidated its ecclesiastical organization. Immediately after the Restoration an Ulster Presbyterian delegation which had travelled to London to present an address to the new king was advised by London Dissenters to remove impolitic references to the renewal of the Covenant and the suppression of prelacy, much to the disgust of their brethren at home.[29] After 1672, when the first royal bounty was granted, the Ulster presbyteries helped to put down a handful of militant Scottish Covenanters agitating against the establishment, leaving themselves open to accusations of betrayal from their own rank and file.

But there were very close links between Ulster and south-west Scotland, where the Covenanters were strongest, and long-standing ties were reinforced by fresh waves of immigration in the late seventeenth century. Beginning in the 1670s, there was a flow of Presbyterians from the west of Scotland caused by economic difficulties and religious persecution. Then, in the late 1690s, came a huge influx, estimated by contemporary churchmen as between 50,000 and 80,000 people.[30] After the rout at Bothwell Bridge the Ulster countryside became a natural haven for fugitive preachers

---

[25] *The Declaration, Protestation and Testimony of a Poor Wasted, Desolate, Misrepresented and Reproached Remnant of the Suffering Anti-Popish, Anti-Prelatick, Anti-Erastian, Anti-Sectarian, True Presbyterian Church in Scotland, United Together in Truth and Duty* (n.p., [1715]).

[26] Hutchison, *Reformed Presbyterian Church*, 56–7.

[27] [William Tisdall], *The Conduct of the Dissenters of Ireland* (Dublin, 1712), 2, 48, 68; id., *The Nature and Tendency of Popular Phrases* (Dublin, 1714[?]), 12, 17.

[28] [James Kirkpatrick], *An Historical Essay upon the Loyalty of Presbyterians* ([Belfast], 1713), 505, 523–6, 540–50.   [29] Reid, *Presbyterian Church in Ireland*, ii. 246–51.

[30] W. Macafee and V. Morgan, 'Population in Ulster, 1660–1760', in Peter Roebuck (ed.), *Plantation to Partition: Essays in Ulster History in Honour of J. L. McCracken* (Belfast, 1981), 53–4, 58.

like Alexander Peden, a Scottish soothsayer whose prophetic powers and miraculous escapes from the authorities became legendary.[31] It is interesting to note that tales of Peden's adventures would be circulated in Antrim over a hundred years later by United Irish propagandists.[32]

Three militants—Michael Bruce, John Crookshanks, and Andrew McCormick—had already toured parts of Ulster in the 1660s, where they were acclaimed by 'the common sorts of people' as the upholders of the true Kirk. Before their return to Scotland they mustered vast assemblies in open defiance of the magistrates.[33] Crookshanks and McCormick were later killed in Scotland at the battle of Rullion Green,[34] but Michael Bruce, the founder of the great Irish clerical dynasty of that name, published two sermons which still survive and provide us with a rare glimpse of Covenanting oratory. One of these fiery discourses, *The Rattling of the Dry Bones*, taunts the Presbyterians with their betrayal of the true religion and looks forward to a great rejuvenation of the Kirk.[35] The 'stirring of dry bones' (a text taken from Ezekiel 37: 7–8) would later become a favourite metaphor of revivalist preachers, signifying an outpouring of the Holy Spirit. Similar commotions attended the preaching of David Houston, regarded today as the founder of the Reformed Presbyterian Church in Ireland. This 'indiscreet and turbulent licentiate' was admonished by the presbyteries of Antrim and Route in 1671 for ministering to large crowds of people at unusual hours and places in opposition to their settled ministers, and was finally deposed in 1687.[36]

Such loyalty to the Covenanting ideal was not sufficient to produce a large-scale defection from the mainstream Church. It took a series of theological controversies to bring into doubt the commitment of the Church of Scotland to orthodox standards. The first focused on the trial of John Simson, the Glasgow Professor of Divinity, between 1714 and 1717. Simson's quick avowal of the Westminster Confession managed to salvage his career but failed to calm the fears of his vigilant opponents. The second followed the republication of Edward Fisher's *The Marrow of Modern Divinity*, a dialogue which had first appeared in London in 1646. The doctrine of free grace expounded by its central character, Evangelista, stemmed from the English puritan tradition. Universal atonement was of course contrary to the Calvinist doctrine of election, and the book was consequently denounced by the General Assembly. However, a small group of ministers was attracted by Fisher's defence of piety against formal religious observance. The Assembly's severe treatment of the *Marrow* appeared in sharp contrast to its failure to discipline Simson and provoked a protest from the popular preacher Ebenezer Erskine.

---

[31] For examples see [F. J. Bigger], 'Alexander Peden, the "Prophet"', *UJA*, 2nd ser., 9 (1903), 116–27. For the capture of a Scottish rebel in Ireland after Bothwell Bridge, see R. M. Young (ed.), 'News from Ireland: Being the Examination and Confession of William Kelso, &c., 1679', *UJA*, 2nd ser., 2 (1896), 274–9.

[32] Samuel McSkimmin, *Annals of Ulster, or, Ireland Fifty Years Ago* (Belfast, 1849), 49–50.

[33] Reid, *Presbyterian Church in Ireland*, ii. 276–7.   [34] Cowan, *Scottish Covenanters*, 64.

[35] Michael Bruce, *The Rattling of Dry Bones: or, A Sermon Preached in the Night Time at Chapel-Yard in the Parish of Carluke. Clydesdale 1672* (n.p., [1672]). Like Peden, Bruce was credited with prophetic powers: see *DNB*.   [36] Reid, *Presbyterian Church in Ireland*, ii. 328–31.

The lines of division revealed by these issues were further deepened by the continuing controversy concerning the exercise of lay patronage in the Scottish Kirk. According to the 1690 settlement, ministers were to be chosen by the elders and heritors, subject to the approval of the congregation. By the Patronage Act of 1712, however, congregational control of the Church was overturned and the rights of local gentlemen to present their own nominees was restored. The General Assembly had apparently sacrificed one of the fundamental principles of the Presbyterian polity, thus failing to defend the Scottish Church against the encroachments of the new British State. When the regulations enforcing patronage were tightened up in 1732, Erskine launched an outspoken attack on the Assembly. The following year he and three other ministers withdrew and formed the 'Associate Presbytery'. And so the Secession was born.

The Seceders and Covenanters in Ireland

As we saw in the last chapter, fears of heresy at this time were not confined to Scotland. The allegations made against Simson, which the Seceders exploited in their attacks on the Church of Scotland, had also fuelled the fears of the pro-subscription party in Ulster. Although the Patronage Act, which had focused the resentments of the Seceders, had no exact equivalent in Ireland, the synodical majority rule of 1733 gave disproportionate weight to the views of the wealthier members of congregations.[37] The effect of this resolution was to exacerbate rather than ease the problem of disputed settlements, with the result that congregations, paralysed by disagreements over ministerial candidates, often lay vacant for several years. These tensions, combined with the reluctance of the Synod to erect new congregations and hence subdivide the already stretched *regium donum*, created ideal conditions for the Seceding apostles who began to visit Ireland shortly after the institution of the Associate Presbytery.

As early as 1736, 280 families from the Lisburn area sent a petition to Scotland requesting the services of a Secession minister. In this case dissatisfaction was directly linked to the progress of New Light sentiment in the Synod: the trouble had started when Gilbert Kennedy, suspected of heterodoxy, had been sent to Lisburn in 1732. Kennedy was forced to leave by popular opposition, but his replacement proved to be no more acceptable, and so the congregation renounced the jurisdiction of the Synod of Ulster and contacted the Associate Presbytery.[38] The commotion which followed at nearby Lylehill, however, illustrates the full range of motives which might lead to a congregational schism. The people of this village had previously attended worship in Templepatrick under the care of William Livingston, a leading subscriber of unquestionable orthodoxy. Templepatrick, however, was some distance away, and what seems to have offended the Lylehill people was the refusal of the Synod to sanction the erection of a separate congregation at a more convenient location. The quarrel was further complicated by a land dispute between Livingston and Samuel

---

[37] Reid, *Presbyterian Church in Ireland*, 237.   [38] Ibid. 243.

Henderson, leader of the breakaway group, reminding us of the importance of personal antagonisms.[39] The reasons for the Seceders' success thus ranged from fears of the New Light malaise, to the structural obstacles which prevented the Synod from expanding its base, to disagreements within congregations over such practical matters as the site of a meeting-house.

In 1745 the Revd Isaac Patton accepted a call from Lylehill and became the first Seceding minister in Ulster. Other emissaries from Scotland soon followed, itinerating through the countryside and attracting large crowds. By 1750, when the first Associate Presbytery in Ireland had been formed, congregations had been set up in Lylehill, Lisburn, Moira, Ray, Ballyroney, Drumachose, Ballybay, Bangor, Armagh, Aghadoey, Ballykelly, Balteagh, Dunboe, Kilraughts, Ballymoney, Derrykeichan, Boardmills, and Markethill. More followed at Aughnacloy, Clonnanees, Newbliss, Castleblayney, and Loughagery near Hillsborough. This expansion represented a considerable achievement, given the difficulties faced by the Seceding ministers who preached to the impoverished Ulster congregations. In the minutes of the various Seceding presbyteries and synods there are repeated cases of clergymen being forced to emigrate to America 'owing to necessitous circumstances'.[40]

The prominence of several villages from the Ulster borderlands suggests that the Seceders' rigid brand of Calvinism may have thrived on the frontier where the Catholic population seemed most threatening.[41] But the Secession thrived in parts of Antrim and Down too. The strength of the local native Irish is probably only one of several factors which determined the spread of the Secession. Another possibility is that the challenge to the Synod may have represented internal tensions within the Ulster Scots population. Writing in 1755, Thomas Clark of Cahans observed that some of the early adherents of the Secession were 'Scotchmen by birth, who had been long acquainted with members of the Associate Presbytery'.[42] Henry Montgomery, who had grown up in the 1790s, claimed that suspicion of the non-subscribers was particularly strong amongst recent immigrants from Scotland.[43] He describes the dissident minority of the Templepatrick congregation as 'chiefly Scotch Calvinists, or their descendants'.[44] Since the whole congregation was composed of Ulster Scots, it may be that Montgomery was making a distinction between long-settled families and those who had come over in more recent waves.

Numerous other factors helped to create a receptive audience for the new sect. The Seceders were able to cash in on the conservatism of Ulster Presbyterians, not just by their firm adherence to the orthodox standards of the Westminster Confession, but also by their fidelity to the old rituals and folk-culture of the plantation settlement. The clergy had an ambivalent relationship with popular tradition. On

---

[39] Ibid. 247–8.

[40] See e.g. the minutes of the Associate Presbytery of Moira and Antrim, 1774–86, PRONI, D. Stewart Papers, D1759/1D/22, p. 1.

[41] The Seceders were concentrated in south Armagh, Monaghan, and west Down: see Alan Gailey, 'The Scots Element in Northern Irish Popular Culture', *Ethnologia Europaea*, 8 (1975), 8.

[42] Thomas Clark, *New Light Set in a Clear Light* (Dublin, 1755), 90.

[43] Henry Montgomery, 'Outlines of the History of Presbyterianism in Ireland', *The Irish Unitarian and Bible Christian*, 2 (1847), 224.   [44] Ibid. 228.

the one hand, they struggled to reform such superstitious practices as the building of bonfires on Midsummer's Eve, the use of charms on 1 November, and the consulting of spaemen (fortune-tellers).[45] On the other hand, they offered rituals and magic of their own.[46] David Hempton and Myrtle Hill have recently observed that the 'zealous activities of the Presbyterian sects offered an important outlet for popular piety, which in less rigidly Calvinist circles was enthusiastically expressed by Moravians, Methodists, and other evangelicals'.[47] Those sections of the laity who lamented the coldness and formality of New Light sermons were not disappointed by the hell-fire performances of the Seceders. It was said of Isaac Patton that

His manner in the pulpit was ardent and excited—sometimes almost wild: and, as he preached extempore, he never hesitated in the middle of his sermon, to attack individuals, or even classes of individuals, who by any look or motion incurred his disapprobation.[48]

While polite Presbyterians looked with distaste upon the traditional festivity of communion services, the Seceders were more in tune with popular feeling:

At Mr Patton's summer sacrament, several thousands usually congregated: the Meeting-House was choked up: two ministers were preaching at opposite ends of the green: tents, for all kinds of refreshments, were erected on the sides of the neighbouring highway: and drunkenness and folly profaned the day of rest. Crowds of dissolute or thoughtless persons came from Belfast; and, over a wide circuit of country, 'Lyle Fair' was considered a favourite place of amusement.[49]

Summer communion services were huge occasions, usually held outdoors. Up to seven congregations might converge on the same day, and many who had no intention of communicating would come just to hear the sermons.[50] These sacramental gatherings were also regarded as ideal opportunities for acquiring a suitable husband or wife. The 'Blacksmith', a Scottish moderate who frowned upon such vulgar customs, described the whole affair as an 'odd mixture of religion, sleep, drinking, courtship, and a confusion of the sexes, ages, and characters'. While the parson preached from his 'tent' or platform, 'sweating, bawling, jumping, and beating the desk', crowds of men and women who had often travelled great distances would congregate around the barrels of ale which were carted into the field, or fall asleep on the grass.[51] His criticisms were echoed by the orthodox minister of Saintfield, County Down, who complained that the outdoor meetings of the Seceders were characterized by drunkenness and debauchery. Young men and women frolicked in the ditches while their parents were at worship, and outside the meeting-house were *'stalls of merchandise*, fraught with every rarity of the season which can delight the

---

[45] David Stewart, *The Seceders in Ireland with Annals of their Congregations* (Belfast, 1950), 423.

[46] L. E. Schmidt sheds light on these aspects of Presbyterian worship in *Holy Fairs: Scottish Communions and American Revivals in the Early Modern Period* (Princeton, 1989).

[47] Hempton and Hill, *Evangelical Protestantism*, 26.

[48] These performances were staged in barns, private houses, and in the open air: Montgomery, 'Outlines', 229–30. Montgomery had attended Patton's Sunday school as a boy.   [49] Ibid. 231.

[50] *A Letter from a Blacksmith to the Ministers and Elders of the Church of Scotland*, signed A. T. Blacksmith (London, 1759), 8.   [51] Ibid. 9–10.

lustful eye, or gratify the luxurian palate!'[52] In general, the Ulster sources back up the unflattering picture of Scottish sacramental gatherings presented by Burns in 'The Holy Fair':

> The lads an' lasses, blythely bent
> To mind baith *saul* an' *body*,
> Sit round the table, weel content,
> An' steer about the *Toddy*.
> On this ane's dress, an' that ane's leuk,
> They're makin observations;
> While some are cozie i' the neuk,
> An' forming *assignations*
> To meet some day.[53]

It must be remembered that the modern image of the dour, abstemious Ulsterman is a Victorian creation. It took many flashes of evangelical fervour, of which the 1859 revival was only the most sensational, and a generation of temperance crusaders to tame the more unruly elements of this rumbustious popular culture.

The Reformed Presbytery was no less eager than the Secession to extend its sphere of operations to the north of Ireland. In 1744, just one year after its formation, two 'mountain ministers', as they were nicknamed in Ireland, were dispatched to preach to the Irish societies who had maintained a correspondence with the Scots since the late seventeenth century.[54] In the 1750s John Cameron and John Cuthbertson were sent from Scotland on itinerant missions, and in 1757 William Martin, the first Irish Covenanting minister, was ordained in the open air on the road from Ballymoney to Rasharkin in County Antrim. Cuthbertson shortly after emigrated to Pennsylvania, where he was instrumental in winning over his sect to the revolutionary cause,[55] while his companion John Cameron joined the Synod of Ulster, a foretaste of the organizational instability which dogged the Reformed Presbyterian Church throughout the century. Over the next thirty-five years it seems that only eleven more ministers were ordained. Of these, Martin and three others also emigrated to America. As a result, the first Reformed Presbytery in Ireland collapsed and was not reconstituted until 1792, leaving the clergy under the direct supervision of the Scottish Church. By 1792 there were six ministers presiding over twelve congregations at Newtownards, Knockbracken, Rathfriland, Creevagh, Ballylane, Dervock, Kilraughts, Bready, Letterkenny, Ballygey, Kellswater, and Cullbackey.[56] Obviously the poor, scattered congregations of Ulster could not compete with the attractions promised by the growing Presbyterian population across the Atlantic, but the shadowy nature of the church structure gives a misleading impression of

---

[52] Thomas Ledlie Birch, *Physicians Languishing Under Disease: An Address to the Seceding, or Associate Synod of Ireland* (Belfast, 1796), 33–6.

[53] 'The Holy Fair', in *The Poems and Songs of Robert Burns*, ed. James Kinsley, 3 vols. (Oxford, 1968), i. 128–37. [54] Hutchison, *Reformed Presbyterian Church*, 190.

[55] W. L. Fisk, 'The Diary of John Cuthbertson, Missionary to the Covenanters in Colonial Pennsylvania', *Pennsylvania Magazine of History and Biography*, 73 (1949), 441–58.

[56] More details can be found in Adam Loughridge, *The Covenanters in Ireland* (Belfast, 1984), 28.

Covenanting support. In addition to his congregations each pastor itinerated over a wide circuit of 'preaching stations', supervising scattered 'meetings'. William Stavely, the best-known of these preachers, was based at Knockbracken outside Belfast, but he organized congregations in Down, Armagh, and Monaghan.[57] In the troubled years of the 1790s, when the militancy of the Reformed Presbyterians held particularly strong attractions, the Revd Henry Henry would ask, 'Why are the covenanting ministers so much followed by the multitude?'[58]

Relations between these two sects and the General Synod were inevitably turbulent. Some of the Synod's ministers had initially hoped that the new missionaries would join them in the fight against the New Light tendency. These sympathizers could not bring themselves to abandon the Synod, however, and when they too found their congregations under threat, all hopes of an alliance vanished.[59] Paradoxically, the fact that the vast majority of ministers who attacked the Secession and the Reformed Presbytery in print were Old Light merely shows how little separated these groups. After the initial expulsions of the 1720s and 1730s the New Lights, with their small but wealthy congregations, had little to fear, but the Old Lights and the Seceders were competing for the same market. The Synod's anxious warnings against Seceding intruders perhaps stemmed from an awareness of the totemic value which the Solemn League and Covenant still possessed among its own people.[60] Old Light ministers occupied an unenviable position. They often found themselves assailed with their own arguments as the Secession and Reformed Presbytery decried the contamination of the General Synod with Arminian and Socinian errors. Caught between two stools, they lost the battle for the leadership of orthodox Calvinism.

Both the new sects relentlessly harried the Synod for its betrayal of the Covenants, and, in particular, for its collaboration with the Irish government. Declaring that the Reformed Presbytery was the last remnant of the true Church in the British Isles, William James of Derry blasted the General Synod for refusing to assert the divine right of presbytery. The members of the Synod, he claimed, had succumbed to erastianism by accepting the *regium donum* and swearing the oaths of assurance, abjuration, and allegiance, thereby accepting a king devoid of all scriptural qualifications and implicating themselves in the preservation of episcopacy. And to top it all, they had taken these oaths by touching and kissing the Bible, 'which idolatrous custom is clearly refuted by many learned divines'.[61]

---

[57] Montgomery, 'Outlines', 266–7.

[58] [Henry, Henry], *An Address to the People of Connor, Containing a Clear and Full Vindication of the Synod of Ulster: From the Aspersions of the People Called Covenanters. Written in the Name of Sanders Donald: Late Sexton of Connor* (Belfast[?], 1794), 24.

[59] See John King's 'Reasons Against a Disruption in the Synod', in Thomas Witherow (ed.), *Historical and Literary Memorials of Presbyterianism in Ireland*, 2 vols. (Belfast, 1879–80), ii. 83.

[60] Pamphlets against the Secession were written by Charles Lynd of Coleraine, Samuel Delap of Letterkenny, John King of Dromara, Robert Peebles of Loughgall, and John Semple of Anahilt, all orthodox; by contrast the only New Light minister to take up the challenge was the old controversialist Alexander Colville. The Covenanters came under fire from John Holmes and Henry Henry. These pamphlets, some of which are now lost, are listed in Witherow (ed.), *Memorials*.

[61] William James, *Homesius Enervatus* (Londonderry, 1772), 13–14, 52–5, 60–1.

This last point was the subject of fierce contention. From the Restoration until the 1798 rebellion and beyond, the greatest test of Presbyterian attitudes to the state arose from the swearing of oaths, especially oaths of allegiance. The ministers of the Synod had long conformed to the official practice of kissing and touching the book as they testified, but the Seceders and Covenanters insisted upon swearing with an uplifted hand, according to scriptural teaching. The practical consequences of these qualms could be serious: Seceders and Covenanters were not only unable to use the courts for civil cases, but were also vulnerable to harassment. Perhaps the most famous case concerns the Scottish preacher Thomas Clark who was ordained at the new Seceding congregation of Cahans in County Monaghan in 1751. Before taking up his post Clark had distinguished himself by a scurrilous attack on the Synod of Ulster, and in 1752 he was reported for disaffection to the government by James Jackson, the New Light minister of nearby Ballybay. There was no evidence to support such a charge—indeed, Clark had fought against the Jacobite rebels in 1745. He had, however, objected to the phraseology of the abjuration oath, and rejected the practice of kissing the book as superstitious.[62] On this occasion Clark was fined 40 shillings; later in the same year he absconded to Scotland following another summons, and in January 1754 two elders of the Ballybay congregation finally succeeded in having him imprisoned for a short time.[63] As we shall see, legislation was later passed to take account of Seceding susceptibilities, but as late as 1812 Edward Wakefield noted 'a repugnance to judicial oaths' as one of the popular prejudices of the Presbyterian north.[64]

The rejection of the Hanoverian regime as anti-scriptural and uncovenanted was not just a rhetorical gesture. The minutes of the Reformed session of Antrim, which contain many examples of members being rebuked for swearing by touching and kissing the Gospels in order to administer wills or to vote at elections, attest to Covenanting alienation from the political culture of the Revolution settlement.[65] It is impossible to understand the dilemma faced by many Presbyterians during the war between Britain and revolutionary France unless we realize that these militant preachers still conceived of their allegiance to royal authority in theological terms. Nothing could be calculated to antagonize them more than the state of emergency announced in 1796. As martial law was imposed throughout Ulster, magistrates were instructed to administer an oath of allegiance to the populace, pledging loyalty to George III, the Hanoverian succession, and 'the Laws and Constitution of this kingdom'.[66]

The Irish Seceders were informed by their Scottish superiors that this formula implicitly sanctioned the ecclesiastical establishment and was therefore inconsistent

---

[62] Two pamphlets were written on the subject: Thomas Clark, *Remarks upon the Manner and Form of Swearing by Touching and Kissing the Gospels* (Glasgow, 1772), and William Stavely, *Truth Restored, or the New Mode of Swearing Religious Oaths by Touching and Kissing a Book Examined* (Newry, 1775). These are listed in Witherow (ed.), *Memorials*, ii. 85 and 329, but there are no surviving copies.

[63] Witherow (ed.), *Memorials*, ii. 88–90; Reid, *Presbyterian Church in Ireland*, iii. 314–15.

[64] Edward Wakefield, *An Account of Ireland, Statistical and Political*, 2 vols. (London, 1812), ii. 740.

[65] Minutes of the Reformed session of Antrim, PRONI, CR5/9A/1.

[66] There is a copy of the oath in E. R. McC. Dix, 'Ulster Bibliography: Coleraine', *Ulster Journal of Archaeology*, 2nd ser., 13 (1907), 22–3.

with their testimony.[67] One Burgher minister, the Revd John Lowry, accordingly forbade his Tyrone congregation to take the oath of allegiance, and refused the sacrament to one member who had taken the Yeomanry oath, thus arousing the suspicion of the local authorities.[68] Such incidents have been read by historians as evidence of United Irish commitment, but this is not necessarily the case.[69] In Ballymena, on the other hand, the Seceders requested that they be allowed to take the oath, but with uplifted hand, according to their own practice.[70] Elsewhere, too, harassed clergymen succumbed to loyalist pressure. Among others, the Revd James Biggar of Newtownards admitted that he had taken the oath, though he had sworn only to maintain the constitution in civil matters, specifically excluding all approbation of the ecclesiastical supremacy and hierarchy of the Church of England. Even such conditional allegiance was unacceptable, however: the Scottish Synod sympathized with Biggar's predicament but nevertheless censured his conduct.[71]

If this situation was bad for the Seceders, it was intolerable for the more intractable members of the Reformed Presbytery. Samuel Brown Wylie explained the stark choice which faced the members of his hardline sect: they could take the oath of allegiance, risk being shot or hanged by the army, or flee the country. 'Unwilling either to pollute their consciences or become the victims of ruthless cruelty, they chose the last: exile from their dearly beloved country.' And so Wylie left for Philadelphia in the autumn of 1797, accompanied by the Revd William Gibson from Ballymena and John Black, his fellow probationer.[72] In the spring of 1798 they met up with James McKinney, another exiled radical from Ulster, to form a presbytery in Philadelphia. Among the more unusual products of the revolutionary crisis in Ireland we must therefore include the Reformed Presbyterian Church of the United States.[73]

The political theology of the Seceders and the Covenanters

Although armed resistance was ruled out, the pursuit of the covenanted kingdom may also have taken more diverse forms. In 1752, just after the formation of the Associate Presbytery, the Irish ministers referred a series of questions to the Scottish authorities. Was it permissible for them to take the constable oath and church-warden oath? Was it proper to acknowledge the bishops' courts or take benefit of

[67] Stewart, *Seceders*, 102. The Scottish Seceders retained administrative control over their Ulster colony: the Irish Burghers formed their own synod in 1779, and the Antiburghers followed suit nine years later, but these were provincial organizations dependent on the general synods which met in Scotland.

[68] Thomas Forsyth to Dublin Castle, 2 Aug. 1797, NAI, Rebellion Papers, 620/32/50.

[69] It is interesting to note that several years earlier, at the time of the Dungannon reform convention, the same congregation had requested their local MP to present an address of loyalty to the lord lieutenant: W. C. Lindsey to James Stewart, 3 Jan. 1793, PRONI, Stewart of Killymoon Papers, D3167/2/87.   [70] Edward Hudson to Charlemont, 31 June 1797, *Charlemont MSS*, ii. 302.

[71] McKerrow, *Secession Church*, 387.

[72] Samuel Brown Wylie, *Memoir of Alexander McLeod, D.D.* (New York, 1855), 29–30.

[73] Ibid. 31. McKinney had helped to establish a Volunteer company in Dervock after the French Revolution, and published a sermon which was denounced as treasonable; the resulting hostility forced him to leave Ireland in 1793 (ibid. 21).

them for confirmation of testaments and other causes? Should they withhold tithes from an Anglican state? The Synod took the view that serving as constables or church-wardens and using the ecclesiastical courts implied approval of episcopacy, although they did agree to provide financial assistance for any Irish brethren who were imprisoned.[74] With more regard for practical considerations than theoretical consistency, they decided that the payment of tithes did not constitute a betrayal of the Covenant. Later in the same decade, however, Edward Willes, chief baron of the Irish exchequer, reported from the north-eastern circuit that the Seceders were proving troublesome on this head, and it may be no coincidence that the 1750s saw an outburst of Presbyterian agitation over tithes and small dues—the fees demanded for christenings, marriages, churchings, and funerals.[75]

There is also some evidence to suggest that Cameronian radicalism had penetrated the agrarian underworld of the Ulster countryside from an early date. The risings of the Oakboys and Steelboys were motivated by economic grievances—tithes (or rather small dues) and the county cess in the first case, rising rents in the second—which were felt by tenant-farmers of all persuasions. Nevertheless, both rebellions threw into relief the alliance of parson and squire which formed the basis of local government. When several Anglican clergymen took refuge from the Oakboys behind the walls of Derry, a letter was sent to the city authorities by 'the royal, sincere, loyal Hearts of Oak, the reformers of abuses in church and state', issuing this warning:

It is with astonishment we find your mayor has not obeyed our orders to him, which were to turn out of the once loyal city of Londonderry (which our forefathers so bravely defended against a most hellish, damned set of papists, with the poltroon James at their head) those high-flying clergy, I mean those who call themselves high churchmen. Indeed, sir, they are only occasional protestants, which we call hypocrites, who would overset the church of God, as by law established, and our most undefiled Church of Scotland. Mind, sir, the Solemn League and Covenant.[76]

Hardly surprising, then, that the rector of Killeeshil in County Tyrone described the local Dissenters as 'the spawn of Scottish covenanters, avowed enemies to all civil and religious establishments and the most virulent and furious persecutors of the established clergy during the late troubles'.[77]

Opposition to the Church of Ireland featured less prominently in the Hearts of Steel insurrection of 1772, sparked off by the renewal of leases on the Donegall and Upton estates in south Antrim. Nervous Anglicans nevertheless viewed the pattern

---

[74] McKerrow, *Secession Church*, 254–5.
[75] *The Letters of Lord Chief Baron Edward Willes to the Earl of Warwick 1757–62. An Account of Ireland in the Mid-Eighteenth Century* (Aberystwyth, 1990), 38; *A Letter to the People of Ireland, on the Subject of Tythes. By a Friend to the Constitution* (Dublin, 1758), 16–18; *A Second Letter to the People of Ireland, on the Subject of Tythes. With a Particular Address to the Dissenters. To which is Added, a State of the Case of the Inhabitants of the Province of Ulster, in Relation to the Demands of the Clergy. By a Friend to the Constitution* (Dublin, 1758), 5–6.
[76] Quoted in J. S. Donnelly, jun., 'Hearts of Oak, Hearts of Steel', *Studia Hibernica*, 21 (1981), 16–17.
[77] Ibid. 17 n. 39.

of agrarian agitation as evidence of some sort of Presbyterian rebellion.[78] At least one New Light Dissenter agreed with them:

These men were the descendants of ancestors, who, whatever others may term their enthusiasm, their wild, perhaps unscriptural definitions of the holy writs, their obstinacy and perseverance in opposition to hierarchical and political tyranny, were members of the Holy League and Covenant, commonly denominated Covenanters.[79]

As the Hanoverian regime proved its durability, however, these fundamentalists struggled to work out the implications of their seventeenth-century inheritance. A convoluted literature grew up on the subject, sufficiently arcane to deter even the most enthusiastic of students.[80] On public platforms, too, representatives of the two bodies assembled to debate the jurisdictional boundaries of *sacerdotium* and *magisterium*.[81] But the virulence of these disputes should not be allowed to conceal the fact that they shared a common heritage. Their testimonies identified the same inventory of defects in the Established Church, and were remarkably similar not only in content and style but even in arrangement. First and foremost, they confirmed their allegiance to the Presbyterian model of church government. Subscribing to the doctrine of the two kingdoms, they asserted that Jesus Christ alone was head of the Church and that the attempts of statesmen to regulate religious affairs were infringements of his kingly rights.[82] In the Scriptures, God had laid down a particular form of polity, by kirk sessions, presbyteries, synods, and assemblies, on which both were agreed. They were uncompromising also on the right of congregations to elect their own pastors.

Both Seceders and Covenanters, moreover, claimed direct descent from the seventeenth-century Kirk, looking back to the 'second reformation' of 1638–49 as the pinnacle of Scottish godliness. They recognized the perpetual obligation of the Covenants and made them terms of communion. The Revolution Church was condemned as erastian: William III, it was insisted, should have sworn the Covenants before his coronation and taken the opportunity to re-establish 'all the ordinances of God in purity, according to their scriptural institution'.[83] The existence of the 'blasphemous royal supremacy' prevented them from taking the oaths of allegiance

[78] Eliza O'Neill to Elizabeth Tobin, 7 Apr. 1772, in W. H. Crawford and B. Trainor (eds.), *Aspects of Irish Social History 1750–1800* (Belfast, 1969), 45.

[79] James Caldwell, 'Particulars of a North County Irish Family', PRONI, Caldwell Papers, T3541/5/3, p. 74.

[80] *Address by the Associate Presbytery, to Reasons of Dissent, Given . . . by the Reverend Mr Thomas Nairn . . . Together with a Declaration and Defence of the Associate Presbytery's Principles Anent the Present Civil Government* (Edinburgh, 1744); [William Fletcher], *The Scripture-Loyalist: Containing a Vindication of Obedience to the Present British Government in Things Lawful* (Glasgow, 1784); id., *The Scripture-Loyalist Defended, from Unfair and False Reasoning* (Falkirk, 1795); William Steven, *Answers to Twelve Queries, Proposed to the Serious Consideration of the Reformed Presbytery, and their Followers* (n.p., 1794); id., *Letter Second to the Reverend William Fletcher* (Glasgow, 1798); John Reid, *Truth no Enemy to Peace. Animadversions on the Rev. Mr Fletcher's Defence of his Scripture-Loyalist* (Falkirk, 1799).

[81] Reid, *Presbyterian Church in Ireland*, iii. 364.

[82] The Associate Presbytery, *Act, Declaration and Testimony* (Edinburgh, 1737); the Reformed Presbytery, *Act, Declaration and Testimony*, 3rd edn. (Edinburgh, 1777).

[83] Reformed Presbytery, *Act, Declaration and Testimony*, 57.

and abjuration.[84] Consequently, they thought it necessary to bear testimony against the 1689 settlement, the Hanoverian succession, and the Patronage Act. Nor did the Irish escape their censure: the Covenanters described the Church of Ireland as 'antiscriptural, anticovenanted, and merely a human and political settlement' and branded the Synod of Ulster 'a synagogue of *Libertines*, a club of *Socinians, Arians, Pelagians*, &c. banded together against Christ'.[85]

It should come as no surprise to learn that these hardliners were also conspicuous for their anti-Catholicism, and they loudly denounced the relaxation of penal laws in England and Ireland in 1778.[86] The Seceder minister of Monaghan, John Rogers, continued to preach against popery at the very height of Volunteer liberality, and was one of two delegates at the Dungannon Convention of 1782 who dissented from the Volunteer overture to the Catholics.[87] The Pope, he insisted, was in the most literal sense the Antichrist, 'the Man of sin and son of perdition; who opposeth and exalteth himself above all that is called God, or that is worshipped; so that he, as God, sitteth in the temple of God, shewing himself that he is God'.[88] After his flight to America the Reformed Presbyterian Samuel Brown Wylie argued that Covenanting immigrants could not become citizens of the new republic because the constitutions of many states tolerated Roman Catholicism.[89]

Where the two bodies parted ways was on the question of political obedience to an uncovenanted state. As in religion, so in politics they had an abundant literature at their disposal. They were able to draw upon a canon which had begun with the Covenants themselves and Samuel Rutherford's *Lex Rex* (1644) to support notions of a direct relationship between God and his people, of civil society as a compact made by ruler and ruled for the common good, and of the people's right to rebel against tyrannical kings. These writings contained a peculiarly Calvinist doctrine of popular sovereignty in which natural law was subordinated to scriptural teaching. As Rutherford had put it, power was derived '*mediately* from God, proceeding from *God* by the consent of the Communitie, which resigneth their power to one or more Rulers'.[90] After the Restoration more stress would be laid on the right of resistance in writings like James Stewart's and James Stirling's *Naphtali, or the Wrestlings of the Church of Scotland for the Kingdom of Christ* (1667), Stewart's *Jus Populi Vindicatum* (1669), written to defend the Pentland rebels, and above all Alexander

---

[84] Ibid. 95.

[85] Ibid. 109, 110. Similar passages can be found in the *Act, Declaration and Testimony* of the Associate Presbytery.

[86] Associate Synod, *A Testimony by the Associate Synod, against the Legal Encouragement Lately Given to Popery* (Edinburgh, 1778); id., *A Warning against Popery. Drawn up, and Published, by Order of the Associate Synod* (Edinburgh, 1779); Reformed Presbytery, *Testimony and Warning Against the Blasphemies and Idolatry of Popery; the Evil and Danger of Every Encouragement Given to It* (Edinburgh, 1779).

[87] John Rogers, *A Sermon Preached at Lisnavein, Otherwise Ballybay New Erection* (Edinburgh, 1780), 19, 24 n. [88] Ibid. 19.

[89] Samuel Brown Wylie, *The Two Sons of Oil; or the Faithful Witness for Magistracy and Ministry upon a Scriptural Basis. Also, a Sermon on Covenanting* (Greensburg, Pa., 1803), 40–5. This pamphlet was also published in Newry in 1806, but I have been unable to trace a copy.

[90] Quoted in I. M. Smart, 'The Political Ideas of the Scottish Covenanters 1638–88', *History of Political Thought*, 1 (1980), 176.

Shields's *A Hind Let Loose*. These tracts furnished a much more popular interpretation of resistance theory than contemporary whig arguments. They also reinforced the view that the Kirk was an instrument of God's providence in the construction of the New Jerusalem.

While the Covenanters agreed with the Seceders that the people had a right to choose the civil magistrate, they believed that the exercise of popular sovereignty was restricted by divine law. Civil government was to be modelled upon a biblical constitution, and the people were to have regard to scriptural qualifications in choosing governors.[91] For the Seceders, on the other hand, these qualifications were 'essential not to the being and validity of the magisterial office, but to its well-being and usefulness'.[92] They pointed out that the early Christians who lived under the pagan emperors of Rome had obeyed 'far worse princes than any of the Hanoverian line'.[93] Anxious to play down the political implications of the Covenant, they tried to side-step the issue by insisting that the civil and ecclesiastical constitutions should be treated separately. But given the bizarre character of the British monarchy (increasingly bizarre after 1707) in which the king was bound to uphold episcopacy in England and presbytery in Scotland, this distinction was far from clear-cut. As long as political obligation was bound up with religious belief and dynastic loyalty such a position was ultimately untenable. When the state signalled the beginning of its withdrawal from religious affairs by repealing the Test and Corporation Acts and emancipating the Catholics, the Seceders would find their natural home among the voluntary churches of the nineteenth century. In the meantime, the ambiguity of their political stance was exposed by the ruthless controversialists of the Reformed Presbytery.

Right from the beginning, then, the Secession found itself shying away from the theocratic language of the seventeenth-century Kirk. When the Scottish Associate Presbytery drew up an overture for the renovation of the Covenants in 1742, it condemned

the *dangerous Extreme* that some have gone into, of impugning the present Civil Authority over these Nations, and Subjection thereunto in lawful Commands, on account of the Want of these Qualifications Magistrates ought to have by the Word of God and our Covenants; even although they allow us in the free Exercise of our Religion, and are not manifestly unhinging the Liberties of the kingdom.[94]

This was too much for one Thomas Nairn, who promptly withdrew from the Associate Presbytery to join McMillan's Covenanters. Nairn objected that the obligation to bring the three kingdoms into line with the Presbyterian system was clearly inconsistent with loyalty to George II, who had sworn in his coronation oath to preserve prelacy in England. The Presbytery countered that it was possible to acknowledge the civil authority in '*lawful commands*' while still repudiating the principles of the

---

[91] Reformed Presbytery, *Act, Declaration and Testimony*, 113–16.
[92] Hutchison, *Reformed Presbyterian Church*, 207–8.
[93] For an example of these arguments, see [William Fletcher], *Scripture-Loyalist*. The quotation is taken from p. 27.　　　[94] *Address by the Associate Presbytery, to . . . Thomas Nairn*, p. v.

English Church.[95] It sought to adapt the Covenants to the contemporary situation, since 'several *Expressions* in our Covenants might be mentioned, which can no way *hit* our present *Condition*, and an Application of which unto the same would be very *absurd*'.[96] The Seceders then fell back on the familiar passages of scripture which emphasized the necessity of obedience, above all, 'Render therefore unto Caesar the Things which be Caesar's, and unto God the Things which be God's' (Luke 20: 25), and, 'Let every soul be Subject unto the higher Powers' (Romans 13: 1).[97]

The tensions between the two-kingdoms ecclesiology and the realities of an erastian monarchy, committed to upholding a moderate Anglicanism in two of its kingdoms and a watered-down Presbyterianism in the third, were finally beginning to tell. Rejoicing in their outlaw position as the remnant of the true Church, the Reformed Presbyterians dreamed of a militant Calvinist state in which both civil and ecclesiastical authorities would be mobilized in the suppression of heresy and idolatry. For the Seceders, on the other hand, the price of religious intransigence was gradual withdrawal from the terrestrial realm of politics. Forsaking the revolutionary programme of the Covenant they began to divert their energies towards the preaching of vital religion and the salvation of the individual. This divergence among the heirs of the second reformation can be seen more clearly if we turn to examine the relationship between doctrinal disputes and radical ideology in greater detail.

[95] Ibid. 6–9.　　[96] Ibid. 29.　　[97] Ibid. 56, 62, 66.

4
RELIGION AND RADICAL IDEOLOGY

Two themes have dominated the historiography of Ulster Presbyterianism in the eighteenth century: the intermittent pamphlet warfare generated by doctrinal differences, and the involvement of many Presbyterians in the United Irish conspiracy of the 1790s. Regrettably, the historiographies of Church and State have usually taken separate routes, the one falling to a succession of denominational scholars at the Union Theological College in Belfast, the other to political and social historians, often trained across the road at Queen's University. While the former have usually pursued church history in a rather narrow sense, the latter have seldom shown any taste for the arcana of doctrinal controversy. A central object of this book is to bring these two lines of enquiry together.

The following chapter contains the first thoroughgoing analysis of the Presbyterian contribution to United Irish political thought, in which I shall attempt to build on the themes discussed so far—the theological and ecclesiastical identities of New Light and Old—to construct a more nuanced account of radical ideology. In the first section I outline the various modes of argument which characterized radical writing in the period. In the second I explore how the politics of the Presbyterian pulpit were shaped by the 'rational' religion of the non-subscribers, and inscribed with their distinctive theological priorities. One of these—the extension of religious toleration—explains why New Light ministers were the first to change their opinions on the justice of the penal code. Finally, the Covenanter and Seceder subcultures are examined, and the curious relationship between their seventeenth-century fundamentalism and the United Irish agenda is assessed. My major concern throughout is to demonstrate the influence of theology, ecclesiology, and eschatology on the intellectual climate within which Irish republicanism was able to flourish.

Opposition ideology under the Hanoverians

What modes of argument were open to critics of the Hanoverian political order? Perhaps the most pervasive was the appeal to an ancient constitution. It was a commonplace of whiggish thought that Englishmen possessed certain rights and privileges derived from the Anglo-Saxon past and confirmed by Magna Carta and the Glorious Revolution. The principles of the British constitution were traced back to the Gothic model of limited monarchy or mixed government in which sovereignty was supposedly shared between king, lords, and commons. The demand for parliamentary reform was commonly justified on the grounds that the constitution had shifted from its ancient basis (as the Crown had infringed upon the authority

of Parliament) and must be restored to its original purity. In Ireland this appeal
to antiquity inevitably acquired a 'national' dimension, as patriotic writers from
Molyneux and Swift to Grattan and Flood defended the constitutional rights of
the Dublin Parliament against imperial interference, drawing upon constitutional
history and common law.[1] Presbyterians participated in the development of this
'colonial nationalism', especially in the second half of the century. During the money
bill crisis of 1753, Patriot Clubs had sprung up in the north in support of the
parliamentary opposition, while in the metropolis the leading Dissenting layman
William Bruce published a string of pamphlets defending the privileges of the Dublin
legislature.[2] In the Volunteer era the most forceful blow struck in the propaganda
war for legislative independence was *The Letters of Owen Roe O'Nial*, written by
the Newry non-subscriber Joseph Pollock. First published in 1779 and later printed
together with Molyneux's *Case*, this tract was revered by the northern Presbyterians 'even down to the lowest of their orders'.[3]

To be sure, there was always some ambiguity about the Presbyterian position
within a patriot tradition whose origins lay in specifically Anglican and aristocratic
grievances and whose spokesmen invested sovereignty in Parliament rather than in
the people. Although they agreed that Ireland possessed its own ancient constitution, Dissenters were practically excluded from both the House of Commons and
the legal profession; for this reason, perhaps, they were more receptive to alternative ways of thinking about politics. Pollock rested his plea for constitutional autonomy on natural rights rather than custom, while his friend and fellow pamphleteer
William Drennan denounced the 'superstitious reliance on the continued efficacy
of antient tenure and prescriptive right, that not a little endangers present possession'. Freedom was derived not from 'common law, or statute law, or musty char-
ters', Drennan continued, but from 'the right hands of the people'.[4] Nevertheless,
the propaganda of the Belfast United Irishmen would pay homage not only to Swift
and Molyneux, but also to Anglo-Saxon democracy, Magna Carta, and 1688.[5]

Perhaps the most striking characteristic of recent work by intellectual historians
in this field has been the devaluation of natural rights theories. In particular, the
impact of John Locke's *Two Treatises of Government* (1690), long considered to be
the handbook of British whiggery, has been increasingly questioned. The tendency
over the last twenty-five years has been to stress the conservative nature of political culture after the Glorious Revolution: whig appeals to reason and natural law,
we are assured, were heavily outweighed by references to history and scripture.

[1] J. T. Leersen, 'Anglo-Irish Patriotism and its European Context: Notes Towards a Reassessment',
Eighteenth-Century Ireland, 3 (1988), 7–24, provides a useful introduction.

[2] See e.g. [William Bruce (the bookseller)], *Some Facts and Observations Relative to the Fate of the
Late Linen Bill* (Dublin, 1753); id., *Remarks on a Pamphlet Entitled Considerations on the Late Bill for
Paying the National Debt, etc.*, 4 pts. (Dublin, 1754).

[3] *Fragment of a Letter to a Friend, Relative to the Repeal of the Test* (Dublin, 1780), 20. Pollock's pamphlet was reprinted in John Lawless (ed.), *The Belfast Politics, Enlarged* (Belfast, 1818), 111–54.

[4] [William Drennan], *An Address to the Volunteers of Ireland, by the Author of a Letter to Edmund Burke,
Esq. Containing Reflections on Patriotism, Party Spirit, and the Union of Free Nations* (Dublin, 1781), 4.

[5] *NS*, 7 July 1792 ('Alfred'), 30 June 1792 ('Parliamentary Reform'), 5 Dec. 1792 (editorial).

Writers who alluded to a social contract usually had in mind the relationship between king and Parliament, not government and governed; they avoided the more thorough-going contractarianism of Locke, which raised troubling questions concerning the location and limitations of sovereignty, preferring to take shelter within the familiar edifice of the ancient constitution.[6] Whereas *An Essay Concerning Human Understanding* (1690) brought Locke an international reputation, his *Two Treatises* attracted little attention at first, and was later read as a whig defence of the revolution which rather complacently confirmed the superiority of the English way of conducting politics.[7]

Locke has also been the main target of the school of revisionists led by J. G. A. Pocock, who have argued that the central debate in eighteenth-century political thought revolved around the classical republican themes of virtue and corruption. At first it was suggested that this civic tradition could be used to explain not only the ideological opposition to the Whig oligarchy of Robert Walpole, but also the discontents voiced in the reign of George III by Wilkites, Associators, and even the artisanal societies of the 1790s. Such a wide-ranging application of the civic human-ist paradigm obscures important distinctions between these areas and has attracted criticism from Isaac Kramnick, Joyce Appleby, and others.[8] Kramnick has drawn attention to the appearance of a radical reading of Locke at the time of the American Revolution, and in his more recent pronouncements Pocock himself has come a long way towards accepting the plurality of political languages which existed in the eight-eenth century.[9] Although further research in this area is needed, it is clear that the rediscovery of Locke in the 1760s and 1770s is related to the American constitutional debate on taxation and representation: it is no accident that *Reflections on Representa-tion in Parliament* (London, 1766), the first major demand for parliamentary reform, cites Locke as well as James Otis's defence of colonial rights. It seems also that Locke's appeal was especially strong among Rational Dissenters. James Burgh, author of the reformist compendium *Political Disquisitions* (1774), found no difficulty in com-bining the opposition rhetoric of the commonwealthsmen with a new appreciation of the *Two Treatises*, while Joseph Priestley's *An Essay on the First Principles of Civil Government* (1771) and Richard Price's *Observations on the Nature of Civil Liberty* (1776) presented an extreme version of Locke's resistance theory in which the

---

[6] H. T. Dickinson, 'The Eighteenth-Century Debate on the Glorious Revolution', *History*, 61 (1976), 28–45; J. P. Kenyon, *Revolution Principles: The Politics of Party 1689–1720* (Cambridge, 1977); J. C. D. Clark, *English Society 1688–1832: Ideology, Social Structure and Political Practice During the Ancien Regime* (Cambridge, 1985), 42–64.

[7] John Dunn, 'The Politics of Locke in England and America in the Eighteenth Century', in J. W. Yolton (ed.), *John Locke: Problems and Perspectives* (Cambridge, 1969), 45–80.

[8] Isaac Kramnick, 'Republican Revisionism Revisited', *American Historical Review*, 87 (1982), 629–64; Joyce Appleby, 'Republicanism and Ideology', *American Quarterly*, 37 (1985), 461–73.

[9] See e.g. J. G. A. Pocock, 'Cambridge Paradigms and Scotch Philosophers', in I. Hont and M. Ignatieff, *Wealth and Virtue* (Cambridge, 1983), 235–52; 'Between Gog and Magog: The Republican Thesis and the Ideologia Americana', *Journal of the History of Ideas*, 48 (1987), 325–46. Also important in this respect is James Tully, 'Placing the "Two Treatises"', in Nicholas Phillipson and Quentin Skinner (eds.), *Political Discourse in Early Modern Britain* (Cambridge, 1993), 253–80, which stresses the similarities between Locke and the commonwealth tradition.

people retained the right to reshape the institutions of government whenever they saw fit.[10]

The debate over Locke's role in eighteenth-century political thought is thus far from over. Little research has been done on the Irish dimension of the subject, but what we know so far tends to support the findings of English and American historians.[11] Locke made his entry into the discourse of Irish patriotism through its key text, *The Case of Ireland's Being Bound by Acts of Parliament in England, Stated* (1698), written by his friend and correspondent William Molyneux. But mainstream patriotism followed a prescriptive line of argument; natural rights occupied a subordinate position. Although Molyneux pleaded 'the Cause of the whole Race of Adam', and praised liberty as 'the Inherent Right of *Mankind*', the bulk of his book employed historical and legal precedents to contest the claims of the Westminster Parliament to legislate for the kingdom of Ireland.[12] Later generations of Irish Protestants fell back on the same composite-monarchy model in which Ireland appeared not as a subordinate colony, but as a separate kingdom united to Britain through a common sovereign. Little notice seems to have been taken of Molyneux's use of natural rights until his *Case of Ireland* was reread in the light of hostilities with the American colonies; and even then Irish patriotism, in its Grattanite, aristocratic manifestation, remained fixated on the twists and turns of medieval statute law.[13] Locke too was a beneficiary of the American Revolution, which prompted the first Irish edition of the *Two Treatises*. Over the next decade his name appears frequently in the columns of the *Belfast News-Letter* and the *Belfast Mercury* as a convenient shorthand for the fully-fledged radical case in favour of popular sovereignty, accountable government, and the right of subjects to resist oppression.[14]

As the reputation of Locke has come under fire, the historical standing of the 'real' or 'true' whigs, first identified in Caroline Robbins's *The Eighteenth-Century Commonwealthman* (1959), has soared. Historians have turned away from the state of nature, the social contract, and the right of resistance to focus on ideas of citizenship and public virtue. There can be no doubt that the appearance of a nascent reform movement in the 1760s and 1770s owed much to the canon of the commonwealthsmen,

---

[10] Kramnick, 'Republican Revisionism', 637–46.

[11] An exception is Patrick Kelly's 'Perceptions of Locke in Eighteenth-Century Ireland', *PRIA*, 89C, no. 2 (1989), 17–35. For the use of Locke in the context of the Glorious Revolution debate see Robert Eccleshall, 'Anglican Political Thought after the Revolution of 1688', in D. G. Boyce, Robert Eccleshall, and Vincent Geoghegan (eds.), *Political Thought in Ireland since the Seventeenth Century* (London, 1993), 36–72.

[12] William Molyneux, *The Case of Ireland's Being Bound by Acts of Parliament in England, Stated* (Dublin, 1698), 3.

[13] Patrick Kelly, 'William Molyneux and the Spirit of Liberty in Eighteenth-Century Ireland', *Eighteenth-Century Ireland*, 3 (1988), 133–48. See also Isolde Victory, 'The Making of the 1720 Declaratory Act', in Gerard O'Brien (ed.), *Parliament, Politics and People: Essays in Eighteenth-Century Irish History* (Dublin, 1989), 9–29; Jacqueline Hill, 'Ireland without Union: Molyneux and his Legacy', in John Robertson (ed.), *A Union for Empire: Political Thought and the British Union of 1707* (Cambridge, 1995), 271–96. The poverty of Irish constitutional theory in contrast to the American revolutionaries is explored in R. J. Barrett, 'A Comparative Study of Imperial Constitutional Theory in Ireland and America in the Age of the American Revolution', Ph.D. thesis (Trinity College Dublin, 1958).

[14] Kelly, 'Perceptions of Locke', 27–33.

which was given a new lease of life in Richard Baron's *The Pillars of Priestcraft and Orthodoxy Shaken* (1752). He was aided by the tireless propagandist Thomas Hollis, an admirer of Molesworth, who reprinted the works of Milton, Sidney, and Ludlow.[15] In his textbook of early radicalism, *Political Disquisitions* (1774–5), James Burgh plundered Bolingbroke, Cato's *Letters*, Blackstone, Harrington, Ludlow, Milton, Machiavelli, Sallust, and Tacitus to denounce the corruption of the British polity at the time of the American conflict.[16] Historians in the United States have been greatly influenced by Bernard Bailyn's *The Ideological Origins of the American Revolution* (1967), which describes how the revolutionary ideology of 1776 was adopted from the opposition to Walpole's administration in the 1730s. Bailyn thus focuses on many of the same figures as Pocock: Milton, Harrington, Neville, and Sidney, and from the next century Bolingbroke, Hoadly, Trenchard, and Gordon.

Irish historiography could not long remain immune to the Atlantic republican tradition. Marianne Elliott revealed the importance of the commonwealthsman heritage in her now classic study *Partners in Revolution* (1982). The United Irishmen, she demonstrates, set out as real whigs, 'accepting monarchy but seeking to curb the powers of central government, to preserve fundamental liberties and to secure religious toleration'. They drew inspiration from classical republican writers and from Locke, but found themselves forced into a revolutionary stance by an unresponsive parliament. This verdict is confirmed in her biography of Wolfe Tone which depicts a reluctant revolutionary, raised within the fold of 'colonial nationalism' but thrown into the arms of the French by the repressive policies of the Castle administration.[17] Most recent commentators on United Irish ideology have taken on board the importance of the commonwealth paradigm, although it is fair to say that their use of Pocock has been uncritical and imprecise.[18]

Like their comrades in Britain, Ulster reformers advanced republican arguments concerning the corruption of the House of Commons, the increasing encroachments of the executive, and the civic virtue which resulted from uniting the citizen and the soldier. But an undue concentration on one real whig paradigm reinforces the conservative picture of eighteenth-century political discourse in a misleading way. By the 1760s, classical republicanism was beginning to interact with other elements to produce a new radicalism which should be differentiated from the opposition politics of Walpole's reign.[19] The rallying cries of the Country party can still be heard, but to concentrate on the longevity of this language is to obscure the new tone which characterized the case for reform. The emergence of a new audience

    [15] [Francis Blackburne], *Memoirs of Thomas Hollis Esq.* (London, 1780).

    [16] James Burgh, *Political Disquisitions: or, An Enquiry into Public Errors, Defects and Abuses*, 3 vols. (London, 1774–5).

    [17] Marianne Elliott, *Partners in Revolution: The United Irishmen and France* (New Haven, 1982), xiii, 20–33; ead., *Wolfe Tone: Prophet of Irish Independence* (New Haven, 1989).

    [18] See e.g. the essays in David Dickson, Dáire Keogh, and Kevin Whelan (eds.), The *United Irishmen: Republicanism, Radicalism and Rebellion* (Dublin, 1993). Of particular interest is Tom Bartlett's perceptive discussion of Tone.

    [19] A good general account can be found in H. T. Dickinson, *Liberty and Property: Political Ideology in Eighteenth-Century Britain* (London, 1977), ch. 6.

for radical propaganda, heralded by the publicity campaigns of Wilkes and the importation of American arguments on the relationship between taxation and representation, brought a new focus on the contractarian nature of civil government and the principle of popular sovereignty.[20]

How were these political vocabularies acquired and passed on? One obvious source is the popular reformist texts produced by writers like James Burgh and recycled by hack pamphleteers. Another answer can be found in the intellectual commerce between the meeting-houses of Ulster and the Scottish universities, where the vast majority of Irish Presbyterian clergymen received their education. At Glasgow, and to a lesser extent at Edinburgh, candidates for the ministry encountered a remarkable succession of innovative thinkers who had elevated the study of laws, institutions, and political practices into a new science of government.[21] The originator of this philosophical enterprise, and its most radical exponent, was the charismatic Francis Hutcheson, himself a native of Armagh, who occupied the Glasgow chair of moral philosophy from 1730 to 1746. By the last quarter of the century Hutcheson's real whiggism had given way to the 'sceptical' or 'scientific' whiggism of his two most brilliant followers, Adam Smith and David Hume, who had deconstructed the myth of the ancient constitution in the interests of a more sociological approach to history that located the development of political institutions in their social and economic contexts.[22] The enlightenment of Hume and Smith, which rejected contract theories of government and played down the right of resistance, tended towards a commercial and unionist defence of the Whig establishment.[23] Against their detached, analytical style, however, we must set the warm, didactic enlightenment of Hutcheson and his followers, who stripped classical republicanism of its old Deist overtones and integrated writers such as Harrington into whig-Presbyterian culture. In both Edinburgh and Glasgow the pursuit of virtue directed philosophical discussion, not just in the classroom, but in the pulpits of the Scottish Kirk and in the network of student clubs and debating societies who dedicated themselves to the refinement of taste, the improvement of manners, and the advancement of learning.[24]

The fourth important strand in opposition ideology was the new, democratic radicalism of the 1790s, sometimes referred to as Jacobinism. The term can be justified by contemporary usage, but is slightly misleading, for although the inspiration came

---

[20] John Brewer, *Party Ideology and Popular Politics at the Accession of George III* (Cambridge, 1976), esp. ch. 10.

[21] See, most recently, Andrew Hook and R. B. Sher (eds.), *The Glasgow Enlightenment* (East Lothian, 1995).

[22] Duncan Forbes, *Hume's Philosophical Politics* (Cambridge, 1975); id., 'Sceptical Whiggism, Commerce and Liberty', in A. S. Skinner and T. Wilson (eds.), *Essays on Adam Smith* (Oxford, 1975), 179–201; Donald Winch, *Adam Smith's Politics: An Essay in Historiographic Revision* (Cambridge, 1978), esp. 46–69.

[23] For the conservative tendencies in Scottish Presbyterianism see R. B. Sher, '1688 and 1788: William Robertson on Revolution in Britain and France', in Paul Dukes and John Dunkley (eds.), *Culture and Revolution* (London, 1990), 98–109; Emma Vincent, 'The Responses of Scottish Churchmen to the French Revolution, 1789–1802', *Scottish Historical Review*, 73 (1994), 191–215.

[24] Glasgow had several such societies, including the Parliament of Oceana, whose name gestured towards the seminal work of the classical republican guru James Harrington. See David Murray, *Memories of the Old College of Glasgow* (Glasgow, 1927), 517–18.

from France, the theory came from Thomas Paine, whose republican ideas owed more to Anglo–American traditions than to the French example. It is impossible here to examine Paine's *Rights of Man*[25] in any detail, but two points should be stressed. The first is that, although he was indebted to older libertarian ideas, Paine demonstrated an extraordinary contempt for British political institutions and poured scorn on the conventional pieties of mainstream whiggism. *Rights of Man* was an assault on the sanctity of tradition, and a robust defence of the right of each generation to wipe the slate clean and devise its own constitutional arrangements. Paine repudiated the mixed monarchy revered by whigs, drawing a simple contrast between the representative democracies in America and France, founded upon the principle of popular sovereignty, and the hereditary regimes of the old world, whose authority rested upon conquest and usurpation.

The second point concerns the social constituency of Paine's work. The appeal of *Rights of Man* was partly due to Paine's creation of a democratic political language which exploded the mysteries of government and invited the ordinary working man to think about politics for himself. It also added to anglophone political discourse a sharper sense of class conflict. The crucial factor here was not so much Paine's novel ideas on state welfare as his ability to channel plebeian grievances against the hereditary principle in society, and, in particular, his assault on tithes and taxes. This style of propaganda had its own Ulster practitioners, most notably the Revd James Porter, author of the immensely popular satire 'Billy Bluff and Squire Fire-brand'. Henry Montgomery later recalled that this pamphlet, serialized in the *Northern Star* in 1796 and reprinted in various forms, was almost committed to memory by the entire peasantry of his district.[26] 'Billy Bluff' depicted the northern gentry as corrupt, ignorant, and oppressive. Porter's mockery of the new lords and earls who were springing up 'like mushrooms on a dunghill'[27] may well have cost him his life—local folklore, at any rate, has always attributed Porter's execution in 1798 to the malice of Lord Londonderry, on whom the central villain Lord Mountmumble was said to be based.

Scholars searching for one dominant political language in the radical literature of the late eighteenth century will find instead a confusion of tongues. Reformers recruited a bewildering array of theorists and politicians in their campaigns against parliamentary corruption. 'Lucas', the writer of several letters to the *Belfast News-Letter* in 1783, appealed first to 'JOHN LOCKE; the friend of our Irish Molyneux', and then went on to cite Machiavelli, Bolingbroke, Rapin, Swift, Montesquieu, Blackstone, Price and Priestley, Chatham, Burgh, and the Westminster Committee.[28] These names would recur in the columns of the *Northern Star*, together with Paine,

---

[25] Part 1 of *Rights of Man* appeared early in 1791 and part 2 a year later. For a recent analysis of Paine's work see Gregory Claeys, *Thomas Paine: Social and Political Thought* (London, 1989).

[26] Henry Montgomery, 'Outlines of the History of Presbyterianism in Ireland', *Irish Unitarian and Bible Christian*, 2 (1847), 331.

[27] 'Billy Bluff', *NS*, 2 Sept. 1796. There are vague references to class struggle in the memoirs of the Antrim weaver James Hope, but these were written for R. R. Madden in 1843, and may have more to do with British Chartism than Irish Jacobinism: Madden, *The United Irishmen, their Lives and Times*, 3 ser., 7 vols. (London, 1842–6), i. 218–95.   [28] *BNL*, 29 Aug. 1783.

Godwin, Harrington, and Beccaria.[29] The same breadth of reference can be found in the correspondence of William Drennan, one of the most interesting and entertaining collections of eighteenth-century papers. In the last quarter of the eighteenth century Dr Drennan and his sister Martha McTier discussed the merits of classical writers (Tacitus, Plutarch, Cicero), Scottish moralists and political economists (Hume, Smith), French *philosophes* (Montesquieu, Voltaire, Rousseau, Volney), and English Dissenters (Priestley, Price) in addition to the revolutionary tracts of Paine, Godwin, and Wollstonecraft.[30] But if Ulster reformers spoke the common political languages of the British Atlantic world they did so with their own distinctive inflection. Natural jurisprudence and classical republicanism (in their British manifestations) had evolved within a Protestant, often Dissenting, framework, and religious belief continued to shape the ways in which these paradigms were transmitted, digested, and applied. After all, the terms which dominated radical discourse—liberty, tyranny, virtue, and corruption—all carried religious resonances. Any attempt to recover the full range of idioms that characterized Presbyterian political thought, its ideological sources and structures, must therefore enter the vibrant and fissile world of polemical theology.

The religious origins of Presbyterian radicalism

My kingdom is not of this world.

(John 18: 36)

All commentators on eighteenth-century Irish politics assumed that the religious and political principles of Ulster Presbyterians were intimately connected. To their enemies, the Dissenters of Belfast were 'a turbulent, disorderly, set of people whom no king can govern or no God please', and their hostility to government flowed naturally from their refusal to submit to the ecclesiastical authority of the Church.[31] The old accusation that the central tenets of Presbyterianism were politically suspect, socially subversive, and theologically intolerant retained a surprising currency in Ascendancy circles; Presbyterian was virtually synonymous with republican and leveller in the Anglican mind. Among their admirers, meanwhile, Wolfe Tone believed that the republicanism of the Presbyterians could be traced to 'the genius of their religion', and Thomas Emmet agreed that the Presbyterian love of liberty stemmed 'from religion, from education and early habits'.[32] But what exactly was it about Presbyterianism that apparently predisposed its adherents towards democratic politics?

[29] Simon Davies, 'The Northern Star and the Propagation of Enlightened Ideas', *Eighteenth-Century Ireland*, 5 (1990), 141–52.

[30] Many of the most interesting letters, preserved in PRONI, Drennan Papers, T765 are omitted from the well-known selection published by D. A. Chart in 1931.

[31] Sir Boyle Roche, 1792, quoted in Jim Smyth, *The Men of No Property: Irish Radicals and Popular Politics in the Late Eighteenth Century* (Dublin, 1992), 55.

[32] *Life of Theobald Wolfe Tone*, ed. W. T. W. Tone, 2 vols. (Washington, 1826), i. 48; Thomas Emmet, 'Part of an Essay Towards the History of Ireland', in William James MacNeven, *Pieces of Irish History* (New York, 1807), 9.

The most obvious starting point, perhaps, is the self-governing, representative organization of the Kirk which, it might be suggested, encouraged Presbyterians to adopt a critical stance towards the oligarchic political structures of the Hanoverian state. In his influential work *An Historical Essay upon the Loyalty of Presbyterians* (1713), the Belfast minister James Kirkpatrick made a connection between revolution principles and the Presbyterian church polity:

The Ecclesiastical Constitution of Presbytery does provide such Effectual Remedies against the Usurpations and Ambition of the Clergy, and lays such Foundations for the Liberty of the Subject in Church Matters: that it naturally creates in People an Aversion from all Tyranny and Oppression in the *State* also.[33]

The equality of status between ministers and the right of congregations to choose their own pastors were fundamental to the Presbyterian position. It is not difficult to see how the rejection of ecclesiastical hierarchy in favour of a popular conception of ecclesiastical polity might foster more participatory forms of political association than the deferential models provided by the English and Roman Churches. Reformist notions of government by consent and the delegatory nature of political authority might therefore appear as a natural outgrowth of Presbyterian organization. At a practical level, too, the involvement of laymen in ecclesiastical government may have encouraged political mobilization—the fact that the United Irish directory of Belfast was sometimes known as the 'committee of elders' is certainly suggestive.[34] Yet lay influence in church affairs could cut both ways. An examination of the long-standing controversy over creeds suggests that congregations were often run on oligarchic rather than democratic lines, and that popular pressure was usually mobilized in opposition to those (including Kirkpatrick himself) who embraced theological liberalism.[35] There was no simple correlation between ecclesiastical democracy and 'liberty'.

Closely related to the internal government of the Church was the troublesome question of the relationship between the temporal and spiritual powers. The potentially explosive element in the Presbyterian idea of polity, for heterodox and orthodox alike, was the insistence on Christ's headship of the Church. According to the two-kingdoms doctrine, Church and State constituted separate but complementary spheres. While the civil magistrate was invested with power over external actions, Jesus Christ was sole 'sovereign in his own house', and the government, discipline, and doctrine of the Church had been entrusted to his ministers alone.[36] Presbyterians had traditionally charged popes and prelates with usurping Christ's authority by imposing their own laws and practices on the Church, an accusation which could equally be levelled at the erastian influence of the Hanoverian state. In the eighteenth century only the Covenanters took this doctrine to its logical conclusion; the mainstream quickly came to terms with the existence of the state

---

[33] [James Kirkpatrick], *An Historical Essay upon the Loyalty of Presbyterians* (Belfast[?], 1713), 152.
[34] N. J. Curtin, 'The United Irish Organisation in Ulster: 1795–8', in Dickson, Keogh, and Whelan, *The United Irishmen*, 217.   [35] Above, Ch. 2.
[36] The phrase is taken from the Associate Synod's *Act, Declaration and Testimony* (Edinburgh, 1737), 97.

religion. But the fundamental belief in the spiritual freedom and independence of the Church did not die when the Covenanting tradition went underground; it soon resurfaced in another, more latitudinarian guise. By the last quarter of the century a new hostility to establishment Anglicanism was evident among the more advanced New Light Dissenters, and Presbyterian radicalism was shaped according to their distinctive preoccupations.

Following the Revolution settlement, with its confirmation of Anglican hegemony, Irish Presbyterians were once more compelled to address the problem of Church–State relations on a theoretical plane. According to the received Calvinist line of thought, the task of the Synod was to maintain its separateness and to preserve the standards of orthodoxy until divine providence should bring about the inauguration of the Godly reign envisioned in the Solemn League and Covenant. This was the direction taken by those militant Presbyterians who would later find a home in the Secession or the Reformed Presbytery, considered in the third and fourth sections below. For the Synod's leadership, however, it was plain that the ideal of a Presbyterian regime was unattainable. Without openly breaking with their Covenanting past, they adopted a more pragmatic response to the Anglican Church–State. On a tactical level, what Irish Presbyterians now required was a theory that would reconcile their demand for full participation in public life with the security of the propertied elite. To fend off the accusations of Anglican polemicists, it was essential to play down the seventeenth-century record of resistance and rebellion, to demonstrate their social respectability and theological moderation, while setting out principled grounds for their rejection of authority in ecclesiastical matters.[37] The material for such a theory emerged during the subscription controversy of 1719–26, and was hammered into shape by John Abernethy during the campaign for the removal of the sacramental test in the following decade. While Abernethy and the early non-subscribers adopted a defensive tone, later generations would discover its revolutionary applications.

Sincerity and persuasion were the organizing principles of the New Light divinity. For the orthodox, the religious knowledge necessary to salvation could be found in the doctrinal standards established by the Westminster divines and policed by the courts of the Kirk. These restrictions stood in the way of the process of reconstruction which the learned members of the Belfast Society believed was essential if Presbyterianism was to be brought into harmony with the intellectual standards of a rational age. In addition to the core propositions of Christianity, they believed that the Westminster Confession had encoded many of those 'indifferent things' which had set Protestant against Protestant since the Reformation. More importantly, the New Light ministers viewed the interrogation of ministerial candidates as a species of religious persecution. The Church of the non-subscribers was a merely contractual association, and its teachings were to be maintained and furthered by free speculation and rational persuasion alone. None of these ideas, of course, were

---

[37] It was for this reason, perhaps, that the term 'Protestant Dissenter' was often preferred to 'Presbyterian', which carried the stigma of fanaticism and rebellion.

original to the north of Ireland or to its intellectual centre at Glasgow. By the end of the seventeenth century they had already been widely canvassed in *avant-garde* circles in England, Holland, and Geneva, and they had been moulded into a sophisticated and influential theory of religious liberty by John Locke.

It is well known that the *Second Treatise* came to enjoy a privileged status as the exposition of the principles of the British constitution. It is worth recalling, however, that this work was conceived not as an attack on a propertied oligarchy, but as a legitimation of resistance against the attempts of an Anglican gentry to reimpose religious uniformity. Locke's task was to show that it was possible to oppose the Crown *without* undermining the rationale for the existing social order, and this is one reason why the *Second Treatise* could later be construed as a smug celebration of English political culture.[38] Read from another perspective, however, as an essay in resistance theory designed for an oppressed Dissenting minority and its allies, its implications were more extreme. It is hardly suprising, then, that Locke should have been rediscovered in the 1770s by those English Dissenters—Joseph Priestley, Richard Price, Joseph Towers, and others—who found themselves once more drawn into conflict with an Anglican Parliament over the Test and Corporations Acts.[39]

As a prophet of the whig order, however, Locke's most important contribution probably lay less in his theory of limited government than in his religious and philosophical writings, *A Letter Concerning Toleration* (1689) and *An Essay Concerning Human Understanding* (1690), which became part of the core curriculum in the Dissenting academies.[40] The first provided the foundation-stone of the eighteenth-century case for liberty of conscience. Locke had furnished an epistemological justification for latitudinarianism by showing that diversity of belief was a natural consequence of the limits of human knowledge. He had also condemned the enactment of penal statutes to suppress heterodox opinions. 'No man can if he would conform his faith to the dictates of another', he argued, for true religion consisted in 'the inward and full persuasion of mind and faith is not faith without believing'. The right to worship God according to one's own conscience was a natural right which could only be curtailed by the civil magistrate in the interests of public security. (This crucial qualification ruled out not only atheists, for whom oaths of allegiance could have no ultimate sanction, but also Roman Catholics, who were allegedly absolved by their priests from civil obligations to heretical rulers.)[41]

[38] Yolton, 'Politics of Locke in England and America'. On Locke generally see John Dunn, *The Political Thought of John Locke* (Cambridge, 1969); Richard Ashcraft, *Revolutionary Politics and Locke's Two Treatises of Government* (Princeton, 1986); James Tully, *An Approach to Political Philosophy: Locke in Contexts* (Cambridge, 1993).

[39] In addition to Kramnick, 'Republican Revisionism Revisited', see Kathleen Wilson, 'Inventing Revolution: 1688 and Eighteenth-Century Popular Politics', *Journal of British Studies*, 28 (1989), 349–86; R. B. Barlow, *Citizenship and Conscience: A Study in the Theory and Practice of Religious Toleration in England During the Eighteenth Century* (Philadelphia, 1962), ch. 6.

[40] J. G. A. Pocock, 'The Varieties of Whiggism from Exclusion to Reform: A History of Ideology and Discourse', in id., *Virtue, Commerce and History: Essays on Political Thought and History, Chiefly in the Eighteenth Century* (Cambridge, 1985), 225, 229; D. L. Wykes, 'The Contribution of the Dissenting Academy to the Emergence of Rational Dissent', in Knud Haakonssen (ed.), *Enlightenment and Religion: Rational Dissent in Eighteenth-Century Britain* (Cambridge, 1996), 118.

[41] For Locke and toleration see Barlow, *Citizenship and Conscience*, 35–42. The quotation is from p. 37.

Locke's justification of religious pluralism was absorbed into polemical theology through the Bangorian controversy, ignited by Benjamin Hoadly's 1717 sermon *The Nature of the Kingdom of Church of Christ*. The unfortunate Bishop of Bangor had produced an ingenious but dangerously subversive reading of the text, 'My kingdom is not of this world', intended to defend the erastian church management of the court Whigs from their non-juring and High Church enemies. Christ was sole sovereign in his spiritual kingdom, Hoadly argued, and had left behind no visible, human authority, to judge over the consciences of his people. Any of his subjects who claimed the authority to make new laws or to reinterpret old ones, to meddle with individual conscience by introducing temporal rewards and punishments, or to enforce spiritual authority with the aid of the civil magistrate, were thus guilty of usurping Christ's prerogatives, just as the false Church of Rome had done.[42] Taken to their logical conclusion, these principles undermined the entire theoretical basis for the Church as a corporate society, linked to the civil power, and they were instantly disowned by the great majority of Whig churchmen. In the north of Ireland, however, where 'a perfect Hoadly mania' quickly spread among the younger ministers, the radical potential of this doctrine was swiftly recognized.[43]

The offensive against the sacramental test had relied initially upon prudential considerations rather than abstract principles of natural justice. Presbyterians demanded full citizenship within the Protestant nation on the grounds that their exertions had secured the survival of the Protestant interest at the time of the Revolution, and that the continuing threat from Catholic Ireland required an alliance between Churchmen and Dissenters. Their apologists struck that note of unrequited loyalty which is such a familiar feature of Ulster Protestant discourse. The classic defence of Protestant Dissent was Kirkpatrick's *Essay upon the Loyalty of Presbyterians*, cited as a source in Presbyterian polemics even in the 1790s, which was designed to prove that Presbyterians had been loyal to the principle of limited monarchy throughout the commotions of the seventeenth century.[44]

At the same time, however, Presbyterian propaganda contained theological and rights-based arguments which became more pronounced as the century wore on. Whereas earlier controversialists had attacked the Church of Ireland on the grounds of liturgy and ecclesiastical polity, Kirkpatrick took the view that all Protestants were agreed in '*the* Substantials *and* Vitals *of Religion*'.[45] Although he believed that the Church should be independent of state supervision, he avoided the militant claims which had been voiced in the seventeenth century, most famously in the

---

[42] For a brief account of the Bangorian controversy see Norman Sykes, *Church and State in England in the Eighteenth Century* (Cambridge, 1934), 290–7.

[43] The quotation is from a letter written by Francis Hutcheson in 1718, quoted in J. S. Reid, *History of the Presbyterian Church in Ireland*, ed. W. D. Killen, 3rd edn., 3 vols. (Belfast, 1867), iii. 115–16.

[44] See also [John McBride], *A Sample of Jet-Black Prelatick Calumny* (Glasgow, 1713). Kirkpatrick was cited by all parties during the discussions on the augmentation of the *regium donum* that took place between 1800 and 1803: see e.g. John Sherrard, *A Few Observations on the Nature and Tendency of the Changes Lately Proposed to be Made in the Constitution of the Protestant Dissenting Church* (Belfast, 1803), 22; Andrew Knox, 'Observations on the Situation of the Irish Presbyterians', in *Memoirs and Correspondence of Viscount Castlereagh*, ed. Charles Vane, 12 vols. (London, 1848–51), iv. 256 n. 1.

[45] [Kirkpatrick], *Historical Essay*, p. iv.

Solemn League and Covenant. In particular, he denied that Presbyterian principles demanded the extirpation of episcopacy or that the authority of the Kirk was superior to that of the civil magistrate.[46] Instead, he contended that, while the magistrate had the power to punish and restrain principles which threatened the security of the state, he had no right to interfere with religious beliefs, for 'God is *Lord* of *Conscience*, and therefore it does not belong to *Caesar*'.[47] Dissent from the Anglican Church was defended not because the Kirk was the only true church, but on the grounds that every man had the right to make up his own mind in matters of religion.

This strategy was advanced a step further by the Revd John Abernethy and the Dublin bookseller William Bruce, who orchestrated the anti-test agitation of 1731–3.[48] Abernethy refrained from attacks on episcopal government and conceded that ecclesiastical authority must be exercised under the check of the civil power.[49] Like Kirkpatrick, he contended that the test was inconsistent with the principles of civil liberty and constituted a violation of the original compact whereby men had entered civil society.[50] He also borrowed from the epistemological theories of John Locke, asserting that 'a Diversity of Opinions in Matters of Religion is utterly unavoidable in the present State of Imperfection', and was perfectly compatible with the public good.[51] The authority of the magistrate existed to protect the life, liberty, and property of the subject; he could not interfere with religious beliefs unless these were dangerous to society.[52] Abernethy's rejection of the confessional state, like his opposition to the practice of subscription, was thus founded upon his belief that the imposition of human creeds infringed upon the individual's right of self-determination. His friend and colleague, James Duchal, explained his dissent from the Established Church in the same Lockian language:

It is evident, that where conscience is to be the sole guide, authority can have no place; that no man can have authority over any other; and that no man can invest another with authority over himself; nor is it less evident that no man can promise a constant adherence to any system, no, nor even to his own present principles, for that is a matter quite out of his power.[53]

The lobbying and pamphleteering of the 1730s made little impression on a solidly Anglican House of Commons, and for forty years there was no further attempt to raise the subject of the test. As William Bruce had presciently observed, only the threat of a revolution would dislodge the alliance of clergy and gentry.[54] On public occasions, nevertheless, Presbyterian ministers reiterated their opposition to the exercise of civil jurisdiction in affairs of conscience. At the time of the Jacobite rebellion of 1745 the Revd Alexander Maclaine reminded the members of his Antrim

---

[46] [Kirkpatrick], *Historical Essay*, 540–50.   [47] Ibid. 20.

[48] Abernethy's anti-test pamphlets, which were written with the assistance of the Dublin bookseller William Bruce, were later collected together in *Scarce and Valuable Tracts and Sermons* (London, 1751).

[49] Abernethy, *Tracts*, 9.   [50] Ibid. 27–33.   [51] Ibid. 44–5.   [52] Ibid. 3.

[53] Duchal to William Bruce, 1 Oct. 1742, printed in T. D. Hincks, 'Notices of William Bruce and of his Contemporaries and Friends, Hutcheson, Abernethy, Duchal and Others', *Christian Teacher*, NS 5 (1843), 78.

[54] William Bruce to 'Will', 2 Feb. 1733, PRONI, Bruce Papers, D2673, uncatalogued.

congregation that they lived in comparative security, and warned them not to press their political claims at such a critical moment, but he also asserted that

the end of Government is no other than the Good of the Governed; nor is there any other just reason to be assigned for making any other alteration in that Equality which is original in Mankind, and for exalting some to Places of Power and Magistracy while others are in the Condition of Subjects.[55]

In the same year, Gilbert Kennedy of Second Belfast set out a systematic account of the origins of civil society using contract theory and affirming the right of resistance. 'The great end of Government, and of Mens [*sic*] entering into civil Societies', he wrote, 'is the Preservation and Security of their just Rights, Liberties and Properties, against unjust Force and Violence.'[56] Citing Locke's *Second Treatise*, he argued that all men were originally equal, that all power was derived from the voluntary consent of the community, and that the sole business of the executive was the welfare of society.[57] While affirming the superiority of the Hanoverian order he boldly condemned the magistrate who

presumes to Model the Religious Sentiments of his Subjects, to think and judge for them in matters of Religion; not only to restrain such Opinions as are inconsistent with Peace and good order in the State, which to be sure is the business of every chief Magistrate; but to impose under severe and heavy Penalties particular Forms of and Modes of Worship; and the belief of Doctrines, no way essential, but disputable and trifling.[58]

Abernethy's writings on the sacramental test were widely circulated not only in Ireland but also in England, where the slow emergence of 'Rational Dissent' from English Presbyterianism stimulated Dissenting antagonism towards all civil establishments of religion.[59] In 1746 Micaiah Towgood published *The Dissenting Gentleman's Answer, to the Rev. Mr Whites's Three Letters*, the standard justification of English nonconformity, which accused the Established Church of restricting Christian liberty by introducing human articles of faith. Three years later, John Jones's *Free and Candid Disquisitions* (1749) highlighted the unscriptural aspects of Anglican liturgy. Within the Anglican Church itself, Francis Blackburne's *Confessional* (1766) sparked off a campaign against subscription to the Thirty-Nine Articles which culminated in the unsuccessful Feathers Tavern petition of 1772 and the resignation of a small number of Anglican clergymen led by Theophilus Lindsey and John Jebb. Hostility to the establishment was reinforced by Blackstone's condemnation of nonconformity in the fourth volume of his *Commentaries on the Laws of England* (1769), which provoked retaliatory pamphlets from the Rational Dissenters Joseph Priestley and Philip Furneaux. All of these anti-establishment polemics were read by Irish

[55] Alexander Maclaine, *A Sermon Preached at Antrim, Dec. 18, 1745, Being the National Fast* (Dublin, 1746), 23, 11.

[56] Gilbert Kennedy, *The Wicked Ruler; or, The Mischiefs of Absolute Arbitrary Power: A Sermon Preach'd at Belfast, December the 18th, 1745. Being the Day of General Fast, Appointed by the Government* (Belfast, 1745), 4.

[57] Ibid. 6, 16, 18–20. See also id., *The Great Blessing of Peace and Truth in Our Days. A Sermon Preach'd at Belfast on Tuesday, April 25th, 1749. Being the Day of Public Thanksgiving for the Peace* (Belfast, 1749).

[58] Kennedy, *Wicked Ruler*, 7–8.   [59] Barlow, *Citizenship and Conscience*, 78–9.

Dissenters.[60] Towgood's popular treatise, which was reprinted in Belfast, Newry, Armagh, and Dublin, was hailed by one Ulster minister as 'the best defence of the principles of Dissenters in the English language'.[61]

The later radicalization of Presbyterian principles was evident in the pamphlet warfare which followed the publication of Richard Woodward's *The Present State of the Church of Ireland* in 1786. The Bishop of Cloyne attacked the Presbyterians partly because the 'levelling spirit' of their Church found its natural political corollary in republicanism, but he singled out the 'leading' Presbyterians who differed from their brethren in Geneva, Switzerland, Holland, Germany, and Scotland in that they rejected the very idea of a national church: 'Their principles do not, like those of the Roman Catholicks, tend to set up, but merely to pull down, an Ecclesiastical establishment.'[62] Two semi-official replies, published by William Campbell, pointed to Scotland and Geneva to show that Presbyterianism was not incompatible with state-supported churches, though the author confessed that his own opinion was against them. He preferred to take his stand on the more favourable ground of history, showing that the Ulster Scots had been sent to Ireland by the British monarchy to secure the loyalty of the northern province and that they had often risked their lives to that end.[63]

In contrast to the politique moderation of Campbell's lengthy historical surveys, however, Samuel Barber of Rathfriland fired off two sharply polemical volleys against the corrupt priestcraft of the Church of Ireland.[64] To some extent Barber's objections to the establishment were practical ones. Was it not absurd, he challenged, that the same state which maintained prelacy in England and Ireland had established Presbyterianism in Scotland and Roman Catholicism in Quebec?[65] He roundly condemned the tithe system, which hindered industry and agriculture, and pointed out the injustice of asking the Irish to support a church which ministered to only an eighth of the people.[66] In a passage which outraged some of his own colleagues he even went on to suggest that if there had to be an established church it should be that of the majority.[67] His fundamental complaint, however, was doctrinal in

---

[60] 'Intended Defence', reprinted in J. F. Larkin (ed.), *The Trial of William Drennan* (Dublin, 1991), 128; Revd William Bruce, 'The Progress of Non-Subscription to Creeds', *Christian Moderator*, 2 (1827–8), 353–4.   [61] Sherrard, *A Few Observations*, 21 n.

[62] Richard Woodward, *The Present State of the Church of Ireland* (Dublin, 1787), 10, 19. The same line is taken in [George Grace], *Presbyterio-Catholicon: or A Refutation of the Modern Catholic Doctrines, Propagated by Several Societies of Catholic Presbyterians, and Presbyterian Catholics, in a Letter to the Real Roman Catholics of Ireland* (Dublin, 1792), 48.

[63] William Campbell, *A Vindication of the Principles and Character of the Presbyterians in Ireland; Addressed to the Bishop of Cloyne* (Dublin, 1787), 8–9, 34, 72; id., *An Examination of the Bishop of Cloyne's Defence of his Principles* (Belfast, 1788), 9. For the background see James Kelly, 'Relations between the Protestant Church of Ireland and the Presbyterian Church in Late Eighteenth-Century Ireland', *Eire-Ireland*, 23 (1988), 38–56.

[64] Samuel Barber, *Remarks on a Pamphlet, Entitled The Present State of the Church of Ireland, by Richard, Lord Bishop Cloyne* (Dublin, 1787). His arguments were reiterated in his *Reply to the Reverend Mr Burrowes and the Reverend Mr Ryan's Remarks etc.* (Dublin, 1787).   [65] Barber, *Reply*, 11.

[66] Barber, *Remarks*, 6, 30–7, 45–7.

[67] Ibid. 34. See Joseph Pollock's response in his letter to William Campbell, 9 Mar. 1787, PHSI, Campbell MSS.

character. Citing the key text of John 18: 36—'My Kingdom is not of this World' —Barber maintained that the idea of a state religion was excluded from the system of church polity laid out in the New Testament; that primitive Christianity had flourished without the aid of the civil power; and that its progressive degeneration could be dated from the moment when *magisterium* and *sacerdotium* had first been joined in partnership.[68] Secular involvement in clerical affairs led inevitably to tyranny:

the whole object of the legislator's province, when he meddles with a kingdom, where he has no power, is to decree rites and ceremonies, and to chain down the soul to a certain system of opinions; to provide large revenues for the teachers of the national faith, and to oppress and persecute all who, like Daniel, refuse to worship, kneel or bow, as the act directs.[69]

The radical assault on the confessional state culminated in William Steel Dickson's *Three Sermons on the Subject of Scripture Politics*, a United Irish manifesto published in the wake of the Ulster convention of 1793. The sermons, which date from 1781, 1792, and 1793, have a common theme, the connection between the kingdom of Christ and the kingdoms of this world. In the first, an exegesis of the now familiar text of John 18: 36, Dickson set out to establish his premiss that true religion was 'inseparably connected' with the science of politics since they shared the same goal, 'the happiness of mankind'.[70] Although the Scriptures had not laid down any specific form of government, God had prescribed in the Bible the standards by which kings were to rule.[71] But this assertion that Christian morality ought to be the basis of all civil association was coupled with a conception of the Church as an independent society, sovereign within its own sphere: 'the Messiah's kingdom did not originate from worldly policy, doth not affect pomp, and perishable wealth, disclaims every idea of being extended by violence, or supported by oppression'.[72] Since Christ's kingdom is not of this world, it follows that any attempt to regulate patterns of belief or modes of worship constitutes a usurpation of his authority as head of the Church.[73]

Unfortunately, as Dickson detailed in his second and third sermons, this relationship between the temporal and spiritual powers had been warped since the reign of the emperor Constantine. The teachers of religion, whose office it was to expose 'the partiality, oppression, and tyranny of rulers', had taken their seats with statesmen, sacrificing the mild spirit of Christianity to their worldly ambitions.[74] Religion had been perverted by kings and princes to justify war and conquest, and its ministers reduced to 'the echoes of political mandates'.[75] Worse still, as the sad chronicles of the seventeenth century demonstrated, the clergy of all sects had propagated their exclusive creeds by the persecution of their competitors; religion had been 'fortified by penal statutes, and guarded by gibbets, racks, and flames'.[76] In Ireland the Presbyterians who had fought so bravely at Derry and Enniskillen had been barred by placemen and pensioners from every honour and office of the State. The same

---

[68] Barber, *Remarks*, 8, 12–13.   [69] Ibid. 11–12.
[70] William Steel Dickson, *Three Sermons on the Subject of Scripture Politics* (Belfast, 1793), 12.
[71] Ibid. 7, 49.   [72] Ibid. 6.   [73] Ibid. 18.   [74] Ibid. 33, 55.   [75] Ibid. 16.
[76] Ibid. 15.

faction, now trading under the name of the Protestant Ascendancy, had bound the Catholics 'with the twisted chains of mental darkness, and corporal incapacity, by a body of laws, which humanity views with horror, justice reprobates, and religion pronounces *accursed*'.[77] With this ringing affirmation of religious liberty, Dickson demonstrated how New Light arguments for liberty of conscience had been transformed into the universalist idiom of the inalienable rights of man.

Opposition to religious establishments of all kinds, then, was the logical terminus of the New Light rejection of creeds and confessions. The anti-subscription movement took Protestant individualism to extreme lengths, where the entire fabric of corporate religion appeared to be dissolved. In their struggle for freedom of worship Dissenters had been driven to demand this right for Protestant, Catholic, and Dissenter alike; the conflict between Presbyterians and the establishment was thus generalized into a struggle between toleration and religious tyranny. The persistence of error, superstition, and bigotry was increasingly attributed to the idols which Church and State had made of religious subscriptions or declarations. In this way Dissent became self-defining, and toleration was seen as an end in itself.[78] There was some justice in Samuel Johnson's scathing depiction of (English) Dissenters as sectaries 'of whose religion little now remains but hatred of establishments'.[79]

If Presbyterian radicalism had its roots in a common religious heritage, it was the New Light Dissenters such as Dickson and Barber who determined its characteristic eighteenth-century tone. As a close-knit community, self-consciously learned, independent, and politically aware, the congregations of the non-subscribers formed a communications network through which new religious and political ideas were accumulated. The New Lights were the first to grasp the importance of the French Revolution, and to advocate the creation of an independent, non-sectarian republic on the French model. But this essentially latitudinarian critique of state-supported religion was soon echoed by other Presbyterians who had no sympathy for New Light divinity. Even Thomas Ledlie Birch, a member of the staunchly orthodox Presbytery of Belfast, upheld the sanctity of freedom of conscience. 'That Civil Liberty must be the forerunner of Religious Reformation' was indisputable, he believed, 'for without it there could be no free discussion, or embracing of truth when discovered'.[80] The involvement of traditionalists like Birch in the United Irish movement certainly proves that there was no necessary correlation between liberal politics and latitudinarian religion, although their commitment to religious pluralism was no doubt held in tension with their own rigid credal allegiances.

While the New Lights constituted the vanguard of Presbyterian radicalism, however, we should also be alert to the limits of their position. In Chapter 2 it was suggested that the virulence of the dispute over compulsory subscription might be explained partly in terms of a widening gap between elite and popular forms

---

[77] Dickson, *Three Sermons*, 34.
[78] R. E. Richey outlines similar developments in English Dissent in 'The Origins of British Radicalism: The Changing Rationale for Dissent', *Eighteenth-Century Studies*, 7 (1973–4), 179–92.
[79] Quoted in Clark, *English Society*, 317.
[80] Thomas Ledlie Birch, *Seemingly Experimental Religion* (Washington, Pa., 1806), 5.

of culture; the urbane social constituency of non-subscription was threatened not only by the credal restraints laid down by clerical establishments, but by the narrow sectarianism of the lower orders. Their battle for intellectual freedom had little to do with the grievances of the ignorant masses, and they had good reason to fear social upheaval; as the United Irish movement became more militant many of them defected to the forces of order. The enlightenment philosophy of the New Lights cannot explain the mobilization of the thousands of farmers and weavers who 'turned out' in June 1798. At this point their brand of radicalism blended with seventeenth-century ideas of the Presbyterian polity, which survived in their purest form among the members of the small Reformed Presbytery and seem to have mobilized much larger sections of the population in the 1790s. To account for the strength of Ulster radicalism we must also examine the persistence of this older, more sectarian strain of scripture politics.

'The Rights of God and Man': the Covenanters

One from among thy brethren shalt thou set king over thee: thou mayest not set a stranger over thee, which is not thy brother.

(Deuteronomy 17: 15, 16)

In its Calvinist origins and in its espousal of the right of resistance, the political theory of the mountain men had close affinities with radical whiggism. The classic treatise *Vindiciae Magistratus* (1773), written by the Covenanting clergyman John Thorburn, quoted liberally from Locke, Grotius and Pufendorf, Harrington, Sidney, and Hoadly, as well as *A Cloud of Witnesses* and *The Hind Let Loose*. But the popular contractarianism of the Covenanting tradition was a far cry from the ancient constitution cherished by the Hanoverian elite. For the Covenanters, civil society had been constituted not merely to preserve the property of the individual, but for divine ends:

that magistracy or government which is God's ordinance, and to which obedience and subjection is due, for *conscience-sake*, must be such, whose human institution, or actual formation and constitution by men, is conform unto, and in pursuance of the divine institution; or unto the moral preceptive will of God.[81]

The Covenanters tried to remain aloof from the constitutional debates which echoed through the northern province after 1775, for while many members instinctively agreed that the defects in the electoral system should be addressed, they felt that the corruption of the ecclesiastical constitution presented a much more urgent problem. Indeed, parliamentary reform was always seen as a means to the end of securing the true religion. Popular energies, it was felt, should be directed towards the complete package of reforms enshrined in the Solemn League and Covenant. In Scotland the Reformed Presbytery therefore castigated those who had joined the Friends of the People on the grounds that parliamentary reform was distinct from

---

[81] John Thorburn, *Vindiciae Magistratus: or, the Divine Institution and Right of the Civil Magistrate Vindicated* (Edinburgh, 1773), 5.

their own grievances against the State, that the radical societies had no proper moral position, and that they approved of the erastian constitution.[82] In a public fast issued in 1795 the Presbytery warned its adherents that among the reformers were many 'stated enemies of God and Religion' and, worse still, 'abettors of the man of sin, and supporters of such schemes as tend to suppress religion, and prevent the success of the Messiah's kingdom'.[83]

This last warning was repeated across the Irish Sea, where the skilful exploitation of a vast array of popular grievances by the Belfast republicans ensured that the Reformed Presbyterians could not escape the revolutionary contagion. A 'Seasonable and Necessary Information', repudiating tumultuous and disorderly assemblies, was drawn up by the Scottish Reformed Presbytery and printed in the *Northern Star*.[84] The Irish Covenanters nevertheless became deeply infected with Paineite ideas, and the extent of their involvement in the '98 rebellion is much greater, proportionately, than that of any other Presbyterian denomination. Of the six ministers who formed the Reformed Presbytery in 1792, three at least were implicated. James McKinney helped to establish a Volunteer company in Dervock after the French Revolution, and published a sermon which was denounced as treasonable. The resulting hostility forced him to emigrate in 1793.[85] William Gibson, and later Joseph Orr, toured Antrim around 1796 preaching to large crowds and prophesying the 'immediate destruction of the British monarchy'.[86] As we have already seen, Gibson was accompanied into exile by the two students then under the care of the Reformed Presbytery, John Black and Samuel Brown Wylie.

Undoubtedly the best-known Covenanting rebel was William Stavely, who had built up the Church almost single-handed. Stavely was arrested on 13 June 1798 and charged with preaching seditious doctrines. When asked to sign a proclamation offering exile in return for information, he protested that he had never taken the United Irish oath, had never co-operated with Roman Catholics, and was unable to join the republicans 'because their principles are deistical, [and] their practice very immoral'. Stavely further insisted that he had cautioned his followers

to beware of and keep at a due distance from, all those sinful associations now existing . . . yet alas! some have been seduced away from their duty to God; and at the expense of breaking their religious vows and obligations, have apostatized from the Covenanted Testimony.[87]

In the light of the account of Covenanting principles outlined above, Stavely's denial seems entirely plausible, and has been quoted approvingly by the historian of the Reformed Presbyterian Church in Ireland.[88] Yet, when commissioners from the

---

[82] Matthew Hutchison, *The Reformed Presbyterian Church in Scotland: Its Origin and History 1680–1876* (Paisley, 1893), 234–5.

[83] Reformed Presbytery, *Act of the Reformed Presbytery for a Public Fast* [Glasgow, 1795], 3.

[84] *NS*, 10 Oct. 1796; E. W. McFarland, *Ireland and Scotland in the Age of Revolution: Planting the Green Bough* (Edinburgh, 1994), 9.

[85] Samuel Brown Wylie, *Memoir of Alexander McLeod, D.D.* (New York, 1855), 21.

[86] Samuel McSkimmin, *Annals of Ulster; or Ireland Fifty Years Ago* (Belfast, 1849), 53–4.

[87] Copy of a narrative drawn up by William Stavely, 24 Aug. 1798, PHSI, Stavely Papers.

[88] Adam Loughridge, *The Covenanters in Ireland* (Belfast, 1984), 47–8.

Scottish Presbytery interviewed him in 1802 following reports of dissensions among the Irish Covenanters, they discovered that Stavely had not only taken the United Irish oath himself, but had initiated others, contributed money for unknown purposes, and, as part of a baronial committee, planned an arms raid.[89]

There is no puzzle about the attraction of revolutionary principles for Stavely and his fellow preachers. Following in the tradition of Rutherford, Shields, and Thorburn, they tapped into the Calvinist doctrine of popular sovereignty, as the handful of Covenanting sermons which survive show. The most important is Samuel Brown Wylie's *The Two Sons of Oil* (1803), a comprehensive discussion of the relationship between magistracy and ministry written after his flight to the United States. 'Civil government', he observed, 'does not, as some modern politicians affirm, originate either in the people, as its fountain, or in the vices consequent upon the fall', but is given by the Creator. Consequently all civil constitutions must be modified according to His Word. So while the immediate end of government is the common good, its ultimate purpose is the advancement of the glory of God.[90] A similar line was taken by James McKinney in his 'A View of the Rights of God and Man' (1793). Spurred to write by the growing association in the popular mind between civil liberty and Deism, McKinney aimed to reconcile Paineite ideas with Calvinist theology, for 'were it not for the persuasion I entertain, that Christianity will purify and support the rights of man, fond as I am of liberty, I do not believe I would give a shilling to bring about a revolution in any nation upon earth'.[91]

As we have seen, the mountain ministers were trying to reconcile the democratic tenets of the Jacobins with traditional Calvinist theology. Stavely actually penned a lengthy refutation of the *Age of Reason* in which he congratulated Paine on his vindication of the rights of man but challenged him to a face-to-face debate on the authority of divine revelation.[92] The theological foundations of Stavely's own radicalism were revealed in three millenarian tracts which he had reprinted in Belfast the previous year. These were John Owen's *The Shaking and Translation of Heaven and Earth*, Robert Fleming's *A Discourse on the Rise and Fall of Antichrist, wherein the Revolution in France and the Downfall of the Monarchy in that Kingdom are Distinctly Pointed Out*, and James Bicheno's *The Signs of the Times*, all of which supplied compelling arguments for regarding the French Revolution as the first round in the final battle against Antichrist.[93] In 1795 Stavely also set out his own thoughts on the calculation of prophetic time. The European states which had risen from the Roman Empire, he claimed, were the ten crowned horns of the beast whose destruction

---

[89] Quoted in Hutchison, *Reformed Presbyterian Church*, 236.

[90] Samuel Brown Wylie, *Two Sons of Oil; or The Faithful Witness for Magistracy and Ministry upon a Scriptural Basis. Also, A Sermon on Covenanting* (Greensburg, Pa., 1803), 9, 12.

[91] James McKinney, 'A View of the Rights of God and Man', *The Covenanter*, 1 (1831), 160.

[92] William Stavely, *Appeal to Light; or, The Tenets of Deists Examined and Disapproved* (Belfast, 1796), 60 n.

[93] Other millenarian tracts published at this time include *An Examination of the Scripture Prophecies Respecting the Downfall of Antichrist . . . and the late Revolution in France Shewn to be Plainly Foretold* (Belfast, 1795); *Extracts from the Prophecies of Richard Brothers* (Belfast, 1795); *Prophetical Extracts Particularly such as Relate to the Revolution in France* (Strabane, 1795).

had been foretold in the Books of Daniel and Revelations. In collaboration with the Church of Rome, the kings of Europe had sinfully assumed the prerogatives of Jesus Christ by taking such titles as 'eldest son of the church' and 'defender of the faith'. They had 'set up their laws in opposition to the laws of this heavenly King, and arrogated a headship over the church, which no mortal on earth is qualified for'.[94]

In common with other millenarians, Stavely saw the French Revolution as the key to understanding the apocalyptic prophecies. France, having overthrown the House of Bourbon and humbled the Roman Catholic Church, had been chosen as God's instrument for toppling the monarchies of Europe. The brand of radicalism espoused by the Covenanting clergy was never worked out on a theoretical level, and the unstable mixture of millenarian theology and Jacobin principles which they brought to the ranks of the radicals can only be guessed at. It is worth noting, however, that an analogous process was taking place in some Catholic areas: in the secret oaths of the Defenders traditional Catholic iconography was joined by revolutionary symbolism.[95]

The Seceders and the sin of rebellion

Let every soul be subject unto the higher powers.

(Romans 13: 1)

The progress of the Secession was marred by internecine conflict from the very beginning. The imposition of an oath requiring the burgesses of Edinburgh, Glasgow, and Perth to swear allegiance to 'the true religion presently professed within this realm' threw the Associate Presbytery into confusion. In 1747 the Seceders split into two rival factions, the Burghers and Antiburghers, a division reproduced in Ulster despite its irrelevance to the Irish situation.[96] But this was just the most destructive of a succession of disagreements concerning the position of a covenanted church under the Hanoverian regime. The general effect was to update the Covenant to make it more palatable for an eighteenth-century audience. Great pains were taken to distance the Secession from the extremism of the second reformation. The Westminster divines had envisaged the rule of a covenanted king under whom Church and State would be fused in the pursuit of godliness; the preachers of the gospel would be backed up by the sword of the civil magistrate in the extirpation of popery and prelacy. In 1743, however, when the Seceders renewed the Covenants, they condemned those who rejected the legitimacy of the civil power, declaring that 'it was not suitable to their present circumstances, to blend civil and ecclesiastical matters in the oath of God'.[97] They avoided the word 'extirpation' because it had

---

[94] William Stavely, *War Proclaimed, and Victory Ensured; or, The Lamb's Conquests Illustrated* (Belfast, 1795), 55–6.

[95] Thomas Bartlett, 'Select Documents XXXVII: Defenders and Defenderism in 1795', *IHS* 24/95 (1985), 374.

[96] David Scott, *Annals and Statistics of the Original Secession Church: Till its Disruption and Union with the Free Church of Scotland in 1852* (Edinburgh, 1886), 36.

[97] John McKerrow, *History of the Secession Church*, rev. and enlarged edn. (Glasgow, 1841), 474.

been used in 'a *sanguinary* sense, for propagating religion by offensive arms quite contrary to the minds of our reformers'.[98] When the Burgher synod published a new edition of its 'Testimony' in 1778 it acknowledged that 'the enforcing of religious duties with civil penalties, and, in too many instances, blending the affairs of church and state with one another, is totally inconsistent with the spiritual nature of Christ's kingdom'.[99]

These tensions finally came to the surface in Scotland in the 1790s when both synods explicitly rejected the use of 'compulsory measures' in the pursuit of godliness. The state could no longer be seen as a vehicle for reformation, and the idea of a covenanted king was finally laid to rest. In 1796 the Antiburghers declared that the Westminster Confession should not be construed as condoning the punishment of good subjects on account of their religious opinions.[100] A new testimony drawn up in 1805 defined covenanting as a purely religious ordinance and disclaimed any methods of furthering reform inconsistent with liberty of conscience. A handful of ministers led by Archibald Bruce left the synod, protesting that covenanting was 'a kind of civil and political transaction, or at least a politico–ecclesiastical one'.[101] The Burghers revised their testimony also, and when the two bodies were eventually reunited in 1818 the articles of union played down the connection between the Church and the original Covenanters.[102] This retreat from their seventeenth-century engagements left the way open for a rapprochement between the Seceders and the authorities. On the coronation of George III the Antiburgher synod in Scotland published an address expressing their attachment to the new monarch, and praising 'the best-modelled government throughout the known world'.[103] Soon the Burghers would be calling on their maker to bless King George in their public fasts.[104] In 1788 both synods celebrated the centenary of the Glorious Revolution, a remarkable volte-face which outraged the hardline Antiburgher Archibald Bruce.[105]

In Ireland, meanwhile, the Seceders were learning to live with their status as a dissenting group in an Anglican state. No longer content to await the collapse of episcopacy, they began to look around for influential patrons. In 1780 the Antiburghers met to petition the House of Commons for liberty to swear oaths according to the form prescribed by the Church of Scotland.[106] Two years later the necessary act was introduced by John O'Neill and Isaac Corry, two Ulster MPs whose help had been enlisted by the Antiburghers.[107] Meanwhile the Burghers had secured the good offices of another northern member, Sir Richard Johnston. An address to the lord lieutenant, forwarded by Johnston in 1782, reveals the extent to which they were prepared to overlook the political principles set out in their own testimony:

---

[98] Associate Presbytery, *Address by the Associate Presbytery, . . . by the Revd Mr Thomas Nairn* (Edinburgh, 1744), 38–9.   [99] McKerrow, *Secession Church*, 594.

[100] Ibid. 474.   [101] Ibid. 466.   [102] Ibid. 579, 658.

[103] Ibid. 271–3.   [104] Ibid. 524.   [105] Ibid. 344–5, 566.

[106] Meeting at Hillhall, 12 Jan. 1780, Minutes of the Presbytery of Moira and Lisburn, 1774–86, PRONI, D. Stewart Papers, D1759/1D/22, p. 24.   [107] Meeting at Moira, 20 July 1782, ibid. 45.

Our principles, civil and religious are not new, they are those that were adopted and professed by the Church of Scotland at the glorious Revolution, and at the happy Accession of the illustrious House of Hanover. . . . Loyalty to our Prince, and Obedience to his Government are the true *Political* characteristics of the Dissenters of our *Persuasion.*[108]

The relief act conceded little—Seceders were still prohibited from giving evidence in criminal cases, serving on juries, and holding public office[109]—but it represents the end of the Secession's self-imposed exile, and it anticipates the more spectacular U-turn which took place in 1784.

During 1783–4, the Synod of Ulster was negotiating an increase in the *regium donum*, described in detail in Chapter 6 below. At the same time, a number of prominent New Light ministers were leading the 'independent' opposition to the Hillsborough interest in the Down election. Consequently, the Synod's commissioners came up against the backstairs influence of the largest landowner in the country. When the augmentation of the bounty was at last announced, the sum granted to the Synod was £1,000 rather than the £5,000 they had been led to expect. But Hillsborough's desire to humiliate his enemies did not stop there. He also secured a share of the bounty for the Secession, a move nicely calculated to rub salt in the Synod's wounds. The Seceding clergymen, who had taken such pride in their complete independence from the uncovenanted state, now meekly accepted their £13 annual subsidy.[110] The pay-off was revealed in the *Belfast News-Letter* of 24 February 1784 when a petition against parliamentary reform orchestrated by Hillsborough appeared. Alongside the local squires and parsons who expressed satisfaction with the 'present happy Constitution' were the names of two Seceding ministers, Thomas Mayn and Samuel Edgar.

How can we account for this ignoble bargain? The obvious explanation is financial difficulty. A quick glance at the minutes of any Seceding presbytery reveals the problems experienced by ministers in extorting their stipends from poor congregations. The *regium donum*, on the other hand, was a regular payment from a reliable source.[111] It is also true that the Seceders had little love for Hillsborough's opponent, Robert Stewart, a well-known patron of the New Light tendency, and frowned upon those ministers who had used their pulpits for political ends. Although several Seceding ministers had served in Volunteer companies, the church authorities repeatedly complained about the profanation of the sabbath by military parades and 'carnal converse about worldly affairs'.[112] Ultimately, however, the decision to accept payment from the Hanoverian monarchy can only be explained in the context of a slow withdrawal from the public religion of the second reformation.

This is not to say that the Seceders were completely insulated from the currents of republicanism which swept through late eighteenth-century Ulster. In 1791 they

---

[108] Meeting at Clonnanees, June 1782, Minutes of the Secession (Burgher) Synod, 1779–1814, PRONI, CR3/46/1/1, p. 21.   [109] Reid, *Presbyterian Church in Ireland,* iii. 347–8.
[110] Ibid. 356.
[111] David Stewart, *The Seceders in Ireland with Annals of their Congregations* (Belfast, 1950), 90, 97.
[112] Meeting at Monaghan, June 1781, Minutes of the Secession (Burgher) Synod, 1779–1814, PRONI, CR3/46/1/1, p. 13; John Rogers, *A Sermon Preached at Lisnavein* (Edinburgh, 1780), 41 n.; Reid, *Presbyterian Church in Ireland,* iii. 376 n. 92.

too welcomed 'the wonderful revolution in France' as a sign of the impending down-fall of Antichrist.[113] Three years later the *Northern Star* office printed a sermon by Josias Wilson of Donegore which included extracts from Robert Fleming and Richard Brothers, the self-proclaimed nephew of Jesus Christ.[114] Another Seceding clergy-man, John Tennent of Roseyards, sympathized with the radicalism of the *Northern Star*, although he argued that no pact should be struck with the Catholics until they had renounced their errors, and he deplored the licentious behaviour of the secret societies.[115] It is arguable, however, that these radical individuals were exceptions. In the early nineteenth century Tennent's son, Robert, and another Seceder named John Barnett were particularly prominent in radical circles, but they belonged to the tiny Associate Presbytery of Primitive Seceders. Their leader, James Bryce of Killaig, had broken with the Secession and refused his *regium donum* in 1811.[116] In his ecclesiastical principles he came much closer to the Covenanters than to his own erstwhile colleagues. Of the *regium donum* he wrote:

This connexion between church and state is called Babylon, or spiritual adultery; in other words, all churches, receiving legal support from the civil power are, in the language of prophecy, committing fornication with the kings of the earth.[117]

The most significant testimony to the political transformation of the Secession is the fact that only two ministers, James Harper and Thomas Smith, were implicated in the rebellion, and one of these had been turned in by a fellow clergyman, Adam Boyle.[118] Others meanwhile demonstrated their support for the British constitution. John Nicholson preached a sermon on the sinfulness of plots and conspiracies which was later sent to the *Anti-Jacobin Magazine*.[119] The attempts of Francis Pringle to dissuade the people of Gilnahirk from rebellion aroused such hostility that he was forced to emigrate to America.[120] A poem later dedicated to him by one of the 'rhyming weavers' praised the loyal stance of the Associate Presbytery of Down:

---

[113] See the 'Reasons for a Fast' drawn up at Armagh, June 1791, Minutes of the Secession (Burgher) Synod, 1779–1814, PRONI, CR3/46/1/1, p. 74.   [114] Advertised in *NS*, 20 June 1796.

[115] John Tennent to William Tennent, 31 Jan. 1792, 6 Feb. 1796, PRONI, Tennent Papers, D1748/A/1/317/1, 7.

[116] In 1809 the Secession's *regium donum* had been increased on the condition that it accepted a classification system similar to the one imposed on the Synod of Ulster: Reid, *Presbyterian Church in Ireland*, iii. 419.

[117] James Bryce, *A Narrative of the Proceedings of the Associate (Antiburgher) Synods, in Ireland and Scotland, in the Affair of the Royal Bounty, with Remarks on Ordination* (Belfast, 1816), 52–3 n. 1. John Brims, 'The Covenanting Tradition and Scottish Radicalism in the 1790s', in Terry Brotherstone (ed.), *Covenant, Charter, and Party: Traditions of Revolt and Protest in Modern Scottish History* (Aberdeen, 1989), 50–62, shows that several Scottish Secession ministers were involved in radical politics. It is interesting to note that the most prominent of these, Archibald Bruce, was opposed to evangelical trends, and occupied a position somewhat similar to that occupied by Bryce in Ulster. His *A Serious View of the Remarkable Providences of the Times* (Glasgow, 1795) is a fascinating exposition of Presbyterian millenarianism.

[118] Stewart, *Seceders*, 290.

[119] John Nicholson, *A Lecture and Sermon: Preached at Belfast* (Belfast, 1799). The copy in the British Library was sent to the *Anti-Jacobin Review and Magazine* in October 1799.

[120] Francis Boyle, *Miscellaneous Poems* (Belfast, 1811), 85–6. See also [Anon.], 'Biographical Sketch of the Reverend Francis Pringle', in J. P. Miller (ed.), *Biographical Sketches and Sermons, of Some of the First Ministers of the Associate Church in America* (Albany, 1839), 417–24.

On proper subjects still you fix,
The church and state you never mix;
Nor dip so deep in politics
    About the throne,
As Clergymen of other sects,
    That I have known.[121]

As Pringle's fate illustrates, loyal clergymen could not always carry their flocks with them. Elements among the laity doubtless continued to take the Solemn League and Covenant in a literal sense. Thus one loyalist reported to the government in 1796 that, although the Seceding clergymen could be relied upon, their followers were 'very generally infected'.[122] That the ministry struggled to restrain such popular disaffection is beyond doubt. The annual fast-day addresses drawn up by their presbyteries and read from each pulpit denounced the discussion of political subjects on the sabbath, the spread of sinful, oath-bound associations, and the greed which drove men to rebellion. The Burgher Presbytery of Down admitted that the severity of the administration had contributed to the breakdown of order, but reminded its people that 'a remarkable extent of religious liberty is still enjoyed, even when our rulers, owing to the state of the country, might have taken occasion to close our houses of worship and prevent our synodical or other assemblies'.[123] All laymen who had taken part in the rebellion were rebuked by kirk session.[124]

A study of their political theology suggests that the new conservatism of the Seceders, signalled by their acceptance of the *regium donum* in 1784, stemmed from their gradual renunciation of the Solemn League and Covenant and their concentration on an inward spirituality which looked forward to the evangelical tone of nineteenth-century Presbyterianism. The link between loyalty and evangelicalism is most clearly demonstrated in the career of Samuel Edgar of Ballynahinch, one of the signatories to Hillsborough's petition. Edgar's parish was a centre of republican activity—his communion goblets and tankards were stolen and melted down to make bullets for the United Irishmen—but he himself exerted all his influence against the rebellion. As professor of theology for the Secession, he was also a prominent advocate of missionary schemes both at home and abroad, and a convert to interdenominational co-operation between the Protestant churches.[125] Similarly, the unfortunate Francis Pringle was an early advocate of the missionary societies which had sprung up in London and Scotland.[126] In terms of political theology, then, the

---

[121] Francis Boyle, 'An Address to the Associate Presbytery of Down', in *Miscellaneous Poems*, 104.

[122] Thomas Whinnery to John Lees, 13 Sept. 1796, NAI, Rebellion Papers, 620/25/57. The same view was expressed in Thomas Ledlie Birch, *A Letter from an Irish Emigrant to his Friend in the United States* (Philadelphia, 1799), 29.

[123] Minutes of the Burgher Presbytery of Down, 3 July 1798, in W. H. Crawford and Brian Trainor (eds.), *Aspects of Irish Social History 1750–1800* (Belfast, 1969), 103.

[124] Meeting at Ballyroney, 25 Sept. 1799, Minutes of the Burgher Presbytery of Down, PRONI, D. Stewart Papers, D1759/1D/17, p. 386. For other examples of Seceding loyalty, see W. C. Lindsey to James Stewart, 3 Jan. 1793, PRONI, Stewart of Killymoon Papers, D3167/2/87; Hudson to Charlemont, 31 June 1797, *Charlemont MSS*, ii. 302.

[125] W. D. Bailie, *Edengrove Presbyterian Church 1774–1974* (Newcastle, Co. Down, 1974), 13.

[126] Francis Pringle, *The Gospel Ministry, an Ordinance of Christ; and the Duty of Ministers and People: A Sermon, at the Opening of the Associate Synod of Ireland, in Belfast—July 12, 1796* (Belfast[?], 1796).

Secession was the exception that proves the rule. Before the onset of a political reaction among its clergy the Ulster Presbyterians had no established conservative vocabulary of their own. To be sure, there was a language of loyalty, which celebrated William III and the Hanoverians as protectors of Protestantism and Dissent, but Presbyterians stood outside the culture of deference sustained by the Anglican confessional state. While Paine's *Rights of Man* was easily superimposed upon a pre-existing radical sensibility, Burke's doctrine of prescription struck no deep roots among the various groupings within the Presbyterian community. In their revisions of the Covenant, however, the Seceders were clearing the way for the devotional revolution of the nineteenth century—for a more introspective, otherworldly outlook which concentrated on the salvation of the individual rather than the transformation of society.

Conclusion

It would be convenient if an analysis of theological controversy could somehow isolate a single gene that programmed radicalism into the Presbyterian Church. Unfortunately, political affiliations were not structured by religious allegiances in any simple way, but resulted from a subtle combination of theological inheritance, social factors, and political circumstances. Ulster radicalism cannot be understood outside the experience of exclusion from the institutions of the state, the social conditions of the north of Ireland, and a deep-seated ambivalence towards a British government which was both the upholder of Anglican ascendancy and the ultimate guarantor of Protestant security. Presbyterianism, furthermore, was neither homogeneous nor static, but was fragmented and filtered through a series of doctrinal schisms. Unlike the monolithic edifices of its Anglican and Roman rivals, this fractured culture allowed theories of both religious and political dissidence to take hold and flourish.

The intellectual inheritance of the Scottish Reformation offered a rich and complex legacy of resistance and radicalism which provided a common platform on which Presbyterians of all theological preferences could unite. The basic principle that Jesus Christ was the sole lawgiver in the Church, though applied in a variety of ways, was shared by all strands of Presbyterian opinion. In its most extreme manifestation, the older 'prophetic' theology called for Church and State to be brought together to create a society in social and political conformity to the word of God, a vision still shared by those groups which adhered to the Solemn League and Covenant. In an age of social and political disruption, it retained its attraction for poorer Presbyterians in the Synod of Ulster, the Secession, and most of all the Reformed Presbytery. The political theology of the Covenanters, which asserted that all government, temporal and spiritual, must be based on those patterns allegedly found in the Scriptures, was violently at odds with the development of an erastian, parliamentary regime. The apocalyptic mood of the 1790s was exploited by enlightened republicans from Belfast who wished to harness the energies of the lower orders to the United Irish programme, a process described more fully in Chapter 8.

In their insistence on the supremacy of individual conscience over received authority, the New Lights also regarded themselves as the genuine heirs of the Reformation heritage. The call to separate Christianity from human policy echoed the fundamental Protestant dichotomy between human corruption, evidenced in the false ceremonies and beliefs which had debased the Church, and divine truth as embodied in the Scriptures. While their political principles were no doubt derived from a common Presbyterianism, however, they also reflected the rationalism of non-subscribing divinity. The vital ingredient here was not Arianism, for Arianism did not possess a distinct identity in eighteenth-century Ireland.[127] Far more important to the evolution of radical ideology was the non-subscribers' battle for freedom of enquiry, and their conviction that civil and religious liberty were inextricably linked. A young probationer expelled from the Presbytery of Bangor following his involvement in the '98 rebellion reminded his former colleagues of the 'REPUBLICAN MORALITY' which they had all preached: 'that religion is a personal thing—that Christ is head of the church—that his kingdom is not of this world—that the WILL OF THE PEOPLE should be the SUPREME LAW'.[128] Here was the authentic voice of New Light radicalism.

The tensions between these various positions had vital implications for the United Irish movement. The political theology of the Seceders and Covenanters remained primarily sectarian in character. Each saw itself as the true church-in-exile; there was no attempt to construct alliances across denominational boundaries in opposition to Anglican hegemony. The role of New Light divinity in delegitimizing the established order was very different. While the Seceders and Covenanters merely rejected the establishment, the non-subscribers who dominated the Synod of Ulster rejected the establishment principle itself, drawing on natural jurisprudence to develop a theory of resistance grounded on a general right to worship God freely. In conclusion, however, it is worth recalling just how much these groups had in common. All subscribed to the same dichotomy between human fallibility and divine omnipotence which underlay the renunciation of Rome. Their understanding of history revolved around an epic struggle between scriptural religion and superstitious traditions. All believed that the headship of the Church had been usurped by civil governments who interfered with ecclesiastical affairs, and above all by the papacy. The remainder of this book describes how, in the domestic and international crises of the late eighteenth century, these various antagonisms forced their way to the surface.

---

[127] There is little purchase, it seems, in Jonathan Clark's argument that the Trinitarian controversy was the *primum mobile* of ideological conflict between 1688 and 1832. Within Ulster Presbyterianism, at least, formulations of Trinitarian doctrine were indistinct and the emergence of a moderate consensus within the Synod allowed the issue to recede.

[128] Quoted in W. T. Latimer, 'David Bailie Warden, Patriot, 1798', *UJA*, 2nd ser., 13 (1907), 29–38.

PART II

The Superior Diffusion of Political
Information Among Them

5
THE IMPERIAL CRISIS, 1775–1783

PRESBYTERIAN radicalism began not with the French Revolution, as historians have sometimes assumed, but with its American predecessor. In February 1797, when United Irish agitation in Ulster was reaching its height, Dr William Richardson, Anglican vicar of a village near Armagh, wrote a long letter to the Duke of Abercorn expounding his own fascinating analysis of the political crisis. He began by tracing the origin of the troubles of the 1790s to the dispute between Britain and its colonies:

American Topics during the War inflamed and discontented more than before, American Success gave Courage to the Factious, and the Volunteer Army Confidence in their own Strength. During the Contest, deep political Schemes were formed, and Belfast I think took the Lead. That they had a deliberate Plan of Revolution formed in 1780, I think I can demonstrate. Some time ago talking with a Loyalist Farmer on the novelty of some political Doctrines, he said they were not new, for they had been taught them all at Belfast at the great Volunteer Review in 1780. On asking Particulars he said at the Houses where they were billeted and sumptuously entertained gratis, the master came to them where they were drinking, sat down with them, entered into Politicks, told them their Grievances, taught them how they were to obtain Redress, and conjured them never to think of laying down their Arms until they had made the Nation Free.[1]

Richardson was not alone in identifying the American revolt as the first crack in the eighteenth-century order. The loyalist historian of the '98 rebellion, Sir Richard Musgrave, maintained that communication with the citizens of the United States had reawakened the republican disposition of the northern Dissenters and, combined with the success of the first Dungannon meeting in 1782, had taught them that an armed assembly could dictate to Parliament.[2] When the radical Dr William Drennan came to chart the polarization which had led to the rebellion he too began with the American war, which had 'created and diffused a belief, that the Constitution as renovated at the revolution and accession, had again shifted from its foundation'.[3]

At first glance, it would seem that the decade or so after 1775 has not suffered from neglect by Irish historians. Few episodes, after all, have been subject to such heavy scrutiny as the rise of the Volunteers, the inauguration of 'Grattan's parliament', and the Anglo-Irish relationship in the 1780s. Most of the existing literature, however, concentrates on the high politics of the period; there has been less consideration of the experiences of the rank-and-file members of the Volunteers who were drawn into the public sphere for the first time. In this chapter my principal

[1] Richardson to [Abercorn], 22 Feb. 1797, PRONI, Abercorn Papers, T2541/IB3/6/5. I have modernized the punctuation in this quotation.
[2] Richard Musgrave, *Memoirs of the Different Rebellions in Ireland* (Dublin, 1801), 152.
[3] William Drennan, *A Letter to the Right Honourable Charles James Fox*, 2nd edn. (Dublin, 1806), 11–12.

concern is not with the well-known *événements* of 1782, nor with the course of Anglo-Irish relations in the 1780s; my aim is rather to convey something of the depth of the rapid politicization of Ulster society which took place as Anglo-American ties were dissolved.

Ulster Presbyterians and the American Revolution

On the morning of 18 April 1775, at Lexington Green in Massachusetts, the first shots were fired in what became known as the American War of Independence.[4] The ensuing conflict, which lasted until 1783 and saw military operations in four continents, led to the loss of the jewel in Britain's first imperial crown. Inevitably, the dismemberment of the Empire produced domestic troubles within the British Isles; one recent survey has described the American war as the 'most anguished period of internal turmoil and external retreat before the experience of war and decolonization in the years 1939–79'.[5] Eventually, the American rebellion would create the backdrop against which the Irish elite was able to negotiate a new commercial and constitutional settlement with London. As we shall see in the next chapter, the imperial crisis also required an adjustment of the balance of power within Ireland. The colonial campaign forced British subjects everywhere to rethink the costs, benefits, and moral implications of the imperial project; it questioned not merely the constitutional framework of the Empire, but the basis of the eighteenth-century British state itself. Among the Ulster Presbyterians, who had been effusively loyal under William III and the first two Hanoverians, its effect was to delegitimize the imperial monarchy of George III.

Irish Presbyterians and American colonists belonged to the same intellectual, cultural, and political world. The long crisis which followed the conclusion of the Seven Years' War therefore placed domestic disputes in a wider context, enabling Irish radicals to portray the conflict as part of a conspiracy against liberty throughout the Empire. There were obvious parallels between the colonists' case and Irish constitutional demands, now taken up by a small group of 'patriots' in the House of Commons, and the American cause accordingly attracted widespread sympathy among the Protestant elite. Although they would eventually repudiate the British constitution, the colonists had initially taken their stand on the ground of the ancient constitution, claiming the '*hereditary Rights of British Subjects*', inherited from their forefathers and enshrined in American laws and customs.[6] It was feared that, if British supremacy over the colonies was established, the subjection of Ireland could not

---

[4] For a valuable general account see Stephen Conway, *The War of American Independence 1775–1783* (London, 1995), ch. 8.

[5] Geoffrey Holmes and Daniel Szechi, *The Age of Oligarchy: Pre-Industrial Britain 1722–1783* (London, 1993), 290.

[6] Jack Greene, *Peripheries and Centre: Constitutional Development in the Extended Polities of the British Empire and the United States, 1606–1788* (Athens, Ga., 1986), chs. 1–7; the quotation is from p. 34. J. G. A. Pocock, 'The Revolution against Parliament', in id. (ed.), *Three British Revolutions: 1641, 1688, 1776* (Princeton, 1980), 265–88.

be far behind.[7] American arguments echoed the writings of Molyneux and Swift, and looked to Irish history for precedents,[8] just as Irish politicians came to adopt the new techniques of non-consumption agreements, conventions, congresses, and committees of correspondence. It was in the north, however, that the Irish–American connection was closest. As one Dissenting clergyman wrote:

A few Generations lead us back to the Origin of American Colonization, when the Inhabitants of the British Isles first explored its pathless Desarts [*sic*], in Quest of that Liberty and Peace which their Country denied them: And every succeeding Year has transported Multitudes from every Corner of these Lands, so that there is scarcely a Protestant Family, of the middle and lower Classes among us, who does not reckon Kindred with the Inhabitants of that extensive Continent.[9]

By 1776 the departure of emigrant ships from Londonderry, Belfast, and Newry was a familiar feature of Ulster life. A recent study has estimated that at least 200,000 left the province over the first three-quarters of the eighteenth century, the vast majority of them Presbyterians. This figure represents a huge proportion of a population which numbered somewhere between 400,000 and 600,000 during the period.[10] Although half of the total was made up of individual emigrants travelling as indentured servants or 'redemptioners', family and business networks were often transplanted to the colonies; on occasion, entire communities emigrated *en masse*, as when the Revd Thomas Clark led 300 families from his Ballybay congregation to the new world in 1764.[11] Prior to the revolution it was the rural poor who were most likely to seek a better life in the New World. The haemorrhage of artisans and farmers from the northern ports was a source of great consternation in Ulster where it was feared that the resulting depopulation was damaging not only to Protestant security in Ireland, but also to the economy. In 1773 the *Belfast News-Letter* regretted that 'the North of Ireland has in the last five or six years been drained of one fourth of its trading cash, and the like proportion of the Manufacturing people'.[12] When

---

[7] Francis Dobbs, *A History of Irish Affairs, from the 12th of October, 1779, to the 15th of September, 1782* (Dublin, 1782), 8–9.   [8] Greene, *Peripheries and Centre*, 98, 131.

[9] William Steel Dickson, *Sermons on the Following Subjects (I) On the Advantages of a National Repentance, (II) On the Ruinous Effects of Civil War, (III) On the Coming of the Son of Man, (IV) On the Hope of Meeting, Knowing, and Rejoicing with Virtuous Friends in a Future World* (Belfast, 1778), 45.

[10] K. A. Miller, *Emigrants and Exiles: Ireland and the Irish Exodus to North America* (Oxford, 1985), 152; Miller's is now the best account of Presbyterian emigration, but R. J. Dickson, *Ulster Emigration to Colonial America 1718–1775*, 2nd edn. with a new introduction by G. E. Kirkham (Omagh, 1988) is still useful. For Ulster–American politics and culture see Maldwyn A. Jones, 'The Scotch-Irish in British America', in Bernard Bailyn and P. D. Morgan (eds.), *Strangers within the Realm: Cultural Margins of the First British Empire* (Chapel Hill, NC, 1991), 284–5; D. N. Doyle, *Ireland, Irishmen, and Revolutionary America, 1760–1820* (Cork, 1981); E. R. R. Green, 'The Scotch-Irish and the Coming of the Revolution in North Carolina', *IHS* 7/26 (Sept. 1950), 77–86; D. F. Norton, 'Francis Hutcheson in America', *SVEC* 114 (1976), 1553–5; Caroline Robbins, '"When it is that Colonies May Turn Independent": An Analysis of the Environment and Politics of Francis Hutcheson (1694–1746)', *WMQ*, 3rd ser., 11 (1954), 214–51.

[11] Thomas Clark, *Pastoral Letter to the Associate Congregation of Presbyterians in Ballybay New Erection* (Monaghan, 1807).

[12] [Henry Joy (ed.)], *Historical Collections Relative to the Town of Belfast* (Belfast, 1817), 114.

shipping resumed after the war, losses were even greater, despite the introduction of legislation to curb emigration, and they now stretched into the ranks of the upwardly mobile—shopkeepers, schoolmasters, and physicians.[13]

Historians have related the patterns of Ulster emigration to economic distress and the social dislocation caused by fluctuations in the linen industry and the commercialization of Irish agriculture. Presbyterian sensitivity to the burdens imposed by the Anglican establishment ensured that the act of emigration quickly acquired an ideological complexion, however, as passengers to the New World imagined themselves escaping from Irish slavery into the land of liberty. In the light of the colonial conflict the decision to leave Ireland could be interpreted as a declaration of loyalty. A County Down land agent recorded in 1775 that the young men on board one emigrant ship 'went avowedly to aid their Dissenting brethren in America, as well as to get clear (of what they call) oppression at home'. The same writer found pro-American sentiment was manifesting itself in resistance to recruitment into the army.[14]

The pro-American sympathies of the Ulster Presbyterians should be seen in the context of a wider Dissenting radicalism whose most famous exponents were Richard Price, Joseph Priestley, Thomas Hollis, Capel Lofft, John Jebb, James Burgh, and Richard Baron. As the heirs of the commonwealthsmen, these activists shared a common ideological vocabulary with their transatlantic brethren, rooted in the interwoven struggles for civil and religious liberty which had taken place under the Stuarts. The canon of this 'real whig' tradition ran from Milton, Harrington, and Sidney to Nevile, Molesworth, Gordon, and Trenchard, sustaining a reading of English history which originated during the civil war and had been recycled by the opponents of Walpole's administration.[15] For decades these real whigs had struggled to preserve British liberty by defending the independence of the House of Commons against the encroachments of the Crown. Their assault on the Whig establishment was generally restricted to demands for more frequent elections and the removal of placemen and pensioners from the Commons, a vision of politics often referred to as the 'Country' platform. By the middle of the 1770s, however, the radical critique had come to focus on the deficiencies of the electoral system itself. For the next seventy years the chief demands of reformers turned upon the redistribution of seats to reflect the changing population and prosperity of the nation, and the widening of the franchise. It has been convincingly argued that the vital step in shifting attention to the limits of the electoral process was the American assertion that there should be no taxation without representation.[16] There was another important way in which the breach with America transformed English opposition politics that did

---

[13] Miller, *Emigrants and Exiles*, 170–1; M. A. Jones, 'Ulster Emigration, 1783–1815', in E. R. R. Green (ed.), *Essays in Scotch-Irish History* (London, 1969), 46–68.

[14] John Moore to Arthur Annesley, 4 Oct. 1775, in W. H. Crawford (ed.), *Letters of an Ulster Land Agent 1774–85 (The Letter-Books of John Moore of Clough, County Down)* (Belfast, 1976), 5.

[15] The classic study of the American commonwealthsmen is Bernard Bailyn's *The Ideological Origins of the American Revolution* (Cambridge, Mass., 1967).

[16] John Brewer, *Party Ideology and Popular Politics at the Accession of George III* (Cambridge, 1976), ch. 10.

not become fully apparent until the 1790s. This was the republican strain injected into British political discourse by Tom Paine. *Rights of Man*, as much as *Common Sense*, was informed by Paine's American experience; his demolition of the hereditary principle which propped up the monarchy and aristocracy was a product of the colonial debate.[17]

If the prominence of Dissenting intellectuals in radical activity reflected historical ties between the nonconforming sects and whig ideology, it was also an indication of the eighteenth-century assumption that civil and religious liberty were closely related. In the canon of the commonwealthsmen the growth of popery loomed as large as the encroachments of tyrannical kings. America possessed powerful symbolic significance as the traditional asylum for nonconformist refugees, and as a primitive society free of the social inequalities and corrupt manners which characterized the Old World. For Dissenters it was no accident when attempts to impose new taxes on the American colonies in the 1760s were accompanied by plans to establish an Anglican episcopate there. The pattern was apparently repeated in 1774, when the Coercive Acts passed in response to the Boston Tea Party coincided with the introduction of the Quebec Act. This statute both recognized the establishment of 'popery' in Quebec and provided for the government of the province by royal prerogative rather than parliamentary institutions, a nice illustration of the dual nature of the menace perceived by the American settlers.

The colonial struggle could thus be depicted as a war of religion as well as a collision of rival constitutional positions. As American historians have amply documented, the imperial crisis was interpreted in providential terms; denominational loyalties were important in mobilizing popular support for the patriot cause, and religious faith invested constitutional controversies with a sense of immediacy which helps explain the resort to armed resistance in 1775.[18] In Ireland, orthodox Presbyterians placed the revolution within the same apocalyptic framework employed by many American Calvinists. One Seceding minister who had emigrated from County Monaghan to Pennsylvania informed his Irish friends of the anxiety and terror excited by news of Anglican bishops coming to the colonies. 'The blood of many Christians', he warned, 'is to be found on the skirts of the[ir] surplices.'[19] New Light Dissenters voiced the same concerns, albeit in more enlightened language. Many would have read Richard Price's extravagant claim that next to the introduction of Christianity the American Revolution 'may prove the most important step in the progressive course of human improvement'.[20] As late as 1792 the Revd Samuel Barber of Rathfriland advised his brethren to turn their eyes

[17] Gregory Claeys, *Thomas Paine: Social and Political Thought* (Boston, 1989), ch. 2.

[18] Patricia Bonomi, *Under the Cope of Heaven: Religion, Society, and Politics in Colonial America* (New York, 1986); Carl Bridenbaugh, *Mitre and Sceptre: Transatlantic Faiths, Ideas, Personalities, and Politics, 1689–1775* (New York, 1962); T. M. Brown, 'The Image of the Beast: Anti-Papal Rhetoric in Colonial America', in R. O. Curry and T. M. Brown (eds.), *Conspiracy: The Fear of Subversion in American History* (New York, 1972), 1–20; J. C. D. Clark, *The Language of Liberty 1660–1832: Political Discourse and Social Dynamics in the Anglo-American World* (Cambridge, 1994).

[19] Thomas Clark to William Weir, 17 May 1771, PRONI, Weir MSS, D1140/1.

[20] Colin Bonwick, *English Radicals and the American Revolution* (Chapel Hill, 1977), 157.

westward to the expanding American empire where every man worshipped God as his conscience dictated.[21]

As the rift between the colonies and Britain widened, parallels between the Ulster Presbyterians and their American relatives became more explicit. At a Belfast town meeting in April 1770 a toast was drunk to 'the American Colonies, and may the Descendants of those who fled from Tyranny in one Country never be forced to submit to its galling Yoke in another'.[22] The Revd William Campbell of Armagh later wrote that the Presbyterians of Ulster believed that the Americans were fighting on their behalf, and that the liberties of the Empire at large depended on the result. He described the pride of the Ulster Presbyterians when they heard that their friends and relatives composed 'the flower of Washington's army . . . still, as their fathers had been, the determined enemies of tyranny and arbitrary power, which ever pursued them, and by a strange fatality from the same quarter, *England*'.[23] The connections were made plain in 1776 when a Belfast edition of William Molyneux's classic *The Case of Ireland's Being Bound by Acts of Parliament in England Stated* was produced, with a preface drawing parallels between the encroachments on American constitutional rights and the restrictions placed on Irish trade.[24]

Northern expressions of solidarity with the American rebels naturally attracted criticism. Presbyterian sympathy for the colonial cause alarmed the defenders of Church and State, reopening old divisions between Anglicans and Dissenters. One vicar in Tyrone, finding himself surrounded by 'rebels', grumbled that 'The king is reviled, the ministry cursed, religion trampled underfoot.'[25] In Ballymoney, County Antrim, members of the Established Church withdrew from a village club following disagreements with the local Dissenters over the colonial crisis. The Declaration of Independence, John Caldwell recalled, was considered 'an outrageous daring against the spiritual power, as well as the temporal, of the Lord's anointed, and created a lasting feud amongst the hitherto happy residents'. His grandfather prayed for those fighting for civil and religious liberty across the Atlantic, and the local women played their part by making clothes for colonial soldiers. When news of Bunker's Hill reached Ballymoney Caldwell was taken by his nurse to a bonfire to celebrate the American triumph.[26] At a commemoration of the battle of Aughrim in Tandragee, County Armagh, a toast was drunk to 'The memory of the saints and martyrs that fell at Lexington'.[27] In Belfast, where reports of the war were eagerly awaited, there could be no doubt where sympathies lay. In December of 1777 William Drennan, an Irish medical student at Edinburgh, wrote home to congratulate his relatives on the

---

[21] Samuel Barber, MS sermon on Revelation 18: 20 (1791), Presbyterian Historical Society of Ireland, 18–19. See also 'Extract from a letter from a merchant in Philadelphia to his brother-in-law near Saint-field', *BNL*, 26 Apr. 1791; 'Common Sense' [John Keogh], 'To the Presbyterians of Ulster', Sept. 1792, PRO, HO, 100/38/5.   [22] [Joy], *Historical Collections*, 110; for further examples, see p. 117.
[23] William Campbell, 'Sketches of the History of the Presbyterians in Ireland' (1803), PHSI, Campbell MSS, 235–6.
[24] 'The Publisher's Advertisement', in William Molyneux, *The Case of Ireland's being Bound by Acts of Parliament in England Stated* (Belfast, 1776).
[25] Philip Skelton to William Knox, 22 Nov. 1777, 'Additional Manuscripts of Captain H. V. Knox', in HMC, *Report on MSS in Various Collections*, vi (1909), 446.
[26] John Caldwell, 'Particulars of a North County Irish Family', PRONI, Caldwell Papers, T3541/5/3, p. 4.   [27] R. B. McDowell, *Irish Public Opinion, 1750–1800* (London, 1944), 43.

surrender of General Burgoyne at Saratoga. The British empire, he declared, was 'degenerating into a state of political dotage, prophetical of its final dissolution'.[28]

The war impinged directly upon domestic life throughout the three kingdoms, and clergymen, like other public figures, were faced with political choices which could not easily be avoided.[29] 'To have offered up prayers for success to the English arms', opined the Revd William Campbell, 'would have been a prostitution of character, a solemn mockery of things divine, approaching perhaps to blasphemy.'[30] The fast-days appointed by government, always controversial since they reminded Presbyterians of the royal supremacy of the Established Church, were generally ignored, and some preachers even used these occasions to criticize government policy. William Steel Dickson began a long and turbulent political career with two such sermons, 'On the Advantage of National Repentance' and 'On the ruinous effects of Civil War', preached to his Ballyhalbert congregation on 13 December 1776 and 27 February 1778 respectively. Dickson had been absorbed in parochial and family duties until the outbreak of the war jolted him into action: 'Having paid considerable attention to jurisprudence, in the course of my studies, and read Locke, Montesquieu, Pufendorf, etc. etc. my mind instantly revolted against the mad crusade; and, while I regretted its folly, I execrated its wickedness.'[31] He therefore began to apply biblical principles to current events, an exercise he would later call 'scripture politics'. These two sermons provoked a general outcry and accusations of disloyalty in his neighbourhood.[32] Dickson was the first of a series of Dissenting preachers who interpreted the war as divine punishment for the corruption prevalent in British society. He alerted his congregation to the disastrous consequences of the conflict —the restrictions on commerce, the burden in taxation, and the danger of invasion by France and Spain.[33] He also warned of the wickedness of fighting with brother Protestants. The colonists were not only kinsmen, after all, but Protestants who had fled religious persecution at home and had recently fought alongside British troops against the French. Similar sentiments can be found in an anti-war ballad published in Belfast in 1776, which reminded 'all Protestant brethren' that 'A house that is divided | Will never stand but fall'.[34]

[28] Drennan to Martha McTier, 13 Dec. 1777, D. A. Chart, *The Drennan Letters* (Belfast, 1931), 4.

[29] The war prompted a wave of Anglican loyalism in England, described in Paul Langford, 'The English Clergy and the American Revolution', in Eckhart Hellmuth (ed.), *The Transformation of Political Culture in England and Germany in the Late Eighteenth Century* (Oxford, 1990), 275–307; and J. E. Bradley, 'The Anglican Pulpit, the Social Order and the Resurgence of Toryism during the American Revolution', *Albion*, 21 (1989), 361–88. We know little about the response of the established clergy in Ireland, but see Thomas Leland, *A Sermon Preached in the Church of St. Anne's, Dublin, on Wednesday the 10th of February, 1779; being the Day Appointed by Authority for a General Fast and Humiliation* (Dublin, 1779), for a measured defence of the government. [30] Campbell, 'Sketches', PHSI, Campbell MSS, 236.

[31] William Steel Dickson, *A Narrative of the Confinement and Exile of William Steel Dickson* (Dublin, 1812), 7.

[32] Ibid. 8. Another fast-day sermon, William Blakely's *The Nature and Foundation of Civil Government, and Duty of Subjects. A Sermon from Romans 13: 1–3, Preached in Carrickfergus on December 13, 1776, Being the Fast Day Appointed by Government* (Belfast, 1777), has unfortunately been lost: see Thomas Witherow (ed.), *Historical and Literary Memorials of Presbyterianism in Ireland*, 2 vols. (Belfast, 1879–80), ii. 329. James Bryson's MS sermons, preserved in QUB, contain a sermon preached on the American war on 13 Dec. 1776. [33] Dickson, *Sermons on the Following Subjects*, 19–23.

[34] *A New Song Called the Beautiful Phoenix, Together with the Battle of Bunker's Hill* (Belfast, [1776]).

Among Ulster businessmen, sympathy for colonial liberties was coupled with fears for the disruption of trade. On 4 November (William III's birthday) 1775, a town meeting of Belfast's principal inhabitants complained of the injury done to manufacturers by the loss of American trade and petitioned the King 'to sheath in mercy the sword of civil war; that a foundation may be laid for a speedy and happy restoration of that *old constitutional system*'. Among the 250 signatures were many names which would soon be prominent in Belfast radicalism: Waddell Cunningham, Henry Joy, the Revd James Crombie, Samuel McTier, Dr Alexander Haliday, Thomas McCabe, Gilbert McIlveen, and Robert Simms.[35] The situation grew worse early in 1776 when the British government banned the export of provisions except to Britain and the loyal colonies.

The united front presented by Ulster Presbyterians appears in sharp contrast with Scottish opinion. Although the colonies found powerful advocates among the Seceders and the 'popular party' in the General Assembly, the 'Moderate' regime of William Robertson threw its weight behind the government.[36] Irish students at Edinburgh, like the young William Drennan, were disgusted by the vocal support of Robertson and the 'Moderate literati' for the British war effort. Drennan, son of the minister of the Belfast First Congregation, had already obtained an MA degree from Glasgow, and was now studying medicine under the guardianship of his sister, the redoubtable Martha McTier. After the outbreak of hostilities he wrote home detailing with dismay the subscriptions of the professors and of the college Speculative Society towards the war effort. By way of contrast he recorded the views of the Irish students:

We spent a pleasant evening on the Fast Day which the Scotch spent in humiliation and prayer. We made every science which we knew of produce a toast applicable to politics and many of them were excellent. We concluded with unanimously wishing that all the tyrants in Europe had but one neck, that neck laid on the block and one of us appointed executioner.[37]

The General Assembly of the Church of Scotland was the scene of virulent debates during these years as the popular party made several unsuccessful attempts to pass motions condemning government policy. Unfortunately, the minutes of the Synod of Ulster are confined to ecclesiastical finances and the supply of ministers, but other sources have survived which show that the war was also debated in Ireland. In an unpublished history of Irish Presbyterianism, William Campbell recorded that the Ulster Presbyterians condemned the war as 'unjust, cruel, and detestable'. In 1778, he notes, reports of disloyalty in the north were so common that the Dissenters were advised by friends in the Irish Parliament to clear their name. The Dublin ministers accordingly met in March with several leading 'Protestant Dissenting

[35] [Joy], *Historical Collections*, 118–21.

[36] R. K. Donovan, 'The Popular Party of the Church of Scotland and the American Revolution', in R. B. Sher and J. R. Smitten (eds.), *Scotland and America in the Age of the Enlightenment* (Edinburgh, 1990), 81–99; D. I. Fagerstrom, 'Scottish Opinion and the American Revolution', *WMQ*, 3rd ser., 11 (1954), 252–75.

[37] Drennan to Martha McTier, 23 Nov. 1777, 20 Jan. [1778], 2 Mar. [1778], PRONI, Drennan Papers, T765/13, 20, 26.

gentlemen', including Lord Templetown and Robert Stewart, the MP for Down. Stewart suggested an address condemning the ministry and the war, Templetown countered that the crisis called for a declaration of loyalty, and eventually the whole affair was dropped. A draft address circulated in the north was also rejected, because the northern clergy wanted an unqualified denunciation of the war and the government.[38]

Unfortunately for the Irish elite the year of American independence also saw the first general election to be held under the Octennial Act. Ulster Presbyterians had already been angered by the passage of an act of Parliament in 1774 excluding them from voting at the vestry meetings of the Established Church. This local example of taxation without representation met with a storm of protest. In response to thirty-nine petitions from towns and parishes all over the province, the act was repealed by a bill introduced by Thomas Conolly when Parliament reassembled in 1776.[39] Conolly, one of the MPs for County Derry, had been forced to act by a widespread rebellion among his tenants who, under the leadership of the Revd Benjamin McDowell, had published resolutions condemning the Vestry Act and threatening to vote for an independent candidate at the next election.[40] McDowell, who had been born in New Jersey and educated at Princeton, reminded his people of the imperial context of this conflict: 'our friends and fellow subjects bleeding in defence of their rights in one part of our dominions, the Roman Catholic religion and military despotism established by law in another'.[41] In William Drennan's opinion, the Presbyterian victory could be attributed to the dispute with America.[42]

In Derry the repentant Conolly held on to his seat, but in Antrim the Dissenters won a stunning victory by electing James Wilson against a conjunction of the landlords who dominated that county—Hertford, Antrim, Donegall, and Massareene. Wilson, a half-pay naval officer who had resigned his commission rather than be forced to choose between disobeying the king and killing '*kindred fellow-subjects and countrymen*' in America, had given assurances that he would notify his constituents of all proposed legislation and would vote according to their instructions.[43] Both he and his running mate subscribed to a test promising to refuse any place or pension, to vote for the amendment or repeal of Poynings' Law, and to support 'a more fair

[38] Campbell, 'Sketches', PHSI, Campbell MSS, 236–7; William Bruce, 'Facts Relating to the Protestant Dissenters of Ireland, Beginning from the Year 1778', PRONI, Bruce MSS, D2673, uncatalogued, 2–3.

[39] *Journals of the House of Commons of the Kingdom of Ireland*, 19 vols. (Dublin, 1796–1800), ix. 176–85.

[40] The resolutions are reprinted, along with an inquiry by Conolly's agent into his tenants' opinions, in W. H. Crawford and B. Trainor (eds.), *Aspects of Irish Social History 1750–1800* (Belfast, 1969), 156–62.

[41] [McDowell], 'To the Free Electors of the County of Londonderry', *London-Derry Journal*, 9 Sept. 1775, repr. in Crawford and Trainor, *Aspects of Irish Social History*, 70.

[42] Drennan to Martha McTier, 3 Apr. [1776], *Drennan Letters*, 1.

[43] [Joy], *Historical Collections*, 123–4, 127–8. Wilson was promised an annuity of £500. When this was not regularly paid he became a government supporter and was rewarded with the command of a revenue cruiser: see G. O. Sayles, 'Contemporary Sketches of the Members of the Irish Parliament in 1782', *PRIA* 56C, no. 3 (1954), 233. For the importance of American issues in the 1776 election, see *Letters Addressed to the Electors of the County of Antrim. By a Freeholder* (Belfast, 1776), pp. x–xix. Two independents were also elected for Donegal with Dissenting support: Desmond Murphy, *Derry, Donegal and Modern Ulster 1790–1921* (Derry, 1981), 4.

and equal representation of the people in parliament'.[44] Such pledges won over the Dissenting congregations who began to declare their support in the *Belfast News-Letter*.[45] In Belfast itself the townspeople defied their landlord, Lord Donegall, to vote for Wilson. It seems that a convention had arisen whereby Donegall's tenants cast one vote according to his directions and the other according to their own preferences. On this occasion, however, Donegall demanded both votes, and Dr Alexander Haliday, recognized leader of the Belfast whigs, wrote to him protesting that the town needed at least one proper representative.[46]

After the cessation of hostilities the American republic continued to stimulate Irish radicalism by providing a model for a reformed constitution. By 1783 the constitutions of the new American states, according to a contributor to the *Belfast News-Letter*, were 'in the hands of every person of reading'.[47] The benefits of the republican system of government and the egalitarianism of American society were recurrent themes in Ulster–American correspondence during this period. John Gamble, who toured the north of Ireland in 1819, was shown hundreds of emigrant letters boasting that American citizens were not obliged 'to uncover the head, or to bend the knee, to any stern Lord, arrogant Squire, proud Vicar, or, above all, upstart Agent'.[48] The increasing prosperity of the United States, usually attributed to its republican system of government, was frequently contrasted with the poverty of the heavily taxed Irish peasantry.[49] After the suppression of the '98 rebellion the United States once more became a haven for Presbyterian radicals, for whom America was still 'the land of freedom and of liberty . . . accounted like the land of promise flowing with milk and honey . . . to those labouring under Egyptian bondage'.[50]

To sum up then, the American Revolution can be seen as a decisive turning point in the development of Presbyterian attitudes towards the establishment. In the middle of the eighteenth century, 'patriotism' in Ireland had united libertarian sentiment with vigorous support for imperial expansion. In the light of recent colonial policies, however, it was no longer clear that the British government stood on the side of civil and religious liberty. The War of Independence abruptly terminated the support which most Dissenters had willingly given to the Whig regime since the Revolution Settlement. Simultaneously, the colonial debate brought questions of sovereignty and representation into sharper definition. In future years the new republic would offer a model of an alternative political structure without restrictions on political participation or religious worship. Perhaps the most important consequence of the American war, however, was an indirect one. The removal of troops,

---

[44] [Joy], *Historical Collections*, 131–2. The inhabitants of the county borough of Carrickfergus drew up a similar test for their candidates: *BNL*, 31 May 1776.

[45] Martha McTier to Drennan, 19 Jan. [1776], PRONI, Drennan Papers, T765/1.

[46] Martha McTier to Drennan, 1 Apr. [1776], *Drennan Letters*, 1.

[47] *BNL*, 29 Aug. 1783.

[48] John Gamble, *A View of Society and Manners in the North of Ireland* (London, 1813), 367.

[49] Job Johnson to John, Robert, and James Johnson, 27 Nov. 1767, John Dunlop to Robert Rutherford, 12 May 1785, John Nevin to James Nevin, 10 Apr. 1804, PRONI, T3700, T1336/1/27, D2966/57/1; E. R. R. Green, 'Ulster Emigrants' Letters', in id., *Essays in Scotch-Irish History*, 87–103.

[50] John Kerr, 10 May 1810, quoted in Miller, *Emigrants and Exiles*, 190.

combined with the entry of France and later Spain into the war, left Ireland open to invasion. In 1778, as the exploits of the American privateer John Paul Jones exposed the vulnerability of the northern coastline, the Ulster Presbyterians began to make plans to defend their liberty and property from enemies both external and internal.

Citizens-in-arms: the political culture of Volunteering

The creation of the first Volunteer companies in 1778 was partly the result of the deficiencies of the Irish militia, a local auxiliary force which existed to defend the island against both domestic insurrection and foreign invasion, and had in fact been called out in 1715, 1719, 1745, 1756, and 1760.[51] Under existing legislation the king, lord lieutenant, and lords justice were able to issue commissions authorizing the gentry to raise companies of infantry and troops of cavalry for the protection of their counties. Lack of equipment and organization, demonstrated in February 1760 when Thurot captured Carrickfergus and threatened Belfast, led to calls for the creation of a properly armed and disciplined force, and this concern for security was combined with patriot ideology when Henry Flood campaigned unsuccessfully for new militia legislation in the 1760s and 1770s. Demands for militia reform became all the more urgent in 1776 when 4,000 regular troops were withdrawn from Ireland for service across the Atlantic, yet official reluctance to arm the people and financial difficulties stood in the way.

It was this vacuum which compelled the citizens of Belfast to form an independent volunteer company on St Patrick's Day, 1778, declaring publicly their refusal to accept commissions or pay under the Crown or to take any military oath.[52] The example of Belfast was quickly emulated throughout the northern counties; as the Earl of Charlemont, commander-in-chief of the Ulster army, later wrote, 'the dragon's teeth were sown, and the fertile soil everywhere produced a plenteous crop of soldiers'.[53] The movement spread south at the end of that year and accelerated dramatically when Spain entered the war in 1779. Numbers jumped from 15,000 in April to 30,000 in September, to over 40,000 in December. By the middle of the following year up to 60,000 men had enrolled, almost half of them in Ulster.[54] Initially at least, they were drawn from the middle classes of the towns and the better-off tenant-farmers who could afford the necessary uniforms and equipment, said to cost £80 for a horseman and £20 for a foot-soldier.[55] Although the officers were usually recruited from the landed gentry, the rank and file in Ulster were Presbyterians.

Most accounts of the 1780s focus on the alliance between the Volunteers and the patriot MPs which eventually renegotiated the imperial relationship between

[51] No comprehensive study of the Volunteers has been published, but see P. D. H. Smyth, 'The Volunteer Movement in Ulster: Background and Development 1745–85', Ph.D. thesis (QUB, 1974); id. '"Our Cloud-Cap't Grenadiers": The Volunteers as a Military Force', *Irish Sword*, 13 (1978–9), 185–207.   [52] Ibid. 185–7.

[53] 'Lord Charlemont's Memoirs of his Political Life', *Charlemont MSS*, i. 51.

[54] Smyth, '"Cloud-Cap't Grenadiers"', 195.

[55] Lord Pembroke to Lord Carmarthen, 2–11 Aug. 1781, *Pembroke Papers (1780–1794): Letters and Diaries of Henry, Tenth Earl of Pembroke and his Circle*, ed. Lord Herbert, 2 vols. (London, 1950), ii. 207.

Britain and Ireland. As the Volunteer army gained strength, a series of dramatic concessions was extorted from an English government weakened by the American war: the restrictions on Ireland's colonial trade were abolished, the Declaratory Act was repealed, and the right to legislate for Ireland renounced at Westminster. These victories, which owed as much to the changing international situation and to political developments in London as to the Volunteer conventions held in Ulster, were followed by a long, ineffective campaign for the reform of the Irish House of Commons. In this chapter, however, I want to turn from the high politics of volunteering—now well-trodden ground—to examine the experience of military and political mobilization at a local level. For the rank and file of Ireland's citizen militia, volunteering was an exciting adventure, an affirmation of citizenship, and proof that Ireland had at last taken its place among the nations of Europe.

Although the Volunteers eventually received official sanction when votes of thanks were passed in both Houses of Parliament in October 1779, their organization was, strictly speaking, illegal. From the beginning, many of the gentry were clearly suspicious of the companies which had sprung up on their estates. Many landed gentlemen joined to keep their tenantry under control; others simply jumped on the bandwagon when volunteering acquired a certain cachet.[56] Chichester Skeffington, brother of the Earl of Massareene, reluctantly agreed to raise a corps in Antrim town rather than injure his electoral interest there.[57] James Hamilton, agent on the Abercorn estates and captain of one of the Strabane companies, complained that 'Volunteering is as troublesome as electioneering, and is attended with a great deal of expense.' He conceded that the appearance of Volunteers had put an end to local crime and disturbances, but still had misgivings about their rapid expansion and their interference in politics.[58]

For the time being, however, the enthusiasm for volunteering was unstoppable. Ireland's gallant and glamorous defenders were celebrated in ballads, plays, and poems, in paintings, and on pottery.[59] For a historian of popular culture the symbolism of flags, banners, uniforms, toasts, glasses, goblets, and medals would make a fascinating subject, for it is from 'such trivia as songs and diversions, mottos and colours', as William Drennan observed, that national feeling can be discovered.[60] Although the ritual aspects of the movement have never been studied, it is clear from memoirs that the bright uniform of the Irish Volunteers left an indelible impression on everyone who wore it. In 1780 one traveller wrote:

---

[56] Francis Hardy, *Memoirs of the Political and Private Life of James Caulfeild, Earl of Charlemont* (London, 1810), 194; Dickson, *Narrative*, 12.

[57] A. P. W. Malcomson, 'Election Politics in the Borough of Antrim, 1750–1800', *IHS* 17/65 (1970), 46.

[58] Hamilton to Abercorn, 5 May 1780, PRONI, Abercorn Papers, T2541/IA1/29; see also Hamilton to Abercorn, 28 May 1780, ibid., T2541/IA1/13/34.

[59] See e.g. *The Patriot Soldier; or, Irish Volunteer. A Poem by a Member of the First Belfast Company* (Belfast, 1789).

[60] [Drennan], 'The Volunteers of Ireland', in William Guthrie (ed.), *An Improved System of Modern Geography*, Royal Irish Academy edn. (Dublin, 1789), 496.

On my last visit to Ireland I thought the people feverish, but I now think they are nearly frantic; every male above the very ragged gave the military salute; nothing hardly is spoke of but Volunteers; the Battle and Siege of Derry lately performed in mock array.[61]

Volunteering also provided an excellent excuse for balls and parties. From 1778 onwards the two Belfast companies patronized the Belfast theatre, and command performances were staged regularly to mark the great festivals of the whig calendar such as William III's birthday. The most popular play was Addison's tragedy *Cato*, traditionally associated with the whig cause. When the curtain fell there would be boos and hisses for 'the Aristocracy of Ireland' or cheers for 'the American Congress', and the musicians were called on to play the Volunteers' March and other patriotic airs.[62]

The highpoint of the Volunteer calendar was the summer review season, when companies from all over Ulster converged on the county towns. It was the appointment of exercising officers and reviewing generals that gave the scattered corps the appearance of a unified movement. The largest annual reviews, held in the Falls meadows outside Belfast, were great social events, lasting several days and attracting thousands of spectators. Dozens of companies made their way to Belfast from all over the province and were provided with accommodation. These gatherings were festive occasions for the whole community. In the evenings the local ladies were invited to dine with the officers and the reviews were often accompanied by assemblies and balls. Although the attendance figures recorded for these events vary considerably, there was general agreement that the largest gathering of Volunteers ever held took place in Belfast in 1781, when, according to Francis Dobbs, 5,383 Volunteers took part.[63]

If volunteering was, as one observer found, 'a trade of recreation', it was also an opportunity for political agitation.[64] On the final day of each review it was customary for the exercising officer to present an address to the reviewing general (often Charlemont himself), which was drafted by an assembly of delegates from all the companies present.[65] These reviews, particularly the Belfast ones, provided an opportunity for radicals to flex their muscles on their own home ground. Many rural visitors to Belfast would have received an education in democratic debate at these gatherings. In 1781 Sir John O'Neill, MP for Randalstown and colonel of the First Royal Regiment of Volunteers, found himself struggling to dilute the resolutions passed by the 'violent characters' of Belfast, which he described as 'the Boston of this country'.[66] His concern was echoed by an English aristocrat also present at the same occasion:

[61] James Steuart to Abercorn, 29 Aug. 1780, PRONI, Abercorn Papers, T2541/IA1/13/47.
[62] W. S. Clark, *The Irish Stage in the County Towns 1720–1800* (Oxford, 1965), 238–9, 243, 251. F. M. Litto, 'Addison's *Cato* in the Colonies', *WMQ*, 3rd ser., 23 (1966), 431–49, explores the American resonances of this play.   [63] Dobbs, *Irish Affairs*, 43.
[64] Pembroke to Carmarthen, 2–11 Aug. 1781, *Pembroke Papers*, ii. 207.
[65] Many of these addresses were written by William Drennan and can be found in his MS notebook, PRONI, T965/6.
[66] John O'Neill to Richard Jackson, 23 July 1781, PRONI, Hezlett Papers, D668/24/1/3.

The Original Armers of the people begin to tremble & make less secret than prudence ought to suggest, that the Catholicks alone can reduce to proper bounds the Republican spirit of the Presbiterians [*sic*], *vi*, & *armis*. During the Review Belfast was a perfect Boston & treason, I dare venture to say, was more freely spoke in the former.[67]

The practice of volunteering rested on a number of ideological suppositions, the most important of which was the eighteenth-century ideal of the citizen-soldier. 'The possession of arms', wrote William Drennan, 'is indeed the prime distinction of a freeman from a slave.'[68] Volunteering offered an opportunity for the middling ranks to affirm their civic identity, particularly important for Dissenters who were barred from public office until the repeal of the Test Act in 1780. In the early days especially there was considerable opposition to the Volunteer interference in polit- ical matters, hence the first resolution of the 1782 Dungannon convention which asserted that Irishmen, by taking up arms, did not forfeit the rights of citizens. A conception of the citizen-in-arms, ultimately of classical inspiration, implicitly sanc- tioned the intervention of the Volunteers in Irish politics, and appealed to the real whig instinct which saw an armed citizenry as the best method of preserving liberty.

By declaring that they would accept no financial assistance from the government nor swear any oath which bound them to use their military capabilities at the gov- ernment's request, the Belfast First Volunteer Company set a precedent which was soon followed in other districts in the north. It was this written engagement, as Peter Smyth has pointed out, which marked the appearance of a new concept of the inde- pendent Volunteer.[69] These associating principles varied from company to company, reflecting local conditions. The articles of association of the First Armagh Com- pany, used as a model by other local corps, included the pledge that except on the battlefield it would be governed by the democratically expressed wish of the majority.[70] The First Company of Newry Volunteers, led by Joseph Pollock, an elder of the non-subscribing congregation, a barrister, and author of the radical *Letters of Owen Roe O'Nial* (1779), resolved that their object was to defend their country against foreign and domestic enemies, 'to resist Usurpation and maintain the Constitution'.[71] The Volunteers of nearby Rathfriland associated to 'defend our civil and religious liberty and to keep the peace in our town and neighbourhood'. The moving spirit in Rathfriland was the New Light minister Samuel Barber, whose influence is re- flected in the fines imposed in the rules for speaking, laughing, swearing, drunken- ness, and being absent from public worship.[72] In County Monaghan the Lisnavein Independent Rangers pledged 'to defend ourselves from our natural enemies; to evidence our loyalty to his Majesty King George, and our attachment to our *civil*

---

[67] Pembroke to Carmarthen, 2–11 Aug. 1781, *Pembroke Papers*, ii. 203.

[68] [Drennan], 'Volunteers of Ireland', 495.

[69] Smyth, '"Cloud-Cap't Grenadiers"', 192–3. Outside Ulster, Volunteer corps seem to have adhered to more traditional notions of militia service.

[70] T. G. F. Patterson, 'The County Armagh Volunteers of 1778–1793', *UJA*, 3rd ser., 4 (1942), 40.

[71] Minute-book of the First Newry Volunteers, 1 Aug. 1780, PRONI, T3202/1A, p. 4.

[72] Andrew Morrow, 'The Revd Samuel Barber, A. M., and the Rathfriland Volunteers', *UJA*, 2nd ser., 14 (1908), 108.

constitution, founded upon Revolution principles; for the establishing of which our fore-fathers fought and bled; and which, at this time, require the exercise of every real friend of our civil and sacred privileges'.[73] The Lisnavein company was recruited from a Seceding congregation; the emphasis on their attachment to the *'civil* constitution' was probably necessary since the Solemn League and Covenant bound the Seceders not to recognize the Established Church.

As the examples of Barber and Rogers show, many Presbyterian clergymen, like Steel Dickson, exchanged the 'rusty black' for the 'glowing scarlet'.[74] Most conspicuous were the prominent New Light ministers like William Bruce of Lisburn, Andrew Craig of Moira, Boyle Moody of Newry, William Crawford of Strabane, James Crombie and James Bryson of Belfast, William Campbell of Armagh, and Robert Black of Derry. Seceders also took part, as we have seen, and during the Volunteer revival of 1792–3 the Covenanters would join in too.[75] Many of these ministers held rank, but their most distinctive contribution to the Volunteers was the preaching of political sermons to companies. At least twenty of these drum-head sermons were published, but many more were recorded in the pages of the provincial press, and since Volunteer services were regular occurrences for several years we can safely assume that this figure represents only a tiny proportion of those actually preached.[76]

The primary aim of these orations was, of course, to bolster the resolution of Ireland's defenders in the face of the French threat. All stressed the importance of love of country, described as a benevolent patriotism rather than a narrow attachment to their home.[77] Ulster Presbyterians imagined their 'country' not in terms of an ethnic homeland, but as a system of legal rights and privileges which their ancestors had brought to Ireland and fought to preserve. In all these sermons the British constitution was contrasted with continental despotism. The Volunteers were reminded that they lived in a free country governed by the rule of law, where their rights, liberties, and properties were secure, even if, as one minister conceded, it

[73] John Rogers, *A Sermon Preached at Lisnavein, otherwise Ballybay New Erection, on Saturday, June 10, 1780. To the Lisnavein Independent Rangers, Trough Volunteers, Lisluney Volunteers, and Monaghan Rangers* (Edinburgh, 1780), 9.   [74] Dickson, *Narrative*, 9–10.

[75] The names of many Volunteer chaplains are listed in T. G. F. Patterson, 'The Volunteer Companies of Ulster, 1778–1793', *Irish Sword*, 7 (1965–6), 91–116, 204–30, 308–12, and 8 (1967–8), 23–32, 92–7, 210–17.

[76] Unfortunately, some of the published sermons have not survived. Nineteenth-century historians had access to James Carmichael, *The Protestant Volunteer Characterised, and the Warrantableness and Necessity of his Appearing in Arms Stated and Illustrated from Judges 5: 2–9. A Sermon Preached December 21, 1779, at Donacloney, to the Volunteers of that Congregation* (Newry, 1780), and Samuel Livingstone, *The Obligation Men are Under to Exert Themselves for the Defence of their Country. A Sermon Preached before the Clare Volunteers on the 9th of January, 1780* (Newry, 1780): see Witherow (ed.), *Historical and Literary Memorials*, ii. 333. John Bell, *Righteousness the Best Friend of Bravery. A Sermon delivered in Hill-hall Meeting-House, December fifth, M.DCC LXXIX; on a Visit of Drumbridge Volunteers and Published at their Request* (Belfast, 1780) is listed in the catalogue of the Ulster Museum, but appears to have been mislaid.

[77] James Crombie, *A Sermon on the Love of Country. Preached before the First Company of Belfast Volunteers, Sunday 19th July 1778* (Belfast, 1778); for benevolence see William Crawford, *The Connection betwixt Courage and the Moral Virtues Considered, in A Sermon Preached before the Volunteer Company of Strabane Rangers, on Sunday the Twelfth of September, 1779* (Strabane, 1779), 3–4, 8–9.

sometimes seemed that the constitution was 'in a consumptive state, and that nox-ious vermin are feeding and fattening upon its discharged humours'.[78] Above all, it was stressed that the British system guaranteed the free exercise of religion, whereas the Catholic states of Europe had trampled on the sacred right of private judge-ment. Only Samuel Barber of Rathfriland brought up the disagreeable subject of the sacramental test.[79]

In their glorification of the independent Volunteer, these clergymen drew upon a fund of images and ideas which went back through Machiavelli to the city-states of ancient Greece and Rome. It was a cardinal principle of classical republicanism that the institution of a citizen militia was the best safeguard against the rise of cor-ruption and arbitrary power in the state. By participating in national defence the citizen elevated the public good over his private interest, and was therefore able to release that civic virtue which was essential for the preservation of liberty. His anti-thesis was the professional soldier or, even worse, the foreign mercenary, whose appearance on the historical stage was associated by republican theorists with imper-ial expansion. As states grew larger and richer, and society became commercialized, they observed, the duties of defence had been entrusted to standing armies, while virtuous citizens became corrupted by luxury. The professional soldiers had no nat-ural ties to the liberty and property of the people; like placemen and pensioners they were subservient to the court. History demonstrated that the standing armies established by great empires had always usurped the reins of government.[80]

The case against professional armies had been formulated in England by com-monwealthsmen such as James Harrington, and restated by Toland, Trenchard, and Molesworth during the standing army controversy of 1697–8, when William III's Whig regime embarked on a series of expensive continental wars. In Harrington's *Oceana* the militia, or *comitia centuriata*, and the *polis* were two faces of a single national community. As J. G. A. Pocock explains, 'the county assemblies are at once the assemblies of the electorate and musters of the militia; the citizens are exercising by their ballots the freedom they manifest in their arms, and casting their votes in the course of their military drill'.[81] The identification of the citizen with the soldier was thus complete. In Scotland, meanwhile, the militia ideal had been closely associated with national independence by Andrew Fletcher of Saltoun in the decade before the Anglo-Scottish union, and more recently by Alexander Carlyle and Adam Ferguson.[82]

Now the same issues were rehearsed once more in Dissenting meeting-houses across Ulster. In one of three published Volunteer sermons, James Crombie of Belfast

---

[78] Robert Sinclair, *Fortitude Explained and Recommended. A Sermon, Delivered before the Larne Volunteers, the First of August, 1779* (Belfast, 1779), 23.

[79] Samuel Barber, MS sermon preached to the Castlewellan Rangers and Rathfriland Volunteers, 24 Oct. 1779, PHSI, 13. This sermon was later published, but I have been unable to find a copy.

[80] For a typical account of the virtues of a citizen militia and the dangers of a standing army see the letter signed 'H' in *Belfast Mercury*, 11 Jan. 1785.

[81] J. G. A. Pocock, 'Machiavelli, Harrington, and English Political Ideologies in the Eighteenth Century', *WMQ*, 3rd ser., 22 (1965), 556–7.

[82] John Robertson, *The Scottish Enlightenment and the Militia Issue* (Edinburgh, 1985).

drew examples from the Old Testament as well as classical sources to show the superiority of citizen armies and the depravity of foreign mercenaries. 'The free states of ancient times', he wrote, 'owed their greatness to their native citizens in arms, and to them were indebted for their deliverance from the hostile attempts of foreign enemies.'[83] His colleague James Bryson, preaching to the Belfast Union Volunteers in November 1778, declared that

An armed yeomanry, as it is the original spirit of our constitution, which the worst Examples of the worst of times have not yet dared to prohibit by the force of Law, is our true defence; because it is ever with us, and because it must ever render us objects both of affection and respect to those that govern us. These associations throughout the land breathe the spirit of ancient Liberty and Virtue which early made us free.[84]

Volunteer chaplains accordingly dwelt upon the disastrous consequences of severing the tie between citizen and soldier. Like Pocock's 'neo-Harringtonians', they ransacked the history books to show how standing armies had ever been used as instruments for establishing absolute monarchies and enslaving free nations. Andrew Alexander of Urney, County Tyrone, described how, after their Asiatic conquests, the Romans had dropped their arms to wallow in opulence, ease, and luxury, committing public defence to hirelings. Ambitious nobles were allowed to sap the foundations of liberty until eventually Caesar overthrew the republic.[85] In Rathfriland, County Down, Samuel Barber explained that Rome had maintained its republican government as long as a military spirit prevailed among its people, but had succumbed to tyranny when overseas wealth brought with it luxury and corruption.[86] There seemed little doubt that the British Empire had reached such a critical juncture. Volunteer preachers regularly lamented the decay of British spirit, the dismemberment of the Empire, the ruin of commerce, and the exposure of their coasts to enemy fleets. Britain's very success, it seemed, was its downfall: as foreign riches encouraged extravagant tastes, degenerate manners, and national complacency, the misguided policies of the king's advisers were allowed to go unopposed.[87]

---

[83] James Crombie, *The Expedience and Utility of Volunteer Associations for National Defence and Security in the Present Critical Situation of Public Affairs Considered, in A Sermon Preached before the United Companies of the Belfast Volunteers, on Sunday the First of August, 1779* (Belfast, 1779), 31.

[84] James Bryson, MS sermon dated 22 Nov. 1778, Bryson, MS sermons, 13 vols., QUB, vol. 7, 35–6.

[85] Andrew Alexander, *The Advantages of a General Knowledge of the Use of Arms. A Sermon Preached before the Strabane, Finwater, and Urney Volunteers and Strabane Rangers, in the Meeting-House of Urney, October 1779* (Strabane, 1779), 13–14.

[86] Barber, Sermon Preached to the Castlewellan Rangers, PHSI, 7–8.

[87] Crombie, *Expedience and Utility of Volunteer Associations*, 8–14; William Steel Dickson, *A Sermon on the Propriety and Advantages of Acquiring the Knowledge and Use of Firearms in Times of Danger. Preached before the Echlinville Volunteers on Sunday the 28th of March 1779* (Belfast, 1779), 15; Crawford, *Courage and the Moral Virtues Considered*, 18–19; Alexander, *Use of Arms*, 21. For other examples of the genre, see William Nevin, *The Nature and Evidence of an Over-Ruling Providence Considered. A Sermon, Preached before the Downe Volunteers, and Fuzileers [sic], on the 5th of September, 1779* (Belfast, 1779); and Hugh Delap, *An Inquiry, Whether, and How Far, Magistracy is of a Divine Appointment, and of the Subjection Due Thereunto. A Sermon Preached in the Old-Bridge Meeting-House near Omagh, the 14th of November 1779 before the Omagh and Cappagh Volunteers* (Strabane, 1779).

According to classical republican theory, the bearing of arms went hand in hand with participation in the political process. The Irish Volunteer was the embodiment of this ideal. William Drennan predicted that military exercise, which involved the 'levelling of all civil distinctions of rank and fortune', would produce political solidarity, fostering 'an independence and republicanism of spirit' among the lower ranks, and eradicating the ties of deference and dependence which bound together landlord and tenant.[88] The Volunteers prided themselves on their democratic organization: in many companies officers were elected by ballot, prompting James Hamilton's wry observation that 'those whom Volunteers call their commanders must obey their orders'.[89] Companies were commonly referred to as 'associations' and must be seen in the context of the contemporary English reform movement led by Christopher Wyvill. In the 1780s Volunteer units became the basic building blocks of a new political machine. Just as individual corps had been grouped into brigades and battalions, it was almost inevitable that the democratic assemblies scattered throughout the land should be organized on a nationwide basis. The conventions which followed were, in effect, shadow parliaments; as many noted, they constituted an overt challenge to the legitimacy of the House of Commons.

As resolutions were debated at meetings, reviews, and conventions, the Volunteer army seemed to offer nothing less than an alternative political structure in which the middling ranks were fully represented and delegates could be held accountable to their constituents. If these conventions reminded contemporaries of American revolutionary practice, they also corresponded to British radical theory. At the time of the American conflict the most authoritative radical treatise was the three-volume textbook *Political Disquisitions* (1774–5), compiled by James Burgh, a Scottish Presbyterian who became master of the Dissenting school at Newington Green, London. Burgh had proposed the institution of a Grand National Association for Restoring the Constitution, with branches in England, Scotland, Ireland, and America. Once elected, this representative body would discover the political sentiments of the 'people of property', and recommend legislation to the Commons. Burgh's scheme for an anti-parliament was taken up by Dr John Jebb of the Society for Constitutional Information, who recommended the election of a popular body of delegates which would have the right to dictate policy to the House of Commons and ultimately to dissolve Parliament in the event of a deadlock.[90] Jebb's suggestions found favour with radical Volunteers like Joseph Pollock; they may also have influenced William Drennan and William Bruce, both of whom argued that the Volunteer conventions of the 1780s had the authority to withhold taxes until Parliament acceded to their demands.[91]

---

[88] [William Drennan], *A Letter to Edmund Burke* (Dublin, 1780), 15–16.

[89] James Hamilton to Abercorn, 5 Dec. 1779, PRONI, Abercorn Papers, T2541/IA2/2/115.

[90] T. M. Parsinnen, 'Association, Convention and Anti-Parliament in British Radical Politics, 1771–1848', *English Historical Review*, 88 (1973), 506–10.

[91] Joseph Pollock to Drennan, 11 Sept. 1780, PRONI, D456/2; Drennan to Martha McTier, [1783], [c.Sept. 1783], PRONI, Drennan Papers, T765/59, 105; Drennan to Bruce, 26 Apr. 1784, PRONI, Drennan–Bruce Papers, D553/26; Bruce to Henry Joy, 26 May 1784, Linenhall Library Belfast, Joy MSS, 14/17.

The popular, democratic impulse which underlay volunteering was demonstrated in the summer of 1782 when the northern companies made it clear that they had no intention of surrendering their role as custodians of national liberty. Following the concession of legislative independence, a split developed in the ranks as some argued that Ireland should rest satisfied with the 'simple' repeal of the Declaratory Act, while others proposed that the patriots should push for a formal disavowal by the Westminster Parliament of the power to legislate for Ireland.[92] On one level, this 'renunciation' dispute can be seen as a personality clash between the two parliamentary spokesmen Henry Flood and Henry Grattan. Flood had been upstaged during the struggle for what has passed into history as 'Grattan's Parliament', and was eager to recover his position as leader of the Irish patriots. But the renunciation issue also raised questions about the long-term role of the Volunteers in Irish politics.

Most of the prominent Volunteer leaders, including Grattan, Charlemont, Francis Dobbs, and Joseph Pollock, took the view that the national emergency had passed and the time had come for the Volunteers to withdraw from the political arena. Dobbs and Pollock were delegates for Ulster on the Volunteer National Committee which met in Dublin on 18 June and drew up an address expressing their satisfaction with the repeal of the Declaratory Act. Three days later, a second Volunteer convention met in the Dissenting meeting-house at Dungannon and unanimously adopted this address.[93] In Belfast it was felt that the National Committee had deliberately delayed the publication of its resolutions to avoid political debate in the north. Three days was not sufficient time for the delegates to refer back to their companies for instructions on how to vote, and so the actions of the National Committee were condemned as an attempt to stifle Volunteer democracy. On 27 June the Belfast First Company therefore reprimanded the three Ulster members of the National Committee, Dobbs, Pollock, and Mervyn Archdall. A week later, as preparations were going ahead for the summer review, the First Company elected Flood an honorary member and issued a call for renunciation and another convention. The simple repeal of the Declaratory Act, they declared, was not enough.[94]

On 31 July 1782, 4,000 Volunteers assembled at Belfast for the annual summer review. As usual, the exercising officer drafted an address to be presented to Charlemont on the final day. On this occasion the exercising officer was Francis Dobbs, eager to vindicate his conduct and to win an endorsement for the simple repealers. Belfast was now, however, 'the very focus of Flood'.[95] It may seem surprising that

---

[92] In the British Parliament the cause of renunciation found an unlikely spokesman in the shape of Lord Beauchamp, son of Lord Hertford, who owned a large estate around Lisburn: see [Francis I. S. Conway, Viscount Beauchamp], *A Letter to the First Belfast Company of Volunteers, in the Province of Ulster. By a Member of the British Parliament* (London, 1783) and [Charles Coote, earl of Bellamont], *A Letter to Lord Viscount Beauchamp, upon the Subject of his Letter to the First Belfast Company of Volunteers, in the Province of Ulster* (London, 1783), and the address of the First Company to Beauchamp in [Joy], *Historical Collections*, 227–9.   [93] Dobbs, *Irish Affairs*, 84–91.

[94] 'An Address from the Belfast First Volunteer Company to the Officers and Privates of the Several Companies to be Reviewed at Belfast, 31st July, 1782', printed in Dobbs, *Irish Affairs*, 97–119; [Joy], *Historical Collections*, 209–12.

[95] Drennan to Bruce, n.d., PRONI, Drennan–Bruce Papers, D553/3.

an apparently semantic squabble should arouse such passions. Many were concerned not so much with the technicalities of this dispute, however, as with the fact that Dobbs had contravened the constitutional rules of Volunteer democracy. At issue was the accountability of Volunteer delegates to their constituents as much as the Anglo-Irish relationship. Dr Drennan, who leaned towards renunciation, has left a fascinating account of the debate:

Innumerable were the knots of every denomination of people that every evening during the review agitated the great national, and very knotty question of renunciation vs. repeal. . . . Papers of all sorts and sizes, some prepared by [Amyas] Griffith, some by [the Revd James] Bryson and some by *Flood* were every hour distributed through the Camp and the Garrison. Each Party seemed confident and equally afraid.[96]

Dobbs took a rather more unfavourable view of the thousands of anonymous handbills dispersed through the ranks, lamenting that 'Every private was taught, that he was competent to legislate, and consequently to express his sentiments on the most speculative points.'[97] The debate itself was scheduled to take place in Bryson's meeting-house, with spectators paying a small admission fee for the benefit of the poor, but the crowd was so great that the meeting was adjourned to the Exchange Rooms. The Volunteers set off through the town, 'attended by the majesty of the people'. Altogether there were 250 delegates, four for each corps. To Drennan the assembly appeared like 'a military Parliament' with the Light Infantry standing guard at the door. Dobbs opened the debate, reading his proposed address to Lord Charlemont expressing satisfaction with the repeal of the Declaratory Act. He was supported by Pollock and, to the surprise of many, the Revd Robert Black of Dromore, famous for his eloquence at the first convention. On the renunciation side, Flood himself was present but had resolved not to speak, leaving the merchant Robert Thompson and the Revd James Bryson to make his case.[98] After a debate of eleven hours the delegates voted against Dobbs's address by 31 to 29.

An act was duly passed early in 1783 whereby London formally surrendered the right to legislate for Ireland, but by this stage the split between repealers and renouncers had been exacerbated by the government's decision to raise new fencible regiments, a move interpreted as an open challenge to the independent Volunteers. In Belfast the new force was condemned as a threat to liberty, and resolutions were passed urging the townspeople to ostracize any man who accepted a position.[99] The extreme language of these resolutions, inspired by Robert Thompson and Thomas McCabe, alienated many of the 'respectable whigs', and forty-two citizens, led by Dr Haliday, signed counter-resolutions.[100] Charlemont sympathized with the popular indignation aroused by the new government force, but he was particularly alarmed by a meeting of the Ulster regiment which had resolved not to co-operate with the

[96] Drennan to Bruce, n.d., July 1782, PRONI, Drennan–Bruce Papers, D553/4. Amyas Griffith was a customs official at Carrickfergus; James Bryson was minister of the Second Congregation and chaplain to the First Volunteer Company.   [97] Dobbs, *Irish Affairs*, 138.
[98] Drennan to Bruce, n.d. [July 1782], PRONI, Drennan–Bruce Papers, D553/4.
[99] Town meetings, 9 Sept., 5 Oct. 1782, [Joy], *Historical Collections*, 216, 219–21.
[100] Ibid. 223; Drennan to Bruce, 28 Oct. [1782], PRONI, Drennan–Bruce Papers, D553/5.

fencibles in the event of an invasion.[101] Party feeling in Belfast ran so high that Thompson and McCabe struck their names off the First Congregation because their minister, James Crombie, had taken the opposing side.[102] The government was forced to abandon the fencible scheme, leaving those who had already accepted commissions—including the unfortunate Dobbs—in an invidious position. In April 1783 the Belfast radicals were still raising their glasses to toasts such as 'May the first who thought of the Fencibles die without the benefit of clergy', adding to Haliday's disgust with the 'busy tribunes' of the town.[103] Reading through the debates on the renunciation issue, one can clearly discern the origins of the much more damaging split of the next decade.

Between 1779 and 1782 the Volunteers had been content to function as the military arm of the patriot faction in the Irish Parliament. After the concession of Irish 'independence', it seemed to the northern radicals that the best guarantor of Ireland's liberties was not the corrupt House of Commons, but the Volunteer army. The real question now was who ruled Ireland—Dublin Castle or Dungannon? The renunciation issue revealed that Belfast was prepared to challenge the political and social order of eighteenth-century Ireland. 'It is a Perilous adventure this Town is engaged in', commented Drennan, 'to alter the voice of four Provinces and two Parliaments.'[104] In 1783 the struggle for power within the Volunteer army would shift more decisively, as the middle classes of Belfast and Dublin seized the initiative. Many of the respectable gentlemen dropped out, while Charlemont fought a rearguard action to keep his army out of the radicals' hands.

---

[101] Charlemont to William Crawford, 27 Sept. 1782, *Charlemont MSS*, i. 418.
[102] Drennan to Bruce, n.d., PRONI, Drennan–Bruce Papers, D553/6.
[103] [Joy], *Historical Collections*, 231–2; Haliday to Charlemont, 17 Apr. 1783, *Charlemont MSS*, i. 425.
[104] Drennan to Bruce, n.d., PRONI, Drennan–Bruce Papers, D553/3.

6
THE FAILURE OF REFORM,
1783–1785

THE secession of the Americans from the imperial system had demonstrated the truth of Wolfe Tone's famous aphorism that England's difficulty is Ireland's opportunity. A unique combination of military defeat abroad and Catholic quiescence at home had forced the British government to concede, first, 'free trade' in 1779, and then legislative independence three years later. Just as important, however, was the revolution in Ireland's internal affairs effected during the same period. The Volunteers had mobilized public opinion on an unprecedented scale, bringing 'the people' into politics for the first time; it was natural that the nation-in-arms should now push for domestic reforms that would render the House of Commons accountable to the new balance of political forces in the country. In the first part of this chapter I shall examine the role of the north in the long and ineffective campaign for the reform of the House of Commons which dominated Irish politics between 1783 and 1785.

The strategic and military requirements of the British war effort also upset the political equilibrium between the three main denominations. In 1780 the Presbyterians were restored to the benefits of full citizenship by the abolition of the sacramental test, a concession which came much too late to have any conciliatory effect; in the second section of this chapter I shall focus on the changing relationship between the Synod of Ulster and the government in the years that followed. Of more profound and far-reaching consequences were the measures taken to secure Catholic compliance during the imperial crisis. The penal system was at last breached, as the Relief Acts of 1778 and 1782 swept away the legal restrictions affecting Catholic landownership and ecclesiastical organization. With the sudden re-emergence of the Catholics as a political force, the Volunteers found it necessary to adopt a more conciliatory tone towards their disenfranchised countrymen. In the final section, I shall describe the disagreements over the Catholic question which eventually derailed the reform movement in 1785, exposing the contradictions of the Protestant patriotism which lay behind the 1782 settlement.

Presbyterians and parliamentary reform

Ulster Presbyterians had called for parliamentary representation to be widened as early as 1776, when James Wilson stood for election in County Antrim. In the following years, however, internal reform was put on hold as popular energies were absorbed in the patriot cause. Now, with Ireland apparently free from English influence, the Ulster Volunteers returned to the deficiencies of the electoral system.

Radicals were well aware that legislative independence was the work not of parliament, but of the Volunteers; 'It was the people that spoke and government complied', as the Revd William Bruce boasted.[1] Within a few years the revolution of 1782 would become the object of ridicule. Without reform, declared William Drennan, Ireland's free trade and legislative independence merely enriched a corrupt aristocracy; oppression from abroad had been exchanged for despotism at home.[2] Although the campaign was actually launched in the columns of the *Dublin Evening Post*, it was the Ulster middle classes who set the pace throughout 1783. A third Dungannon meeting was organized, followed by a Grand National Convention in Dublin in November. Peace had been made with the Americans in February, however, and the administration, now under the firm leadership of Northington, was no longer prepared to be intimidated. With the election of 1783 behind them, MPs were also less susceptible to popular pressure; secure in their seats for another seven or eight years, their misgivings about the whole Volunteer enterprise came to the fore. The House of Commons thus felt bold enough to reject two reform bills introduced by Henry Flood in November 1783 and March 1784.

During the general election parliamentary reform was naturally an important issue. Buoyed up by the successes of the Volunteers, the 'independent interest' scored a series of spectacular victories. In County Antrim neither Lord Hertford nor Lord Antrim dared to put up a candidate, and two prominent Volunteers (both with large estates in the county, admittedly) were returned unopposed. Hertford's discomfort was doubled when two more Volunteer officers, Todd Jones and William Sharman, defeated his nominees in the pot-walloping borough of Lisburn. There was less cause for celebration in Belfast, a corporation borough, where the inhabitants had unsuccessfully petitioned Lord Donegall to appoint Captain Waddell Cunningham of the First Volunteer Company as one of the town's representatives.[3] The following year, however, Cunningham, described by Hillsborough as 'a rank American Republican', triumphed at a by-election for the county borough of Carrickfergus, and Belfast enjoyed a brief moment of revenge before Donegall's men had Cunningham unseated on a charge of bribery.[4]

The centrepiece of this struggle between the Presbyterians and the Ulster aristocracy took place in County Down. One of the most populous and prosperous counties in the kingdom, Down boasted a large gentry and a wealthy middle class. It also possessed an extensive electorate: out of a population of 200,000 in 1790, around 6,000 freeholders were qualified to vote. The Presbyterians, concentrated in the north and east, made up about half of the population and were disproportionately strong among the merchants and manufacturers.[5] Electoral politics were dominated by two great interests. The first was the Hill family, holders of the earldom of Hillsborough

---

[1] [Revd William Bruce], *The History of the Last Session of Parliament, Addressed to the Right Honourable the Earl of Charlemont*, signed Gracchus (Dublin, 1784), 5.

[2] William Drennan, *Letters of Orellana, an Irish Helot, to the Seven Northern Counties not Represented in the National Assembly of Delegates* (Dublin, 1785), 12, 18–19.

[3] Drennan to Bruce, [Feb. 1783], PRONI, Drennan–Bruce Papers, D553/12.

[4] Hillsborough to Northington, 11 Feb. 1784, BL, Pelham Papers, Add. MS 33101, fo. 50.

[5] Peter Jupp, 'County Down Elections 1783–1831', *IHS* 18/70 (Sept. 1972), 178–9.

and later the marquisate of Downshire, and perhaps the most powerful landowners in Ireland. Hillsborough's chief rival was Robert Stewart of Mount Stewart, created Lord Londonderry (at first baron, eventually marquis) in 1789, and his son, also named Robert, the future Viscount Castlereagh. In terms of acreage the Stewarts, although substantial landowners, were not in the same league as the Hills, but they could hope to profit from their strong Presbyterian connections.

At the 1776 election the two families had divided the county's representation between them, Stewart and Hillsborough's son, Lord Kilwarlin, each taking a seat. A complicated three-cornered contest arose at the next general election in 1783, when Edward Ward, son of Lord Bangor, announced his intention to stand on the independent interest. Stewart declared his neutrality, but eventually both he and Ward were forced to seek alliances with Hillsborough, Ward emerging the victor. A bribery petition presented by Stewart was thrown out of the House, causing Hillsborough's friends to rejoice at this 'fatal blow to the pride of our Dissenters'.[6] At the next election, which took place in 1789–90, Robert Stewart, jun., a member of the Northern Whig club, formed a coalition with Ward to challenge Kilwarlin, who had now succeeded to his father's title. After a contest which lasted sixty-eight days and cost over £36,000, Ward finally dropped out and the county seats were split between the two families once more.[7] Robert Stewart, initially hailed as a radical whig, was marked out as traitor when he took office under Pitt. His sins were compounded when, as Viscount Castlereagh, he put down the '98 rebellion and steered through the Act of Union. The Down Presbyterians finally exacted their revenge by ousting him in 1805.

The trend of recent Hanoverian historiography has been to emphasize the reciprocal nature of the relationship between patron and voter. A series of studies has demonstrated that there was more life in the unreformed electorate than was once thought, and it is now accepted that landlords built up their electoral interests through complicated ties of deference rather than the coercion of their tenantry.[8] The Ulster evidence certainly reveals the reality of oligarchic dominance, but also the sometimes subtle and sophisticated ethics of electioneering. Many voters accepted that Hillsborough had fulfilled his local responsibilities to the county community, exhibiting public beneficence as well as private favours. 'Though in the North of Ireland four-fifths of the Voters are Dissenters,' wrote William Richardson in 1797, 'I do not recollect a single Election carried upon that Interest, although perpetually tried by their Ministers.' In the county of Down, where the Presbyterian interest was strongest, the 'personal Qualities and private Friendships' of the Hills had always prevailed.[9]

If these contests reveal the weakness of the independent interest, however, they also attest to the vitality of Dissenting ideology and organization. The elections of

---

[6] John Moore to Arthur Annesley, 19 Nov. 1783, W. H. Crawford (ed.), *Letters from an Ulster Land Agent 1774–85* (Belfast, 1976), 44.   [7] Jupp, 'County Down Elections', 182–3.

[8] The latest is Frank O'Gorman, *Voters, Patrons, and Parties: The Unreformed Electoral System of Hanoverian England 1734–1832* (Oxford, 1989).

[9] William Richardson to [Abercorn], 22 Feb. 1797, PRONI, Abercorn Papers, T2541/IB3/6/5.

1783 and 1790 produced an avalanche of squibs, poems, and songs. Hundreds of Presbyterians participated in parades, processions, and public meetings. Drennan later maintained that these electoral contests had been responsible for sharpening political awareness in the north.[10] A quick glance through the columns of the *Belfast News-Letter* or the *Belfast Mercury* for 1783 will reveal numerous addresses and declarations of support from the Committee of the Independent Interest and from the Constitution Club, which had branches in both Lisburn and Belfast.[11] Admittedly the organization of the Stewart camp in 1783 was far from perfect—at one point Martha McTier, whose husband Samuel was an election agent, complained that there was 'no council, no cockades, no forty shilling freeholders registered'.[12] The situation was much improved in 1790, however, when the independents' committee published daily lists of the poll, containing a breakdown of the votes cast, in Downpatrick and eighteen other towns in the county.[13] Stewart owed a great debt to the Dissenting clergy for their sponsorship, particularly in 1783. Steel Dickson, who served on one of the election committees, rode around the county on horseback throughout the three months of the poll.[14] Others, like Joseph Little of Killinchy, Moses Neilson of Kilmore, Samuel Barber of Rathfriland, and Thomas Ledlie Birch of Saintfield, also played a conspicuous part. Indeed, Samuel Barber so irritated the Hills that Kilwarlin burst into the Rathfriland meeting-house one Sunday to launch a personal attack on him.[15]

During these contests, two rival conceptions of the political process came into collision. In 1790, for example, Arthur Hill (now Earl of Hillsborough, following his father's elevation to Marquis of Downshire) emphasized his contributions to county communications—the post, inland navigation, and, most recently, the construction of a lighthouse. Against the tangible ties of local patronage, the Stewart party tried to raise ideological issues of national importance. Independent pamphleteers pointed out that the Hill family had always sided with England on questions of trade, that Downshire had pushed the Stamp tax onto the American colonies, had opposed the repeal of the sacramental test, and had supported the Vestry Act.[16] Playing on his Presbyterian origins, Robert Stewart also posed as the friend of civil and religious liberty.[17] Constant attempts were made in the press to link the independence of the county to that of the country. At the Carrickfergus election of 1784, electors were encouraged to vote for Cunningham because his experience as a merchant qualified him to represent the area, because of his part in securing free trade

[10] William Drennan, *A Letter to the Right Honourable Charles James Fox*, 2nd edn. (Dublin, 1806), 13.

[11] Many of these were later collected together in [Anon.], *An Historical Account of the Late Election of Knights of the Shire for the County of Down* (n.p., 1784).

[12] Martha McTier to Drennan, [Aug. 1783], in D. A. Chart (ed.), *The Drennan Letters* (Belfast, 1931), 15.

[13] Jupp, 'County Down Elections', 183.

[14] William Steel Dickson, *A Narrative of the Confinement and Exile of William Steel Dickson* (Dublin, 1812), 16, 20.

[15] W. D. Bailie, 'The Revd Samuel Barber 1738–1811: National Volunteer and United Irishman', in J. L. M. Haire (ed.), *Challenge and Conflict: Essays in Irish Presbyterian History and Doctrine* (Antrim, 1981), 78.

[16] See the collection of 144 pamphlets, broadsides, and poems from the 1789–90 Down election, PRONI, MIC 361.   [17] *Historical Account of the Late Election*, 17.

and legislative independence, and because it was essential to support 'the Independency of our County, in Opposition to the unconstitutional lordly influence which has nearly reduced us to the condition of a rotten Borough'.[18]

What was 'independence'? To the adherents of the old Country outlook, the independent freeholder was a gentleman possessed of sufficient land to render him free from economic pressures—that is, landlord coercion. It was his task to ensure the election of virtuous representatives to the House of Commons who would defend the constitution against the corrupting influence of the court. The 'independent interest' was therefore the party of the people, fighting to keep the county free from the influence of the Crown; but it also had a more specific meaning, denoting the smaller landowners of the county, who sometimes formed coalitions in order to bring down the great magnates. In County Down there was an abundance of families— the Wards, Blackwoods, Prices, Fordes among them—who regarded themselves as pillars of the independent interest. Parliamentary candidates who raised the banner of independence did not necessarily abjure the corrupt electioneering tactics of the unreformed system, however; they expected to command the votes of their tenantry just as much as their opponents.[19]

The idea of independence also had more popular connotations. In the late eighteenth century, 'independency' was counterposed to aristocracy. It represented a challenge to an electoral system based on the paternalistic relationship between landlord and tenant. County Antrim, for example, was said to be divided into 'the Independent Interest, or the party of the people' and 'the Aristocratic, or the Lords' faction', the latter consisting of three or four great peers who allegedly had been conspiring to reduce the county to the position of a pocket borough since 1715.[20] The characteristic contribution of Dissenting propagandists to electioneering was to stress the moral rather than the material basis of independence. One pamphleteer at the Carrickfergus election protested against the notion that voting was a matter of interest rather than conscience:

To this I will answer, that a *Christian* is to make conscience the guide of *every* Part of his Conduct, and if we are 'to give an Account of every idle Word in the Day of Judgement', it must surely be a Matter of Conscience, how we give our Vote, in choosing the Person who is to assist in making Laws for our Lives, Liberties and Properties.[21]

He then rebuked those freeholders who had refused to vote for Waddell Cunningham on the grounds that they were in arrears or had a lease up for renewal, warning them that they should fear God more than their landlords. The Revd Moses Neilson,

---

[18] John Moore, *To the Electors of the County of the Town of Carrickfergus* (n.p., 1784), 4. A copy of this pamphlet can be found in PRONI, Malcolm Papers, D3165/4/1.

[19] For an example see Robert Stewart to the Earl of Moira, 21 July [1789], PRONI, Castlereagh Papers, D3030/33/2A.

[20] Tom Neitherside, *A Candid Review of the Merits of the Present Candidates for the County of Antrim: Containing a Short History of the Contested Elections for the County, for a Century Past* (n.p., 1790), 16–17. For the struggle between independency and aristocracy in Antrim see also *Letters Addressed to the Electors of the County of Antrim. By a Freeholder* (Belfast, 1776); *An Address to the Freeholders of the County of Antrim, Respecting the Choice of Representatives, to Serve in the Ensuing Parliament. By an Irishman* (Belfast[?], 1789).   [21] Moore, *To the Electors of Carrickfergus*, 2.

chairman of the committee of County Down independents in 1783, called on the other Dissenting ministers to inspire their congregations with a love of liberty. 'Their votes are not their own,' he reminded them, 'they have them in trust from GOD: to him they will answer for their conduct on this occasion in a more solemn and awful manner than it is possible for them to do to any landlord or agent.'[22] Also devoted to this theme was a series of letters which Drennan published in the *Belfast Mercury* under the name of the martyred commonwealthsman Sidney, stressing that the right of suffrage was a sacred trust, and the task of the freeholder a solemn and religious duty.[23] One is reminded of the New Light emphasis on the moral sovereignty of the individual and the sanctity of the right of private judgement as well as traditional republican ideas of self-government.

For many reformers the ideal of the independent elector was linked to a conception of the MP as a deputy to whom authority was merely delegated on trust. This vision of representative democracy was underlined by the use of two devices by the independent interest: the issuing of instructions to their representatives, and the imposition of tests or pledges upon candidates. The practice of issuing instructions to representatives can be traced back to the early seventeenth century, and had recently been revived by radical whigs in England during the 1774 election. We have already seen that James Wilson, the Presbyterian candidate for the Antrim contest of 1776, had promised to consult his freeholders on proposed legislation. At the election of 1783 much was made of Kilwarlin's refusal to sign a test obliging him to vote according to his constituents' instructions; in Lisburn, on the other hand, Todd Jones assured his constituents that he was obliged to vote on all matters in conformity with their directions—by representing them he was 'executing a trust which may be relinquished, but must never be violated'.[24] This was the democracy of the Volunteers, where active participation in the political process was not limited to the hustings, but was exercised continuously throughout the life of a Parliament.

While the Down election dragged on, preparations were being made for another provincial assembly to push the reform issue to the centre of Irish politics. Unlike its predecessors, which were orchestrated by the patriot leaders in Dublin, the 1783 Dungannon convention had its origins in a Belfast meeting of Volunteer delegates on 9 June, which had unfurled the banner of reform.[25] The following month, the representatives of forty-five companies assembled at Lisburn and summoned a convention to discuss the subject of 'A MORE EQUAL REPRESENTATION OF THE PEOPLE IN PARLIAMENT'. A committee of correspondence was appointed to consult with leading reformers on both sides of the water and draft a programme of constitutional reconstruction. Although a handful of the local gentry was elected, including the chairman William Sharman, the committee also contained

[22] *Historical Account of the Late Election*, 59.
[23] Sidney's letters appeared in the *Belfast Mercury* in August 1783. They included a recommendation of an electoral test which was read in all the meeting-houses in Belfast: Martha McTier to Drennan, [*c*.Sept. 1783], *Drennan Letters*, 16.
[24] William Todd Jones, *A Letter to the Electors of the Borough of Lisburn* (Dublin, 1784), 6.
[25] *BNL*, 17 June 1783.

prominent Presbyterians such as the Belfast merchants Waddell Cunningham and Robert Thompson, the Revd Robert Black of Derry, Dr Alexander Crawford of Lisburn, and the Revd Andrew Craig, New Light minister of the same town.[26] The moving spirit seems to have been Henry Joy, proprietor of the *Belfast News-Letter*. As secretary, he fired off a series of letters to Grattan, Charlemont, Pitt, John Jebb, Christopher Wyvill, John Cartwright, the Earls of Effingham and Abingdon, the Duke of Richmond, and Richard Price; Joseph Priestly was apparently overlooked.[27]

At this convention the tensions always latent within the Volunteer ranks at last came to the surface. On one side stood the moderates, those gentlemen who were essentially parliamentarians and who distrusted popular participation in politics, led by Charlemont and his deputy, the County Tyrone MP James Stewart. The Volunteer earl was unenthusiastic about the prospect of another convention; frequent political assemblies, he apprehended, were boosting the confidence of the Volunteers, rendering them susceptible to dangerous and extreme measures.[28] Although he sympathized with parliamentary reform, he feared that the composition of a detailed plan constituted an 'improper and perhaps unconstitutional' interference with the powers of the legislature.[29] Rather than openly oppose the convention, however, Charlemont determined to persuade the delegates to adopt a more moderate course.

On the other side stood the radicals, who appreciated that it was not parliamentary oratory but 'some rhetorical flourishes of the firelock' that had effected the revolution of 1782.[30] The radical camp had no one to match the enormous prestige of the 'Volunteer earl', but two alternative leaders had emerged. The first was Henry Flood, whose forwardness in the renunciation dispute had earned him honorary membership of the Belfast First Volunteer Company. The second was the flamboyant and eccentric Frederick Augustus Hervey, Earl of Bristol and Bishop of Derry, something of a loose cannon on the Irish political scene. Hervey's well-known opposition to the penal code earned him the hatred of most of his fellow churchmen. According to the Archbishop of Cashel, the earl-bishop was half mad: 'Those who know him best, seem to doubt whether he is a Papist, a Dissenter, a Protestant, a mixture of all, or totally undetermined with respect to the choice of his religion.'[31] After a tour of the continent the bishop had returned to Derry in 1780, and was soon impressed by 'that Elastick uncontroulable spirit that pervades the six Northern Counties'.[32] From his headquarters in Derry he set about wooing the northern Presbyterians. In 1783, for example, when William Bruce was dining at Downhill, the earl-bishop declared himself in favour of disestablishment and offered to propose a motion to that effect at the oncoming Dungannon convention.[33] In the same year he donated

---

[26] [Anon.], *History of Proceedings and Debates of the Volunteer Delegates of Ireland on the Subject of a Parliamentary Reform* (Dublin, 1784), 1–2.

[27] Martha McTier to Drennan, [Sept. 1783], *Drennan Letters*, 18.

[28] 'Memoirs', *Charlemont MSS*, i. 112–15.   [29] Ibid. 113.

[30] The phrase is Drennan's: *An Address to the Volunteers of Ireland* (Dublin, 1781), 13.

[31] Charles Agar, Archbishop of Cashel, to Sir George Macartney, 17 Feb. 1780, PRONI, Macartney Papers, D572/7/52.

[32] Bishop of Derry to John Thomas Foster, 17 Apr. 1782, PRONI, J. L. Foster Papers, T2519/7/2/10.

[33] William Bruce, memoir of a tour of the north, 1783, PRONI, Bruce Papers, T3041/3/1.

£50 towards the costs of the new meeting-house built by the Belfast First Congregation.[34] The Irish government was thus confronted by the paradoxical spectacle of the Presbyterian radicals of the north rallying to a bishop of the Established Church. In the event, both Hervey and Flood were prevented from taking part in the Dungannon proceedings by attacks of the gout: Flood was stricken a few miles from Dungannon (rather conveniently, thought some), while the earl-bishop was forced to retire after the first day. And more importantly for the radicals, both men were also victims of their own ambitions. Flood by this time was more interested in a seat in the British House of Commons, while the Bishop of Derry's fitful and idiosyncratic interventions in Irish politics were directed towards his own eccentric agenda.

The case for reform was founded upon the doctrine of popular sovereignty. Radical propagandists constantly reminded their public that all political power was originally lodged in the people. As 'Lucas', the author of a series of letters in the *Belfast News-Letter*, declared, 'THE GRAND CONTROUL OF THE PEOPLE over their deputies is a *Fundamental* in the constitution'. The state of representation in Ireland clearly bore no relation whatsoever to this principle. The liberties of the people, Lucas explained, had been usurped by a corrupt aristocracy. He denounced the rotten boroughs with their insignificant electorates, the pot-walloping boroughs open to the highest bidder, the corporations with their non-resident burgesses, the free boroughs which lay under the thumb of the proprietor of the soil, and the counties 'where by the wretched nature of tenures and the absurd qualification of voters' the landlords had reduced their tenants to slaves, stripping them of 'the greatest natural right—that of thinking and acting as *free agents*'. Lucas calculated that 200 members (two-thirds) of the House of Commons were returned by the borough patrons, this in addition to their unconstitutional influence in the counties. The only remedy was to restore the system of representation to its former health, to fix parliaments at an annual period, and to disqualify dependants from voting in the House.[35] It was necessary to redress the imbalance in the constitution by the interposition of the people, and in the Ireland of the 1780s 'the people', of course, meant the Volunteers.

Central to the radical critique of the electoral system was the aristocratic control of the Lower House and the patronage which the Crown exercised through the appointment of pensioners and placemen. But the attack on corruption, once limited to denunciations of court influence, was now firmly focused on the issue of representation, clearly reflecting the interests of the disfranchised borough populations of the northern towns. Although in retrospect it is the broadening of the franchise which seems the key demand, the reformers accorded as much importance to the redistribution of seats: the slogan 'a fair and equal representation' refers not so much to the extension of the franchise as to the adaptation of the electoral system to take account of the decay of old boroughs and the rise of new trading centres.

On 8 September the Volunteers returned for a third time to the 'Mons Sacer' at Dungannon, thought to be the most central town in Ulster. Five hundred delegates

---

[34] Martha McTier to Drennan [spring, 1783], *Drennan Letters*, 10.　　　[35] *BNL*, 26 Aug. 1783.

crowded into the Dissenting meeting-house in Scotch Street, representing 278 corps out of a possible total of 400. James Stewart of Killymoon, Charlemont's friend, was elected chairman.[36] They began with a ringing declaration that Irishmen could not be free unless governed by laws of their own consent. The majority of the House of Commons, they complained, was chosen not by the people but returned by the mandate of peers and commoners; the balance of the constitution had therefore been destroyed, creating a danger of monarchical or aristocratic tyranny. It was resolved that parliaments should be made annual and the vote given to 'all those who are likely to exercise it, for the public good'. An appeal was then made to the other three provinces to join in a National Convention dedicated to reform, and representatives from the Ulster gentry were chosen. The committee of correspondence published the results of its inquiries and deliberations on constitutional reform, recommending annual parliaments, vote by ballot, the redistribution of seats with compensation for borough patrons, and the exclusion of placemen and pensioners from the Commons. In the counties the franchise was to be granted to Protestants possessing £20 worth of property, as well as to the 40-shilling freeholders, and in the towns these two categories were joined by £5 householders. The vital question of Catholic participation in elections was referred to the discretion of the national body.[37]

The 'Grand National Convention', which accordingly met in Dublin on 10 November 1783, proved a bitter disappointment to the northern radicals. The assembly, led by the Earl of Charlemont and boasting a total of fifty-nine MPs and six peers, was hopelessly divided on fundamental issues—indeed, many delegates seemed to doubt the propriety of meeting at all—and much time was lost on procedural points and trivial disagreements. After several chaotic days Flood produced his own plan, a much more moderate document than the Dungannon recommendations: annual parliaments had become triennial, the secret ballot was dropped, and the Catholic question was ignored. To Charlemont's horror, Flood, dressed in his Volunteer uniform, was appointed to take the bill to the Commons while the convention was still sitting, a move which was interpreted as a crude attempt to force reform upon the Irish Parliament at the point of a bayonet. The bill was indignantly thrown out by 158 votes to 49 as insults were heaped upon the convention. Some radicals regretted that the Volunteers had not taken the opportunity to overawe the House of Commons. Drennan, complaining that Flood was 'too wise, too cool, *perhaps* too selfish, to be a Luther in civil reform', thought that the convention should have marched on Parliament House.[38]

The reform agitation now moved from the metropolis back to the provinces as county meetings were summoned to endorse the convention plan. It was hoped that this more orthodox method of proceeding might draw a less hostile response from College Green. When the freeholders of Down met at Downpatrick in January to draw up their petition, the Earl of Hillsborough exerted his influence to ensure that

---

[36] The number of corps represented can be broken down as follows: Antrim, 59; Derry, 50; Down, 42; Tyrone, 35; Donegal, 24; Monaghan, 23; Armagh, 23; Fermanagh, 8; Cavan 4: *BNL*, 12 Sept. 1783.
[37] *History of Proceedings and Debates of the Volunteer Delegates*, 6–15.
[38] Drennan to Bruce, [Dec. 1783], PRONI, Drennan–Bruce Papers, D553/17.

the meeting would be a failure. In a letter to Dublin Castle he requested that more troops be sent to Belfast, warning the Lord Lieutenant that 'The turbulent Spirit encreases everywhere and the Dissenting Parsons do their utmost to foment it.'[39] Hillsborough was prone to conspiracy theories, especially where the Presbyterian clergy was concerned, but his warnings were not without foundation. The Dissenting ministers had now grown used to extra-parliamentary politics: 'I live almost in a Flame', wrote one, 'I am accustomed to it and even begin to like it.'[40] Hillsborough organized a counter-petition expressing satisfaction with the 'present happy Constitution', and managed to secure the support of two Seceding ministers in return for his services in getting them a share of the *regium donum*, the annual grant given to the Synod of Ulster by the Crown.[41] The Seceders had objected to the use of Presbyterian pulpits as political platforms, and regarded the Stewarts as supporters of the New Light party in the Synod. Nevertheless, their arrangement with Hillsborough was a staggering betrayal of the Dissenting interest and caused much bitterness between the two Presbyterian bodies.

Following petitions from twenty-two counties and towns, Flood once more introduced his bill in March 1784. This time he was defeated by 159 to 85. By now, Charlemont was using all his influence in the north to ensure that the Volunteer meetings abstained from political pronouncements. In February 1784 he wrote to Dr Haliday in Belfast begging him to prevent the Volunteers from deliberating upon political matters.[42] The Bishop of Derry, on the other hand, was once more the centre of attention. For some time he had been the recipient of addresses from Volunteer corps in the north, and he obligingly responded in the press with strongly worded attacks on parliament. After the Grand National Convention he had advised the Strabane Volunteers to withhold supplies until the government accepted the reform plan, a gesture taken with a pinch of salt by Drennan who retorted that the bishop himself should set an example.[43] Following a string of addresses to companies from St Johnstown, Londonderry, Armagh, Coleraine, and elsewhere, hinting that the Volunteers should pursue their aims by force of arms, the chief secretary consulted lawyers about the possibility of prosecution.[44]

The final act in the reform farce was the election of another assembly, this time named the National Congress, which met in Dublin in October 1784. Unlike its predecessors, the congress was a purely civil body, with delegates chosen by freeholders from each county or town. In most counties the high sheriff refused to summon the freeholders, and unofficial meetings had to be called in order to return delegates. Many of the more respectable reformers had by this stage dropped out, tipping the balance towards the northern radicals, represented by the Revd William Bruce, the Revd Sinclare Kelburn, Robert Thompson, Henry Joy, and William

[39] Hillsborough to Northington, 11 Feb. 1784, BL, Pelham Papers, Add MS 33101, fo. 50.
[40] Barber to Campbell, 3 March 1784, PHSI, Campbell MSS.
[41] The petition appeared in *BNL*, 24 Feb. 1784.
[42] Martha McTier to Drennan, [about Feb. 1784], *Drennan Letters*, 22.
[43] Drennan to Martha McTier, [around Nov. 1783], ibid. 11.
[44] Pelham to Portland, 14 Dec. 1784, BL, Pelham Papers, Add. MS 33000, fos. 460–3. Many of the bishop's letters were published in the *Dublin Evening Post* between Nov. 1783 and Jan. 1784.

Drennan.[45] The meeting got off to a bad start, as several gentlemen immediately rose to declare their disapprobation of assembling at that period, their faith in the Irish parliament, and their conviction that the proceedings of the congress would only hinder reform.[46] After a vague declaration reiterating the urgent need for reform, the meeting was adjourned. A second session of the congress in January 1785 was much better attended, but achieved no more. It was notable primarily for the appearance of Drennan's brilliant pamphlet *Letters of Orellana, an Irish Helot*, defending the right of the people to assemble, associate, and petition. Although tremendously popular in the north, this best-selling tract proved to be the swansong of the Ulster Volunteers. The subject of reform was growing 'unfashionable', as Drennan noted, and was now seldom mentioned in 'genteel company'.[47]

The Synod of Ulster and the Castle

By the close of the American war, Ulster Presbyterians had emerged as a powerful interest in Irish politics for the first time in over half a century, courted both by the patriot leadership at College Green and by the administration. It was natural that they should expect some official recognition of their enhanced status. While they pressed for the purification of parliament, their ministers therefore opened negotiations with Dublin Castle in the hope of strengthening their ecclesiastical position. Following the repeal of the test in 1780, the Synod and its allies in the House of Commons worked for an augmentation of the *regium donum* and the establishment of an educational institution for the ministry. Once more, the redress of grievances was belated, begrudged, and clumsily handled. The administration's disregard for Presbyterian sensitivities fed the Synod's persecution complex, reinforcing the historical identity of a church which had lost much of its doctrinal coherence.

The dominance of the Anglican elite in Ireland was not based simply on legal weapons such as the sacramental test, but on a broader monopoly of social prestige and economic opportunity which long predated the 1704 act. Nevertheless, the initial impact of the test clause on the social structure of Presbyterianism was probably greater than historians have suggested.[48] Their political representation, already negligible, was halved to a meagre four MPs. In the important towns of Belfast and Derry, Dissenters were forced to resign their seats on the corporation. More importantly, the test almost certainly played a part in eroding the landed base of the Dissenting interest: by the 1730s it was believed that no more than twenty

---

[45] Thomas Orde informed Pitt that the reform movement was now led by Henry Joy, William Bruce, the Dublin radical Napper Tandy, and his brother George of Lisburn: 9 Jan. 1785, PRO, Chatham Papers, 30/8/329, fos. 201–5.

[46] Letter from Archibald Hamilton Rowan to the Newtownards Reform Club, *BNL*, 22 Feb. 1785.

[47] Drennan to Bruce, [17 Mar. 1785], PRONI, Drennan–Bruce Papers, D553/38.

[48] For an attempt to gauge the social and psychological effects of anti-Dissenter legislation see Ian McBride, 'Presbyterians in the Penal Era', *Bullán: An Irish Studies Journal*, 1/2 (Autumn 1994), 73–86. The traditional picture of the test act has been revised by David Hayton in 'Exclusion, Conformity, and Parliamentary Representation: The Impact of the Sacramental Test on Irish Dissenting Politics', in Kevin Herlihy (ed.), *The Politics of Irish Dissent, 1650–1800* (Dublin, 1997), 52–73. I am grateful to Dr Hayton for allowing me to read a copy of this important paper prior to publication.

of their number possessed sufficient land to qualify them for commissions of the peace.[49] Henceforth, for the vast majority of northern Presbyterians, exclusion from public office no doubt constituted a merely hypothetical form of discrimination, but the sacramental test remained on the statute book, the most concrete symbol of their degradation.

The last repeal campaign, mounted in the early 1730s, had received the backing of Sir Robert Walpole's ministry in London, but had run aground against the overwhelming hostility of the Irish House of Commons. In 1780 the situation was reversed, with patriot parliamentarians taking up the Presbyterian cause in spite of metropolitan disapproval. The first signs of a revival in Presbyterian fortunes came with the introduction of Luke Gardiner's Catholic Relief bill in May 1778. The Dublin MP Sir Edward Newenham, supported by some of the northern members, had the bill amended to include the abolition of the test, but this extra clause was deleted in London lest its passage should trigger a parallel campaign among English Dissenters. (Under the terms of Poynings' Law, bills returned by the English Privy Council could only be passed or thrown out; no further debate was allowed.) Over the following year, however, military setbacks in the colonies, combined with the alarming expansion of the Volunteer movement in the north, forced the government to reconsider its position. At the beginning of the next parliamentary session Newenham and his friends renewed their exertions, and a second Dissenters' relief bill was eventually returned from England unaltered to come into effect in 1780.[50]

The intense controversy aroused by Gardiner's bill can only be understood in the context of the American war. By sponsoring a measure of relief the government hoped at least to secure the loyalty of the Catholic population at a time when a French invasion of Ireland seemed possible, and at best to stimulate Catholic enlistment in the British army.[51] For patriots, however, the conciliation of papists could be seen as part of a conspiracy against the liberties of Protestant subjects throughout the Empire. Rumours circulated that regiments of Irish Catholics were to be used to put down the American colonists. In Britain the protests of opposition whigs, the Popular party in the Scottish Kirk, and George Gordon's Protestant Association all testified to the link between pro-American sympathy and anti-popery.[52] In Ireland, meanwhile, Grattan drew a parallel between Gardiner's bill and the 'establishment'

---

[49] For the decline of the Dissenting gentry see T. C. Barnard, 'Identities, Ethnicity and Tradition among Irish Dissenters, c.1650–1760', in Kevin Herlihy (ed.), *The Irish Dissenting Tradition, 1650–1750* (Blackrock, Co. Dublin, 1995), 34–5; S. J. Connolly, *Religion, Law and Power: The Making of Protestant Ireland 1660–1760* (Oxford, 1992), 163.

[50] J. S. Reid, *History of the Presbyterian Church in Ireland*, ed. W. D. Killen, 3rd edn., 3 vols. (Belfast, 1867), iii. 343–4. See also James Kelly, '1780 Revisited: The Politics of the Repeal of the Sacramental Test', in Kevin Herlihy (ed.), *The Politics of Irish Dissent, 1650–1800* (Dublin, 1997), 74–92. I am grateful to Dr Kelly for permitting me to read this essay in advance of publication.

[51] See R. K. Donovan, 'The Military Origins of the Roman Catholic Relief Programme of 1778', *Historical Journal*, 28 (1985), 79–102.

[52] Ibid.; R. K. Donovan, 'The Popular Party of the Church of Scotland and the American Revolution', in R. B. Sher and J. R. Smitten, *Scotland and America in the Age of Enlightenment* (Edinburgh, 1990), 81–99; Colin Haydon, *Anti-Catholicism in Eighteenth-Century England: A Political and Social Study* (Manchester, 1993), 200.

of popery in Canada by the Quebec Act of 1774.[53] The stage was set for a brilliant example of the dangers involved in tampering with Ireland's triangular balance of power.

There is no doubt that the adoption of the Dissenters' cause was an obstructionist tactic on the part of the patriot MPs. They suspected, rightly, that the test clause would be removed from the bill by the English Privy Council, currently pre-occupied with the demands made by its own 'Rational Dissenters', thus provoking a constitutional debate in which the patriots could oppose the administration on the congenial ground of safeguarding Irish parliamentary independence. If, on the other hand, the bill was returned to Ireland with the test clause intact, these MPs would at least have placed the Presbyterian electorate in their debt.

Opposition to Gardiner's proposal came from Hercules Rowley, MP for County Meath, James Wilson, MP for County Antrim, Isaac Corry of Newry, and Sir Richard Johnston of Coleraine. All had northern connections and were to some extent receptive to Presbyterian feeling; this was particularly true of Wilson, who claimed to be acting on the instructions of his constituents. Newenham, who had proposed the amendment on 15 June, represented a Dublin constituency which still contained many Presbyterian merchants, and he had also entered into correspondence with Dissenters in Antrim, Derry, and elsewhere. The Revd William Bruce, noting that 'the clause was not solicited by any Dissenters; nor were the Dissenters in the least active during its progress', suggested that Newenham and Corry had backed the measure simply to boost their electoral support.[54] With Grattan apostrophizing about popish conspiracies and an 'affront to the Presbyterians of the country', however, it would not be long before their natural sense of persecution was rekindled.[55] When the Catholic Relief Act was passed—minus the test clause—a petition was drawn up in Belfast complaining of government impartiality and asserting the entitlement of Presbyterians to 'all the rights of free-born subjects'.[56] The Belfast petition was eventually laid aside lest it should distract attention from the campaign for free trade, a telling indication of Presbyterian priorities at this time.[57]

Whereas the test issue had stimulated the publication of over two dozen pamphlets between 1731 and 1733, almost all hostile to the Dissenters, the parliamentary manoeuvres of 1778–80 called forth just one defence of the monopoly of public office long cherished by Anglicans as the central bulwark of their established status. This very rare tract, *Fragment of a Letter to a Friend, Relative to the Repeal of the*

---

[53] R. E. Burns, 'The Catholic Relief Act in Ireland, 1778', *Church History*, 32 (1963), 181–206. This article, on which the following paragraphs are based, draws upon the manuscript notes of Commons debates made by Sir Henry Cavendish, almost the only source for the subject. The original manuscript is in the Library of Congress.

[54] William Bruce, 'Facts Relating to the Protestant Dissenters of Ireland, Beginning from the Year 1778', PRONI, Bruce MSS, D2673, uncatalogued.

[55] The quotation is from Burns, 'Catholic Relief Act', 202.

[56] William Campbell, 'Sketches of the History of Presbyterians in Ireland', PHSI, Campbell MSS, 244.

[57] Ibid. 244–5. Although there were no petitions in favour of repeal from the north, the same period saw petitions from Belfast, Derry, Lisburn, Newry, Banbridge Armagh, Monaghan, and Dungannon on the state of trade: *Journals of the House of Commons of the Kingdom of Ireland*, 19 vols. (Dublin, 1797), x. 11–85.

Test (1780), rehearsed the conventional case against Presbyterianism. The agrarian protests of the Hearts of Oak and Hearts of Steel were dredged up as evidence that Presbyterians had 'an *Itch* of Rebellion' flowing through their veins, while their support for the American cause revealed the 'rank *Republicanism*' disguised by their repeated declarations of loyalty to the House of Hanover.[58] At the bottom of this disaffection lay their theological and ecclesiological principles. The anonymous author conjured up seventeenth-century images of fanatical Calvinists whose Confession of Faith obliged them to stamp out rival creeds and whose insistence on the absolute sovereignty of the Kirk dissolved the bonds of civil society itself. Hardly preferable was the non-subscribing position adopted by 'a few of the more polished and fashionable dissenters', whose rejection of all ecclesiastical authority threatened the State–Church alliance which stood at the heart of the national constitution.[59]

Earlier in the century the Anglican hierarchy had used its weight in the House of Lords and its influence in England to frustrate government attempts to tamper with its privileges. On this occasion, however, the activities of the church lobby were belated and ineffectual. The alarm was raised by Charles Agar, Archbishop of Cashel, who was in close contact with George Macartney, a former chief secretary in the Irish administration. Their one hope, suggested Macartney, was Lord North's fear that the admission of Irish Dissenters to public office would make it impossible to deny the claims of their English brethren, but even Macartney confessed that the two situations were different, 'for the Dissenters here [Engand] are an inconsiderable body compared with the rest of the peoples but in Ireland they are much more numerous than the established church'. Nevertheless, he suggested, a petition drawn up by the Church of Ireland might furnish Lord North with the necessary excuse.[60] In the end, Agar and Primate Robinson, agreeing that a petitioning campaign would subject the parochial clergy to intolerable abuse, decided on a joint letter from the Irish bishops to the Archbishop of Canterbury. As a second line of defence they drafted a declaration which might be substituted for the test, requiring the office-holder to swear that 'I do not believe the public worship of the Church of Ireland as by law established to be sinful or idolatrous and that I do not hold myself bound in conscience to use my endeavours to subvert the said public worship.'[61] Even this fall-back position failed, confirming the extent to which the confessional state had been weakened in Ireland.

How should this curious episode in Irish parliamentary politics be evaluated? The restoration of full citizenship was not recorded in the minutes of the Synod of Ulster, nor did it receive much space in the double-decker history of Ireland published just three years later by the Revd William Crawford of Strabane. The author of the *Fragment* was probably right to predict that Anglican concessions would not earn the gratitude of Dissenters, but merely fuel their new-found assertiveness.[62] Indeed

---

[58] *Fragment of a Letter to a Friend, Relative to the Repeal of the Test* (Dublin, 1780), 18–20.
[59] Ibid. 8–12.
[60] [Macartney] to Agar, 21 Jan. 1780, in *Macartney in Ireland 1768–72: A Calendar of the Chief Secretaryship Papers of Sir George Macartney*, ed. Thomas Bartlett (Belfast, 1978), 326.
[61] Ibid. 328–9.   [62] *Fragment of a Letter*, 30.

the abolition of the test was quickly followed by an act confirming the legality of Presbyterian marriages.[63] If anything, the 1780 legislation merely demonstrated that a more fundamental reform was required if the grand juries and borough corporations were to be made accountable. It was not until well into the nineteenth century that the Ascendancy began to be dismantled, by a process which began with the Great Reform Act and the Municipal Corporations Act in the 1830s, and culminated in the destruction of landlordism under the Wyndham legislation of 1903 and its further extension in 1909.[64]

The real significance of repeal lies less in its consequences than its origins. A study of the Commons debates in 1778–9 reveals the emergence of a parliamentary lobby responsive to the interests of the Presbyterian electorate. One MP wrote to the Earl of Hillsborough of 'the leaders of the Dissenters, who may justly be called the leaders of faction, such as your Stewarts, Rowleys, Montgomerys, Lord Charlemont, etc'.[65] In addition to the handful of MPs who came from Dissenting families, such as Robert Stewart, the Irish parliament also contained a number of figures who might be called 'friends of Dissent'. Undoubtedly the crucial factor in cementing this relationship between Presbyterian ministers and Episcopalian gentlemen was the mobilization of the Volunteers. The Revd William Campbell of Armagh noted that the mingling of Anglican and Dissenter, and particularly the custom of marching to worship on Sundays—church one week and meeting the next—had eroded episcopalian prejudice.[66] It was through the annual Belfast reviews, for example, that Charlemont became a firm friend of Dr Haliday. William Campbell, the Synod's commissioner during the 1780s, was chaplain of Charlemont's Armagh regiment, while Crawford held the same post in James Stewart's Tyrone regiment.[67]

The friends of Dissent also included northern whigs and radicals such as Sir John O'Neill, Archibald Hamilton Rowan, and William Todd Jones. There can be no doubt, however, that the greatest champion of the Dissenting interest was James Stewart, MP for the 'independent' constituency of County Tyrone, and Charlemont's mouth-piece in the Lower House. Stewart's seat was in fact uncontested from his first election in 1768 until 1812, due to the balance of power which existed among the Tyrone grandees; nevertheless, as a small landowner he clearly saw the value of courting the Presbyterian freeholders. Among his papers there survives an address from the Dissenting congregation of Cappagh, thanking him for a contribution of ten guineas to the expense of a new meeting-house, for faithfully

[63] For Presbyterian agitation on the marriage issue, see William Campbell to Grattan, 15 June 1782, PRONI, Fitzwilliam/Grattan papers, T3649/1. There was still some question about the validity of Presbyterian marriages where one of the parties was not a Protestant Dissenter, a question not resolved until 1844.

[64] A parliamentary survey in 1884 revealed that 72.6 per cent of Ulster JPs were Episcopalians, 14 per cent Presbyterians, and 8.5 per cent Roman Catholics: Richard McMinn, 'Presbyterianism and Politics in Ulster, 1871–1906', *Studia Hibernica*, 21 (1981), 132.

[65] Robert Ross to Hillsborough, 7 Sept. 1778, PRONI, Downshire Papers, D607/B/31.

[66] Campbell, 'Sketches', PHSI, Campbell MSS, 247.

[67] Stewart met Crawford at a Volunteer review in the summer of 1781: Stewart to Charlemont, 2 Aug. 1781, PRONI, Stewart of Killymoon papers, D3167/1/2.

representing his constituents, and declaring that 'we do hold ourselves in duty bound to you, our country and every [one] of us to support your interest on all future occasions to establish you as our first representative of the County of Tyrone'.[68]

With the test issue at last resolved, one major area of potential controversy remained. Between 1775 and 1803 the question of the Synod's relationship with the establishment focused on the *regium donum*.[69] This state subsidy which Presbyterian ministers received directly from the Crown had its origins in a grant of £600 made by Charles II and doubled by William in 1691.[70] At the end of Anne's reign it was briefly suspended following Anglican complaints that the money had been used to set up new congregations, but the grant was restored after the accession of George I, and increased to £1,600 in 1718 in recognition of Presbyterian support for the Hanoverian succession. The royal bounty was a lump sum divided evenly between the clergy. Consequently, the rapid multiplication of congregations in the early eighteenth century, combined with inflation, seriously diminished its value: in 1783 the Synod calculated that the *regium donum* now amounted to less than £9 for each minister.[71] A number of attempts to have the bounty increased in the 1740s were unsuccessful, but the grant was enlarged three times in the last quarter of the century.[72] In 1784 it was supplemented by an extra £1,000, raising it from £1,600 to £2,600; six years later it was bumped up to £6,329. 16s. 10d.; and in 1803 it was more than doubled to £14,970. 18s. 10d.[73]

The royal bounty was of more than material value. It gave the Synod of Ulster a degree of official recognition: the grant was paid directly by the monarch, and the extra sums added by William and George I were proudly considered as rewards for Presbyterian loyalty. Receipt of state assistance left the Synod open to the charge, gratefully exploited by Seceders and Covenanters, that it had sold its independence and compromised with prelacy and erastianism, but the *regium donum* was viewed very differently by most ministers. The Scottish settlers in Ulster had originally been comprehended within the Church of Ireland and had accordingly received the tithes of their own congregations until deprived of this privilege by Oliver Cromwell. When the royal bounty was granted after the Restoration it was therefore regarded not only as a reward for services to the Crown, but as compensation for the tithes which they hoped one day to reclaim.[74]

---

[68] Cappagh Protestant Dissenters to James Stewart, 21 July 1789, Stewart of Killymoon papers, D3167/2/75.

[69] During the same period the Synod also pressed for the creation of a Presbyterian university in Ulster, but unfortunately there is insufficient room to deal with this subject here. The best source is the Campbell MSS in PHSI.

[70] Robert Black, *Substance of Two Speeches, Delivered in the General Synod of Ulster* (Dublin, 1812), app. v.

[71] Petition of the Presbyterian ministers of the General Synod of Ulster to the King, [Dec. 1783], PHSI, Campbell MSS.

[72] *RGSU*, ii. 307 (1744); 347 (1749); Reid, *History of the Presbyterian Church in Ireland*, iii. 285 n. 5; James Duchal to Thomas Drennan, 4 June 1747, PRONI, D. Stewart Papers, D1759/3B/6, p. 11.

[73] Black, *Substance*, 78.

[74] Thomas Ledlie Birch, *Physicians Languishing under Disease* (Belfast, 1796), 31 n.; William Bruce to Castlereagh, 9 Apr. 1800, *Castlereagh Correspondence*, iii. 268.

Inevitably, the fate of the *regium donum* became linked to the political threat posed by Presbyterian radicalism. The issue was first broached in November 1783, when Charlemont informed the Synod that Lord Northington and Thomas Pelham, then Lord Lieutenant and chief secretary respectively, would look favourably upon an application for an augmentation of the grant. For some years the possibility of such a boon had been floated by northern MPs, but it was not until the previous month that the Revd William Crawford had met James Stewart to discuss the matter.[75] When the Synod's committee convened in December, fears were voiced that the government was trying to counteract Volunteering and the campaign for representative government in the north. There was also opposition to the method of proceeding, some ministers arguing that application should be made to parliament rather than the king. Notwithstanding these suspicions, it was decided to respond positively to the Castle's offer, and William Campbell was duly dispatched to Dublin as the Synod's commissioner.[76]

In his discussions with the Castle administration Campbell could count on the support of several whiggish parliamentarians, including Henry Grattan, William Brownlow, Thomas Dawson, Hercules Rowley (the last two both colonels in the Volunteer army), the radical Lisburn MP William Todd Jones, and Travers Hartley, representative for the city of Dublin and sometime member of the Strand Street Dissenting congregation.[77] Meanwhile, in London, Lord Templetown had been soliciting the favour of Charles James Fox.[78] Both Rowley and Templetown were descendants of Arthur Upton, the Templepatrick landlord who had played a leading role in the Synod's affairs in the early decades of the century.

In fact, Northington had already accepted the wisdom of augmenting the state grant to the Synod. On 7 November he had informed Charles James Fox of his opinion that any sum which increased government influence over the northerners was money well spent.[79] But talks between the Synod of Ulster and the Castle were soured from the beginning by the Lord Lieutenant's concern that the Presbyterians were being led astray from 'the true Whig principles'.[80] The backdrop to these negotiations was the meeting of the 1783 national convention, where the Bishop of Derry had made overtures to both Catholics and Dissenters. After the earlier provincial convention at Dungannon, Pelham had noted the violent language of the earl-bishop and several Dissenting ministers.[81] The Dublin meeting, in which William Bruce, then minister of the Strand Street congregation, had played a prominent part, was denounced by the administration as an insult to the Irish parliament.[82] Campbell anxiously assured Northington that he disapproved of the Volunteer agitation and that most of his colleagues were opposed to Catholic emancipation.[83] He immediately wrote to ascertain public sentiment in Ulster and received replies

[75] Crawford to William Campbell, 23 Sept. 1783, PHSI, Campbell MSS.
[76] Campbell, journal, PHSI, Campbell MSS, pp. 1–3.   [77] Ibid. 6–9, 16.
[78] Portland to Pelham, 27 Oct. 1783, BL, Pelham Papers, Add. MS 33100, fo. 382.
[79] Northington to Fox, 7 Nov. 1783, BL, Northington Letterbook, p. 226, Add. MS 38716, fo. 137.
[80] Campbell, journal, PHSI, Campbell MSS, p. 18.
[81] Pelham to Portland, 10 Sept. 1783, BL, Pelham Papers, Add. MS 33100, fo. 310.
[82] Campbell, journal, PHSI, Campbell MSS, pp. 17–19.   [83] Ibid. 19–21.

from Crombie, Bryson, Barber, Black, Crawford, and ten other ministers. The accusations of sedition levelled by Northington and Pelham drew the predictable retort that all political activity was moderate and constitutional, and that Presbyterians remained true to the political principles held by their forefathers in 1641 and 1688.[84]

It was the wrath of the Earl of Hillsborough, incurred by Presbyterian agitation during the Down election of 1783, which finally scuppered the Synod's hopes. Through his influence the *regium donum* was raised by only £1,000, while the Secession ministers, two of whom had signed a County Down petition against parliamentary reform, were given their own bounty of £500.[85] Although the Synod's memorial had mentioned no specific sum, it was widely known that an addition of £5,500, the amount required to give every minister £40, was desired. Campbell was bitterly disappointed when on 11 February he was informed of the Castle's decision. Northington hinted that the blame lay with 'unfavourable representations' of the state of the north, specifically mentioning the interference of the Volunteers on behalf of Waddell Cunningham in the recent Carrickfergus election.[86] There is no doubt as to his source of information: on 8 February he had received a letter from Hillsborough complaining about Volunteer intimidation and calling for troops to be sent to the Belfast area.[87] Soon after, Hillsborough wrote to the Lord Lieutenant thanking him for the troops and warning him that it was impossible to buy off the 'Dissenting Parsons'.[88]

Although Northington tried to soften the blow by suggesting that the sum should be regarded as an 'earnest' of a further enlargement, the Synod was understandably indignant.[89] It was widely known that Hillsborough had been responsible for the reduction of the £5,000 originally on offer, and the admission of the Seceders, the Synod's bitter rivals, to the royal favour added insult to injury.[90] Crawford of Strabane considered the 'paltry sum' as a deliberate slight. 'We now plainly see the light in which we are considered by government', he observed; 'they do not think the services of our forefathers, our loyalty and zealous attachment to the constitution as worthy of any notice.'[91] John White of Stewartstown, John Smith of Loughbrickland, James Crombie, and Samuel Barber all expressed their resentment in letters to Campbell.[92] One minister, Thomas Ledlie Birch of Saintfield, was so disgusted that he resigned his share of the bounty and repudiated the principle of state provision for religion.[93]

The concessions made to the Synod of Ulster during the war for America, although important victories, only made those inequalities which still remained all the more intolerable. For the repeal of the sacramental test the Presbyterians had the Volunteers,

---

[84] Ibid. 33–4, and the enclosed letters.   [85] Dickson, *Narrative*, 291 n.

[86] Campbell, journal, PHSI, Campbell MSS, p. 53.

[87] Hillsborough to Northington, 8 Feb. 1784, BL, Pelham Papers, Add. MS 33101, fo. 48.

[88] Hillsborough to Northington, 11 Feb. 1784, ibid., fo. 50.

[89] Campbell, journal, PHSI, Campbell MSS, pp. 49–50, 53.

[90] Dickson, *Narrative*, 291 n. Dickson claimed that the original figure was £10,000, but there is no evidence to support him.   [91] Crawford to Campbell, 15 Feb. 1784, PHSI, Campbell MSS.

[92] These are appended to his journal.

[93] See Birch's letter to the Lord Lieutenant in *Belfast Mercury*, 14 Jan. 1785.

rather than the Castle, to thank, while the ham-fisted treatment of the *regium donum* affair, and the ease with which the administration gave way to the Earl of Hillsborough, invalidated the conciliatory intentions behind the measure. Neither of these gains could dent the persecution complex of the Ulster Presbyterians, or reduce their hypersensitivity to government interference in church affairs. When the legality of Presbyterian marriage rites was questioned in 1782, Campbell dispatched a blunt letter to Henry Grattan explaining how easily the folk-memories of betrayal and persecution could be revived: 'They call back to their recollection the treatment of their fathers in former days—& consider & dwell on the insults and wrongs they endured as the reward of their having restored or defended the Constitution.'[94] It remains to be seen whether this renewed antagonism would lead, as the government feared, to a reappraisal of traditional attitudes towards their Catholic countrymen.

The rock of religion: reform and the Catholic question

> The Puritans, a restless faction,
> Ripe ever for rebellious action;
> Did not resolve with pious zeal,
> To over turn our common-weal:
> But, doubtful of their single strength,
> Determined to go every length,
> Their point to gain at any rate,
> With Papists they confederate . . .
>
> *Drawcansir: or, The Mock Reform*[95]

A central part of the mythology which surrounds the Irish Volunteers concerns their support for the Catholic cause. Historians have made much of the softening of anti-Catholic feeling which accompanied the heyday of Protestant patriotism.[96] Two gestures of goodwill have often been cited to demonstrate the point. The first is the famous declaration of liberality contained in the Dungannon manifesto of 15 February 1782. The thirteenth resolution passed on that day affirmed the sanctity of the right of private judgement, and the fourteenth went on to state:

Resolved, therefore, That as Men, and as Irishmen, as Christians, and as Protestants, we rejoice in the relaxation of the Penal Laws against our Roman Catholic fellow-subjects, and that we conceive the measure to be fraught with the happiest consequences to the union and prosperity of the Inhabitants of Ireland.[97]

The second great date in the history of Volunteer ecumenics is 30 May 1784, when the Belfast First Company marched to St Mary's Roman Catholic chapel, having

---

[94] Campbell to Grattan, 15 June 1782, PRONI, Fitzwilliam/Grattan papers, T3649/1.

[95] *Drawcansir: or, The Mock Reform. An Heroic Poem* (Dublin, 1784), 5.

[96] There is an excellent, if slightly romanticized, account in Patrick Rogers, *The Irish Volunteers and Catholic Emancipation (1778–1793)* (London, 1934).

[97] The resolutions can be found in [Henry Joy (ed.)], *Historical Collections Relative to the Town of Belfast* (Belfast, 1817), 180–5.

collected £84 for the benefit of the congregation.[98] Together with the admission of Catholics to corps all over the country and the raising of the Catholic question at the Grand National Convention of November 1783, these signals were taken as evidence of a plot hatched by Dissenters and Catholics to overthrow the government. In August Fitzgibbon apprehended that 'The Puritans of the North are Become Advocates of Religious Tolerance, and the Catholics Profess a strong Predilection for Republican Government—The Puritans tell them[,] If you will Assist us in Reforming the Constitution, we will Assist you in shaking off Every Restraint which the Laws of Ireland now Impose upon you.'[99] The partisan historian Richard Musgrave believed that it was during the Volunteer campaigns that 'the flirtation between John and Peter' had begun.[100]

The first Dungannon convention which assembled in February 1782 is the climax of the Volunteer legend. Although the vast majority of the delegates present were Dissenters, the proceedings were dominated by the northern gentry. The meeting was in fact managed by the patriot opposition in the Irish parliament—Charlemont, Flood, Grattan, Stewart of Killymoon, and Dobbs—who had drafted most of the resolutions concerning the independence of the Irish parliament and the evils of Poynings' Law.[101] A number of Presbyterians were appointed to the standing committee, however, including Joseph Pollock, captain of the Newry First Volunteers, Waddell Cunningham, captain of the Belfast First Company, Robert Thompson, the Revd Robert Black who was captain of a Dromore corps, and the Revd William Crawford of Strabane who was chaplain of the First Tyrone Regiment. It is interesting to note that some of these Dissenters had a hand in the Dungannon resolutions. Pollock had helped Dobbs frame the first resolution, defending the right of Volunteers to debate political subjects, 'that a citizen by learning the use of arms, does not abandon any of his civil rights', and Robert Thompson had drawn up resolution twelve, calling for a ban on the consumption of Portuguese wine. Most importantly, the fourteenth resolution, thrown in at the last minute at the suggestion of Grattan, was proposed by Pollock, seconded by Black, and supported by Crawford.[102] This was not because the northern Presbyterians were particularly forward in their support for toleration; on the contrary, Pollock and Black were asked to speak because of a widespread perception that the Ulster Presbyterians were especially prejudiced against the Catholics.[103]

The Volunteers were of course heirs to a political tradition in which Protestantism and liberty were inextricably linked. Their flags and emblems carried the usual Orange iconography and they frequently celebrated Protestant anniversaries like the Siege

---

[98] Examples of similar ecumenical gestures can be found in the *Londonderry Journal* from this period.

[99] Fitzgibbon to William Eden, 29 Aug. 1784, PRONI, Sneyd Papers, T3229/1/2. See also Edward Cooke to Eden, 14 May 1784, ibid., T3229/2/3.

[100] Richard Musgrave, *Memoirs of the Different Rebellions in Ireland* (Dublin, 1801), 50. The references are to John Calvin and St Peter.

[101] Francis Dobbs, *A History of Irish Affairs* (Dublin, 1782), 52.

[102] Ibid. 52, 59; Samuel McSkimmin, 'Memoranda referring to the County Antrim Volunteers', PRONI, T2822, p. 8.

[103] Joseph Pollock, *Letter to the Inhabitants of the Town and Lordship of Newry* (Dublin, 1793), 160 n.

of Derry and the battles of the Boyne, Aughrim, and Culloden. Their aggressive Protestantism was inevitably reinforced by the threat of invasion by the two great Catholic powers of France and Spain. The Bourbon monarchy was the traditional protector of Irish Jacobitism, and most Volunteer sermons had accordingly stressed the need to watch the popish enemy within as well as the French. There is some evidence, however, to show that anti-Catholic feeling had mellowed somewhat among the Dissenting elite. Joseph Pollock pointed out that in other European states, like Switzerland and the United Provinces, Catholics and Protestants happily coexisted under the same constitution. He recommended the 'gentle, gradual' extension of religious toleration.[104] As early as March 1779, William Steel Dickson of Portaferry had preached a sermon to the Echlinville Volunteers proposing the admission of Catholics to their ranks. The outcry which followed was so great that Dickson was forced to remove this passage from the sermon before publication, substituting instead a plea that the Volunteers should not let the gravity of the international situation reopen old wounds at home.[195] Another Volunteer preacher, Samuel Barber of Rathfriland, also cautioned his men against sectarian animosity. 'The present generation', he pointed out, 'have behaved peaceably and quietly tho' as a religious society they have been subjected to penal laws too shocking to enumerate.'[106] He finished off by envisaging a day when all Irishmen would worship God freely according to their own consciences. To these names we can add Robert Black and William Crawford, who had supported the Catholic resolution at Dungannon. Crawford's belief that Ireland had entered a more tolerant age enabled him to adopt a philosophical view of the wars of religion in *A History of Ireland* (1783), a two-volume celebration of the revolution of 1782 which was published by subscriptions collected from the Ulster Volunteers. In the preface Crawford notified his readers, who included many Dissenting clergymen, that he differed from most previous Protestant historians in his treatment of Roman Catholic grievances. The 'benevolent reader', he anticipated, would be horrified by the 'inhuman treatment to which the natives were exposed from the rapacity of the English adventurers', the imposition of the Reformation on Ireland, and the hardships endured by Roman Catholics for their religious beliefs.[107]

Pollock, Barber, Dickson, and Crawford all belonged to the New Light tendency in Ulster Presbyterianism, however; their opposition to creeds and confessions made them more sensitive to any state interference in religious matters. That liberal views were making headway among the New Lights was confirmed by two addresses sent to the *Belfast News-Letter* by the Presbyteries of Bangor and Killyleagh, echoing the sentiments of the fourteenth resolution of the Dungannon manifesto. These two

---

[104] Owen Roe O'Nial [Pollock], 'Letters to the Men of Ireland', in John Lawless (ed.), *The Belfast Politics Enlarged* (Belfast, 1818), 131–2, 134.

[105] Dickson, *Narrative*, 10–11; see also id., *A Sermon on the Propriety and Advantages of Acquiring the Knowledge and Use of Firearms in Times of Danger. Preached before the Echlinville Volunteers* (Belfast, 1779), 25.

[106] Samuel Barber, Sermon Preached to the Castlewellan Rangers, PHSI, Barber MSS, p. 11.

[107] William Crawford, *A History of Ireland from the Earliest Period, to the Present Time*, 2 vols. (Strabane, 1783), vol. i, p. vii.

presbyteries were firmly anti-subscription. The latter made explicit the connection between pro-Catholic sympathy and heterodox theology by referring to the penal code as 'a black branch grafted upon the blasphemous doctrine of imputed sin'.[108] Interestingly, the Killyleagh address incurred the censure of the General Synod, not because of its political content, but because the resolution had breached the theological truce which then prevailed in Irish Presbyterianism.[109]

The sort of liberal sentiments expressed at Dungannon and in Crawford's book should be seen in the context of a growing feeling among the Protestant elite that the penal laws were counter-productive and outdated. Such views had been expressed in a number of pamphlets in the 1760s and 1770s. Presbyterians were far from leading this trend. Next to the Bishop of Derry, the staunchest supporters of the Catholics at this time were William Todd Jones, a small landowner from County Down and MP for Lisburn, and Peter Burrowes, a Dublin barrister. It is clear too that liberal Protestants drew a line between ecclesiastical discrimination, meaning the restrictions imposed on church organization, and the civil disabilities which guaranteed that Ireland remained a free, Protestant kingdom attached to the British Empire. Many Protestants spoke as if the penal code had been entirely abolished by 1782, since full religious toleration had been conceded. Furthermore, outside New Light circles anti-popery retained its vital, literal force, as the hysterical reaction to Dickson's sermon revealed. Another Volunteer sermon, preached by John Rogers, the Seceding minister of Cahans, County Cavan, may be more representative of the attitudes of Old Light Presbyterians at this time. Rogers regretted the fact that many 'enlightened' Protestants failed to see the continuing threat posed by the papacy. After rehearsing the old arguments for identifying the Pope as Antichrist, and reasserting old myths about the persecution of heretics, the deposition of Protestant princes, and the dispensing of oaths made with Protestants, Rogers defended his right to warn the Volunteers against popery.[110] Rogers was also one of two delegates at the Dungannon convention who voted against the fourteenth resolution.[111]

As the Volunteers moved on to consider the reconstruction of the electoral system it was inevitable that the question of Catholic enfranchisement should be discussed. In the old nationalist historiography there is a teleological tendency to assume that the clamour for Catholic emancipation followed on logically from the attainment of parliamentary independence. According to this view it was natural that the Volunteers, having secured parliamentary independence, should attempt to heal the divisions between Ireland's sects. It is certainly true that all Irish patriots were acutely aware that their country had been weakened by religious divisions. While many felt that this problem must be addressed, however, it was believed that the lifting of all restrictions would have led to the renewal, not the end, of religious conflict. Behind the penal code lay the familiar Protestant bogeys of a court of claims, a Catholic establishment, and discrimination against Protestants. These apprehensions were

[108] *BNL*, 8 Mar., 17 May 1782.   [109] *RGSU*, iii. 45.

[110] John Rogers, *A Sermon Preached at Lisnavein, Otherwise Ballybay New Erection, on Saturday, June 10, 1780. To the Lisnavein Rangers, Trough Volunteers, Lisluney Volunteers, and Monaghan Rangers* (Edinburgh, 1780), 17–25, 36–7.   [111] Rogers, *Irish Volunteers and Catholic Emancipation*, 70.

encouraged by Northington, the Lord Lieutenant, who saw that the best way to defeat the Volunteers was to 'Create Confusion in their Deliberations' and to exploit the alarm of many members at the introduction of the Catholic demands.[112] Radicals like Drennan recognized that the Catholic question was being exploited to sidetrack the reform debate. He therefore tried to prevent the penal laws emerging as the dominant issue. For Drennan the question was one of tactics: 'Why should we drive the wedge with the *blunt* end foremost?'[113]

We have already seen that the Ulster committee which led the reform movement in 1783 had consulted a number of authorities in Britain and Ireland when formulating its programme. Although they were not asked specifically to comment on the penal code, several of the English correspondents declared themselves in favour of some degree of Catholic enfranchisement. The Rational Dissenters Richard Price and John Jebb dealt with the matter most fully. These two men were also the most likely to impress the New Light Presbyterians: Price was widely admired as a moral philosopher and a defender of the American Revolution; Jebb for his principled opposition to religious creeds, which had led him to resign his position at Cambridge and quit the Church of England. Price began with the general principle that it was unjust to deprive any man of his rights on account of his religious opinions. The threat from Irish papists, he advised, derived not so much from their religious tenets as from the penal laws themselves which alienated them from the constitution. In a postscript, however, Price alluded briefly to Ireland's peculiar circumstances, acknowledging that the Ulster reformers may know of objections to emancipation of which he was not aware.[114] Jebb took a similar position, admitting that there may be local difficulties but condemning the injustices of the popery laws. If the Catholics were emancipated, he predicted, they would become attached to the public, and 'their prejudices would be softened'.[115]

By way of contrast, the Irish reformers consulted by the committee of correspondence replied with vague statements, and ignored the religious aspect of reform. Their letters were 'poor, trifling, polite, short and unsatisfactory', complained Mrs McTier.[116] Flood and Charlemont were both resolutely opposed to Catholic involvement. When the committee of correspondence sided with the English reformers, including in their report an assertion that the constitution could never be completely settled until the franchise was extended to persons of all religions, Charlemont's allies insisted that the resolution be abandoned.[117] Instead, it was decided that the question of Roman Catholic participation should be left to the National Convention.[118] It is not necessary to recount the absurd debates of the Grand National Convention here; suffice it to say that there was uncertainty as to what the Catholic demands actually were, and when a false report was read claiming that the Catholics had

---

[112] Northington to Charles J. Fox, 17 Nov. 1783, BL, Northington Letterbook, p. 207, Add. MS 38716, fo. 128.   [113] Drennan to Bruce, [Nov. 1784], PRONI, Drennan–Bruce Papers, D553/34.
[114] *A Collection of the Letters which Have Been Addressed to the Volunteers of Ireland, on the Subject of a Parliamentary Reform* (London, 1783), 86–8.   [115] Ibid. 119.
[116] Martha McTier to Drennan, [Sept. 1783], *Drennan Letters*, 18.
[117] 'Memoirs', *Charlemont MSS*, i. 117.
[118] Ibid. 113; 'Heads of a Plan of Parliamentary Reform', *BNL*, 3 Oct. 1783.

withdrawn their claims, the Volunteers grasped the opportunity to shelve the question. The confusion which surrounded the issue was encouraged by the opponents of the Catholics, but it also reflected doubts within the Catholic Committee itself, torn between the Castle and the Volunteers.[119]

Although there had been Roman Catholics in some corps from the very beginning, it was about this time that some northern companies began to welcome publicly members of all religious persuasions. To entrust Catholics with the right to bear arms, it should be remembered, was an important step towards recognizing them as citizens. On 13 May 1784 the Belfast First Company threw open its ranks to persons of all denominations, followed a few days later by the Newry First Volunteers.[120] Soon Catholics had been admitted to companies in Downpatrick, Strabane, and other towns.[121] In some areas, however, there was opposition: John Caldwell recalled how his father, a New Light Presbyterian and commander of the Ballymoney company, had struggled hard to secure the admission of a Roman Catholic neighbour.[122]

As summer approached, both Belfast and Newry met to discuss the Catholic question. On 8 July 1784 a Belfast town meeting adopted the resolutions of the Dublin Aggregate Committee calling for the gradual extension of suffrage to their Roman Catholic brethren, '*preserving unimpaired the Protestant Government of this country*'. A petition was accordingly drawn up by a committee comprising Kelburn, John Brown, Robert Thompson, Waddell Cunningham, and Henry Joy.[123] A few days later at the annual review these sentiments were approved and presented to Lord Charlemont. The 'Volunteer earl' rejected the address, on the grounds that such a move would hinder the cause of reform.[124] This scene was repeated across the province. At Newry the Volunteers followed Belfast's lead, proposing an address in favour of the Catholics. Drennan, who had drafted the motion, confided to his sister that he had in mind a '*gradual*' extension of the suffrage, beginning with 500 or 1,000 people.[125] Although he was confident that the Newry review would endorse the address despite Charlemont's known opposition, it was actually defeated by a large majority.[126] In Derry, too, Charlemont succeeded in having Catholic resolutions withdrawn, on the Earl-Bishop's own home ground.[127] It was at this time also that the Peep O' Day Boys began their raids on Catholic homes in County Armagh. This recrudescence of sectarian feeling, like the more general reassertion of traditional Protestant fears, was part of a delayed backlash following the relief acts of 1778 and 1782. The apparent triumph of liberalism at the Dungannon convention should not be allowed to obscure the fact that the same year also saw the

[119] For a full account see Rogers, *Irish Volunteers and Catholic Emancipation*, ch. 3.

[120] Minute-book of the First Newry Volunteers, pp. 16–19, 4 May 1784, PRONI, T3202/1A.

[121] Rogers, *Irish Volunteers and Catholic Emancipation*, 147; for Strabane, see James Hamilton to [Abercorn], [Jan. 1784?], PRONI, Abercorn Papers, T2541/1A1/14/7.

[122] John Caldwell, 'Particulars of a North County Irish Family', PRONI, Caldwell Papers, T3541/5/3, p. 63.   [123] Joy, *Historical Collections*, 298.

[124] Ibid. 298–311.   [125] Drennan to Martha McTier, [1784–5], *Drennan Letters*, 28–9.

[126] Drennan to Martha McTier, n.d., PRONI, Drennan Papers, T765/158.

[127] Charlemont to Haliday, 27 Aug. 1784, *Charlemont MSS*, ii. 6.

first attempts of conservatives to articulate the new concept of Protestant Ascendancy. While the former proved to be an essentially transient phenomenon, the latter was soon to demonstrate its resilience.

It is difficult to gauge the extent of Presbyterian support for Catholic emancipation at this time. The Protestant–Catholic rapprochement came during the twilight of volunteering when the annual reviews attracted relatively poor numbers. Nevertheless, it seems clear that the advanced radicals in Belfast had accepted the case for a limited measure of enfranchisement. At the National Convention, Charlemont noted that 'even a few of the northern dissenters, by their speeches or acquiescence, appeared already to indicate the approaches of that strange madness, by which they were not long after activated'.[128] The *News-Letter* had certainly swung behind the Catholics. After the 1784 review it printed two letters signed 'T', arguing for the admission to the electorate of Catholics holding £50 in land in actual fee. The writer, Henry Joy, anticipated many of the arguments employed on behalf of the Catholics in the 1790s. He explained to his readers how the British government had kept Ireland in chains by fostering differences between the Catholics and Dissenters. He warned that the government would try to detach the Catholics from the common interest and add their weight to the opposite scale. In North America, he pointed out, Protestants had extended the suffrage to all descriptions of Christians, and he referred to the opinions of Price, Jebb, and Cartwright that Irish Protestants should follow their example.[129] A week later he added:

If, as informed Protestants, we wish to sap the very foundation of *superstition*;—if we want to give rank to Ireland among the Nations,—it is only to be done by unequivocal testimonies of our affection and regard for those who at present constitute so great a part of its inhabitants.[130]

Outside Belfast and Newry, however, support for the Catholics seemed to depend on the influence of the Bishop of Derry, who had now withdrawn from the political scene as suddenly as he had appeared. When the Revd William Campbell wrote to several colleagues in 1784 in an effort to gauge political attitudes in Ulster, he found several of his co-presbyters implacably opposed to any further relaxation of the penal code and convinced that if the right of suffrage was granted to Roman Catholics there would be a great wave of emigration from the north.[131] 'There are a few—and very few—weak men', he informed Charlemont, 'that are led away by some abstract ideas of what they call the common rights of mankind, which may do very well on religious toleration, or in books of natural jurisprudence, but never can have place in civil society.'[132] Interestingly, Campbell detected a resurgence of support for reform in Ulster after the removal of the Catholic question from Irish politics in late 1784.[133]

---

[128] 'Memoirs', *Charlemont MSS*, i. 125.   [129] *BNL*, 23 July 1784.

[130] Ibid., 30 July 1784. In 1783 an anonymous Belfast pamphleteer had called for 'a severe and attentive revision of the Penal Laws, which are at present a disgrace to equal justice, and a public satire on humanity': *A Letter to Henry Flood, Esq. on the Present State of Representation in Ireland* (Belfast, 1783), 25.

[131] Campbell, journal, PHSI, Campbell MSS, pp. 21, 118–22.

[132] Campbell to Charlemont, 9 Oct. 1784, *Charlemont MSS*, ii. 7–8.

[133] Campbell to Charlemont, 25 Dec. 1784, ibid. 16.

When the Dublin reformers summoned the National Congress to meet in October 1784, Charlemont did his best to ensure that the meeting would be a failure. Jones, as always the champion of the Catholic cause, was disgusted to find that the reformers had already made up their minds and would not even consider his arguments. Drennan's attitudes had undergone an alteration. Now he believed that when the Catholics 'acquire in *general* more property, more independence & republicanism of spirit, they will then be worthy of the boon—At *present* I would dread the weight of catholic influence in that house'. His main concern was that the question should not paralyse the convention.[134] In his 'helot' letters he therefore seized on dubious reports that the Catholics had withdrawn their claims until parliamentary reform was granted. His close friend and correspondent William Bruce also believed that the Catholic experiment had failed. As the congress opened he hoped that in future the Volunteers would 'abjure the errors of popery' and concentrate on 'the simple question of reform unembarrassed by religious disputes'.[135]

In fact, the Protestants never recovered the unanimity which had made possible the revolution of 1782. A secret investigation ordered by Dublin Castle in 1784 revealed that the Volunteer organization had entered terminal decline. County Antrim, the heartland of volunteering, could still muster 3,573 men, but the other northern counties lagged far behind—Armagh, for example, managing only 500. A couple of Roman Catholic corps were reported in Down and Donegal, but surprisingly few Catholics were to be found elsewhere—only six or seven in any of the Antrim corps. It was reported that the collapse of volunteering in the northern counties had been hastened by the Belfast resolutions in favour of Roman Catholics.[136] In preparation for the Belfast review of 1786 a company was raised in Newry from the remnants of the others, but the new corps was greeted sceptically by Drennan: 'This is just a frolic of young lads to show their silver at the review and will die the day after.'[137] The following year, when James Stewart of Killymoon proposed a field day at Strabane, he was informed that it was almost impossible to assemble enough members to do the old Tyrone battalion credit.[138]

Like William Bruce, Drennan was determined to keep the Volunteer spirit alive. Throughout 1784 he and Bruce discussed plans for a new radical periodical, to be published weekly by a committee based in Dublin. Drennan suggested many names— 'The Commoner', 'The Free-Speaker', 'The Independent', 'The Helot', and his own favourite, 'The Philanthropist'. Presbyterian radicals like Joseph Pollock and the Revd James Crombie were consulted, and other potential contributors ranged from the veteran whig Dr Haliday to the Glasgow philosopher Dugald Stewart.[139]

---

[134] Drennan to Bruce, [30 Oct. 1783], PRONI, Drennan–Bruce Papers, D553/16. See also Drennan to Martha McTier, [autumn 1783], *Drennan Letters*, 21.

[135] Bruce to [Joy], 7 Oct. 1784, Linenhall Library Belfast, Joy MSS, 14/19.

[136] James Kelly, 'Select Documents XLIII: A Secret Return of the Volunteers of Ireland in 1784', *IHS* 26/103 (1989), 268–92.

[137] Drennan to Martha McTier, 3 May 1786, *Drennan Letters*, 41–2.

[138] Richard Carleton to Stewart, 11 June 1787, PRONI, Stewart of Killymoon Papers, D3167/2/71.

[139] Drennan to Bruce, [Feb. 1784], [Feb. 1784], [21 Sept. 1784], [Nov. 1784], PRONI, Drennan–Bruce Papers, D553/20, 21, 31, 34; James Crombie to Drennan, [1784], PRONI, D456/5.

Drennan did get as far as drafting a prospectus which made it clear that the periodical would be a vehicle for literary nationalism as well as reform propaganda.[140] At the same time, he proposed to Bruce the creation of a new reform club, organized along the lines of a Masonic lodge, bound to secrecy by oath, to be called the Irish Brotherhood.

The Brotherhood was first suggested by Drennan in an anonymous pamphlet in 1780, when he proposed the formation of an inner cell of dedicated reformers within the Volunteers.[141] Throughout the 1780s he occasionally returned to this idea, always as a means of giving fresh life to the flagging companies. In February 1784 he advocated the establishment of an oath-bound society dedicated to 'the complete liberation of the Country'. Patriotism, he felt, was too general and too weak—'We want to be condensed into the fervent enthusiasm of sectaries.'[142] When Bruce joined the rather aristocratic Reform Club set up in Dublin in the summer of 1785, Drennan wrote to him:

Ten or 12 Conspirators for Constitutional freedom would do more in a day than they would do in ten—I should like to see a Constitutional *Covenant* drawn up, solemnly recapitulating our political creed, and every man who chose sh'd subscribe his name to it—This would be a knocking down club . . . I would sign such a confederation of compatriots with my Blood. Oh! I think I see Marcus Cato looking down from heaven, austerely smiling while he calls us Prattlers—mere Prattlers.[143]

It would be six years, however, before Drennan's Irish Brotherhood, renamed the Society of United Irishmen, would make its appearance.

Conclusion

By 1785 Presbyterian radicalism had run out of steam. The great triumphs of 1779 and 1782 had been followed by a long war of attrition in which the Irish elite had successfully eroded support for the Volunteers. Some radicals had hoped that an alliance of reformers and Catholics would break this deadlock, but overtures towards the Catholics, tentative though they were, had alienated Protestant support without bringing any tangible benefits. Over the next few years reviews were occasionally held in the north and diehards turned out to go through the Volunteer motions, but the reform issue was dead. Neither the hopes aroused by William Pitt's reform bill, nor the storm caused in Ireland by his commercial propositions, succeeded in arresting the decline of radicalism. It soon became apparent that the much vaunted 'Constitution of 1782' had been a hollow victory. In the last two chapters, however, I have tried to argue that the significance of volunteering lay not just in what it achieved but in what it represented. The Irish Volunteer was the embodiment

---

[140] Drennan to Bruce, [20 Oct. 1784], PRONI, Drennan–Bruce Papers, D553/33.

[141] [Drennan], *Address to the Volunteers of Ireland*. A sketch of a Volunteer test appears on the back of the title page.

[142] Drennan to Bruce, [Feb. 1784], PRONI, Drennan–Bruce Papers, D553/20.

[143] Drennan to Bruce, [16 May 1785], PRONI, Drennan–Bruce Papers, D553/43. See also Drennan to Bruce, [26 July 1785], ibid., D533/45.

of the civic virtue so prized by republican writers. The debates of these years represent the beginnings of popular politics in the north and the emergence of a new, self-conscious public eager to assert its authority. The experience of electing officers and delegates, participating in debates, writing addresses, chairing meetings, and serving on committees provided a vital political education for thousands of northern Dissenters. Although the reformers ultimately failed to obtain their demands, the Ulster Volunteers had created a provincial political culture outside the structures of the constitution. It was a culture which was republican in the classical sense, founded on the active participation of the arms-bearing citizen. If radicalism had lost its momentum after 1785, the machinery for popular mobilization was still there.

PART III

Sincere and Enlightened Republicans

7
THE UNITED IRISHMEN

IN April 1789, a month before the States General met at Versailles, Dr Haliday wrote to Charlemont lamenting the torpor which had descended upon Belfast. Since the failure of Pitt's bill in 1785, the reform movement had fizzled out. In Ireland, as in England, the government steadily regained confidence following the end of the American war and the economic recovery which accompanied it. During the campaigns of 1784–5 the House of Commons had rejected reform bills with contempt and had found it was able to attack the Volunteers. Meanwhile, in the counties, landlords quietly suppressed Volunteer activity on their estates and discouraged political meetings. The restoration of political stability had enabled the Protestant Ascendancy to regain the upper hand: lacking immediate issues, and a leader of national status, the Volunteer machine soon fell into disrepair. Even in Belfast, the capital of the reformers, public meetings were dominated by the sovereign and the corporation. 'In short' complained Haliday, 'the spirit of commerce, here as elsewhere, monopolises the human mind, and most of our merchants are infinitely more anxious about their own credit than that of parliament or the nation.'[1]

After the collapse of the *ancien régime* in France, of course, nothing would ever be the same. The impact of French affairs was considerably delayed, however, and the lesson drawn from them by Irish radicals has often been misunderstood. The Irish press quickly relayed news of the initial triumphs of the Revolution, and the debates of the French assemblies were reported in detail. As early as November 1789 the revolutionary drama was celebrated on the Irish stage when 'Gallic Freedom, or the Destruction of the Bastille' was performed at the Theatre Royal in Dublin.[2] It was not until two years after the storming of the Bastille, however, that the full implications of French events for the British constitution were spelled out.

By this time the forces of reform were already regrouping. Political debate had been stimulated by the regency crisis, which gave the English Whigs hopes of office and the Dublin legislature the chance to prove its independence by appointing the Prince of Wales regent of Ireland.[3] Earlier in the same year reformers had celebrated the centenary of the Glorious Revolution. In Belfast the occasion was marked by *feux de joie* from the Volunteers, and Haliday drew up a string of toasts for a dinner attended by 300 whigs.[4] Across the water, a group of Rational Dissenters who had

---

[1] Haliday to Charlemont, 11 Apr. 1789, *Charlemont MSS*, ii. 96.

[2] R. B. McDowell, *Ireland in the Age of Imperialism and Revolution, 1760–1801* (Oxford, 1979), 351–2. In 1793 the same theatre would stage 'Democratic Rage', a tragedy mourning the end of Louis XVI, an indication of how perceptions of the Revolution had changed.

[3] For Belfast opinion on this question see Henry Joy to Charlemont, 31 Mar. 1789, *Charlemont MSS*, ii. 89–90; Drennan to Martha McTier, [Dec. 1788/Jan. 1789], Martha McTier to Drennan, [*c*.28 Dec. 1788], PRONI, Drennan Papers, T765/245, 246A.

[4] Haliday to Charlemont, 13 Feb. 1788, *Charlemont MSS*, ii. 70.

for some time been agitating for the repeal of the Test and Corporation Acts established the London Revolution Society. It was to this body that Dr Price preached his famous sermon *On the Love of Country* at the Old Jewry on 4 November 1789, advancing a radical interpretation of the Glorious Revolution as grounded on the principle of popular sovereignty. The Williamite Settlement, he argued, had established three vital principles:

First; The right to liberty of conscience in religious matters.
Secondly; The right to resist power when abused. And,
Thirdly; The right to chuse our own governors; to cashier them for misconduct; and to frame a government for ourselves.[5]

To some extent there was little novelty here: Price's creed was based on a Rational Dissenting reading of John Locke, and his views had already attracted considerable attention during the American conflict. But his ardour had been rekindled by the fall of absolutism across the Channel which seemed to presage 'a general amendment beginning in human affairs'. In a famous peroration which demonstrates how closely civil and religious liberty were intertwined in the Dissenting mind, Price envisaged 'the dominion of kings changed for the dominion of laws, and the dominion of priests giving way to the dominion of reason and conscience'.[6]

It was this linkage of England's Dissenting tradition with the assault on the old order in France that prompted the publication of Burke's *Reflections on the Revolution in France* in November 1790, which in turn provoked Thomas Paine to write the best-known pamphlet of the period, *Rights of Man* (March 1791). While Paine transformed the terms of political discourse, it is important to realize that the pamphlet war over the French Revolution was superimposed on top of an existing debate. Burke's rhetoric harked back to an older literature which defended Anglican civility against the dangers of religious enthusiasm, and to some extent the fissures of the 1790s followed lines of division already carved out by the struggle over the Test and Corporation Acts.

The controversy over the new French regime provided the central dividing issue in Irish politics. The two great protagonists were in time presented with fitting honours: Burke a degree from Trinity College Dublin, Paine membership of the Society of United Irishmen.[7] At first, the reaction to Paine was overwhelmingly favourable, as *Rights of Man* was serialized in the Irish papers, and a thousand copies were sold in Belfast.[8] An early note of caution was sounded by the Earl of Charlemont, however, who welcomed the emancipation of the French but objected to the conclusions which Paine had drawn about the British constitution. 'He does, indeed, tear away the bandage from the public eye, but, in tearing it off, there may be some danger of injuring the organ,' he warned Haliday. Echoing Burke, he remarked that 'There is no science in which theory and practice differ more than in the science

[5] Richard Price, *A Discourse on the Love of Our Country* (London, 1789), 34.
[6] Ibid. 49–50.   [7] McDowell, *Ireland*, 353.
[8] Martha McTier to Drennan, [Mar. 1795], PRONI, Drennan Papers, T765/548.

of politics', and pointed out that no government had been more tyrannical than the democracy of Athens.[9]

As British and Irish spectators discussed the merits of the French Revolution, the parameters of political debate were redefined, splitting public opinion between 'aristocrats' and 'democrats'. Gallic slogans and motifs were adopted by radicals, now branded as 'Jacobins' by their enemies, while the fashion for short hairstyles earned them the nickname 'croppies'. This identification of native radicalism with the French Revolution brought mixed blessings. Initially, the reform movement received a huge boost as Volunteers celebrated Bastille Day, and later the victories of Valmy and Jemappes, in the northern towns. But as the tempo of events in France accelerated, the United Irishmen found themselves apologizing for revolutionary excesses such as the September massacres of 1792 and the bloodletting of the Terror. Reformers were now cast as violent fanatics who conspired to overturn Church and State. Above all, the execution of Louis and the declaration of war focused conservative hostility on the United Irish societies, now depicted as allies of the French regicide regime.

The French Revolution and the Radical Revival, 1791–1794

All this, however, lay some years ahead. The revival of political activity in Ireland at first took a more conventional shape. During the Commons debates on the regency bill several important 'connections' in the House had co-operated together in opposition, and in August 1789 they endeavoured to put their alliance on a more formal basis with the formation of the Irish Whig Club. With the encouragement of Charlemont, Dr Haliday established a sister society, the Northern Whig Club, in Belfast in February 1790.[10] Among the sixty members were Charlemont himself, Lord Moira, the MPs John O'Neill and Hercules Rowley, the Wards of Bangor, William Brownlow, and other local gentlemen, including Robert Stewart, the future Viscount Castlereagh.[11] The predominance of landed gentlemen raised objections from the Belfast merchants, however, and the following month there was some talk of founding a separate branch in the town.[12]

The Northern Whigs were soon furnished with a declaration of principles by Haliday, similar to the 'Country' programme adopted by the Dublin branch but with a distinctively northern flavour. A preamble traced the pedigree of the Northern Whigs back through the Volunteers of 1782 and the Patriot Clubs of the 1750s to the Glorious Revolution. Added to the hackneyed calls for the abolition of places and pensions, the encouragement of trade, and the preservation of Irish Parliamentary independence was a bold description of the British constitution as a 'regal commonwealth'. Even more controversial was Haliday's vague assertion that 'as religion

---

[9] Charlemont to Haliday, 9 May 1791, *Charlemont MSS*, ii. 139–40.
[10] Haliday to Charlemont, 14 June 1789, Charlemont to Haliday, 4 Dec. 1789, ibid. 99–100, 109–10.
[11] Haliday to Charlemont, 17 Apr. 1790, ibid. 125; Charles Hamilton Teeling, *Personal Narrative of the 'Irish Rebellion' of 1798* (London, 1828), 270.
[12] Haliday to Charlemont, 1 Mar. 1790, *Charlemont MSS*, ii. 117.

is of the utmost importance to every individual, no person ought to suffer civil hardships for his religious persuasion, unless the tenets of his religion lead him to endeavour to subvert the state'.[13] Haliday later defended this clause, insisting that the right of conscience was the most sacred of all, but he then went on to reassure the Volunteer earl that as long as Catholics held subversive principles they had to be restrained by the magistrate.[14] Inevitably, however, the return of the reform issue brought with it the vexed question of the penal laws. In the months ahead Charlemont watched helplessly as the northern capital succumbed to the 'mal Catholique'.[15]

As the second anniversary of the storming of the Bastille approached, it was decided that the Northern Whigs should make arrangements for a celebration in Belfast.[16] There were already signs that Haliday's moderate whiggism was giving way to more extreme sentiments, however. William Drennan, who had finally escaped the drudgery of Newry to set up medical practice in Dublin, was once more pushing his plan for a Masonic-style society with renewed enthusiasm. Writing to his brother-in-law, Samuel McTier, Drennan outlined his scheme for an 'Irish Brotherhood':

A benevolent conspiracy—a plot for the people—no *Whig* Club—no party title—the Brotherhood its name—the Rights of Men and the Greatest Happiness of the Greatest Number its end—its general end Real Independence to Ireland, and Republicanism its particular purpose.[17]

A prospectus, minus the reference to republicanism, was later circulated in Belfast. William Bruce, who had moved to the First Belfast Congregation on the death of James Crombie, disapproved of the idea, as did Henry Joy, but McTier's associates in the Volunteers were enthusiastic. When a Volunteer committee was appointed to draw up resolutions for the 14th, Drennan was therefore contacted and asked to contribute an address.[18] At the same time, they approached a young Dublin barrister, Wolfe Tone, whose *Review of the Conduct of Administration* (1790) had recently been reprinted by the Northern Whigs.

The Bastille Day celebrations thus became the focus for the dissensions emerging in the ranks of the reformers. The anniversary was marked by a spectacular parade to the White Linen Hall, as the Volunteer companies carried through the streets portraits of Franklin and Mirabeau, and a huge standard depicting the storming of the Bastille on one side, and a Volunteer freeing a shackled Hibernia on the other. Three resolutions drawn up by Tone were proposed. The first two were passed, condemning English influence in Irish affairs and proposing parliamentary reform as the remedy. The third, asserting that the widening of the franchise should be accompanied by an abolition of religious distinctions, was rejected.[19] Reporting

---

[13] Haliday to Charlemont, 18 Feb. 1790, *Charlemont MSS*, ii. 114–16.
[14] Haliday to Charlemont, 11 Mar. 1790, ibid. 119–20.
[15] Charlemont to Haliday, 31 Nov. 1791, ibid. 179.
[16] Haliday to Charlemont, 16 June 1791, ibid. 140.
[17] Drennan to Samuel McTier, 21 May 1791, *Drennan Letters*, 54.
[18] Samuel McTier to Drennan, 2 July 1791, PRONI, Drennan Papers, T765/302.
[19] [Revd William Bruce and Henry Joy (eds.)], *Belfast Politics* (Belfast, 1794), 52–65.

to the Marquis of Abercorn, the County Tyrone MP Thomas Knox expressed his alarm at the idea of a coalition of Dissenters and Catholics, but he dismissed the show put on by the Belfast radicals: 'It has always been the way with these Gentry to flourish and parade upon political subjects, and you may rely upon it that no mischief whatever will come from it.'[20] Presbyterian radicalism still operated within the constraints imposed by the Catholic threat.

The breakthrough came in August with the appearance of Tone's *Argument on Behalf of the Catholics of Ireland*. The pamphlet was aimed specifically at the northern Dissenters, and 10,000 copies were struck off in Belfast.[21] Within a couple of months Haliday informed Charlemont that Tone had made many converts to the Catholic cause:

The tide here runs strong in favour of the 'Argument'; too strong at present to be directly resisted, it can only be eluded by an oblique course; not but there are many who retain their old horrors and dread of Popery as much as ever, but they are looked on as 'men of the little mind' as Ossian says.[22]

By this stage Haliday himself confessed to some uncertainty on the question of Catholic suffrage. The rationale behind the penal code had certainly been shaken by the French Revolution, he admitted, and he proposed that the educational system should be opened to the Catholics as a first step to enfranchisement.[23] By thus 'enlightening their minds and humanising their tempers', the Protestants might prepare the next generation of Catholics for the exercise of civil liberty.[24] This change of attitude was reinforced by *realpolitik*: Haliday perceived that the Catholic population was 'up at auction' and urged that the reformers should make a bid for their support before the government did. To this end he proposed that the Whig Club should express wishes for a further mitigation of the penal laws at its next meeting.[25] Such tentative overtures drew the predictable reply from Charlemont: 'There is no arguing from analogy between Ireland and any other country upon the globe, not only on account of the disparity of numbers, but on account of those never-to-be-forgotten claims.'[26]

How can we explain the transformation of many Belfast reformers from commonwealthsmen to United Irishmen? After the collapse of the reform campaigns of the 1780s, the challenge of recasting the language of Irish radicalism to accommodate the Catholic majority became unavoidable. It was not until the storming of

---

[20] Knox to Abercorn, [17 July 1791], PRONI, Abercorn Papers, T2541/IB1/2/27. Knox reported that a proposal for uniting the Dissenters and the Catholics had been defeated in the Volunteer committee by a majority of one, and afterwards by 10 to 1 in the body at large.

[21] Thomas Addis Emmet, 'Part of an Essay Towards the History of Ireland', in W. J. MacNeven, *Pieces of Irish History* (New York, 1807), 16. Other pamphlets addressed to the northern radicals include William Todd Jones, *A Letter to the Societies of United Irishmen of the Town of Belfast* (Dublin, 1792), and id., *Reply to an Anonymous Writer from Belfast, Signed Portia* (Dublin, 1792).

[22] Haliday to Charlemont, 5 Nov. 1791, *Charlemont MSS*, ii. 160.

[23] Haliday to Charlemont, 4 Dec. 1791, ibid. 179–80.

[24] Haliday to Charlemont, 29 Dec. 1791, ibid. 185–6.

[25] Haliday to Charlemont, 10 Dec. 1791, ibid. 180.

[26] Charlemont to Haliday, 15 Dec. 1791, ibid. 182.

the Bastille, however, that Dissenters tackled this problem. The reports of French politics which filled the radical press emphasized the extension of religious toleration under the revolutionary regime, drawing the lesson that a Catholic country was not only capable of exercising the rights of citizenship, but was outstripping the Protestant states in its promotion of civil and religious liberty.[27] The weakening of papal authority on the international stage had raised the possibility that Irish Catholics, if emancipated from the penal laws, might embrace the doctrines of 'rational' Christianity. For some time Catholic propaganda had been carefully designed to counteract traditional myths regarding 'popery' and to break the old equation of religious belief with political loyalty. The culmination of this campaign was the Declaration of the Catholic Committee issued on St Patrick's Day 1792. In this document, which was read by the Revd Sinclare Kelburn to a Belfast town meeting in 1792, the temporal jurisdiction and deposing power of the Pope and the principle that 'no faith be kept with heretics' were denied; papal infallibility and the power of priests to forgive sins were dismissed; the Catholic Committee declared itself content with the existing land settlement, Established Church, and Protestant government.[28] Combined with the democratic reorganization of the Dublin Catholic Committee, events on the international scene seemed to herald a new era of liberty.[29] Defending the formation of the Society of United Irishmen to the sceptical William Bruce, Drennan argued that the 'intermingling of sects' was the best way to spread ideas of civil and religious liberty among the Catholics. Echoing the revolutionary optimism of Richard Price, he looked forward to 'the destruction of the fatal alliance between church and state which has been the great support of Despotism, and the ruin of true religion—a reform which will bring on another and a purer reformation'.[30]

The significance of the French Revolution, then, lay not only in the downfall of Bourbon despotism but also in the dismantling of the Roman Catholic Church in the country that had been regarded as Britain's natural enemy much of the preceding century. It is against this background that we should set the success of *An Argument on Behalf of the Catholics*; Tone's accusation that it was Protestant bigotry which had produced Catholic ignorance caught the mood of *fin de siècle* expectancy which had marked the Bastille Day celebrations in the northern capital. He reminded those who feared the Catholics that effigies of the Pope had been burnt in Paris and that English Catholics were seceding from their Church.[31] Many of the Belfast radicals became convinced that the relaxation of the penal laws

[27] For some interesting examples see *NS*, 7 Nov. 1792 ('Aristides'), 17 Nov. 1792 ('Corrector'), 12 Dec. 1792 ('Extract of a letter from Saintfield'). For reports of the treatment of Protestants in France, the confiscation of church lands, etc., see *BNL*, 8 Jan. 1790, 2 Mar. 1790, 11 Jan. 1791, 20 May 1791.

[28] Richard Musgrave, *Memoirs of the Different Rebellions in Ireland* (Dublin, 1801), 80–1; *Declaration of the General Committee of the Catholics* (Dublin, 1792).

[29] See e.g. Drennan's toast to 14 July enclosed in Drennan to Samuel McTier, 3 July 1791, PRONI, Drennan Papers, T765/303.

[30] Drennan to Bruce, [early Nov. 1791], PRONI, Drennan–Bruce Papers, D553/72.

[31] Tone to John Chambers, June 1790, quoted in Hereward Senior, *Orangeism in Ireland and Britain, 1795–1836* (London, 1966), 26–7.

was the best way of breaking the bond between the Irish Catholic and his priest. Antipopery was not just a quaint atavistic footnote to United Irish ideology; for the Presbyterians, at least, it formed a seminal part of the republican vision.

Following the popularity of his pamphlet, Tone was invited to Belfast, the town which he would come to regard as his 'adopted mother', by a group of radical Volunteers in October.[32] All were Presbyterian businessmen: in addition to McTier, they included the woollen draper Samuel Neilson, the mill owner William Sinclair, the tanners William and Robert Simms, and Henry Haslett and William Tennent, both shipbrokers. These men, Tone discovered, had formed 'a Secret Committee, who are not known or suspected of co-operating, but who, in fact, direct the movements of Belfast'.[33] On 14 October they met for the first time as the Society of United Irishmen. A manifesto, drawn up by Tone, announced their goal as 'a complete and radical reform of the representation of the people in Parliament'. In order to counteract English influence a union of all Irishmen was essential, and it was therefore resolved that 'no reform is practicable, efficacious, or just, which shall not include *Irishmen* of every religious persuasion'.[34] It is interesting to note that Tone and Russell found the Belfast Presbyterians ignorant of the Dublin Catholic Committee and its activities; indeed, Tone himself had not made contact with the Catholics until after the publication of his *Argument*.[35] Other societies soon followed in Antrim and Down; most importantly, however, a branch was quickly established by the Dublin reformers. Although the colourful Napper Tandy assumed the role of leader, the tone was initially set by the northerner William Drennan, who drew up the oath of the United Irishmen and was to pen most of their declarations over the next two years.

The emergence of the United Irish societies produced an open rift between Drennan and his erstwhile comrade Bruce. Though differing in temperament, both men were products of the New Light elite, connected by their parents to the great luminaries of early non-subscription, Abernethy, Duchal, and Hutcheson. In the 1780s they had come to prominence as two of the most influential Dissenters at the advanced edge of the reform coalition. In the 1790s, however, the two men came to embody the split personality of Presbyterian radicalism. Now convinced that reform could only be achieved by a complete separation from Britain, Drennan enthused that only a revolutionary convulsion could purify the body politic. He spoke up for the Catholics, whom he thought 'more enlightened and less under the trammels of Priesthood than is imagined', and complained that Bruce spent too much time denouncing popery. He himself found the Dublin Catholics 'rather aristocratical', and was cautious about how far the franchise should be extended to them, but he believed that they presented no threat to the land settlement.[36] Bruce, on the other hand, stuck to his preference for a 'gradual' extension of civil liberties to the Catholics.

---

[32] Tone to Russell, 1 Sept. 1795, NAI, Rebellion Papers, 620/16/3.

[33] *The Life of Theobald Wolfe Tone*, ed. W. T. W. Tone, 2 vols. (Washington, 1826), i. 141.

[34] The full address is reprinted in Marianne Elliott, *Wolfe Tone: Prophet of Irish Independence* (New Haven, 1989), 139–41. [35] *Life of Tone*, i. 52, 141.

[36] Drennan to Bruce, [summer 1791], [early Nov. 1791], PRONI, Drennan–Bruce Papers, D553/70, 72.

Rather than hand over the government of the country to 'a people ignorant, illiberal, intolerant, superstitious and justly exasperated against their future subjects', he proposed that the Protestants should first redress their wrongs and make sure of their goodwill.[37] Shortly after the formation of the United Irishmen Tone recorded a 'furious battle' over the Catholic question at McTier's house, as Bruce, 'an intolerant high priest', restated the conventional case for the penal laws, predicting that Catholic enfranchisement would lead to a religious inquisition and the confiscation of Protestant property.[38] Drennan went on to become chief scribe of the Dublin United Irishmen, and a rather half-hearted ally of the Catholics, later withdrawing into romantic nationalism when the movement assumed a conspiratorial form.[39] Bruce, on the other hand, became spokesman for the old whigs of the north, and eventually a powerful advocate of the Act of Union.

The rupture in the Presbyterian camp was given dramatic expression at a town meeting convened on 28 January 1792 to draw up a petition for emancipation. The Revd Sinclair Kelburne was in the chair. The radicals were represented by Dr John Campbell White, Robert Thompson, Robert Getty, and Samuel Neilson, with John Holmes, Dr Haliday, and Bruce leading the moderate opposition. While stressing their commitment to the cause of reform, Bruce and his friends dissented from the petition on the grounds that premature enfranchisement would result in tumult and confusion, as the Catholics attempted to recover the forfeited estates and restore their Church to its former established position; only when the power of the priesthood over the laity had been reduced, the lower orders educated, and the memories of ancient wrongs and recent oppression had subsided, could the penal code be abolished. On the United Irish side, it was argued that the government had set the Catholics and Dissenters against one another to deprive both of their rights, and that reform would never be attained without a union of Irishmen. The National Assembly was held up as proof that Catholics were capable of forming a free government; it was suggested that the penal laws had debased their nature, and that the best means of dispelling Catholic ignorance was the extension of the franchise. But the most forceful argument was a simple plea on the basis of natural right, that every man contributing by his labour or learning to the well-being of the state had a right to a voice in the government, and that it was unjust to ask for an equal representation while three-quarters of the population were excluded from the vote.[40] After an exhaustive debate the petition was signed by over 600 citizens, while 253 dissentients produced a counter-declaration recommending that the penal laws should be lifted gradually or 'from time to time'.

Although the moderates found themselves in a minority, they included many of the influential reformers in Belfast, most obviously Dr Haliday, William Bruce, Henry

---

[37] [William Bruce] to Drennan, 19 Nov. 1791, PRONI, Additional Drennan Papers, D456/6.

[38] *Life of Tone*, i. 55.

[39] For Drennan's anxieties that the Catholics would betray the Dissenters by making separate terms with the government see PRONI, Drennan Papers, T765/315, 320, 321B, 341, 351, 359, 368, 477. His mistrust was exacerbated by personal pique caused by the Catholics' refusal to employ him as a physician.   [40] [Bruce and Joy], *Belfast Politics*, 5–32.

Joy, and Waddell Cunningham. Thomas Knox wrote that the amendment was supported by 'all the principle People', whilst those who signed the petition came mainly from 'the middling & lower class', including Catholics from the Belfast area.[41] To some extent the schism in the town did indeed reflect social distinctions. The Belfast economy was dominated by the general merchants who managed the town's embryonic financial institutions as well as directing its foreign trade. The best-known perhaps was Waddell Cunningham, involved in numerous trading, manufacturing, and banking concerns, who would leave £60,000 on his death. Other well-established families included the Blacks, the Gregs, the Batts, and the Joys, names which can be found among the minority in 1792. Together they made up a mercantile elite in which business partnerships and family ties intersected. Outside this circle was a number of upwardly mobile men, often migrants from the countryside, who specialized in a single line of business.[42] Such were the Tennent brothers, sons of the Seceding minister of Dervock, Samuel Neilson, the son of the minister of Ballyroney, and the shipbroker Henry Haslett, who came from Limavady. In 1790 some of these younger businessmen had formed a shipping company which patronized Ritchie's shipyard, and christened their vessels with names such as 'Shamrock', 'Hibernia', and 'St Patrick', and in the following year they set up the Belfast General Insurance Company.[43]

These businessmen were responsible for the launching of the United Irish society, and, at the same time, they collaborated in another business venture, the extraordinarily successful newspaper the *Northern Star*. Late in 1791 they wrote to radicals throughout Ulster asking for collections of subscriptions. Not surprisingly, a number of Presbyterian ministers were canvassed, including Futt Marshall of Ballyclare, John Lindsay of Ballymena, James Cochran of Ballywalter, William Magee of Lurgan, Matthew Trumble of Monaghan, William Sinclair of Newtownards, Samuel Barber of Rathfriland, Thomas Ledlie Birch of Saintfield, Alexander Patton of Tandragee, and Hugh Jackson of Ballybay.[44] Over the next five years the paper gave a voice to the northern radicals, providing them with leadership and unity, popularizing the works of Paine, Godwin, and others, and reporting the debates and resolutions of the French: in a sense, the *Northern Star* was the United Irish movement.

The Dissenting clergy was once more prominent at Bastille Day 1792, when sixteen Volunteer corps from Antrim and Down, amounting to 790 men, assembled in Belfast.[45] Tone, now agent of the Catholic Committee, travelled north with the

[41] Knox to Abercorn, 30 Jan. 1792, PRONI, Abercorn Papers, T2541/IB1/3/9.

[42] In 1807, the Revd James Armstrong wrote: 'I have often heard in conversation, that, within the last forty years the influx of young men from the country has been so great as to outnumber the ancient inhabitants of Belfast.' See his *Observations on the State of Education in Belfast; in a Letter to James MacDonnell Esq. M.D. etc.* (Belfast, 1807), 25–6.

[43] This information on the Belfast economy is taken from N. E. Gamble, 'The Business Community and Trade of Belfast 1767–1800', Ph.D. thesis (University of Dublin, 1978), 20–41, 79, 91–2, 111–12.

[44] Prospectus for the *Northern Star*, 1791, PRO, HO, 100/34, fo. 50; letters to Samuel Neilson, Robert Caldwell, and Robert Simms re *Northern Star*, NAI, Rebellion Papers, 620/19/42.

[45] The parade was attended by 5,000 altogether; of the 790 Volunteers, 194 belonged to Belfast corps: see Samuel McSkimmin, *Annals of Ulster; or, Ireland Fifty Years Ago* (Belfast, 1849), 14–15.

Catholic leaders, Keogh, McCormick, and McKenna. As on the previous occasion, two addresses were proposed, one (to the French) communicated by Drennan, and one by Tone. Warned that the gradualists, led by Cunningham, Joy, and the barrister Alexander Stewart, were prepared to oppose any pro-Catholic resolutions, Tone was obliged to soften the demand for emancipation in his address. It was eventually passed with an overwhelming majority, following a blistering attack by Steel Dickson on the 'time to time' men. By this stage, however, the more conservative County Down corps had already gone home.[46]

The rest of 1792 saw the radicals triumphant, with more Volunteer corps reviving in preparation for another Dungannon convention.[47] As new companies were raised, the Dissenting clergy was again called upon to provide ideological direction in this crisis; more than ever, ministers saw themselves as not only leaders of a religious community, but also as the moral spokesmen for a body politic. Political sermons were preached by the Revds John Glendy of Maghera and John Wright of Donegore to mark the victories of the French army.[48] Two ministers of the small Reformed Presbytery, William Stavely and James McKinney, also participated.[49] The Volunteers lacked direction, however. George Knox found that while some men saw their aim as freeing their fellow subjects from the penal laws, others in the same company claimed they had armed to prevent Ireland becoming a popish country.[50]

There had always been links between Freemasonry and volunteering, and in 1792–3 a number of lodges passed radical resolutions and raised companies. The driving force here was James Reynolds, a Presbyterian physician from County Tyrone, who had organized a convention of thirty lodges at Dungannon.[51] In December 1792 he had presided over the formation of a Volunteer association in Cookstown, recruited from the local Masonic lodge and including Presbyterian and other clergymen, linen drapers, and merchants. A meeting of the Cookstown radicals held on 1 January 1793 disclaimed any revolutionary intentions, but affirmed that they held sacred the right of private judgement, and were convinced that the peace and prosperity of the country required 'the speedy abolition of all civil and political distinctions on account of religious opinions, and by a Radical Compleat Reform in the Commons House of Parliament'.[52] The meeting was attended by other leading radicals from the mid-Ulster area, including Dr Caldwell of Magherafelt, and the Revd John Glendy who treated the assembly to a sermon on the rights of man.

County meetings were held to elect delegates in Antrim, Down, Donegal, Londonderry, and Tyrone, despite the opposition of Downshire in County Down,

---

[46] *Life of Tone*, i. 157–60; [Bruce and Joy], *Belfast Politics*, 52–66. Tone commented that some of the country corps were no better than Peep O' Day boys.						[47] McSkimmin, *Annals*, 18.

[48] Ibid. 19 n.

[49] Samuel Brown Wylie, *Memoir of Alexander McCleod, D.D.* (New York, 1855), 21; McSkimmin, *Annals*, 18.

[50] George Knox to Abercorn, 14 Feb. 1793, PRONI, Abercorn Papers, T2541/IB1/4/12.

[51] McSkimmin, *Annals*, 24.

[52] Reynolds to James Stewart, [31 Dec. 1792], and copy of resolution passed at a meeting of 'the friends of liberty and good order, inhabitants of Cookstown and the adjacent country', 1 Jan. 1793, PRONI, Stewart of Killymoon Papers, D3167/2/84, 85.

where Steel Dickson once more acted as spokesman for the radical camp.[53] On 15 February 1793, the eleventh anniversary of the original convention, the delegates met in the Dungannon meeting-house.[54] A number of advanced reformers were present, led by Reynolds, Caldwell, and Dickson, but the meeting also boasted a fair sprinkling of the northern gentry. Dickson preached a sermon, 'fraught with phlogistick principles', which recommended reform and emancipation on biblical grounds.[55] Some idea of the content can be gathered from his collection *Scripture Politics*, published later that year, which included two sermons delivered at the end of 1792. In these discourses he literally preached the United Irish cause. Although the British constitution had been founded on the rights of man, he claimed, its principles had been slowly perverted and the structure transformed into 'a mis-shapen and monstrous pile of venality, corruption, and partiality'.[56] Demanding that the Catholics be liberated from their mental and corporal chains, Dickson urged his audience to attend to the example of France.

On the face of it, the convention was a stunning success for the United Irish platform. It was resolved that the electoral system should be altered to reflect the population and property of the country, and that the franchise should be granted to persons of every religious persuasion. At the same time, due homage was payed to the British constitution, and the republican form of government declared unsuitable for Ireland. Beneath this broad reforming consensus, however, differences were beginning to emerge. In the previous month Louis XVI had been executed, and it was the deterioration of the international situation which threatened to undermine the unanimity apparently displayed at Dungannon. Thus the proposals of Caldwell and Reynolds, that the resolution disapproving of republican government should be dropped, and that the continental powers should be condemned for making war on France, met with bitter hostility. The anxiety produced by European affairs was probably also the cause of Joseph Pollock's wish for more effusive expressions of loyalty to the constitution and fewer disrespectful references to Parliament.[57]

International events were indeed conspiring against the cause of reform. Shortly after the convention closed, Britain entered the war against France and the position of the Irish radicals was transformed. Early in 1793 Volunteer activity in Dublin was suppressed. Government fears had been heightened by the appearance of a francophile 'National Battalion' and a rather incautious call to arms penned by Drennan the previous December. In March, following a military riot in Belfast, volunteering in the northern capital was ended.[58] New legislation declared both armed associations and conventions illegal. At the same time, the British administration leaned

[53] Martha McTier to Drennan, [*c*.Jan. 1793], *Drennan Letters*, 120.

[54] For a general account see *BNL*, 22 Feb. 1793.

[55] Musgrave, *Rebellions*, 124, McSkimmin, *Annals*, 31; Samuel Neilson to Drennan, 17 Feb. 1793, *Drennan Letters*, 136. The mention of 'phlogiston' is a reference to the scientist and radical Joseph Priestley.

[56] William Steel Dickson, *Three Sermons on the Subject of Scripture Politics* (Belfast, 1793), 63.

[57] John Pollock, *Letter to the Inhabitants of the Town and Lordship of Newry* (Dublin, 1793), 14–16, 39, 46.

[58] [Bruce and Joy], *Belfast Politics*, 122–30; *Life of Tone*, i. 270–1; Emmet, 'Pieces', 54; Martha McTier to Drennan, 1 Feb. 1793, Mar. [1793], 1 Apr. 1793, *Drennan Letters*, 43, 47–8.

upon Dublin Castle to ensure the passage of another relief act, granting Irish Catholics the right to vote (though not the right to sit in Parliament) in February 1793.

The years 1792–3 thus proved to be the peak of United Irish influence on 'respectable' opinion. In Belfast, town meetings endorsed the United Irish programme and the Northern Whigs passed a resolution in favour of Catholic emancipation, with 'a solitary and feeble "no"' from Dr Haliday.[59] Even the Synod of Ulster, whose rules forbade pronouncements on political subjects, was moved to intervene. At Lurgan in June 1793, with Steel Dickson presiding as moderator, a declaration was issued calling for a reform of representation and expressing pleasure at the admission of Catholics to the franchise.[60] The assembly also heard a sermon from Thomas Ledlie Birch, which cited the opening of public office to Protestants in France as evidence that the millennium was fast approaching. At such a time, argued Birch, the duty of ministers to bear testimony against corruptions in the state became particularly pressing.[61]

Dickson and Birch, however, were both convinced United Irishmen; other ministers tempered their continued support for parliamentary reform with growing unease at the more extreme views which were then gaining ground. In *The Rights of Kings, and the Duties of Subjects*, a sermon published in 1793, the Revd James Patterson of Ballee acknowledged that the corruption of the democratic part of the constitution had given just cause for popular discontent, but counselled that the proper method for seeking redress was by remonstrance and petition. He condemned the republican prescriptions of Paine on the grounds that kingly government had scriptural sanction, and he denounced talk of the sovereignty and majesty of the people as subversive of the natural order of government. While admitting that the people had the right to disobey wicked kings, he warned that civil disorder would bring anarchy and confusion, exposing the nation to its enemies.[62]

Meanwhile the 'time to time' party in Belfast had been promoting its moderate reform line. Since December 1792, Joy had been running a series of articles in the *News-Letter* entitled 'Thoughts on the British Constitution'. The purpose was to defend the virtues of limited monarchy and balanced government against an onslaught of republican propaganda. Joy did not deny that the British constitution was in need of renovation, but he saw greater dangers in an 'unmixed democracy' which would lead to tyranny.[63] The British system had won the praise of Montesquieu, Voltaire, and Rousseau; it was tried and tested, unlike the French model; and it contained within itself the mechanisms for its own repair.[64] On the question of the franchise, Joy argued that the poor had no stake in society:

[59] [Bruce and Joy], *Belfast Politics*, 87–8 (Northern Whigs, 5 Nov. 1792), 104–8 (general meeting of the inhabitants, 26 Dec. 1792), 118–21 (Declaration and Principles of the Friends of a Parliamentary Reform, 10 Jan. 1793); *Life of Tone*, i. 205; Martha McTier to Drennan, Nov. [1792], *Drennan Letters*, 95. For the mood in Belfast see also Martha McTier to Drennan, 28 Oct. [1792], *c.*Nov. 1792, 3 Dec. [1792], 20 Dec. [1792], PRONI, T765/345, 349, 355, 362.

[60] *RGSU*, iii. 156–7. There was one dissentient, Moses Hogg.

[61] Thomas Ledlie Birch, *The Obligations upon Christians and Especially Ministers to be Exemplary in their Lives* (Belfast, 1794), 18, 29–30.

[62] James Patterson, *The Rights of Kings, and the Duties of Subjects*, passim.

[63] [Bruce and Joy], *Belfast Politics*, 171, 176, 178–80.					[64] Ibid. 173–4, 195.

It is only under a regular government, growing principally out of *the middle orders* (those true sources of the power, virtue and knowledge of all communities) that the occupations of life, which give employment to the working class, can be carried on with spirit or steadiness.[65]

In 1794 Joy's 'Thoughts' were collected together and published in a volume entitled *Belfast Politics*, along with reports of recent political debates and resolutions taken from the *News-Letter* and a series of strictures on the United Irish test written by William Bruce. The book was dedicated to Haliday and Charlemont, and prefaced with a vindication of the moderates, who now claimed to command the majority in Belfast. The suppression of volunteering and the recent military attacks on the town were blamed on the extremism of the United Irishmen and their imitation of French language. As far as emancipation was concerned, Joy and Bruce argued that the prejudices of both Protestant and Catholic would have to be conciliated first, and warned that a denomination devoted to monarchy and hierarchy would support the State and the Established Church rather than the Dissenters.[66] The volume immediately ran into trouble, however. Charlemont regretted the inclusion of the controversial resolutions and debates of the previous two years and doubted the wisdom of publication.[67] Sales were suspended after 80 copies, following reports of government displeasure.[68] The episode showed how difficult it was to steer a middle course in an increasingly polarized situation.

Presbyterian radicalism, construed in the broadest sense as support for parliamentary reform, continued to be split over the question of Catholic representation, the position of the monarchy, the suffrage, the justice of the French war, and the methods by which reform ought to be pursued. The younger generation of radicals who had inaugurated the United Irish programme in Belfast derived support from the Volunteers, especially in the Belfast area, and the number of seasoned radicals active in the 1790s is testimony to the continuities with the reform drive of the previous decade. Particularly prominent was a core of advanced clergymen—Dickson, Birch, Barber, and Kelburn. Just as striking, however, is the number of defections from the vanguard. In Belfast William Bruce, Henry Joy, and Dr Haliday, all stalwarts of the Volunteer heyday, acted as a rallying point for those reformers who opposed the new departure. In Newry, Joseph Pollock, celebrated in 1779 as Owen Roe O'Nial, had drifted in a conservative direction. And in Derry the Revd Robert Black stood forward to speak for the 'sober and rational part of the community' who wished to eliminate parliamentary corruption but opposed the few seditious spirits who aimed to 'overturn the constitution, and to try improved theories'.[69] There are doubts also about the strength of United Irish support in the countryside. Birch informed Tone that his neighbourhood had been converted to the United Irish agenda, and claimed to have his congregation under control, but the formation of a Secession congregation in Saintfield in 1796 indicates some

---

[65] Ibid. 238.   [66] Ibid., pp. vi–xii.

[67] Charlemont to Joy, 18 Apr. 1794, Linenhall Library Belfast, Joy MSS, 11/14.

[68] Joy to Charlemont, 12 Apr. 1794, *Charlemont MSS*, ii. 235–7.

[69] Quoted in Thomas Witherow (ed.), *Historical and Literary Memorials of Presbyterianism in Ireland*, 2 vols. (Belfast, 1879–80), ii. 272.

dissatisfaction with his brand of scripture politics. Many families also withdrew from Dickson's congregation at the time of the Dungannon convention.[70]

Furthermore, the United Irishmen had pinned all their hopes on the outcome of the Dungannon meeting. Everything was staked on the old strategy of concentrating public opinion through the Volunteer machine. In 1793 this avenue was closed. During the same period, prosecutions were commenced against a number of Dublin United Irishmen, leading eventually to the trial of William Drennan on a charge of seditious libel in June 1794. The United Irish societies themselves were outlawed. Scorned by respectable opinion and confronted with government hostility, a group of United Irishmen dispatched Wolfe Tone to Paris to press for French assistance. Meanwhile, the northern radicals looked for support in the plebeian underworld of the Ulster countryside.

Presbyterian radicalism and popular politics, 1794–1798

It has become fashionable to stress the continuities in United Irish activity from the middle-class, constitutional agitation of 1791–4 to the mass insurrectionary activity of 1795–8.[71] There is growing evidence to support this view, drawn principally from Ulster. In contrast to the Dublin United Irish society, which boasted a membership of several hundred and courted publicity, the northern societies had adopted a cell-like structure from the beginning. They also demonstrated greater willingness to reach out to a popular base. As early as 1792 Tone, Neilson, and Barber had made contact with the Defenders in County Down, and Thomas Russell was proselytizing throughout the Ulster countryside between 1792 and 1794.[72] Meanwhile, in Belfast itself, artisans were joining the francophile Irish Jacobin club, a United Irish satellite founded in 1792.[73] The revival of volunteering at the end of that year and the preparations for the Dungannon convention had stimulated a burst of popular political activity which alarmed many observers. George Knox of Dungannon expressed the sentiments of many when he wrote that in the north Paine had led 'every man to think himself a legislator and to throw off all respect for his superiors'.[74] His brother Thomas believed that the Presbyterians were overwhelmingly republican and that their French sympathies made them dangerous subjects. By the beginning of 1793 he had become convinced that reform was necessary to stem the public outcry in the north and to prevent a Volunteer rising.[75]

It would be unwise, however, to conclude that the reform programme of the United Irishmen led inexorably to full-blown separatism. Militant republicanism fed upon

---

[70] *Life of Tone*, i. 173; Thomas Ledlie Birch, *Physicians Languishing under Disease* (Belfast, 1796), 41; W. S. Dickson, *A Narrative of the Confinement and Exile of William Steel Dickson, D.D.* (Dublin, 1812), 28.

[71] Jim Smyth, *The Men of No Property: Irish Radicals and Popular Politics in the Late Eighteenth Century* (London, 1992), 79.

[72] Ibid. 68–70, 117; Nancy Curtin, 'The Transformation of the United Irishmen into a Revolutionary Mass Organization, 1794–6', *IHS* 24/96 (1985), 469–70.   [73] For the Jacobins, see ibid. 471–3.

[74] George Knox to Abercorn, 14 Feb. 1793, PRONI, Abercorn Papers, T2541/IB1/4/12.

[75] Thomas Knox to Abercorn, 11 Jan. 1793, 19 Jan. 1793, 26 Jan. 1793, 11 June 1793, PRONI, Abercorn Papers, T2541/IB1/5/1, 5, 7, 31.

the underlying tensions in Irish society, but its development owed much to a series of unforeseen crises. In the memoirs of several leading United men the ill-fated Fitzwilliam viceroyalty often figures as the point of no return. The appointment of the pro-emancipation Fitzwilliam as Lord Lieutenant came at the end of five years of intense Catholic campaigning which had extorted important concessions but had failed to attain the grand object, admission to Parliament. The expectations frustrated by his abrupt recall led many reformers to abandon all hope of constitutional redress.[76] In Belfast, where a new petition for emancipation received over 1,000 signatures, it was agreed that the day of Fitzwilliam's departure should be observed as a day of 'National Mourning', and all business ceased.[77] Elsewhere, meetings of freeholders demanded reform, and Drennan made a brief political comeback with a pamphlet calling for educational expansion and the extension of the franchise.[78] In the Synod of Ulster, meanwhile, there was anger when the Dublin Dissenters, accompanied by Bruce, presented the new Lord Lieutenant with a loyal address which failed to mention the need for constitutional change.[79] But the chief destabilizing factors of the 1790s were extraneous in origin. From the anti-militia riots of 1793 to the final explosion in 1798, it was the war in Europe which propelled Irish crises. Henceforth, the struggle which had begun in pamphlets and town meetings was played out in the Ulster countryside as reformers and loyalists sought to harness the energies of the common people.

The popular agitation of the 1790s built upon the traditional pattern established by earlier secret societies, sharing many of the same aims and employing the customary intimidatory tactics. The rebel forces who fought at the battle of Ballynahinch would later pass into popular mythology as 'the Hearts of Down', suggesting the continuities which undoubtedly existed in Presbyterian areas between the United Irishmen and the earlier Oakboys and Steelboys. The Catholic Defenders, who spread from south Armagh through the adjacent districts of Down, Louth, Monaghan, and Cavan, were also viewed as the latest of a succession of agrarian societies often lumped together under the label of whiteboyism. Unlike their predecessors, however, the Defenders adopted revolutionary language and drew support from weavers involved in the rural linen industry and artisans from the industrialized towns. Above all, they carried with them a bitter hatred of the Protestant vigilantes of Armagh, who in 1795 acquired a more political and aggressive organization with the formation of the Orange Order.

There can be no doubting the dramatic politicization which took place in the Ulster countryside as thousands were sworn into these organizations. As United Irish propaganda took on a new populist tone Drennan found his political inspiration drying up and his style considered 'too florid and refined for the people'.[80] *The*

---

[76] See e.g. Teeling, *Narrative*, 2.   [77] McSkimmin, *Annals*, 4.

[78] William Drennan, *A Philosophical Essay on the Moral and Political State of Ireland in a Letter to the Earl Fitzwilliam* (Dublin, 1795).

[79] See the letters by Bruce, Matthew Elder, John Sherrard, and Thomas Ledlie Birch in *BNL* and *NS* for February and March 1795; Charlemont to Haliday, 31 Jan. 1795, *Charlemont MSS*, ii. 257–8.

[80] Drennan to Samuel McTier, [29 Jan. 1794], *Drennan Letters*, 184.

Children's Catechism, a handbill printed in Belfast and circulated among the common people in 1794, demonstrates the new virulence with which radicals now assailed monarchy, Parliament, and aristocracy:

Q. What is the greatest *Absurdity* in the World?
A. Ten Millions of People setting up *ONE*, perhaps the meanest, of themselves to govern them—telling *HIM* we are your humble Slaves, whose lives and our Children's lives and properties are at your *Highness*' service.
. . .

Q. What are the common curses of mankind?
A. The habit of affixing great Ideas to little Things—hence the phrase as great as a King, (although a German *Bastard*) the first of which God gave to the Israelites, as a curse to them and their Posterity—this is the divinity of Kings. See Samuel, Chap. viii.

Q. When will *happiness* attend mankind?
A. At the extirpation of SLAVERY, Priestcraft, *king*craft, and *Aristocracy*—thence spring fair *Liberty* and *Equality*, that Men may enjoy the BLESSINGS of GOD in an earthly *Paradise*.[81]

In July of the same year the Anglican squarson Edward Hudson noted that, although Bastille Day celebrations in Belfast and Lisburn had attracted inconsiderable numbers, there were signs of seditious activity among the lower orders. He enclosed a handbill signed by 'one of the people', printed in Newry, which vilified the rich for maintaining a monopoly of political power, keeping the industrious poor in darkness, and fleecing them of their property. The people were urged to 'think of your rulers; think of republics; think of kings; think of the murderous wars they are carrying on; think of the money they are robbing you of to keep you in slavery and ignorance'.[82]

According to Thomas Emmet, new societies emerged among the mechanics, petty shopkeepers, and farmers of Belfast in 1793–4, adopting the United Irish name, and prompting the original members to resume leadership of the radical movement.[83] This version of events, part of Emmet's bid to portray the republican leaders as reluctant revolutionaries, underestimates the extent to which reform agitation had already assumed a conspiratorial form. It was not until mid-1795, however, that the northern organization began to be reconstituted as a network of secret oath-bound units, co-ordinated by a hierarchy of baronial, county, provincial, and national committees.[84] Defender cells, Volunteer companies, Masonic lodges, and reading societies were all subsumed into a loosely structured popular movement under the leadership of the Belfast United men and their allies in the Ulster towns.[85] Initially, the 'system' was confined to Ulster, and although the United Irishmen would later tap discontent in the other three provinces the national leadership was in practice an alliance of the Belfast and Dublin republicans. In the north the provincial executive was run by Neilson, the Simms brothers, William Tennent, Dr White, Henry Joy

---

[81] Handbill preserved in the Linenhall Library Belfast, Joy MSS.
[82] Hudson to Charlemont, 8 July 1794, *Charlemont MSS*, ii. 244–6.   [83] Emmet, 'Essay', 77–8.
[84] McDowell, *Ireland*, 471–5.
[85] For book clubs, see J. R. R. Adams, 'Reading Societies in Ulster', *Ulster Folklife*, 26 (1980), 55–64.

McCracken, and the Catholic Teeling family of Lisburn, the last supplying the crucial Defender link. In Dublin the moderates Emmet and William James MacNeven
were increasingly outflanked by Arthur O'Connor and Lord Edward Fitzgerald.[86]

Who were the United Irishmen? Emmet described the conspirators as farmers, manufacturers, and shopkeepers. One Episcopalian minister from Country Tyrone, dis-
tinguishing between 'deep, intriguing politicians' and 'loosely connected recruits',
identified 'the shopkeepers, petty merchants and Inn-holders in the country towns'
whose trade connected them to 'the great democrats of Belfast and Newry' as the
core of the conspiracy. The County Down magistrate George Anderson also singled
out the 'Republican Merchants' of Belfast and Newry, while James McKay of Mount
Collyer near Belfast reported a seditious spirit spreading among the middling class
of people, 'I mean with the Linen drapers & Shop-keepers, the greatest part of whom
are Presbaterians [*sic*]'.[87] These impressions of the United Irish leadership can be
confirmed by examining the records of state prisoners detained in Belfast after the
rebellion. One typical example lists four Presbyterian ministers and one priest, three
physicians, two schoolmasters, one gentleman, seven merchants and shopkeepers,
a butcher, four farmers, two weavers, and a shoemaker.[88]

What were their aims? Hostile observers were of course agreed that the United
Irish programme was an excuse for plunder. The Bishop of Dromore, for example,
believed that they aimed at 'the Demolition of the great Nobility,—the Confiscation of great Estates—the destruction of the aristocracy and monarchy'.[89] But the
object of the original societies, defined in their test, was limited to the attainment
of an 'impartial and adequate representation' of the people in Parliament, of which
Catholic enfranchisement was an integral part. As in the 1780s, the call for reform
worked better as a vague slogan than as a set of specific demands. It was not until
1794 that the Dublin society finally agreed upon a detailed plan recommending annual
parliaments, the payment of MPs, the equalization of constituencies, the abolition
of property qualifications for parliamentary representatives, and (by a narrow majority) universal manhood suffrage. Historians have often pointed out that the United
Irishmen were not social revolutionaries. Their expectations that a reformed Parliament would reduce taxation and abolish tithes can be seen in the context of
traditional objections to old corruption and to church establishments. As the new
popular societies emerged, however, grievances were focused much more sharply on
the inequalities of the social order. One oath found in Newry early in 1797 declared
that the United Irishmen would 'join the French on landing and would pull down all

[86] McDowell, *Ireland*, 477–8; see also L. M. Cullen, 'The Internal Politics of the United Irishmen',
in David Dickson, Dáire Keogh, and Kevin Whelan (eds.), *The United Irishmen: Republicanism,
Radicalism and Rebellion* (Dublin, 1993), 176–96.

[87] Emmet, 'Essay', 103; Richardson to [Abercorn], 22 Feb. 1797, PRONI, Abercorn Papers, T2541/
IB3/6/5; George Anderson to Downshire, 15 Feb. 1797, James McKay to Downshire, 16 Mar. 1798,
PRONI, Downshire Papers, D607/E/105, D607/F/98.

[88] McDowell, *Ireland*, 481. A full treatment can be found in N. J. Curtin, *The United Irishmen: Popular
Politics in Ulster and Dublin, 1791–1798* (Oxford, 1994), ch. 5.

[89] Thomas Percy, Bishop of Dromore, to Downshire, 9 Mar. 1797, PRONI, Downshire Papers, D607/
E/168. See also Haliday to Charlemont, 26 June 1796, 28 Jan. 1797, *Charlemont MSS*, ii. 293–4, 274–5.

Gentlemen and Magistrates, Tithes, Taxes, Rents, etc.'[90] That the United Irishmen adopted many of the agrarian grievances which had stimulated the earlier risings of the Oakboys and Steelboys can be demonstrated from a document found on Thomas Smyth, secretary to a committee of United Irishmen near Ballynahinch, entitled 'What evils will be removed and what advantages gained by a reform in Parliament'. Top of the list was the abolition of tithes and hearth-money. Cheaper taxes on tobacco and other imported goods came next, followed by abolition of the excise laws, cheap and equal justice, low county cess rates, abolition of customs at fairs, the unshackling of the press to make it cheaper, and the introduction of simple contracts between farmer and landlord without the 'intrusions of moss-bailiffs and bog-trotters'. In sum, as the manifesto concluded, 'THE LAWS will be made by YOURSELVES, or in other words YOU WILL BE FREE'.[91]

After the attempted French invasion at Bantry Bay in December 1796, the United Irishmen received a tremendous boost as thousands of men and women were sworn into the system and others were forced to join.[92] Reports of robberies, assassinations, nocturnal assemblies, and arms raids flooded into Dublin Castle from alarmed gentlemen. For a time it seemed that the legal system was completely paralysed. Although the gaols were full of suspected rebels, juries and witnesses were intimidated, and in many cases convictions could not be obtained.[93] At the 1797 assizes, for example, twenty-three death sentences were passed for political crimes in Ulster, but many were reprieved.[94] At the same time Irish republicanism was provided with its first great martyr, William Orr, a wealthy farmer convicted of administering an unlawful oath to Hugh Wheatley, a Fifeshire fencible. After the trial, letters from local gentlemen and magistrates including Sir John O'Neill, William Sharman, Stewart Banks, and Chichester Skeffington flooded into Dublin Castle recommending leniency. Orr's sponsors even included the Countess of Londonderry, sister of the then Lord Lieutenant, Camden.[95] There was considerable doubt about Wheatley's testimony, and affidavits were sworn by two Presbyterian ministers, James Elder and Alexander Montgomery, stating that Wheatley had later confessed his perjury; but Pelham, the chief secretary, thought that an example was necessary. 'Remember Orr' quickly became the rallying cry of the northern republicans, and his death was commemorated by rings, lockets, and bracelets, and Drennan's popular poem 'The Wake of William Orr'.[96]

As United Irish cells reproduced themselves and organized shows of strength, many magistrates complained that a system of terror was operating in Ulster.[97]

---

[90] George Anderson to Downshire, 28 Feb. 1797, PRONI, Downshire Papers, D607/E/134.

[91] Printed in W. H. Crawford and B. Trainor (eds.), *Aspects of Irish Social History 1750–1800* (Belfast, 1969), 181–2.

[92] For United Irishwomen see Teeling, *Narrative*, 12; McSkimmin, *Annals*, 58.

[93] James Hamilton, jun., to Abercorn, 8 Mar. 1797, 17 Apr. 1797, 21 Apr. 1797, PRONI, Abercorn Papers, T2541/IA2/6/18, 22, 23.   [94] McDowell, *Ireland*, 542.

[95] The letters can be found in PRONI, Camden Papers, T2627/4/77–90; Haliday to Charlemont, 6 Oct. 1797, *Charlemont MSS*, ii. 306.   [96] Musgrave, *Rebellions*, 178; McSkimmin, *Annals*, 91.

[97] For United Irish confidence at this time see [William Sampson], *Advice to the Rich: In a Series of Letters, Originally Published in the Northern Star: by an Independent Country Gentleman* (Belfast, 1796).

By the beginning of 1797, large tracts of the countryside had become virtually ungovernable, and Dublin Castle finally gave in to the demands of the hawkish landlords in the north. First, the powers of the magistrates were greatly extended by the suspension of habeas corpus and the passage of an indemnity act. New offences were created to prevent the administration of illegal oaths, an oath of allegiance was introduced, and new powers were given to magistrates to search for and confiscate weapons. Professor McDowell has estimated that between September 1796 and September 1797 some 500–600 persons were arrested in Ulster for 'political' offences. By the end of 1797 the whole of Down and parts of another five northern counties had been 'proclaimed' in a state of disturbance under the Insurrection Act of 1796.[98] Secondly, the raising of a yeoman auxiliary force, first suggested by Thomas Knox and the Revd William Richardson, was approved. By 1798, 540 corps had been raised, totalling about 40,000 men, a third of whom were mounted.[99] The force was predominantly Protestant and increasingly coloured by the presence in its ranks of the Orange Order, which by 12 July 1796 already numbered around 90 lodges and could count on the backing of a growing phalanx of landed gentlemen, particularly around Armagh.[100]

But the culmination of this official terror came with the imposition of martial law and the bloody campaign launched in March 1797 known as 'the dragooning of Ulster'. Under the command of Generals Lake, Nugent, and Knox, the army, backed up by the yeomen and the militia, began to disarm the rebels. Knox viewed Ulster as England's Vendée, and argued that the disaffected areas should be devastated in the French fashion.[101] Although he believed that the hunt for arms was largely futile, he persisted in military raids in order to inflame the feuding between Orangemen and United Irishmen: 'Upon that animosity', he wrote, 'depends the safety of the centre counties of the North.'[102] In perhaps the greatest single blow struck against radicalism, the *Northern Star* office in Belfast was destroyed by the Monaghan militia in May 1797.[103]

The dragooning of Ulster outraged liberal and radical opinion; from this point onwards, United Irish propaganda concentrated on the confusion and terror created by hangings and half-hangings, house-burnings, floggings, pitch-cappings, and free-quartering (the billeting of troops upon suspected rebels). Conservative opinion was equally shocked. The Revd Edward Hudson was appalled by the atrocities committed by the military in Belfast and in County Derry, where he found that 'The soldiers make no scruple of stripping men, tying them to a tree, and flogging them bitts and bridles.'[104] The Ancient Britons, a Welsh fencible regiment which arrived in Ulster in April, was particularly feared and hated. 'Fathers and sons were murdered', recorded the moderate reformer and ecclesiastical historian William Campbell,

---

[98] McDowell, *Ireland*, 552, 554, 573.   [99] Ibid. 558–9.
[100] Senior, *Orangeism in Ireland and Britain*, 51.
[101] Knox to Abercorn, 12 Mar. 1797, PRONI, Abercorn Papers, T2541/IB3/6/9.
[102] Quoted in Senior, *Orangeism*, 67.
[103] Martha McTier to Drennan, [19] May 1797, *Drennan Letters*, 256.
[104] Hudson to Charlemont, 5 June, 25 June 1797, *Charlemont MSS*, ii. 299–300, 301.

'or torn from their families, put to torture, or sent into banishment, without even the form of a trial—their houses burned; their property destroyed and their wives and children left destitute.'[105]

As Charles Teeling later recalled, the established clergy, whom he christened 'the church militant', were among the most zealous exponents of this policy.[106] At a local level the union of Church and State took the form of a partnership between parson and squire. Indeed Anglican ministers, well integrated into the landed and professional families of the elite, often combined their sacerdotal offices with the more worldly duties of magistrates and land agents. One of the most notorious was the Revd Philip Johnson, vicar of Derriaghy and a magistrate for County Antrim who, along with the Revd Dr Cupples of Lisburn, took a leading part in organizing the loyalists and preached sermons to local Orangemen.[107] In south Armagh one of the few remaining magistrates was the Revd Charles Warburton, who led military manoeuvres to intimidate the rebels and overcame his contempt for plebeian Orangeism.[108] Most zealous of all was the Revd John Cleland, vicar of Newtownards and agent to the Earl of Londonderry.[109] These ministers were very vulnerable and were often exasperated at the lack of protection offered to them by the government. At the end of 1796 the Revd William Hamilton of Fanet in County Donegal informed Dublin Castle that he stood alone against the local Dissenting farmers and called for loyalist reinforcements.[110] Just over a year later he was assassinated at the house of a neighbouring clergyman.[111] Philip Johnson survived several assassination attempts, while Charles Warburton fought off attacks on his home by crowds of rebels.[112]

The terrorist methods employed by the government in 1797 involved great risks. The indiscriminate attacks which accompanied the disarming of Ulster pushed many neutral farmers and weavers into the United Irish system for protection. Membership actually doubled between January and April and popular pressure for a rising steadily mounted.[113] Many moderate reformers objected to the oath of allegiance, which they believed sanctioned the abuses of the unreformed system and required them to uphold unconstitutional laws.[114] A series of freeholders' meetings in the northern counties raised hopes that the spirit of reform was reviving once more. In May 1797 a County Antrim address supported radical causes, condemning the war as unjust and injurious to industry and commerce, and asking for reform of the Commons; in the same year a County Down meeting condemned government policy,

---

[105] William Campbell, continuation of 'Sketches of the History of Presbyterians in Ireland' (1803), PHSI, Campbell MSS, 99.   [106] Teeling, *Narrative*, 87–8.
[107] [Anon.], *A Plain Statement of Facts in Answer to . . . Francis Plowden* (Dublin, 1814; repr. Lisburn, 1905), 4–7, 11; Haliday to Charlemont, 7 Aug. 1796, *Charlemont MSS*, ii. 279.
[108] Warburton to Cooke, 27 May, 31 July 1797, NAI, Rebellion Papers, 620/30/212, 620/31/292.
[109] Dickson, *Narrative*, 39, 168.
[110] Hamilton to Pelham, 22 Dec. 1796, NAI, Rebellion Papers, 620/26/146.
[111] Murphy, *Derry, Donegal and Modern Ulster*, 19.
[112] Warburton to unknown, 13 Apr. 1797, NAI, Rebellion Papers, 620/29/243.
[113] Marianne Elliott, *Partners in Revolution: The United Irishmen and France* (New Haven, 1982), 125.
[114] See e.g. Haliday to Charlemont, 28 Jan. 1797, *Charlemont MSS*, ii. 293–4.

calling for reform and emancipation.[115] Similarly, the recruitment of the Yeomanry met with opposition from northern liberals who still clung to the volunteering ideal. In Belfast, for example, where the Revd William Bristow and the sovereign John Brown urged the formation of a Yeomanry corps in the aftermath of Bantry Bay, a town meeting led by William Sampson, Arthur O'Connor, and Robert Thompson advocated the revival of the Volunteers, and passed resolutions calling for a reform of the franchise in which members of all religious persuasions would benefit. When two Yeomanry units were eventually raised a number of the new recruits reassured the town that they had not forsaken 'the rights and liberties of all the people of Ireland'.[116] There is evidence to suggest, then, that constitutional radicalism, although helpless in the face of events, did not completely die out.

From May, however, Lake tightened his grip and his officers were given authority to act without the sanction of the civil authorities.[117] Combined with the penetration of the United Irish network by spies and informers, Lake's war of attrition at last began to take effect. There could be no greater indication of rebel demoralization than the news that repentant republicans were now swelling the ranks of the Orange Order.[118] There were signs too that the propertied Presbyterians of the countryside, alarmed by the possibility of a French invasion, were beginning to throw their weight behind the Yeomanry.[119] In Belfast almost a hundred citizens had enlisted in the first corps of Yeoman infantry and cavalry, despite the attempts of Arthur O'Connor to restore momentum to the Jacobin movement in the town.[120] Among others, the Revd William Bruce completed his apostasy early in 1797 by taking the Yeomanry oath.[121] Thus it transpired that during the rebellion many of the old Belfast Volunteers found themselves on guard duty with the Fifeshire fencibles, the Monaghan militia, and a contingent of 228 Orangemen.[122] One jubilant loyalist wrote to Lord Downshire:

The number of disaffected fellows now in this Town under Arms for the Protection of their property would astonish you. . . . To see Presbaterian [*sic*] Ministers, with the rich Republican Shopkeepers, sitting in the guard Room at day light in the Morning with their Guns, &c. had, in my Eyes, a wonderful appearance.[123]

[115] Copy of Antrim address, 8 May 1797, PRONI, Camden Papers, T2627/4/73; McSkimmin, *Annals*, 81–2. For doubts about how representative these meetings were see McDowell, *Ireland*, 526.

[116] McDowell, *Ireland*, 561; McSkimmin, *Annals*, 61–7; *BNL*, 13 Mar. 1797.

[117] Elliott, *Partners in Revolution*, 128.

[118] Hudson to Charlemont, 19 May 1797, *Charlemont MSS*, ii. 322–3.

[119] Richardson to [Abercorn], 22 Feb. 1797, PRONI, Abercorn Papers, T2541/IB3/6/5.

[120] John Brown to Thomas Pelham, 4 Jan. 1797, 620/28/31; *Town Meeting. A Handbill, Lately Circulated from the Belfast Post-Office, and Cool Strictures Thereon. By a Townsman* (Belfast, 1797).

[121] Martha McTier to Drennan, 13 Jan. 1797, 30 Jan. 1797, 17 Mar. [1797], Drennan Papers, PRONI, T765/645, 647, 652; *BNL*, 8 June 1798. Bruce was joined by the Revd Patrick Vance of the Second Congregation. [122] Senior, *Orangeism*, 104.

[123] McKey to Downshire, 14 June 1798, PRONI, Downshire Papers, D607/F/244.

8

THE DYNAMICS OF REBELLION: ULSTER IN 1798

As the United Irish societies were transformed into a mass, insurrectionary organization in the mid-1790s, radical ideology was popularized to appeal to the plebeian networks of rural Ulster, whose grievances centred on taxes and tithes. The collapse of the social order in the years before the '98 rebellion must be set against the background of pre-existing tensions between the merchant and manufacturing classes, the tenant farmers, and the landed establishment, some of which have been touched upon in previous chapters. It is the more basic categories of ethnic and denominational identity, however, which hold the key to the geography of Ulster republicanism. In this chapter I shall begin by establishing the ways in which United Irish mobilization was shaped by the magnetic pull of the settlement patterns created by seventeenth-century colonization.[1] The sudden intrusion of the masses into the political sphere released the latent violence stored up in the fractured landscape of the northern province, as tensions between Protestant, Catholic, and Dissenter were brought to the fore.

By paying attention to Ulster's religious topography, it becomes possible to show how the diffusion of radical sentiment was directed by the ancestral fears and aspirations of the three main confessional communities. Each of these groups carried its own origin-myth, its own historical narrative of oppression and persecution, and its own prophetic vision of an alternative future. Millenarianism supplied a shared set of concepts and images, drawn from scripture, history, and tradition, which enabled both individuals and communities to make sense of their experiences. As the common people struggled to find meaning in the unprecedented upheavals which revolution and war had brought to Europe, many observers noted the sudden prevalence of 'false prophecies' throughout the countryside.[2] Among Presbyterians, these visions centred on biblical texts drawn from the books of Daniel and Revelation, believed to foretell the destruction of the Turks, the conversion of the Jews, and, most importantly, the rise and fall of the papal Antichrist. In the second and third sections below we shall investigate the eschatological framework of political thought in the later 1790s and assess the part played by the Dissenting clergy in the insurrections of 1798.

---

[1] For the sectarian friction produced by cultural frontiers see L. M. Cullen, *The Emergence of Modern Ireland* (London, 1981), esp. ch. 10; Kevin Whelan, 'The Religious Factor in the 1798 Rebellion in County Wexford', in P. Flanagan *et al.* (eds.), *Rural Ireland 1600–1900: Modernization and Change* (Cork, 1987), 62–85.

[2] D. W. Miller (ed.), *Peep O'Day Boys and Defenders: Selected Documents on the County Armagh Disturbances 1784–96* (Belfast, 1990), 53.

The ethnic and sectarian dimensions of radicalism

It was in Ulster that the three cultures of Protestant, Catholic, and Dissenter co-existed in conditions of claustrophobic intensity. Taking the province as a whole, it is probably true to say that the Protestant denominations accounted for somewhere between 50 per cent and 60 per cent of the population, with Presbyterians making up rather more than half of this figure.[3] The denominational balance varied greatly from county to county, however. On the basis of an official inquiry of 1766, W. H. Crawford has estimated that Protestants outnumbered Catholics in Antrim (4 : 1), Down (2 : 1), and Londonderry (2 : 1), and constituted half the inhabitants of Armagh and Tyrone. They were outnumbered by Catholics in Fermanagh (9 : 11), Donegal (3 : 4), Monaghan (1 : 2), and Cavan (1 : 3).[4] Unfortunately, this census does not subdivide Protestants into Anglicans and Presbyterians. By reading backwards from nineteenth-century census returns, however, we find that Presbyterians were a majority of the population in County Antrim; the largest single Protestant group in Down and Londonderry; fewer than the Anglicans, although still a substantial element, in Tyrone, Armagh, Donegal, and Monaghan; and a smaller proportion of the inhabitants of Fermanagh and Cavan.[5]

Although Protestants were concentrated in the east of the province, there was a high degree of segregation at the most local level. The surprising feature is not just the continuity of English, Scottish, and Irish cultural forms, but the precision with which territorial boundaries could be demarcated. A detailed breakdown of the population on the Rawdon estate at Moira in 1712 showed that the land could be neatly divided into Presbyterian and Anglican blocs.[6] Ninety years later, a survey of Tyrone commented that the various communities of that county differed so much that they formed 'separate kingdoms':

The people of the baronies of Dungannon and Clogher [areas of English settlement] are much more polished than those of Strabane and Omagh [Scots] generally are. The inhabitants of Strabane and its vicinity seem quite a different race from those of Munterloney [Irish], who are in the same barony.[7]

The resilience of plantation patterns has also been demonstrated by research on local dialects in Northern Ireland. In south Antrim, for example, it was recently found that divisions between Scots and English dialects corresponded exactly with the

[3] In 1835 Presbyterians still outnumbered Anglicans in the northern dioceses of the church by 638,073 to 517,722 despite over a century of emigration: *First Report of the Commissioners of Public Instruction in Ireland*, HC, 1835, xxxiii. 11.

[4] W. H. Crawford, 'Ulster Economy and Society in the Eighteenth Century', Ph.D. thesis (QUB, 1983), 26.

[5] e.g. W. E. Vaughan and A. J. Fitzpatrick (eds.), *Irish Historical Statistics: Population, 1821–1971* (Dublin, 1978), 52–3.

[6] Raymond Gillespie, 'The Presbyterian Revolution in Ulster, 1660–1690', in W. J. Sheils and Diana Wood (eds.), *Studies in Church History*, xv, *The Churches, Ireland and the Irish* (Oxford, 1989), 161.

[7] John Braidwood, 'Ulster and Elizabethan English', in Ulster Folk Museum, *Ulster Dialects: An Introductory Symposium* (Holywood, 1964), 30.

boundaries of the Conway (later Hertford) estates which ran from Lisburn to Antrim town; similar findings were reported in part of Tyrone.[8]

Outside the large towns Presbyterians were still known as 'the Scotch', and many towns possessed a distinct 'Scotch' quarter. All outsiders were struck by the tenacity of Scottish dialect, accent, and 'manners' in Ulster.[9] Edward Willes, Lord Chief Baron of the Irish Exchequer, found that the people spoke 'broad lowland Scotch [and] have all the Scotch phrases'.[10] For John Gamble, a native of Strabane returning after many years in Britain, it was Ulster's Scottish character which set it apart from the other provinces. 'It would appear incredible,' he wrote, 'how pertinaciously they retain the customs and usages of their ancestors.'[11] In the west he found that battles between the 'English colony' of Lifford and the 'Scotch laddies' of Strabane had been common until the early nineteenth century.[12] It is worth stressing the vitality of such local antagonisms because they help us to understand how Ulster society disintegrated so rapidly in the mid-1790s. Touring the north in the 1790s, the French *émigré* de Latocnaye was perplexed by that combination of sectarian warfare and hospitality which still strikes visitors to the region.[13]

The mobilization of republican and loyalist blocs in the 1790s followed the anterior confessional alignments created in the previous century. The basic pattern is clear enough. At the beginning of 1793 the reform convention which met at Dungannon had revealed the central divide in Ulster politics: while Antrim, Down, Derry, Donegal, and Tyrone were well represented, the southern counties of Armagh, Cavan, Monaghan, and Fermanagh could not organize the baronial meetings necessary to elect delegates.[14] Four years later, General Knox observed that the geographical strength of the Jacobins lay in the counties of Down, Antrim, Derry, and parts of Donegal and Tyrone, where the whole population was disaffected; in the rest of the province the United men had encountered some popular resistance.[15] At one extreme, then, we have the Presbyterian heartland in Antrim and Down, with its long tradition of hostility to Anglican oligarchy. In Belfast, which lay outside the orbit of the capital, there was little sense of an immediate Catholic threat. At the other extreme, we have the borderlands of south Ulster where both Orangeism and evangelicalism were able to take root. But recent research by Nancy Curtin and others has presented a much more complicated picture.[16] Presbyterians were split in almost every county,

[8] Antony Alcock, 'The Making of a Nation', in Ulster Society, *Ulster, an Ethnic Nation?* (Lurgan, 1986), 28–9.

[9] Journal of a tour from Dublin to the North, 4 July 1781, QUB, Miscellaneous MSS, Box 1 (1), acc. 58360, pp. 30–1.

[10] *The Letters of Lord Chief Baron Edward Willes to the Earl of Warwick 1757–62. An Account of Ireland in the Mid-Eighteenth Century*, ed. James Kelly (Aberystwyth, 1990), 36.

[11] John Gamble, *Sketches of History, Politics and Manners in Dublin, and the North of Ireland, in the Autumn of 1810* (London, 1811), 153.   [12] Ibid. 280.

[13] Chevalier de Latocnaye [Jacques Louis Bougrenet], *A Frenchman's Walk through Ireland 1796–7*, trans. John Stevenson (Belfast, 1917), 266.   [14] *BNL*, 19 Feb., 8 Mar. 1793.

[15] General John Knox to General Gerard Lake, 11 Mar. 1797, BL, Pelham Papers, Add. MS 33103, fos. 265–6.

[16] N. J. Curtin, *The United Irishmen: Popular Politics in Ulster and Dublin 1791–1798* (Oxford, 1994) is now the best study of United Irish organization in Ulster.

with particular discord in the pivotal county of Armagh, the great Orange wedge which separated the eastern radicals from their comrades in Tyrone and Londonderry.

The strongholds of the United Irishmen, often known more simply as the 'Liberty Men',[17] were to be found in the Presbyterian districts of Antrim and Down. The recruitment figures for May 1797, when the 'system' was at its peak, recorded around 118,000 men in the north, almost 50,000 of whom were in these two counties alone.[18] The northern capital itself had been knocked out of action in 1793 and had never quite recovered. In the following years it was regularly terrorized by the soldiery, and in 1796 de Latocnaye was surprised to find the notorious citadel of radicalism in 'a sort of stupor hardly distinguishable from fear'.[19] Nevertheless, Belfast was still the seat of the Ulster provincial executive and was regarded by all as the epicentre of sedition. A radical communications network radiated out along the trade routes created by the linen industry into its hinterland; one of Downshire's correspondents revealingly remarked that the town had 'poisoned every County within the circuit of its commerce'.[20]

After the foundation of the Belfast United Irishmen, sister societies had appeared in many Antrim towns including Templepatrick, Doagh, Randalstown, Killead, Muckamore, and Sixmilewater.[21] As popular support for the republicans gathered, it became clear that the one great obstacle to United Irish mobilization was the Marquis of Hertford's huge estate at Lisburn, where the zealous Anglican clergyman and magistrate Philip Johnson had organized the Yeomanry in 1796.[22] County Down, the most populous county in Ireland, had also been represented by several societies in the constitutional phase of the movement, the best-known of which was established at Saintfield under the direction of the Revd Thomas Ledlie Birch.[23] It was probably in Down that the alliance of Presbyterian radicals and Defenders worked best. In 1796 Thomas Lane complained to Lord Hillsborough that United Irish emissaries were capitalizing on the fear of the Orangemen to make new recruits: 'These are the villains most to be dreaded. They are Dissenters with true republican principles.' In June 1798 he reported that the 'cloven-footed Presbyterians' had seduced the Catholics in Upper Iveagh.[24] It was often remarked that the merchants and shopkeepers of Newry were not far behind those of Belfast in their dedication to French principles.[25]

---

[17] e.g. Brendan McEvoy, 'The United Irishmen in County Tyrone' (part 1), *Seanchas Ardmhacha*, 3 (1958–9), 306, 312.

[18] Curtin, *United Irishmen*, 69. The exact figures are: Down (26,153), Antrim (22,716), Armagh (17,000), Tyrone (14,000) Derry (10,500), Donegal (9,648), Monaghan (9,020), Cavan (6,880), Fermanagh (2,000), making a total of 117,917.   [19] De Latocnaye, *A Frenchman's Walk*, 251–2.

[20] Edward Alexander McNaghten to Downshire, 26 Nov. 1796, PRONI, Downshire Papers, D607/D/348.   [21] Samuel McSkimmin, *Annals of Ulster* (Belfast, 1849), 9, 13.

[22] William Richardson to [Abercorn], 22 Feb. 1797, PRONI, Abercorn Papers, T2541/IB3/6/5; [Anon.], *A Plain Statement of Facts in Answer to Certain Charges, Adduced by Francis Plowden, Esq. in his History of Ireland, against the Rev. Philip Johnson* (Dublin, 1814; repr. Lisburn, 1905), 4–7, 11.

[23] McSkimmin, *Annals*, 9, 27.

[24] Lane to Hillsborough, 16 July 1796, 24 June 1798, PRONI, Downshire Papers, D607/D/102, F/272.

[25] For Newry see George Anderson to Downshire, 15 Feb. 1797, 14 Mar. 1797, Joseph Pollock to Downshire, 18 Mar. [1797], [21 Mar. 1797], PRONI, Downshire Papers, D607/E/105, 190, 207, 214.

Across the Bann lay 'Orange country', ranging from parts of Down westwards through Armagh to the town of Dungannon. Dr William Richardson, a Church of Ireland clergyman whose parish lay near the Armagh border in County Tyrone, pictured the republican tide breaking against the obstacle of Orangeism in the south, but spreading north of Lough Neagh through Coleraine, Newtownlimavady, Derry, Strabane, Omagh, Aughnacloy, and doubling back to the southern parts of Armagh.[26] In his native Tyrone, the rebels had established a footing among Presbyterian watchmakers, blacksmiths, wealthier farmers, and linen manufacturers, with the towns of Coagh and Cookstown conspicuously disaffected.[27] The south remained loyal, Richardson reported, but 'to the north of us is quite lost. Dungannon is frontier and Stewartstown an advanced post in the enemies [*sic*] country with many Royalists in it. Thence to the Northern Sea scarce a friend.'[28] There were greater numbers of Episcopalians west of the Bann, of course, and it may be that the loyalty of towns like Lurgan can be attributed to Church and King sentiment.[29] On the other hand, Richard Musgrave, no friend to the Dissenters, confessed that outside Antrim and Down many Presbyterians had rallied to the government.[30] In Omagh, for example, an exponent of the Yeomanry scheme had found the local Presbyterians hostile to 'Belfast principles' and belligerently anti-Catholic; 2,000 were willing to enrol.[31] In areas where Roman Catholics predominated, radicalism was frail and the Presbyterians collaborated with their Episcopalian neighbours against the common threat; thus while the government found it difficult to raise Yeomanry corps in Antrim, Down, and Derry, they found numerous recruits in Armagh and Tyrone.[32]

The sectarian warfare of the Armagh/Monaghan border represents the violent legacy of the Ulster plantation in its purest, most concentrated form. This intractable region was a bastion of Gaelic culture, shielded from the spread of the English language by the surrounding mountains. The inhabitants, according to a local Anglican parson, retained 'many traces of Savage life', such as laziness, pugnacity, and drunkenness; they were bound together by close kinship ties; and they cherished the 'hereditary Enmities' which had been handed down from generation to generation.[33] Along this frontier, traditions of banditry had survived well into the eighteenth century, and ethnic friction was kept alive by continued colonization.[34] Around 1733, for example, a group of landed gentlemen in the parish of Creggan encouraged Presbyterians to

[26] Richardson to [Abercorn], 22 Feb. 1797, PRONI, Abercorn Papers, T2541/IB3/6/5.

[27] McEvoy, 'United Irishmen in County Tyrone'.

[28] Richardson to [Abercorn], 22 Feb. 1797, PRONI, Abercorn Papers, T2541/IB3/6/5 on the south; McEvoy, 'United Irishmen in County Tyrone' (part 1), 309.

[29] Richard Musgrave, *Memoirs of the Different Rebellions in Ireland* (Dublin, 1801), 55, 182.

[30] Ibid. 88, 97, 106, 174, 194.

[31] James Buchanan to Edward Cooke, 16 Sept. 1796, NAI, Rebellion Papers, 620/29/133.

[32] Richardson to [Abercorn], 28 Mar. 1797, PRONI, Abercorn Papers, T2541/IB3/6/11; Musgrave, *Rebellions*, 182, 189. Of around 18,000 Ulster yeomen serving in 1798, somewhere between 5,000 and 7,000 were Presbyterians: A. F. Blackstock, 'The Origin and Development of the Irish Yeomanry, 1796–*c*.1807', Ph.D. thesis (QUB, 1993), 382.

[33] Edward Hudson to Charlemont, 7 Dec. 1789, Miller (ed.), *Peep O'Day Boys*, 94.

[34] S. J. Connolly, *Religion, Law and Power: The Making of Protestant Ireland 1660–1760* (Oxford, 1992), 204–17.

settle on their estates and granted a lease for the nominal rent of three peppercorns a year to the Revd Alexander McCombe, a Dissenting minister who was ordained at the Fews barracks in 1734. One result was a sharp increase in sectarian tension: McCombe's first place of worship, a small thatched house near Crossmaglen, was burned down by Roman Catholics.[35] The same fate befell a Seceding meeting-house at nearby Cahans, County Monaghan, in 1779, fuelling the fierce anti-Catholicism of the preachers John Rogers and George Carson, and of the local Volunteer units.[36] Throughout this area, sectarian conflict also possessed a racial edge that had largely disappeared elsewhere. According to John Byrne, our main source for the Armagh troubles of the 1780s and 1790s, the two parties went under the names of 'Scotch' and 'Irish', a reminder of the ethnic animosities between planter and Gael which persisted in south Ulster.[37]

It would be surprising if some Armagh Presbyterians had not joined the ranks of the Orange Order after 1795. There is evidence to suggest that during the first phase of the Armagh troubles, the anti-Catholic raids begun in 1784, the aggressors were Dissenters. The Peep O' Day Boy violence began with a quarrel in the Presbyterian town of Markethill and spread to other areas of Scottish settlement such as Nappagh, Hamiltonsbawn, Newtownhamilton, and Keady, though the location of the disturbances later moved to the north of the county.[38] It appears also that Presbyterians were instrumental in taking the first steps to create a new league to defend Protestantism against the Defenders in the years before the battle of the Diamond. During the elections for the Dungannon convention, James Wilson, a Presbyterian farmer of Dyan, County Tyrone, had tried to organize the Freemasons of Benburb into such an association, before establishing his own oathbound society of 'Orange Boys', although he played no part in the Orange institution which emerged in 1795.[39] Once it had become institutionalized as a gentry-led, church-associated movement, many Presbyterians would have found it less congenial, and there were certainly no Dissenting ministers or prominent laymen among its patrons.[40] The participation of some of their poorer co-religionists was clearly an embarrassment for respectable Presbyterians, and the local ministers and middling ranks seem to have done all in their power to put down the disturbances.[41]

---

[35] John Donaldson, *A Historical and Statistical Account of the Barony of the Upper Fews in the County of Armagh 1838* (Dundalk, 1923), 11–12, 86–7.

[36] Depositions relating to the burning of Freeduff meeting-house, 1743, PRONI, T1392; W. D. Bailie et al., *A History of Congregations in the Presbyterian Church in Ireland* (Belfast, 1982), 259; John Rogers, *A Sermon Preached at Lisnavein, Otherwise Ballybay New Erection* (Edinburgh, 1780), 17–18, 24 n., 36–7.

[37] Miller (ed.), *Peep O'Day Boys*, 54. Byrne also speaks of the 'mountainy Irish' and the 'lowland Scotch', while in south Armagh Catholics called Presbyterians 'Whigs', echoing old seventeenth-century vocabulary of abuse (ibid. 34, 94).

[38] Hereward Senior, *Orangeism in Britain and Ireland, 1795–1836* (London, 1966), 7, 9–10. Lord Gosford, for example, attributed the disturbances in south Armagh to 'a low set of Fellows, who Call themselves Protestant Dissenters': see Gosford to Arthur Acheson, 8 Feb. 1788, D1606/1/125C, printed in Miller (ed.), *Peep O'Day Boys*, 49.   [39] *BNL*, 1 Feb. 1793; Senior, *Orangeism*, 14, 18.

[40] Ibid. 40.

[41] [Revd William Campbell] to Revd Benjamin McDowell, 18 Aug. 1788, PRONI, Bruce Papers, T3041/1/E53, quoted in Miller, *Peep O'Day Boys*, 66.

Armagh, it is true, still found room for the reception of what Thomas Knox called 'the Belfast doctrines'.[42] The Presbyterian congregation of Drumbanagher, led by the United Irishman Alexander Patterson, felt confident enough to make a public stand against Orange brutality.[43] In the mid-1790s the county was integrated into the cellular network of the United Irishmen, and Louis Cullen has recently drawn attention to the importance of Presbyterian radicals in the electoral interest of the Cope family of Loughgall.[44] More surprisingly, perhaps, organized republicanism had reached the Presbyterian communities further south in Cavan and Monaghan. At Stonebridge, County Monaghan, the congregation of the Revd James Whiteside was said to be composed of 'old stiff Presbyterians who incline much to Paine's principles' and asserted their electoral independence.[45] There was also activity in the Ballybay area, where the Revd John Arnold was a United Irishman, and in the Presbyterian centres of Glasslough and Newbliss. In Cavan, meanwhile, the Dissenting enclave of Bailieborough was disaffected, and a number of local preachers were 'up', although attempts to form a coalition of Dissenters and Catholics seem to have met with opposition.[46]

Other evidence, meanwhile, suggests that the Presbyterians had buried their differences with the Anglican establishment as the Defenders spread throughout Louth, Monaghan, and Cavan.[47] Along the Cavan/Meath border, according to one pamphleteer, 'there reside numerous tribes of Presbyterians, called by the common people Scotch' who existed in a state of 'hereditary animosity' with the lower orders of Irish who surrounded them.[48] When sectarian warfare between Defenders and Presbyterians had flared up in 1792 the Scotch had collaborated with the magistrates and clergymen of the Established Church.[49] On one occasion the Revd James McAuley, Seceding minister of Castleblayney, marched his congregation to south Armagh to assist Lord Blayney in putting down the United Irishmen, while 'the Scotch people' of Ballyjamesduff came armed to worship on the sabbath, with sentinels posted on a nearby hill to give the alarm if the Defenders should attack.[50] As in Armagh, then, so generally throughout the borderlands, Dissenters were to be found in both camps. No doubt allegiances here were complicated by the fact that Seceders were particularly strong in Monaghan and Cavan, that they had a history of difficult relations with the parent church, and that their congregations represented relatively late settlements where ethnic friction was still fresh.

Further west, the letters of James Hamilton, agent on the Tyrone and Donegal estates of the Earl of Abercorn, provide some indication of popular feeling. In the

---

[42] McEvoy, 'United Irishmen in County Tyrone' (part 1), 302.   [43] *NS*, 18 Feb. 1796.

[44] L. M. Cullen, 'The Political Structures of the Defenders', in David Dickson and Hugh Gough (eds.), *Ireland and the French Revolution* (Dublin, 1990), 119.

[45] L. T. Brown, 'The Presbyterians of Cavan and Monaghan: An Immigrant Community in South Ulster over Three Generations', Ph.D. thesis (Belfast, 1986), 702.

[46] Ibid. 703–9. The ministers were Robert Montgomery of Bailieborough (Corglass), John Craig of the Burgher congregation at Coronary, Thomas Stewart of Cootehill, and William Moore of Corvalley.

[47] Ibid. 702.

[48] *A Candid and Impartial Account of the Disturbances in the County of Meath, in the Years 1792, 1793, and 1794. By a County Meath Freeholder* (Dublin, 1794), 2.   [49] Ibid. 2.

[50] Brown, 'Presbyterians of Cavan and Monaghan', 707–8.

early months of 1797 Hamilton found he could collect the rent only by employing parties of military. Around this time a series of nocturnal arms raids carried out by large bodies of Liberty Men forced magistrates to place the area under martial law. A few months later he complained of inflammatory handbills strewed on the road at night, and wrote to Abercorn that 'Little Petty Killings in the Night are become very frequent and there are few in which they are not attended with Cruelty'. By May, Hamilton was able to report that almost 250 stands of arms had been given up quietly in the neighbourhood and that the area from Derry to Omagh was quiet; this, however, he attributed to the doubling of the military guards and the nightly patrols, rather than to any change of mood in the countryside.[51] The disaffected parts of the west also included an important pocket of radicalism in Donegal.[52] At the time of the Dungannon convention the Anglican parson of Taughboyne reported resistance to the collection of tithes, taxes, and rents, which he put down to the 'levelling and republican principles' which prevailed among his Presbyterian and Seceding parishioners.[53] After the Bantry Bay scare the United Irish became active in the Laggan area between the rivers Foyle and Swilly, where the Presbyterian farmers were strongest. The site of the trouble, according to the clerical magistrate William Hamilton, was a semicircle cutting into Donegal, with Derry city as its centre.[54] Once again, Dissent and disaffection coincided with remarkable precision.

Finally, turning to County Londonderry, there is much evidence of guerrilla activity in the mid-Ulster towns such as Maghera, Magherafelt, and Coleraine.[55] It was feared that the rebels possessed the whole county except the maiden city itself, which remained the besieged citadel of Protestant legend.[56] Initially, the Derry whigs had welcomed the French Revolution with the same enthusiasm demonstrated by their Belfast brethren. At a Fourteenth of July celebration in 1791, the Paris citizens who stormed the Bastille were compared to the apprentice boys who had closed the city gates against the despot James II; a cheap edition of *Rights of Man* was issued a few months later; and the Catholics found a sympathetic voice in the Revd George Sampson, an Anglican clergyman and father of the prominent United Irish leader William Sampson.[57] But whatever sympathy existed for the Catholic cause soon evaporated. In 1792 'A Citizen of Londonderry' published a collection of extracts from various devotional works to show that the Catholics, despite their declarations of

[51] James Hamilton to Abercorn, 11 Feb. 1797, 4 Apr. 1797, 7 May 1797, PRONI, Abercorn Papers, T2541/IA2/6, 17, 21, 25.

[52] Richardson to [Abercorn], 22 Feb. 1797, PRONI, Abercorn Papers, T2541/IB3/6/5.

[53] Thomas Pemberton to Abercorn, 15 Jan. 1793, 22 Mar. 1793, PRONI, Abercorn Papers, T2541/IA1/19/9, 26.

[54] William Hamilton to Dublin Castle, 15 Feb. 1797, NAI, Rebellion Papers, 620/28/269.

[55] McEvoy, 'United Irishmen in County Tyrone' (part 3), 37–65; R. L. Marshall, 'Maghera in '98', in S. S. McFarland, *Presbyterianism in Maghera: A Social and Congregational History* (Maghera, 1985), 174–8; for Coleraine see John Galt's diary, PRONI, D561/1, p. 33.

[56] Richardson to [Abercorn], 22 Feb. 1797, PRONI, Abercorn Papers, T2541/IB3/6/5; Desmond Murphy, *Derry, Donegal and Modern Ulster 1790–1921* (Londonderry, 1981), 7–11.

[57] *BNL*, 26 July 1791, 6 May 1791; [George Vaughan Sampson], *Remarks on the State of the Catholic Question in Ireland* (Belfast, 1793). The Derry *Rights of Man* can be found in the National Library of Ireland.

liberality, still adhered to the old belief that salvation was exclusive to the Church of Rome, and were not yet sufficiently '*enlightened*' to be emancipated.[58] After Bantry Bay the city was converted into a loyalist base under the command of the zealous magistrate Sir George Hill, whose Londonderry Cavalry arrested suspects, searched for arms, and gathered intelligence in its hinterland.

The United Irish organization naturally reflected the disparate grievances of the rural bodies it had absorbed. Belfast radicals sometimes found it difficult to disguise their suspicion of their Defender allies: the northern supremo Samuel Neilson considered them an 'undisciplined rabble' and feared that the Catholic masses were 'Bigots to a Monarchy'.[59] At ground level the union of Catholic and Dissenter was never fully perfected, and United Irish leaders were troubled by reports of the movement splitting along sectarian lines.[60] In some areas the attempts of agents like McCracken and Hope to knit together the two sects undoubtedly met with striking success. Large numbers of Defenders were certainly sworn into the United Irish system, although information on this process is disappointingly thin. After the appearance of Paine's *Age of Reason*, one informer declared that the Catholic clergy was losing its influence, and papal infallibility was mocked, resulting in 'a strong union between the better class of Papists and Dissenters'.[61] On the other hand, many local observers, like the Revd Edward Hudson and Bishop Thomas Percy, testified to the persistence of confessional quarrels.[62] According to Musgrave, the United Irishmen and the Defenders continued as separate bodies until the end of 1797, despite the efforts of the clergy to overcome the strong antipathies which existed between the 'papists' and the lower class of Presbyterians.[63]

On the outer edges of Ulster, where sectarian conflict was most bitter, Defenderism was inspired by hopes for a reversal of the land settlement and even of the plantation itself. Unable to counteract these passions, the United Irishmen often swam with the tide, actively encouraging the popular perception that the native population was at last about to enter into its rightful inheritance. To this end, sectarian fervour was inflamed by prophecies warning that 'the Scotch' would rise on a certain night and massacre the Catholics, or rumours that the Orangemen had sworn an oath to wade knee-deep in Catholic blood.[64] In May 1794 the Cavan Defenders announced that '*they would destroy every Scotsman or Presbyterian they should find*', while a Donegal farm servant who joined the Defenders was told that the fields would be littered

---

[58] A Citizen of Londonderry, *A Test of Roman Catholic Liberality, Submitted to the Consideration of Both Roman Catholicks and Protestants* (Londonderry, 1792), 26–7, 33; Murphy, *Derry, Donegal and Modern Ulster*, 7–8.   [59] Information of Smith, NAI, Rebellion Papers, 620/27/1.

[60] See e.g. the information of Nicholas Magin, 31 July 1797, PRONI, Cleland Papers, D714/2/6.

[61] [Leonard McNally] to Downshire, 8 Dec. 1794[?], PRONI, Downshire Papers, D607/C/56. See also Thomas Lane to Downshire, 4 Feb. 1796, PRONI, Downshire Papers, D607/D/27, and James Hamilton, jun., to Abercorn, 11 Feb. 1797, Abercorn Papers, T2541/IA2/6/17, for evidence of joint Catholic–Dissenter activity.

[62] Hudson to Charlemont, 3 Aug. 1794, Percy to Hudson, 22 Dec. 1794, *Charlemont MSS*, ii. 246, 256.   [63] Musgrave, *Rebellions*, 104, 180.

[64] McSkimmin, *Annals*, 99; Hudson to Charlemont, 29 May 1796, *Charlemont MSS*, ii. 273; Musgrave, *Rebellions*, 54.

with the bodies of Protestants and Presbyterians.[65] The instability of the 1790s thus acted on a variety of antagonisms. The shape of the rebel forces was often determined by local passions and motivations as Ulster society broke along the criss-crossed lines carved out by the plantation.

The millenarian moment

We have already seen the importance of millenarian ideas in predisposing the Covenanters and, to a lesser extent, the Seceders towards rebellion. Historians of millenarianism have generally concentrated on its popular manifestations, such as the cults which surrounded Richard Brothers and Joanna Southcott.[66] Such outbursts of religious enthusiasm are usually seen as an irrational phenomenon, belonging to a pre-industrial era and expressing the social grievances of the dispossessed. This is essentially the view taken by David Miller, whose 'prophetic' Presbyterianism belongs to a superstitious age which vanished as the linen industry in Ulster moved from the home to the factory. But there was also a scholarly preoccupation with prophetic exegesis that links Isaac Newton and William Whiston with the Rational Dissenters Richard Price and Joseph Priestley.[67] In Ulster the last decade of the eighteenth century witnessed a flowering of eschatological speculation which crossed the entire theological spectrum from Unitarian to Covenanter.

It is true that millenarian beliefs, whilst common enough in the almanacs and chapbooks of the eighteenth century, did not often surface in the published sermons designed for a more select readership. Before the last quarter of the century there was little eschatology in either Scotland or Ireland. The only known example from Ulster is John Abernethy's *A Sermon Recommending the Study of Scripture-Prophecie*, preached to the Synod in 1716.[68] Abernethy's somewhat hesitant forecast that the year 1716 would see the inauguration of the millennium may have seemed rather precipitous to his audience, but he could draw support from the computations of William Whiston, Newton's successor at Trinity College, Cambridge, and of Pierre Jurieu, the Huguenot refugee and biblical scholar whose *Accomplishment of the Scripture Prophecies, or the Approaching Deliverance of the Church* had been published in London in 1687. Otherwise he presented a fairly unremarkable explication of the prophetic writings. His identification of the Pope with the Beast of Revelation

---

[65] Richardson to [Abercorn], 14 Feb. 1797, Abercorn Papers, PRONI, T2541/IB3/6/4; Jim Smyth, *The Men of No Property: Irish Radicals and Popular Politics in the Late Eighteenth Century* (London, 1992), 51, 105, 108; R. B. McDowell, *Ireland in the Age of Imperialism and Revolution, 1760–1801* (Oxford, 1979), 473–4.

[66] See J. F. C. Harrison, *The Second Coming: Popular Millenarianism, 1780–1850* (London, 1979).

[67] See Clarke Garrett, *Respectable Folly: Millenarians and the French Revolution in France and England* (Baltimore, 1975); W. H. Oliver, *Prophets and Millennialists: The Uses of Biblical Prophecy in England from the 1790s to the 1840s* (Auckland, 1978); Jack Fruchtman, jun., 'The Apocalyptic Politics of Richard Price and Joseph Priestley: A Study in Late Eighteenth-Century English Republican Millennialism', *Transactions of the American Philosophical Society*, 73/4 (1983); Iain McCalman, 'New Jerusalems: Prophecy, Dissent and Radical Culture in England, 1786–1830', in Knud Haakonssen, *Enlightenment and Religion: Rational Dissent in Eighteenth-Century Britain* (Cambridge, 1996), 312–35.

[68] John Abernethy, *A Sermon Recommending the Study of Scripture-Prophecie* (Belfast, 1716).

was representative of Protestant readings of the prophecies since the Reformation, and was grounded in the belief that the papacy had usurped the position of Jesus Christ as head of the Church. It was commonly accepted that the Roman Church represented the last of the four great empires spoken of by the prophet Daniel, and that the ten horns of the Beast described in the Book of Revelation signified the crowned heads of Europe, united in their support for papal power.

There were endless debates among church historians concerning the rise of Antichrist in the middle ages, and the significance of Rome's decline since the Reformation. According to Revelation 12: 6, the reign of the Beast would last for a period of 1,260 days, interpreted by scholars as so many years. Many commentators believed that this period had ended with the Reformation. This was only the first of several battles, however, which were commonly identified with the seven vials of Revelation. Although Abernethy associated Antichrist with Rome and the Catholic monarchies of Europe, he also spoke of 'popery' in a more abstract sense, denoting the tendency of all churches to infringe the right of private judgement. In a sermon which predates his open opposition to the Westminster Confession, he asserted that the Protestant Churches still retained antichristian elements within them, and he cited as an important example the enforcement of a conformity by penal statutes. Here were the first signs of the New Light outlook which related the idea of Antichrist to the spirit of persecution which afflicted all churches, and more specifically to the corruption of Christianity by the use of human creeds and confessions.

Apart from the latent millenarianism of Covenanting tracts, the next eschatological work produced in Presbyterian Ulster was a study drafted by the heterodox minister John Cameron around 1785, but not published 'owing to the disturbed state of the country and to some political statements and allusions in the book, which were judged to be unseasonable'.[69] By this time there were already some hints of that enlightened optimism that would characterize *fin de siècle* radicalism. Some of the sermons preached before the Synod's annual meetings reveal a faith in the progressive unfolding of religious understanding which could reach apocalyptic dimensions. In 1774 the outgoing moderator, William Campbell, encouraged his brethren to look forward to a new reformation, an age of enlightenment when the dark clouds of popery and superstition would be dispelled.[70] It was soon possible to draw evidence for such beliefs from the creation of the American republic. Many Irish Presbyterians read Richard Price's *Observations on the American Revolution* (1784), which depicted the new state as the harbinger of 'the empire of reason and virtue' which would govern the last age on earth.[71] The conflict in the colonies had been described by many of its participants in the language of prophecy, and it was natural that Ulster Presbyterians should treat its outcome as an event of cosmic significance.[72]

---

[69] Thomas Witherow, *Historical and Literary Memorials of Presbyterianism in Ireland*, 2 vols. (Belfast, 1879–80), ii. 129.

[70] William Campbell, *The Presence of Christ with his Church in Every Age and Period of it, Explained and Improved* (Belfast, 1774), esp. 34.   [71] Fruchtman, 'Apocalyptic Politics', 1.

[72] Barber, MS sermon on Revelation 18: 20, PHSI, Barber MSS, p. 18. For America, see N. O. Hatch, *The Sacred Cause of Liberty: Republican Thought and the Millennium in Revolutionary New England* (New Haven, 1977); R. H. Bloch, *Visionary Republic: Millennial Themes in American Thought, 1756–1800* (Cambridge, 1985).

The ways in which the cataclysmic events of the 1790s could be fitted into a millenarian scheme can be illustrated by three sermons. The first is Samuel Barber's commentary on Revelation 18: 20, preached before the Synod of Ulster in June 1791. Barber's diary reveals that he had been eagerly following constitutional changes in France—in particular the ecclesiastical reforms—and his sermon is an early attempt to interpret these affairs in the light of the biblical prophecies.[73] The second is William Steel Dickson's *Three Sermons on Scripture Politics*, published in 1793. Although all three sermons are relevant, it is the second one, preached to his Portaferry congregation on Christmas day 1792, which captures the apocalyptic expectations of that year. The last is Thomas Ledlie Birch's *The Obligations upon Christians and Especially Ministers to be Exemplary in their Lives*, another synodical sermon, this time from the annual meeting of June 1793. These three ministers were the most prominent radicals within the Synod; each had a long history of political activism, and each was later arrested in connection with the rebellion. Indeed, one of the charges made against Birch was that his preaching and prayers were of a seditious nature, 'setting forth from Scripture prophecy the extension of the redeemer's kingdom over the whole earth'.[74] But while Barber and Dickson were leading New Lights (Barber seems to have been a Unitarian), Birch was a member of the Presbytery of Belfast which had been set up to safeguard the doctrines of the Westminster Confession.

All three took it for granted that the close of the eighteenth century was, in Birch's words, 'a very advanced and enlightened period of the world, when ignorance and superstition are falling like lightning from Heaven, and knowledge is making very rapid strides'. According to Barber, the destruction of 'Babylon' would be gradual, just as its rise to power had taken place over several centuries. He dated the ascent of Antichrist, which he associated with the alliance between Church and State, to the reign of Constantine, when imperial Rome had been transformed into a Christian power. The Council of Nicaea, summoned by Constantine in AD 325, was singled out as the first occasion when civil authorities had dared to legislate on church matters. This mixture of religion and politics was responsible for the perversion of Christianity into an instrument of war, persecution, and bloodshed. (The legislation in question was of course the orthodox definition of the doctrine of the Trinity, known to posterity as the Athanasian creed, a fact which would have reinforced Barber's distaste.) The Reformation had dealt a severe blow to this antichristian system, but Barber lamented that the Protestant Churches had shaken off papal authority only to succumb to the power of the state. A second reformation was now approaching, however, as evidenced by the recovery of twenty-four million souls from civil and religious captivity. Heartened by the news of French Catholics throwing off the shackles of civil and religious thraldom, Barber urged his hearers to prepare for the collapse of all religious establishments, and the imminent 'fall of the great city Babylon'.[75]

---

[73] Both the sermon, which was never published, and Barber's commonplace book are in PHSI.
[74] Thomas Ledlie Birch, *A Letter from an Irish Emigrant to his Friend in the United States* (Philadelphia, 1799), 22 n.   [75] Barber, sermon on Revelation 18: 20, PHSI, p. 18.

Thomas Ledlie Birch also conjured with the numbers found in Revelation, choosing AD 606 as the date when Antichrist arose, since Pope Boniface had then established his claim as God's representative on earth in league with the emperor Phocas, thus forming the tyrannical partnership of magistracy and ministry.[76] Although he calculated that the destruction of the Beast would not occur until 1848, Birch's interpretation pointed to a series of remarkable setbacks crowded into the period between 1760 and 1790. These predictions had now been fulfilled, he believed, and as evidence he instanced the dispute with America, which had begun with the conspiracy to impose bishops on the colonies, the seizure of the Crimea from the Turks by Russia in 1784, the liberalization of the laws against Presbyterians and Catholics in Ireland, and, lastly, the opening of public office to Protestants in France.[77] The rise of Deism clearly presented something of an embarrassment for Birch, and he later felt it necessary to point out that the French still attended worship, but were merely less bigoted than before. In Ireland he believed that the Catholics had become 'as enlightened as others', having been made aware of the 'worldly policy' pursued by the temporal powers and even by the Pope himself.[78]

Although these sermons differed on various points, they both identified the union of Church and State as the key to the antichristian system. Reviewing the conflicting interpretations of the biblical prophecies, Barber advised his colleagues that the Beast had not taken the shape of one individual, but could be found in those principles which were opposite to the fundamental Christian doctrines, that Christ is the sole king and lawgiver of His Church, and that every man is bound for himself to search the Scriptures. Above all, he denounced the pretensions made by mortals who sat in the throne of God and usurped Christ's authority by making new laws and terms of communion.[79] Antichrist could thus be described in abstract terms as any interference with the sacred and unalienable right of private judgement. Barber's concentration on the importance of individual conscience was rooted in his New Light theology, but the orthodox Birch was in agreement:

by the name Anti-christ we do imagine, that not any man, or class of men, is designed in scripture, but a system now known in the world (particularly under the name of church establishment) planned and carried on, under various agencies, which (as occasion served) has persecuted all religions, and opposed all reformation.[80]

Unlike Barber and Birch, Steel Dickson did not refer directly to the prophetic books. His more figurative references to the commencement of the millennium bear some resemblance to a 'secular', or utopian vision of moral and social improvement. He hailed the French republic as the harbinger of a new age when peace, freedom, and justice would be established throughout the world:

---

[76] Thomas Ledlie Birch, *The Obligations upon Christians and Especially Ministers to be Exemplary in their Lives, Particularly at this Important Period, when the Prophecies are Seemingly about to be Fulfilled in the Fall of Antichrist, as an Introduction to the Flowing in of Jew and Gentile into the Christian Church* (Belfast, 1794), 26–7. [77] Ibid. 28–9, 29–30 n.

[78] Birch, *Irish Emigrant*, 24, 26–7. [79] Barber, sermon on Revelation 18: 20, PHSI, pp. 3–6.

[80] Thomas Ledlie Birch, *Seemingly Experimental Religion* (Washington, Pa., 1806), 15–16.

One great and enlightened nation has burst the chains of prejudice and slavery, disclaimed the idea of conquest for dominion, opened the temple of liberty for all religious denominations at home, and sent forth her arms, *not to destroy*, but *restore* the liberty of the world, and extend her blessings to all who dare, and by daring, deserve to be free.[81]

But Dickson too possessed a prophetic sense of history which revolved around the struggle for religious freedom. He shared the belief that tyranny and oppression had their roots in established religion, which he too traced to Constantine. Christianity had been warped by the attempts of statesmen to interfere with religious belief and regulate modes of worship. All sects were equally prone to this disease, as demonstrated during the upheavals of Stuart England, when 'Catholic burned Protestant, Protestant persecuted Catholic, and the Presbyterians in their momentary triumph, denied toleration to both'. Only when this persecuting spirit was abandoned, and all penal laws were abolished, would the divine prophecies be realized, Dickson argued. 'Then will jealousies cease, discontents vanish, animosities be extinguished, and the pure spirit of the gospel, unadulterated by the politics of the world, warm us into mutual kindness, restore us to confidence, and soothe us into peace.'[82]

Millenarianism thus offered common ground on which both New Light and Old could unite to defend civil and religious liberty from the threat of priestcraft and superstition. It also bridged the gap between the enlightenment ideology of the Belfast radicals and the grievances of the tenant farmers and artisans who made up the rank and file. During the crisis of the late 1790s—a time of economic dislocation, invasion scares, and Lake's brutal military campaigns—the apprehension that human history was approaching its apocalyptic conclusion was not confined to one sect. Edward Hudson, Anglican minister at Lisburn, wrote to Charlemont that 'We are like the Christians in the first century, who every day expected the world would be at an end, and in contemplation of that great event every idea was absorbed. So here, nothing can persuade us but that some great event is at hand.'[83] Martha McTier informed her brother that the lower orders in Belfast had been inflamed by predictions of the second coming.[84] In the district of Dromore, County Down, handbills were circulated describing spectral armies which had been observed marching through the countryside of County Down. Birch recalled that

Some years before the late commotions in Ireland, the sky at night seemed frequently as clothed with a mantle of blood—at other times convulsed with the most lively agitations, resembling the evolutions of an army. Westerly, near the horizon, there was sometimes the resemblance of an immense pile of fuel, the flame just breaking out.[85]

One antiquarian recorded that visions and prophetic dreams regarding the landing of the French were supposed to have been common at this time. Old legends

---

[81] William Steel Dickson, *Three Sermons on the Subject of Scripture Politics* (Belfast, 1793), 35.

[82] Ibid. 33–5.

[83] Hudson to Charlemont, 26 May 1797, *Charlemont MSS*, ii. 300. See also Charlemont to Haliday, 9 June 1797, ibid. 300.

[84] Martha McTier to Drennan, [*c*.Oct. 1798], 28 June 1800, PRONI, Drennan Papers, T765/725, 854. [85] Birch, *Seemingly Experimental Religion*, 20.

and prophecies were revived; new predictions of civil war and bloodshed proliferated.[86] Such millennial hopes and fears inevitably reflected the faultlines which defined Ulster's sectarian geography. Rumours spread that hosts of Orangemen were coming from Armagh to destroy Belfast, while Catholics were terrified by reports, encouraged by the United Irish command, that the Orangemen, or 'black militia', had sworn an oath to exterminate them.[87] Steel Dickson later remembered how the poorer Catholics and Presbyterians who had lived together in peace would run from house to house warning of massacres about to be perpetrated by their neighbours.[88] In an atmosphere of heightened religious tension many people were vulnerable to such appeals. On the Ulster frontier millenarianism could fuse with the otherworldliness and introspection of evangelical Christianity to produce E. P. Thompson's 'chiliasm of despair'. As we have seen, the Secession clergy used this language to counsel their flock against the sin of rebellion. In the Presbyterian east, however, millennial excitement played a critical role in detonating the series of insurrections which erupted in the year of liberty.

United Irish chiefs in Belfast quickly stepped forward to exploit the apocalyptic mood in the countryside. One government informer reported that Neilson had placed 'a foolish old Prophecy' in the *Northern Star* to please the 'Country Readers'.[89] The paper itself ran numerous articles interpreting the European war in providential terms; in the summer of 1796, for example, Bonaparte's Italian victories were hailed as signs of 'the approaching downfall of the Pope'.[90] The *Northern Star* office also printed millenarian tracts such as Fleming's *A Discourse on the Rise and Fall of Antichrist* in 1795, with a preface by the Revd William Stavely and an introduction by the publisher predicting that the 'absolute monarchical form of government, which obtained hitherto in these dominions, will be completely set aside'.[91] Another millenarian tract written by James Tytler, a Scot who fled to Belfast in 1793 before making his way to the United States, claimed that the French 'have in great measure overthrown that monstrous system of superstition and Spiritual tyranny in Scripture called *Babylon the Great*'.[92] In Derry and Antrim, republican emissaries circulated the *Life and Prophecies* (1682) of Alexander Peden, the fugitive Covenanter who had visited Ireland in the 1680s, which foretold a French invasion of the British Isles.[93] Readings of these prognostications to groups of Protestant farmers were arranged by the United Irishmen.[94]

---

[86] McSkimmin, *Annals*, 48–9, 100; Musgrave, *Rebellions*, 54, 69.   [87] McSkimmin, *Annals*, 99.
[88] William Steel Dickson, *A Narrative of the Confinement and Exile of William Steel Dickson, D.D.* (Dublin, 1812), 30–1.   [89] Information of Smith, 1796, NAI, Rebellion Papers, 620/27/1.
[90] *NS*, 20 June 1796.   [91] A copy can be found in NAI, Rebellion Papers, 620/22/63.
[92] James Tytler, *The Rising of the Sun in the West: or the Origin and Progress of Liberty* (Salem, 1795), found among the papers of the United Irishmen, NAI, Rebellion Papers, 620/22/62. For Tytler's links with the Belfast radicals see E. W. McFarland, *Ireland and Scotland in the Age of Revolution: Planting the Green Bough* (Edinburgh, 1990), 136–8.
[93] Eleven editions of this book were advertised in Belfast between 1729 and 1787 and a Newry edition of Peden's *The Lord's Trumpet Sounding an Alarm Against Scotland* was also published sometime before 1798: J. R. R. Adams, *The Printed Word and the Common Man: Popular Culture in Ulster 1700–1900* (Belfast, 1987), 2, 87, 87 n., app. 1.
[94] McSkimmin, *Annals*, 49–50. Catholics preferred the prophecies of Thomas the Rhymer.

The intellectual inheritance of the Covenanters, analysed in Chapters 3 and 4, made them especially susceptible to these apocalyptic warnings. It was said that one Covenanting preacher, William Gibson, entertained crowds with six-hour-long sermons on Revelation 18, with the result that his hearers were 'inflamed to deeds of rebellion, tyranny and murder'.[95] As the result of such preaching the membership of the Reformed Presbytery was boosted at this time by individuals 'distinguished by little else than hatred of the British government'.[96] The ways in which they were persuaded to co-operate with the United Irishmen are described in an intriguing passage of Thomas Emmet's memoirs. The Covenanters, he explains, traditionally believed that reformation could be promoted only by coercion and penal laws, but they were also 'lovers of liberty, and republicans by religion and descent'. United Irish agents argued with them that persecution had failed to reclaim the Catholics, and that the object of the Solemn League and Covenant could only be secured by 'the efforts of reason, which would be best promoted by mixing with the misled, and gradually convincing them of their errors'. To this end, the United Irishmen employed Father James Quigley, a Catholic priest-turned-republican, to tour the Covenanting areas. The appearance of this renegade papist quickened the millenarian pulse with the result that the Covenanters became 'the most active promoters of the system':

Intelligence was dispatched to every part, of his arrival, and from every part they crowded to receive and caress him. But when they learned that this Romish priest was so sincere a lover of liberty, as to have been actually fighting at the capture of the Bastille, their joy was almost extravagant.[97]

Another Jacobin agent attracted crowds by advertising himself as a lapsed papist who had become convinced of the 'true doctrines of Presbyterianism'.[98] Here indeed was evidence of a new age dawning.

The rebellion and after

The '98 rebellion in the north was an anticlimax. The conspiracy had reached its high-water mark in June 1797 when the United Irishmen calculated that they had 121,000 men in Ulster.[99] A year later, partial insurrections broke out prematurely as the leadership, reluctant to rise without French aid, struggled desperately to contain popular excitement.[100] It was the erosion of the northern organization by Lake's campaign that convinced the commanders to bring forward their insurrectionary plans. By this time, however, the command structure had been shattered by the

---

[95] Ibid. 53–4.   [96] Thomas Houston, *The Covenanter's Plea and Narrative* (Belfast, 1841), 2.

[97] Thomas Addis Emmet, 'Part of an Essay towards the History of Ireland', in W. J. MacNeven, *Pieces of Irish History* (New York, 1807), 99–100. According to Samuel McSkimmin thousands gathered in the fields of Antrim and Down to hear a touring Roman Catholic priest preach on 'brotherly love' and 'the renovation of mankind': *Annals*, 46.

[98] R. R. Madden, *The United Irishmen, their Lives and Times*, 3 ser., 7 vols. (London, 1842–6), 3rd ser., i. 312.   [99] McDowell, *Ireland*, 475.

[100] Charles Hamilton Teeling, *Personal Narrative of the 'Irish Rebellion' of 1798* (London, 1828), 126–7; Musgrave, *Rebellions*, 157–8.

imprisonment of the main leaders. Ironically, then, most of the Ulster population, which had received its political education and military training during the heyday of the Volunteers, remained quiet while the insurrection erupted in Wexford, an area of weaker organization.

The fighting in Antrim and Down lasted barely a week. When reports of the Wexford rising reached the north the Ulster commanders hesitated, reluctant to risk their troops until news of a French landing or of success in Leinster. It was left to the 'violent young men' to mobilize the United army.[101] At last, on 7 June, Henry Joy McCracken and James Hope brought out the Antrim rebels; the Down insurgents appeared in the field two days later, delayed by the last-minute arrest of their adjutant-general, Steel Dickson. Two major battles were fought at Antrim and Ballynahinch and a number of smaller confrontations took place at Larne, Limavady, Glenarm, Maghera, Carrickfergus, Newtownards, Broughshane, Portaferry, and Donaghadee.[102] The Ulster rebellion was a fiasco: the Antrim army was crushed before the Down rising got off the ground, and the other counties were paralysed by indecision and fear.

There is some evidence to suggest that the low turnout may have been influenced by attacks on Protestants in the south. Even before the Ulster rebels took the field, reports of atrocities in Wexford were already reaching the north. The civil war in Wexford was much more complicated than the sectarian *jacquerie* of loyalist propaganda, but early reports depicted it as a popish plot, stressing the role of priests, the oaths allegedly sworn by the rebels to murder all 'heretics', and inviting comparisons with 1641.[103] James Hamilton found the loyalty of the north increasing in proportion to the disaffection of the south; the Presbyterians, he believed, would now side with the establishment to save Protestant Ireland.[104] General Knox noted that many Dissenters in mid-Ulster converted from United Irishmen to yeomen when accounts of Vinegar Hill and Scullabogue became known about the end of June.[105] One Anglican minister explained the calm in Ulster outside Antrim and Down thus:

The United Irishmen there who are mostly Presbyterians discovered that the principals of the rebels held out a line to the Roman Catholics directly contradicting that which had been offered in the north last year and they immediately saw that an overturn in the constitution must end in the Presbyterians being overpowered and exterminated by Catholics.[106]

Ironically, the decade of the United Irishmen thus witnessed a reassertion of sectarian identifications. The rebellion itself collapsed amid mutual recriminations. Protestant disillusionment with the Catholic alliance was already swelling the ranks

---

[101] Account of the rebellion by Robert Hunter, NAI, Rebellion Papers, 620/7/75/5.

[102] For the rebellion see McDowell, *Ireland*, 636–43; Curtin, *United Irishmen*, ch. 10; A. T. Q. Stewart, *The Summer Soldiers: The 1798 Rebellion in Antrim and Down* (Belfast, 1995).

[103] Edward Lascelles to Downshire, 4 June 1798, John Patrickson to Downshire, 5 June [1798], 6 June [1798], Richard Annesley to Downshire, 9 June 1798, PRONI, Downshire Papers, D607/F/195, 196, 199, 215.

[104] Hamilton to Abercorn, 3 June 1798, PRONI, Abercorn Papers, T2541/IA2/7/19.

[105] McDowell, *Ireland*, 643; see also Musgrave, *Rebellions*, 74, 97, 107, 181, 189, 558.

[106] Edward Chichester to General George Vaughan Hart, 6 July 1798, PRONI, Hart Papers, D3077/C/3/10–11.

of the Orange Order. Indeed, a report circulated after the rebellion claimed that the Catholic Defenders of Glenarm, led by John Magennis, had refused to serve under the Presbyterian minister Robert Acheson and had deserted the night before the battle of Ballynahinch.[107] According to another story, the Randalstown commander, James Dickey, had renounced his Catholic sympathies before his execution at Belfast, claiming that the destruction of the Protestant Ascendancy would have been followed by a war between Catholics and Dissenters. Such reports were no doubt magnified by triumphant loyalists, but there is ample evidence to show that each side attempted to place the blame for the disaster of 1798 on the other.[108] One Defender song contained the lines:

> Treachery, treachery, damnable treachery!
> Put the poor Catholics all in the front,
> The Protestants next was the way they were fixed,
> And the black-mouthed Dissenters they skulked at the rump.[109]

Of all the participants in the northern rebellion it is the Presbyterian clergy who have attracted most attention. Richard Musgrave, the historian of the '98 rebellion, observed that only the Protestants of the Established Church were steady in their loyalty to king and constitution; he pointed out that the Presbyterian Church had emerged from a republic and its members had tended towards that form of government throughout Europe.[110] Like many others of the Ascendancy class, Musgrave viewed the '98 rebellion as a conspiracy hatched by Catholic priests and Presbyterian ministers. Appended to this book is a list of sixty-three ministers and probationers who were suspected of complicity in the insurrection itself, or at least of membership of the United Irishmen during their military, underground phase. Of these, twenty-two can be identified as New Light and twenty-two as Old Light including Seceders and Covenanters. The remainder cannot be classified, though it seems likely that the majority were orthodox. There is an interesting contrast here with the 1780s, when New Light ministers were more predominant. It should be emphasized, however, that many were innocent of any connection with the rebellion, and the evidence against the others is almost always problematic. In most cases we have to rely on hearsay, informers' reports, and the views of the military and the magistracy (at a time when habeas corpus was suspended)—sources which historians have accepted too readily.

---

[107] Musgrave, *Rebellions*, 181, 553, 557.

[108] Recent work has demonstrated the ways in which the sectarian character of the Wexford rising was magnified by loyalists in order to unify the Protestant population: see e.g. Kevin Whelan, ''98 After '98: The Politics of Memory', in id., *The Tree of Liberty: Radicalism, Catholicism and the Construction of Irish Identity 1760–1830* (Cork, 1996), 135–8; id., 'Reinterpreting the 1798 Rebellion in County Wexford', in Dáire Keogh and Nicholas Furlong (eds.), *The Mighty Wave: The 1798 Rebellion in Wexford* (Blackrock, Co. Dublin, 1996), 9–36. While it has been convincingly argued that historians have sometimes accepted loyalist accounts rather uncritically, we should beware of jumping to the opposite extreme. Ulster Presbyterians should not be seen as the dupes of Ascendancy propagandists, nor should the sectarianism of 1798 be dismissed as a figment of Richard Musgrave's lurid imagination.

[109] R. M. Young, *Ulster in '98: Episodes and Anecdotes* (Belfast, [1893]), 51.

[110] Musgrave, *Rebellions*, 120, 182.

So how many ministers were actually 'up' in 1798? There can be little doubt about the revolutionary credentials of Arthur McMahon, whose activities in Ireland, Britain, and France are well documented.[111] Both official sources and popular reports confirm that Steel Dickson replaced Thomas Russell as commander-in-chief of County Down and that Thomas Ledlie Birch participated in the battle of Ballynahinch.[112] On the other hand, many of the names listed below were innocent victims of loyalist enthusiasm. A correspondent of the Revd William Campbell described how many ministers suffered imprisonment and insults, and lost their property by military violence, 'for no other cause than that of being teachers of a sect *suspected* by government, and for their avowed *liberality* to Catholics', and he mentioned Boyle Moody of Newry as one such case.[113] Another example was William Neilson, who was arrested for incitement to treason as he rose to preach a Gaelic sermon in his father's church at Rademon. He was quickly released after translating the sermon into English at his own trial.[114] The contribution of William Hamilton Drummond to Presbyterian radicalism was limited to a couple of patriotic poems printed at the *Northern Star* office, but a Yeomanry officer put a pistol to his head a few days after the rising, crying, 'You young villain, it is you and the like of you, that have brought this upon us with your infernal poetry.'[115]

In between these two extremes lay the majority of the Presbyterian ministers who found themselves in gaol or emigrant ships during the year of liberty. These include the unfortunate James Porter, hanged in front of his meeting-house. Porter's son believed that he had been a United Irishman, but thought that he had opposed the rising because of insufficient resources and inadequate planning.[116] Porter was charged with taking captive a government messenger at the head of a small party of insurgents, but his son claimed that the rebels had taken the messenger to Porter's house merely to have the letter read. Whatever the truth of the matter, Porter's notoriety as a radical propagandist sealed his fate: he was a constant contributor to the *Northern Star*, wrote frequently for its successor, the *Press*, and was the author of a collection of popular patriotic songs entitled *Paddy's Resource* (1795) and a sermon condemning the war with France.[117] Porter had also undertaken an extremely popular tour of Natural Philosophy lectures which he used as vehicles for political evangelicalism.[118]

---

[111] Marianne Elliott, *Partners in Revolution: The United Irishmen and France* (New Haven, 1982), 146, 160, 171, 217, 269.

[112] Dickson himself always refused to deny that he was a rebel: see *Narrative*, 207–13, 314, and *Retractions; or, A Review of, and Reply to, a Pamphlet* (Belfast, 1813), 60.

[113] William Campbell, 'Sketches of the History of Presbyterians in Ireland', PHSI, Campbell MSS, p. 124.

[114] Aodan Mac Poilin, 'The Most "Expressive and Polished" Language', in *Fortnight: An Independent Review of Politics and the Arts*, 287 (Sept. 1990), 29.

[115] W. H. Drummond, *Posthumous Sermons*, ed. J. S. Porter (Dublin, 1867), pp. iv–viii.

[116] Account of the Revd James Porter, written by James Porter, jun., 1844, PRONI, D3579/2, pp. 4–5.

[117] James Porter, *Wind and Weather: A Sermon on the Late Providential Storm which Dispersed the Fleet off Bantry Bay. Preached to the Congregation of Gray-Abbey, on Thursday the 16th February, Being the Day Appointed by Government for Thanksgiving* (Belfast, 1797), 9–10, 15, 20.

[118] Henry Montgomery, 'Outlines of the History of Presbyterianism in Ireland', *Irish Unitarian and Bible Christian*, 2 (1847), 331; 'Observator', in *NS*, 21 Jan. 1796.

Similar doubts attend the arrest of Samuel Barber of Rathfriland. Again there is no doubt as to Barber's political sympathies: he had joined Wolfe Tone in his attempts to reconcile the Peep O' Day Boys and Defenders of County Down in 1792, and had formed a company of National Guards in that year. According to the informer Nicholas Magin, Barber was a candidate for one of the adjutant-generals of Down.[119] Yet when Barber was tried by court martial on 14 July, the only evidence brought against him was a rather unguarded remark he had been heard to make about the state of the country. Barber insisted: 'I have constantly preached peace, goodwill and obedience to the laws and the following circumstances, that when the rebellion broke out in the County of Down, not one man in my congregation joined in it is proof that I did not preach in vain.'[120]

We know even less of the other exponents of scripture politics. We have already seen that John Glendy, whose arrest was ordered by Castlereagh, preached radical sermons during the Volunteer revival of 1792–3, but one of his American colleagues later recalled of Glendy that 'he denied any other agency in the Rebellion, than was implied in frankly expressing his opinion, and in showing kindness to those who were directly engaged in it'.[121] Robert Acheson was reputedly the leader of a rebel camp on Belair Hill, but three witnesses, including a militia officer, later swore that he had been attempting to persuade the insurgents to give up their arms and surrender to the authorities.[122] William Sinclair of Newtownards was defended by a lieutenant in the local Yeomanry who asserted that he had been forced to become a member of the rebel committee which had taken possession of the town; Sinclair himself insisted that he had prayed twice every Sunday for the king and the government.[123] Another of the 1798 prisoners, James Worrall, found an influential friend in Dr Haliday, who believed that his views were confined to emancipation and reform, and that he had been persecuted by a few individuals merely for his independent stance.[124]

The evidence implicating Presbyterian clergymen in the '98 rebellion is frustratingly inconclusive. The information compiled from government papers, informers' reports, and popular anecdotes cannot be taken as a reliable guide to the events of that confused year. Although we will never know how many ministers were prepared to take up arms against the British and Irish governments, it seems likely that most of the suspects were sympathetic to the goals, if not the means, of the United Irishmen. The same can be said of those radicals who had been active during the first phase of the United Irish movement, like John Wright of Donegore, James

---

[119] Information of Magin, 9 Mar. 1798, PRONI, Cleland Papers, D714/2/16.

[120] Transcription of a letter from Barber to Castlereagh, PRONI, Morrow notebooks, D3696/A/3/1, p. 47.

[121] See the letter from the Revd Thomas Balch in W. B. Sprague, *Annals of the American Pulpit*, 7 vols. (New York, 1857–61), iv. 233.

[122] Depositions of Patrick McHenry, Mary Donaldson, and Andrew Stewart, 12 July 1798; Captain George Stewart to Edmund McNaghten, 18 June 1798, PRONI, McCance Collection, D272/22, 32.

[123] Sinclair to the Misses Fleming, 30 Oct. 1798, PRONI, Bruce Papers, T3041/1/E56; Hugh Gillespie to Downshire, 11 July 1798, PRONI, Downshire Papers, D607/F/313.

[124] Haliday to Castlereagh, 26 Aug. 1798, NAI, Rebellion Papers, 620/4/29/29.

McKinney of Dervock, and James Bryson of Belfast.[125] As in the 1780s, the Church provided the reform movement with ideological guidance: the collection of names listed in the appendix below can therefore be seen as a testimony to the Dissenting contribution to Irish radicalism.

[125] For Wright see McSkimmin, *Annals*, 19, note; for McKinney see Samuel Brown Wylie, *Memoir of Alexander McCleod, D.D.* (New York, 1855), 21; for Bryson see John Anderson, *History of the Belfast Library and Society for Promoting Knowledge, Commonly Known as the Linenhall Library* (Belfast, 1888), 91.

9
CONCLUSION: PRESBYTERIAN RADICALISM IN IRISH HISTORY

AT the beginning of this century, Presbyterian Ulster, which just over a hundred years before had supplied the backbone of the republican movement, had already emerged as the proud bastion of Irish loyalism: pro-British, vehemently anti-Catholic, and increasingly conservative in politics. The aim of this conclusion is to describe what happened to Presbyterian radicalism, both in the immediate aftermath of the rebellion and in the longer term. Some of the explanations for its demise—the rise of evangelicalism, the industrial and commercial expansion associated with the Union, and the increase of the *regium donum*, are well enough understood, and rather than attempt a comprehensive survey I have concentrated on those themes which seem most relevant to this book. At the outset, however, the point to emphasize is that the efflorescence of Ulster radicalism belongs to the interval between the shipwreck of the Catholic aristocracy at the end of the seventeenth century and the emergence of Catholic democracy at the beginning of the nineteenth. The absence of the Catholic threat, and the consequent space opened up for opposition ideologies among Protestants, gave to late eighteenth-century politics a fluidity which has never been recovered.

From rebellion to repeal

In explaining the silencing of Ulster's radical voice, the obvious starting point is the devastating impact of the rebellion itself. In the atmosphere of terror and confusion which followed, active loyalists such as William Bruce and Robert Black were able to seize the initiative in the Presbytery of Antrim and the Synod of Ulster. In 1798 the Synod took the unprecedented step of contributing £500 to the war effort, and in the first decade of the next century pastoral addresses were read annually from the pulpit, exhorting congregations to remain firm in their loyalty to the monarchy and their attachment to the constitution.[1] The upper levels of the United Irish conspiracy, already weakened by legal and extra-legal methods in 1796–8, were now broken by execution, imprisonment, and enforced or voluntary exile. Of those clergymen and probationers involved in radical activities, three had been executed;[2] eighteen or more were incarcerated for various lengths of time;[3] at least twenty had fled or been transported to the United States;[4] and one was serving in the Irish Legion

---

[1] *RGSU*, iii. 208–12.   [2] Robert Gowdie, James Porter, and Archibald Warwick.

[3] Robert Acheson, Thomas Alexander, Samuel Barber, William Steel Dickson, Francis Dill, Alexander Henry, Henry Henry, Adam Hill, Sinclair Kelburn, Benjamin Mitchell, Robert Montgomery, Boyle Moody, Joseph Orr, Robert Scott, John Smyth, William Stavely, William Warnock, and James Worrall.

[4] William Adair, John Arnold, Thomas Ledlie Birch, John Black, James Connell, Francis Dill, William Gibson, John Glendy, James Harper, James Hull, John McNish, John Miles, James Simpson, William Sinclair, Thomas Smith, Robert Steel, James Townsend, Charles Wallace, David Bailie Warden, and Samuel Brown Wylie.

of the French army.[5] Others, no doubt, were disillusioned or demoralized, and had good reasons to keep their heads down. Britain was still at war, after all, and the continuing counter-insurgency activities of the Yeomanry, combined with paramilitary displays of Orange strength, effectively deterred the remnants of the republican movement.

During Emmet's insurrection of 1803, the feeble sequel to the '98, the north remained conspicuously quiet. The merchants and manufacturers of Belfast seem to have heeded the Revd William Bruce's appeal to take up arms against 'those infatuated people, who would subvert that beautiful order of society . . . and betray their country to a ferocious, disorderly and unprincipled enemy'.[6] Two corps of Yeomen were quickly raised, providing an opportunity for erstwhile radicals to demonstrate their respectability: the three lieutenants of the Belfast Volunteer Infantry were William Sinclair, Robert Getty, and Gilbert McIlveen, all former United Irishmen.[7] Lord Hardwicke, the first Lord Lieutenant after the Union, received assurances from his northern correspondents that the men of property were all well affected.[8] When James Hope and Thomas Russell toured the old republican enclaves in Antrim and Down, they found their former comrades unwilling to rise until a French landing had taken place; the strongest response came from 'the lowest orders of the Catholicks', inflamed by local Orange harassment.[9] A transformation of political attitudes was also evident in the district around Derry, where Brigadier-General Hart found the Presbyterians preparing to arm in defence of the government and 'endeavouring to outdo each other in their expressions at least of a determined Loyalty'.[10] As the Orange Order expanded, it was said that some of its most violent partisans were former United men, anxious to atone for their revolutionary enthusiasm by an excess of anti-Catholic zeal.[11]

On the causes of this spectacular conversion all were agreed. As Castlereagh's secretary pointed out, republicanism in the north had already been 'checked and usurped by the cruelties of R.C.s in the late Rebellion and by the despotism of Bonaparte'.[12] Richard Musgrave recorded that in Armagh, Tyrone, Fermanagh, and Donegal, Presbyterians had joined the Orange Order following news of the massacres at Vinegar Hill and Scullabogue. In Fanet, County Donegal, it was reported that the late rapprochement between Dissenters and Catholics had been replaced by mutual suspicion, 'the former dreading the fate of the Protestants in Leinster,

---

[5] Arthur McMahon.

[6] Revd William Bruce, *The Christian Soldier. A Sermon, Preached before the Belfast Merchants' Infantry, September 25, 1803* (Belfast, 1803), 21.

[7] [Henry Joy (ed.)], *Historical Collections Relative to the Town of Belfast* (Belfast, 1817), p. xv n.

[8] Michael MacDonagh (ed.), *The Viceroy's Post-Bag* (London, 1904), 263, 265.

[9] Marianne Elliot, *Partners in Revolution: The United Irishmen and France* (New Haven, 1982), 311–12, 315–16; MacDonagh, *Viceroy's Post-Bag*, 416–18.

[10] George Vaughan Hart to Sir Edward Littlehales, 29 Aug. 1803, NAI, SOC 1025/34.

[11] See the testimony of the Quaker James Christie before the Select Committee on Orangeism, 1835, quoted in D. W. Miller (ed.), *Peep O'Day Boys and Defenders: Selected Documents on the County Armagh Disturbances 1784–96* (Belfast, 1990), 116; E. W. McFarland, *Ireland and Scotland in the Age of Revolution: Planting the Green Bough* (Edinburgh, 1994), 209.

[12] Alexander Knox to Castlereagh, 5 July 1803, PRONI, Castlereagh Papers, D3030/1793/A.

and the latter fearing that the Presbyterians would be revenged of them for the massacre of their brethren'.[13] Musgrave, to be sure, was no impartial observer: his monumental *Memoirs of the Different Rebellions in Ireland* (1801) was typical of the loyalist propaganda which peddled the reductive interpretation of 1798 as a rerun of 1641.[14] The Wexford rising had more complex political and social roots, as recent research has demonstrated, but there can be no doubt that in the north it was viewed primarily as fresh evidence of the incorrigible barbarity of the Catholic population.[15]

This political reaction was compounded by disenchantment with France, as Bonaparte claimed his imperial throne and reached an accommodation with Rome. After the peace preliminaries of 1801 had been signed, there was bitter talk of emigration among the Belfast republicans.[16] Two years later, impressed by the loyalist fervour he found on the north-eastern circuit, Baron St George Daly reported that the Presbyterians could be relied upon during the current crisis because they believed that Emmet's insurrection was an exclusively papist affair, and because they were convinced that if Bonaparte succeeded, 'there would be no *republick*, but on the contrary, despotism and pillage'.[17] In 1805, when Thomas Emmet wrote to his old Belfast associate Robert Simms describing his reasons for moving from Paris to New York, he warned that a French expeditionary force to Ireland would establish a satellite government propped up by a Catholic establishment.[18] The French emperor, once idolized by United Irishmen as the messiah who would inaugurate the reign of liberty, was now execrated as the Caesar who had destroyed it.[19]

Of course, the United Irish system, painstakingly built up in the mid-1790s, did not simply vanish. For several years after Emmet's rebellion Dublin Castle regularly received reports concerning the existence of secret societies and the expectations of French aid which persisted in some quarters.[20] We know that one of these societies, based in Belfast, was named Unitos Fratres, and known among the lower classes as the Ezekielites, but there is little evidence concerning its personnel or activities.[21] In the countryside, meanwhile, undercurrents of disaffection lingered. The following threatening notice, for example, was received by Lord Massareene in 1802:

Myly and Mylys calf present their compliments to the Earle of Masreen [and] expects the plasur of his company for Diner the 2nd of November on Donagor Hill as they know he is so fond of fish will have a nise dish of well drest pikes.[22]

[13] Richard Musgrave, *Memoirs of the Different Rebellions in Ireland* (Dublin, 1801), 74, 97, 181, 189, 558.
[14] Kevin Whelan, ' "'98 After '98": The Politics of Memory', in id., *The Tree of Liberty: Radicalism, Catholicism and the Construction of Irish Identity 1760–1830* (Cork, 1996), 135–8.
[15] Dáire Keogh and Nicholas Furlong (eds.), *The Mighty Wave: The 1798 Rebellion in Wexford* (Blackrock, Co. Dublin, 1996).
[16] McG [James McGuikan] to unknown, 14 Oct. 1801, NAI, Rebellion Papers, 620/10/118/17.
[17] Baron St George Daly to Baron Redesdale, [before 22 Oct. 1803], PRONI, Redesdale Papers, T3030/9/25.
[18] Emmet to Simms, 1 June 1805, PRONI, Emigrant Letters to Robert Simms, T1815/4.
[19] John Gamble, *A View of Society and Manners in the North of Ireland in the Summer and Autumn of 1812* (London, 1813), 143.   [20] Elliott, *Partners in Revolution*, 343.
[21] A. T. Q. Stewart, 'The Transformation of Presbyterian Radicalism in the North of Ireland, 1792–1825', MA thesis (QUB, 1956), 69.   [22] MacDonagh, *Viceroy's Post-Bag*, 262.

'Moily', apparently a mythical cow used to represent the republican movement, was part of the rebel folk culture of the 1790s: when a loyalist was murdered it was said that '*Moily* had got him'.[23]

In rural areas, then, it seems that the United Irish network relapsed into the conventional forms of popular protest from which it had emerged. Freemasonry, which had offered an organizational medium for United activity in mid and east Ulster, seems to have acted as a conduit for continuing radical sentiment in much the same way. Dr William Richardson of Moy noted that the 'tail of the United Irish' had rallied in Masonic lodges and continued to clash with the Orangemen at fairs.[24] After the Union they continued to thrive, their insignia, rituals, and annual St John's Day processions offering an alternative to the popular confessionalism of both the Orange Order and the Ribbonmen.[25]

What about the more public traditions of constitutional reformism which stretched back to the late 1770s? Opposition politics had been briefly rekindled in the County Down by-election of 1805, when the freeholders who had backed the Stewarts in 1783 and 1790 joined forces with the Marchioness of Downshire to deprive Castlereagh of his seat in the imperial Parliament. This was an unusual opportunity, however, created by the ongoing electoral feud between the Hill and Stewart families, and by Castlereagh's severe unpopularity in Down, where he was regarded as a traitor to his country, his religion, and the independent interest.[26] In Belfast itself, the speculative politics for which the town was famous had given way to a flowering of cultural activity. 'The north seems dead and rotting', lamented William Drennan when he returned to his native town in 1807, 'like its flax when sleeping in holes and ditches owing I think in a great measure to the literary talents of Belfast displayed in their vapid newspapers, etc'.[27] Since 1801 the Belfast Literary Society had provided a focal point for citizens with literary and scientific interests; but while its members produced papers covering botany, topography, natural history, antiquities, economics, classics, metaphysics, and medicine, political subjects were, by general agreement, avoided.[28] The dominant figure in the intellectual life of the town was now Drennan's estranged friend William Bruce, minister of the First Congregation, principal of the Belfast Academy, and the moving spirit behind the Literary Society.

But Presbyterian radicalism was soon to rediscover its most articulate voice. William Drennan had been the only Dissenter to register a public protest against the liquidation of the Dublin Parliament, in three powerful pamphlets which fused the familiar appeals to the ancient constitution with a full-blown romantic nationalism.[29] In

---

[23] Samuel McSkimmin, 'Memoranda Referring to the Co. Antrim Volunteers 1778–1790', PRONI, T2822, p. 1.   [24] MacDonagh, *Viceroy's Post-Bag*, 265.

[25] J. H. Lepper and Philip Crossle, *History of the Grand Lodge of Free and Accepted Masons of Ireland* (Dublin, 1925), i. 297.

[26] Peter Jupp, 'County Down Elections 1783–1831', *IHS* 18/70 (1972), 184–5.

[27] Drennan to Martha McTier, 17 Apr. 1807, PRONI, T765/1320.

[28] George Smith *et al.*, *Belfast Literary Society 1801–1901: Historical Sketch* (Belfast, 1902), 4.

[29] William Drennan, *A Letter to the Right Honourable William Pitt* (Dublin, 1799); *A Second Letter to the Right Honourable William Pitt* (Dublin, 1799); *A Protest against an Union* (Dublin, 1800).

1806 he had emerged from political retirement once more with his *Letter to Charles James Fox*, invoking the old tradition of Ulster radicalism, rooted in the right of private judgement, nurtured through sympathy for the Americans, contested elections, and volunteering, and driven into rebellion by oppression in the 1790s. As he admitted, however, his zeal had cooled with the political climate, and his last pamphlet was intended as 'a return to the genuine Whiggish principles as the safeguard of the people's rights and the citadel of the constitution'.[30] The same tone characterized his literary journal, the *Belfast Monthly Magazine*, launched in 1808, which combined support for Catholic emancipation and attacks on Orangeism with a close interest in parliamentary reform and anti-war campaigns across the water. Similarly, the radical meetings organized by Drennan and Robert Tennent often centred on metropolitan personalities and issues such as Colonel Wardle, Francis Burdett, and the Queen Caroline affair.[31] In post-Union Belfast, opposition was emphatically loyal opposition, and reform was pursued within the framework of the British monarchy.

The most celebrated episode in the history of Presbyterian radicalism after the rebellion is the controversy surrounding Belfast Academical Institution which erupted in 1816.[32] Despite frequent discussion of the need for a northern university in the later eighteenth century, Presbyterian approaches to government had secured only vague promises, and their independent academies, intended to rival the divinity faculties of the Scottish universities, never became anything more than grammar schools. By the turn of the century there were three forces pushing for the establishment of a college in Belfast: the business community, which believed that a thriving commercial centre must have strong educational institutions; the Synod of Ulster, which aimed to secure training for its ministers without the inconvenience of travel to Scotland; and those radicals like Drennan who had long regarded a national education system as part of the reform package. These three strands came together in the foundation of the Belfast Academical Institution, which opened a grammar school in 1814 and, following the announcement of an annually renewable grant from Parliament, admitted the first students to its collegiate department the year after.

Not unnaturally, the Irish administration was alarmed by the well-known political opinions of the Institution's proprietors. Although the project had secured the support of several local landlords and magistrates, the moving spirits in the venture were the old United Irish leaders. Among the founders were William Tennent, Robert Callwell, and William Simms, all ex-proprietors of the *Northern Star*, Robert Simms and William Drennan, also United Irishmen, and the Revd Henry Henry, who had been imprisoned in 1798. At the launch of the Institution Drennan had delivered a speech defining the progressive ethos of the new college. Its aims were to offer a useful and liberal education to the young of the province

---

[30] Drennan to McTier, 18 Feb. 1806, *Drennan Letters*, 353–4.

[31] For this neglected period, see R. B. McDowell, *Public Opinion and Government Policy in Ireland, 1801–46* (London, 1952), ch. 2; Stewart, 'Transformation of Presbyterian Radicalism', ch. 4.

[32] The best accounts are Peter Brooke, *Ulster Presbyterianism: The Historical Perspective, 1610–1970* (Dublin, 1987), ch. 7; J. R. Fisher and J. H. Robb, *Royal Belfast Academical Institution: Centenary Volume 1810–1910* (Belfast, 1913).

without distinction of sect or profession, to diffuse knowledge, particularly among
the middling orders, to stimulate the study of the Irish language, and to inculcate
the love of country.[33] Letters exchanged between Robert Peel, then Irish chief secretary, and Castlereagh reveal the government's preoccupation with the influence
of 'democrats' such as Drennan among the managers.[34] The connection between
the Synod of Ulster and the seminary—the Synod had no formal say in the management of the Institution's affairs, but appointed a divinity professor to look after
its students—was condemned by those who recalled the conspicuous role of Presbyterian divines in the 1798 rebellion and feared that 'the republican spirit of the
Presbyterians will pervade the system of education'.[35]

Intriguingly, much government criticism was directed at the constitution of the
college. The affairs of the Institution were to be conducted by a board of twenty
managers (including a president and four vice-presidents) and a board of eight visitors, both to be elected by the proprietors. The franchise was originally granted
to every subscriber of five guineas to the funds, but this qualification was later raised
to twenty guineas to placate the government. In true classical republican fashion,
it was stipulated that a quarter of the board members should vacate their seats annually, though they would become eligible for re-election after one year. The obvious political parallels were not lost on observers, friendly or hostile. When the plan
was first drawn up in 1807, Robert Black remarked contemptuously to Bruce that
it 'put me in mind of the French Constitution with which we were so frequently
amused'.[36] James Knowles, who denounced the Institution following his dismissal
as head English teacher by the board of managers, referred sarcastically to the dic-
tatorial power assumed by Drennan and his colleagues over 'this new Republic, or
rather this new Democracy of Literature'.[37] On the other hand, Drennan, in his
inaugural address, had explained that in this 'little commonweal' the masters constituted the executive and the boards the legislature, both under control of proprietors at large.[38] In this curious way, the old battles of the 1790s were being
fought out in microcosm.

A major confrontation between the administration, on the one hand, and the boards
and the Synod, on the other, became unavoidable after the attendance of several
teachers and members of the governing body at a radical dinner held on the eve of
St Patrick's Day, 1816. At this meeting Dr Robert Tennent, the chairman, seems
to have spoken of passing on the principles of 1782 and 1792 to a new generation,
toasts were drunk in celebration of the American and French Revolutions, and
calls were made for 'A Radical Reform in the Representation of the People in

---

[33] 'Address of William Drennan M. D. at the Opening of the Belfast Academical Institution, 1st
February 1814', in Fisher and Robb, *Belfast Academical Institution*, 204–7.
[34] Robert Peel to Viscount Castlereagh, 2 Dec. 1816, BL, Peel Papers, Add. MS 40181, fos. 241–9;
Castlereagh to Peel, 10 Dec. 1816, ibid., fo. 249.
[35] Fisher and Robb, *Belfast Academical Institution*, 40.
[36] Black to Bruce, Nov. 1807, PRONI, Bruce Papers, T3041/1/E52.
[37] James Knowles, *An Appeal to the Dignified Visitors and the Noblemen and Gentlemen, Proprietors of
the Belfast Acadical Institution* (Belfast, 1817), 10.
[38] Fisher and Robb, *Belfast Academical Institution*, 205–6.

Parliament'.[39] This unguarded behaviour supplied Castlereagh with the pretext to press for alterations to the constitution of the academy which would enable the government to exercise influence over appointments. His real concern, however, was the link with the Synod of Ulster; this was the crux of what he saw as 'a deep laid scheme to bring the Presbyterian Synod within the ranks of democracy' by giving 'Dr Drennan and his associates . . . the power of granting certificates of qualification for the ministry in that Church'.[40]

Despite the considerable pressure exerted by Castlereagh, the proprietors rejected government demands for a say in the Institution's affairs, and the annual grant of £1,500 was duly withdrawn. The Synod too rallied against the threat of state interference, pressing on with the appointment of a divinity professor. If this post-script to Belfast radicalism underlined the continuing independence of the Presbyterian community, however, it also revealed the vulnerability of the radicals after the incorporation of the two kingdoms. When Sir George Hill made a speech in the Commons warning that the principles of Paine and Priestley were being openly taught in Belfast, the boards quickly passed a resolution repudiating any sentiments 'inimical to the Government or the principles of the British Constitution'. The visitors and managers who had attended the St Patrick's Day dinner were persuaded to resign, while the masters undertook not to repeat such an indiscretion.[41] The radicals were pushed onto the defensive, with Drennan denying that politics played any part in the curriculum.[42] One subscriber to the college published a pamphlet condemning the principles of Paine, Voltaire, and Rousseau, paying the usual homage to the British constitution, and distancing the present generation from those ignorant men who had been led away by 'chimerical, inflammable nonsense' to Antrim and Ballyhinch twenty years before.[43] Significantly, the most militant noises came not from the Belfast Presbyterians, but from Jack Lawless, a Catholic journalist who would later lead the O'Connellite invasion of the north in 1828. Denunciations of this 'snake from the south' anticipated the imagery of beleaguered loyalism which would feature so prominently in later unionist rhetoric.[44]

The resistance of the Synod and the Institution to Castlereagh pointed to the future direction of opposition politics in the northern province. When their interests were threatened, Presbyterians time and time again revealed the spirit of defiance and democracy which had characterized their eighteenth-century forebears. At the same time, however, they would be haunted by the experience of revolution and reaction which had brought them so close to destruction in the 1790s. The limits of their liberalism were most clearly delineated in two key areas of conflict: the Catholic question, and the British connection.

---

[39] Ibid. 63; Peter Brooke, 'Controversies in Ulster Presbyterianism, 1790–1836', Ph.D. thesis (Cambridge, 1980), 121–2.

[40] Castlereagh to Peel, 9 Nov. 1816, BL, Add. MS 40181, fos. 225–6.

[41] Fisher and Robb, *Belfast Academical Institution*, 64–5.

[42] William Drennan, *A Retort Courteous to the Remarks of 'Presbyter' relative to the Belfast Academical Institution, Published in the Belfast News-Letter, July 26, 1816* (Belfast, 1816), 20.

[43] *Strictures on the Letter of John Lawless, Esq. to the Proprietors of the Belfast Academical Institution. By Warfield, a Subscriber to the Belfast Academical Institution* (Belfast, 1816), 8, 10.   [44] Ibid. 7, 12.

After 1813, when emancipationists secured their first majority in the House of Commons, support for the Catholic cause in Belfast was directed by the Friends of Civil and Religious Liberty, with William Drennan and Robert Tennent at their head. As the Catholics demonstrated their capacity to act as an independent political force, however, a defensive note crept into the editorials of Drennan's *Belfast Monthly Magazine*. The appearance of the term 'Catholic Ireland' in O'Connellite propaganda was quickly condemned as exclusive and sectarian, and the Catholics were reminded of their debt to the Protestant reformers who had first led them out of 'mental bondage'.[45] The old preoccupation with papal authority and the priesthood resurfaced when the Catholics split over the 'veto'—the question of state influence over the nomination of bishops. In a series of editorials Drennan called on the Catholics to resist the corrupting influence of the Crown, but urged them to declare their independence from Rome too, thus returning to the elective constitution of the ancient church.[46] In 1819, the year before his death, Drennan wrote to Daniel O'Connell, encouraging him in his latest efforts to secure a relief act, and endorsing his recent compromise over the veto issue:

Well, you must balance the *much* you may receive against the *comparatively* little you lose. The Catholic *regium donum* will follow the Presbyterian *regium donum*, but the love of laymen for liberty will overcome and quench the ecclesiastical proneness to prostration.[47]

As we enter the age of O'Connell, an age characterized by the reinvigoration of confessional loyalties, it is hard not to feel that the old United Irishman, with his anticlerical brand of radicalism, had become little more than a curious anachronism.

Equally revealing to the historian was Drennan's happiness to see reform pursued within the parliamentary monarchy of the United Kingdom. Nostalgia for Grattan's parliament was a recurring feature of the *Belfast Monthly Magazine*, but its editorials came to accept the Act of Union as a new social contract, which although brought about by corrupt and dishonourable means, might yet be legitimized by putting Ireland on an equal footing with England:

Then indeed the Irish feeling that still burns under the ashes of national independence may be gradually extinguished. Then the fondest wish of our hearts may be obliterated, and we may at least say to each of our *children*—Be Britons with all your souls—and forget that your Father called himself an Irishman.[48]

He accused the Dublin repealers of selfish motives: where were they when Francis Burdett was attacking the distress which Ireland shared with the rest of the empire? Irishmen should bury old grudges, he urged, and join their brethren in Britain in the fight for a representative Parliament.[49]

From the 1820s, when the old republicanism of Drennan and his comrades gave way to the cautious, constitutional reformism of the *Northern Whig*, the integrity of the United Kingdom would remain an article of faith with Ulster Presbyterians.

---

[45] *Belfast Monthly Magazine*, 5 (1810), 394; 6 (1811), 233.   [46] Ibid. 4 (1810), 142, 225, 464.
[47] Quoted in Oliver MacDonagh, *O'Connell: The Life of Daniel O'Connell 1775–1847* (London, 1991), 166.
[48] *Belfast Monthly Magazine*, 7 (1811), 489.   [49] Ibid. 5 (1810), 223–4.

The trauma of the 1790s, explained Henry Joy, had taught them the indelible lesson that 'adherence to the *British connexion* (so long as Papists form the majority of the inhabitants of this island) is absolutely necessary to their existence'.[50] Far from wishing to break the Union, the new Liberalism called for its full realization, hence the launch of the Ulster Constitutional Association in 1840 to obtain 'an equalization of all rights, franchises and benefits with Britain, and the closest possible assimilation of the laws and institutions of both countries'.[51] As late as the 1840s, the old 1798 veteran James Hope was still to be found chairing Repeal meetings, despite reservations about the nature of O'Connellism. But the vast majority of Presbyterians, of all political and theological parties, united in support of the constitutional connection.[52] Mary Ann McCracken, the sister of Hope's old comrade-in-arms, noted that many of those who had violently disapproved of the Act of Union were now just as opposed to its abolition. She herself viewed the matter 'coolly':

it would be necessary to lay aside the natural feelings of National pride and the love of independence which is not easily done, in order to consider whether the people of this country might not have their liberty and happiness better secured by being an integral part of a great & powerful nation provided that ample justice towards Ireland was strictly observed & that Ireland would have a better chance of justice, when the liberals of both countries were united in our parliament, than when divided.[53]

The simplest explanation for the evaporation of Belfast radicalism is that the Belfast of the 1790s no longer existed. 'We were a small insignificant town at the end of the last century, deeply disaffected and hostile to the British Empire,' recalled the Belfast Chamber of Commerce in 1893. 'Since the Union, and under equal laws', they explained, 'we have been welded to the Empire and our progress has been second to none.'[54] The commercial port of the 1790s had indeed been transformed into a great industrial centre, based on textiles and later shipbuilding and heavy engineering. From a mere 20,000 souls in 1800, the population had leapt to over 75,000 in 1841, and by the end of the century reached almost 350,000.[55] The economic miracle of the north-east was taken as confirmation that Protestantism and prosperity were closely linked, a providential sign that God had blessed the junction of Great Britain and Ireland. In his celebrated challenge to O'Connell, the Revd Henry Cooke had answered the case for repeal by pointing to 'the masted grove within our harbour —our mighty warehouses teeming with the wealth of every climate—our giant manufactures lifting themselves on every side', all attributable to the Act of Union. 'Look at Belfast', he concluded in a famous peroration, 'and be a repealer, if you can.'[56] Even the *Northern Whig*, no friend to Cooke's belligerent Protestantism, welcomed his intervention.

---

[50] Joy (ed.), *Historical Collections*, p. xiii n.   [51] Brooke, *Ulster Presbyterianism*, 185.

[52] R. F. G. Holmes, *Henry Cooke* (Belfast, 1981), 145–6.

[53] Mary Ann McCracken to R. R. Madden, 15 Oct. 1844, PRONI, McCracken Papers, T1210/46.

[54] Quoted in Philip Ollerenshaw, 'Businessmen in Northern Ireland and the Imperial Connection, 1886–1939', in Keith Jeffrey (ed.), *'An Irish Empire'? Aspects of Ireland and the British Empire* (Manchester, 1996), 171.

[55] Leslie Clarkson, 'The City and the Country', in J. C. Beckett *et al.*, *Belfast: The Making of the City* (Belfast, 1983), 153.   [56] Holmes, *Henry Cooke*, 148.

The divergence of the regional economy thus bolstered the northern sense of difference. But industrialization also had other, more disruptive consequences *within* the province. Ulster radicalism had always been strongest in the cradle of Scottish settlement and weakest in more mixed ethnic areas like Armagh. As Belfast expanded, however, its denominational balance was upset by waves of migration from the countryside. Although Presbyterians still dominated the city elite, their share of the total population had fallen to 35 per cent by 1861. From the Lagan valley and from the linen triangle of mid-Ulster lower-class Anglicans poured in, bringing with them the icons and structures of Orangeism, while the Catholic population, focused on the Pound area in the west, swelled to form a third of the inhabitants by the middle of the century. Rural Ulster, with its ritualized patterns of sectarian violence, was transposed into the claustrophobic backstreets of the industrializing city. As early as 1813 an Orange procession in the town precipitated a riot resulting in two deaths; major disturbances would follow in 1857, 1864, 1872, and 1886, as the territorial boundaries between Protestant and Catholic became more sharply defined. Nineteenth-century Belfast was becoming a microcosm of Ulster's three-way confessional divide, much as Armagh had been in the century before.[57]

The politics of evangelicalism

The reorientation of Presbyterian politics in the first half of the nineteenth century was accompanied and facilitated by a sea change in religious attitudes. Traditionally, the triumph of conservative unionism has been linked to the progress of a new evangelical spirit and to the bitterly fought Arian controversy of the 1820s, when the orthodox hero Henry Cooke drove the dwindling band of non-subscribers out of the Synod. In fact, Cooke's ascendancy has been much exaggerated: his friendship with aristocratic families like the Downshires and Rodens and his support for Tory ministries repeatedly threatened to undermine the authority and influence which his services to the cause of godliness had brought him. As recent historiography has shown, a robust Liberal strand survived within Presbyterianism until the Home Rule crisis of 1886, rooted in hostility to landlordism and a historical sense of grievance kept alive by the institutional vestiges of Anglican superiority.[58] While these qualifications should warn us against any simple correlation between religion and politics, it is nevertheless undeniable that Cooke fused together in his own person a particular combination of conversionist theology, social conservatism, and anti-Catholicism which would eventually come to dominate popular politics in the north of Ireland.

At the end of the eighteenth century the crucial point of contact between the Synod and the State was the *regium donum*, which offered financial aid and a degree of social respectability to the clergy. Always a controversial matter, the potential

---

[57] S. E. Baker, 'Orange and Green: Belfast, 1832–1912', in H. J. Dyos and M. Wolff (eds.), *The Victorian City: Images and Realities*, 2 vols. (London, 1973), ii. 789–814.

[58] For general accounts of nineteenth-century Presbyterianism see Brooke, *Ulster Presbyterianism*, chs. 7–9; David Hempton and Myrtle Hill, *Evangelical Protestantism in Ulster Society 1740–1890* (London, 1992); R. F. G. Holmes, *Our Irish Presbyterian Heritage* ([Belfast], 1985), ch. 4.

use of this annual subsidy as a channel of government influence had soured relations between the Synod and the Castle in the 1780s, when William Campbell had obtained an extra thousand pounds per annum. In 1792 the lobbying activities of his successor, the Revd Robert Black of Derry, proved much more successful, and following an address moved in the House of Commons by James Stewart and supported by Henry Grattan, the royal bounty was increased by £5,000.[59] As on the previous occasion, negotiations with the government took place against the background of radical agitation in the north. When Black arrived in Dublin it was rumoured that he had come 'to sell the Presbyterian clergy to government for a pension on condition of their repudiating the Catholics', and the author of an anonymous letter had threatened to tar and feather him.[60] While these two episodes amply testify to the traditional Presbyterian suspicion of the civil authorities, they pale into insignificance beside the storm which blew up in 1800, when the matter was raised once again.

In the aftermath of the '98 rebellion, representatives of the government and the Synod entered into discussions, the one aiming to restore its authority in the country, the other eager to shake off any imputation of disloyalty. The scheme originated with Castlereagh, who wanted to reward 'those who have committed themselves in support of the State against a democratic party in the Synod, several of whom, if not engaged in the Rebellion, were deeply infected with its principles'. It was only 'a considerable internal fermentation' in the body, perhaps even a schism, that would change its temper. The chief secretary believed that it was necessary to introduce a hierarchy into the republican constitution of the Presbyterian Church, and the key to this restructuring was the *regium donum*, for 'the distribution and government of the fund is a natural engine of authority'. It was therefore decided that the grant should be paid directly to the individual pastors, rather than through the Synod as previously, and should be conditional on statements of each recipient's character.[61] Most controversially, the ministers were grouped into three classes according to the size and wealth of their congregations. The first, numbering about fifteen ministers, was to receive £200 per annum each; the second, comprising about seventy, was to be given £70; and a third group of around a hundred ministers would have to settle for £60. These sums were to be paid by an agent, nominated by the Synod and confirmed by the government. A total addition of £8,500 was required.[62] This ambitious plan represented a bold attempt to devise a comprehensive ecclesiastical arrangement which would form an essential part of the Union settlement.

[59] Robert Black, *Substance of Two Speeches, Delivered in the General Synod of Ulster at its Annual Meeting in 1812* (Dublin, 1812), 73. This amount had to be shared by the Synod with the Seceders, the Southern Association, and the minister of the French Church in Dublin. The Synod's share amounted to £3,729. 16s. 10d., a rise from £2,600 to £6,329. 16s. 10d.

[60] Drennan to Samuel McTier, Feb. 1792, *Drennan Letters*, 78–9; Drennan to McTier, 31 Jan. [1793], PRONI, Drennan Papers, T765/381.

[61] Castlereagh to Addington, 21 July 1802, *Memoirs and Correspondence of Viscount Castlereagh*, ed. Charles Vane, 12 vols. (London, 1848–54), iv. 224–6.

[62] 'Plan for strengthening the connection between the Government and the Presbyterian Synod of Ulster', 5 Feb. 1799, ibid. iii. 172–4. There was also talk of a university for Ulster, with places for Presbyterians guaranteed among the students, trustees, and professors.

The full details of the negotiations which took place between 1800 and 1803 can be pieced together from Castlereagh's papers, the records of the Synod, and other sources. They reveal Castlereagh's close relationship with Robert Black and William Bruce, both of whom were firm supporters of the Union. In the Presbyterian book of apostasy, Black comes a close second to Castlereagh himself. A celebrated orator, he had spoken at the Dungannon convention of 1782, and his eloquence had earned him a call to the First Derry congregation. By the reform convention of 1793 his early radicalism had mellowed, however, and he had publicly denounced those 'few seditious spirits' who planned 'to overturn the constitution'.[63] But the vast majority of Dissenting clergymen opposed the classification scheme on the grounds that the smaller congregations were often spread over a large tract of country, necessitating much work, while ministers in large towns had practical advantages as well as additional expenses. Above all, Castlereagh's plan was perceived as a deliberate assault on the 'Presbyterian principle which recognizes no distinction among its ministers but such as are founded in knowledge and virtue'.[64]

When it became clear that the terms of the new *regium donum* were not negotiable, the Synod eventually acquiesced and accepted the government's conditions. But there is little evidence to suggest that the clergy were reduced to the 'subordinate ecclesiastical aristocracy' envisaged by the administration.[65] The angry debates of 1800–3 demonstrate the continuing potency of the Presbyterian ideal of church polity. Dissenting spokesmen, New Light and Old, united to defend the principle of parity among ministers, the right of congregations to elect their own pastors, the scriptural basis of Presbyterian government, and the sinfulness of erastianism. William Drennan, a member of the non-subscribing Presbytery of Antrim, pronounced that 'Bruce and Castlereagh, walking hand in hand, is a new alliance of Church and State', and called for his comrades to rally to 'the old *Presbyterian Principle*' of ecclesiastical independence.[66] The Revd John Sherrard of Tullylish reminded his comrades that 'Jesus Christ is supreme head, and sole law-giver in his church, and that no other authority whatever is to be acknowledged by his disciples'.[67] He was supported by Henry Henry of Connor, an Old Light minister and suspected rebel, who warned that Castlereagh's attempts to make the Synod a creature of the State must be resisted:

[W]hat are the great principles of our dissent? Are they not—*the rights of private judgement?*— *the liberty of conscience*, in opposition to all human authority, in matters of religion?—The acknowledgement of CHRIST *alone* as head of his Church?—And the sufficiency of the word of GOD as the rule of faith and practice?[68]

---

[63] *BNL*, 25 Jan. 1793.

[64] 'Memorial of Bankhead and Little, two of the commissioners of the Synod of Ulster', [*c.*Aug. 1800], PRONI, Castlereagh Papers, D3030/1426.

[65] Alexander Knox to Castlereagh, 15 July 1803, *Castlereagh Correspondence*, iv. 287.

[66] Drennan to Martha McTier, 12 Dec. 1800, PRONI, T765/889; [Drennan], 'A Letter from a Layman to a Layman', MS copy in PRONI, D531/6. See also Drennan to Martha McTier, 9 [Aug.] 1800, *Drennan Letters*, 300.

[67] John Sherrard, *A Few Observations on the Nature and Tendency of the Changes Lately Proposed to be Made in the Constitution of the Protestant Dissenting Church* (Belfast, 1803), 13.

[68] [Henry Henry], 'Presbyter', *An Illustrative of the Present Critical State of the Synod of Ulster in Three Letters* (n.p., 1802), 16.

It was a sign of things to come that, during his later political campaigns, Black seems to have sought out allies among the younger generation of evangelical ministers including the ambitious Henry Cooke.[69] Both Black and his colleague in the Presbytery of Antrim, William Bruce, were advanced liberals in theology, and their pro-government line failed to take root among the New Light party, which had historically identified itself with constitutional reform. In the 1820s, however, Cooke would pioneer a far more formidable and durable conservative coalition which hitched loyalism to the rising forces of evangelicalism and anti-Catholicism. The crucial turning point was the second subscription controversy of the 1820s which led to the withdrawal of the Arian party from the Synod and the adoption of unqualified subscription in 1835, thus paving the way for a reunion with the Seceders in 1840.

In the last quarter of the eighteenth century a spirit of compromise on the subscription issue had allowed the Synod of Ulster to contain the doctrinal differences which had earlier disturbed the peace. It was a situation in which even the young Cooke could maintain friendly personal and professional relations with advanced New Light men.[70] As late as 1824, when the Synod drafted a new code of discipline, a proposal for the reimposition of obligatory subscription was not even seconded.[71] By this date, however, the theological truce was being threatened by two opposing developments. The first was the public avowal by a number of prominent divines of an explicitly heterodox position. In *The Study of the Bible and the Doctrines of Christianity* (1824), the Revd William Bruce not only announced his adherence to the Arian scheme, but boasted that this viewpoint was making progress in both his own Presbytery of Antrim and the General Synod of Ulster. When a parliamentary commission examined Belfast Academical Institution the following year, two of the Synod's ministers, Henry Montgomery and William Porter, seemed to confirm Bruce's claim by acknowledging their rejection of the Trinitarian creed.[72]

The second disruptive factor was the growth of conversionist theology. As we have seen, evangelicalism was not part of the original Presbyterian package, which had been less concerned with the personal experience of faith than formal allegiance to the doctrinal standards and institutional forms of the Kirk.[73] In the opening decades of the new century, however, Ulster Presbyterians began to share in the missionary impulse which had begun to revitalize the British Churches in the wake of the French Revolution. A series of organizations—the Hibernian Bible Society, the Hibernian Sunday School Society, the London Hibernian Society, the Irish Evangelical Society, the Irish Society for Promoting the Education of the Native Irish through the Medium of their Own Language—were formed in the first two

---

[69] Holmes, *Cooke*, 18.   [70] Ibid.

[71] R. F. G. Holmes, 'Controversy and Schism in the Synod of Ulster in the 1820s', in J. L. M. Haire (ed.), *Challenge and Conflict: Essays in Irish Presbyterian History and Doctrine* (Antrim, 1981), 117–18.

[72] Ibid. 119.

[73] It is interesting in this respect to note the recurrence of outside influences in Cooke's career: he had links with Dublin evangelicals—the American-born Presbyterian Benjamin McDowell and the Swiss preacher Cesar Malan—as well as evangelical members of the Anglican ascendancy such as Mountcashel and Roden. See Holmes, *Henry Cooke*, 10–11, 43–4.

decades after legislative union. The Evangelical activists introduced new organizational forms and techniques including itinerant preaching, the distribution of Bibles and tracts, and voluntary societies and groups devoted to temperance and other forms of self-improvement; they also brought the Protestant Churches into direct competition with the Catholic clergy for the first time in over a hundred years. The massive conversionist enterprise of the so-called Second Reformation may have won few souls, but it did much to sour relations with a resurgent Catholicism.[74]

This proliferation of Bible and missionary societies played a significant part in rallying the forces of orthodoxy.[75] They created a new organizational basis for inter-denominational (i.e. inter-Protestant) endeavour, and brought with them new theological standards. Evangelical teaching centred on the experience of salvation, bringing soteriological and Christological questions to the fore. The doctrine of the Trinity could no longer be regarded as a speculative point of divinity. For Cooke, it supplied 'the only foundation of sacrifice and atonement; and sacrifice and atonement are the vital principles of a believer's hopes'.[76] 'A Saviour no better or only a little better than ourselves', he explained to the Synod in 1825, 'can never be a fit object for the faith, the life, the dependence of sinners.'[77]

As long as synodical disputes were presented in terms of ecclesiastical authority, the Arians occupied relatively favourable ground. As Cooke gradually levered the debate on to the doctrine of the Trinity itself, however, the large centre grouping in the Church was forced reluctantly to take sides. When a well-known Arian was appointed to the chair of Hebrew and Greek at the Academical Institution, Cooke launched a campaign to hound the 'infidels' out of the Church. At the Newry synod of 1822 a motion calling for an inquiry into the orthodoxy of professors was withdrawn in the face of opposition from all shades of opinion.[78] Outside the ranks of the clergy, however, Cooke's tireless campaigning was beginning to pay off, and his rising popularity among sections of the Presbyterian laity would boost his position at future meetings.[79] After a series of spectacular clashes in 1827, 1828, and 1829, and an outpouring of controversy in pamphlet and press, the Synod voted to affirm its Trinitarian faith and set up a committee to establish the orthodoxy of candidates for the ministry. In the end, the Arians jumped before they were pushed: seventeen ministers withdrew to form their own Remonstrant Synod in 1829.

While the growing conservatism of the Presbyterian community cannot be explained solely by this evangelical turn, a relationship between the two forces can certainly be demonstrated. A close correlation was already evident among the conspicuously loyal ministers of the Secession who, as we saw in Chapter 4, had begun to demonstrate a pietist revulsion against participation in secular affairs. The rebellion gave this process a massive boost. On 10 October 1798, sixteen Seceders, three ministers from the Synod of Ulster, and four from the Church of Ireland, joined together to found the Evangelical Society of Ulster. Encouraged by the missionary enterprises which had recently surfaced in Britain, they organized prayer meetings,

---

[74] Hempton and Hill, *Evangelical Protestantism*, chs. 3–5.
[75] *First Report of the Commissioners on Education in Ireland*, HC, 1825, xii, app. 261, p. 824.
[76] Quoted in Holmes, *Henry Cooke*, 193.   [77] Ibid. 38.   [78] Ibid. 31.   [79] Ibid. 32.

distributed Bibles and evangelical tracts, and arranged tours for the itinerant preachers of the London Missionary Society. It was quickly agreed that all political and religious controversies should be avoided.[80] Martha McTier, who heard some of these preachers in Belfast shortly after the insurrection, noted that theirs was 'a zealous religion, very judiciously blended with loyalty, and avowing no principles inconsistent with any church but that of the New Light Dissenter'.[81]

Concentrated in the Armagh area, the society was dominated by Burgher Seceders, and the moving spirit seems to have been George Hamilton, the Burgher minister in the primatial city itself. Both Seceding synods expressed alarm at the intrusion of itinerant ministers into their congregational boundaries, the improper qualifications of the evangelicals, and their vague opinions on church government. The Burgher synod cautioned its presbyteries against compromising their views on discipline and worship, and the Antiburghers rebuked one of their number who had joined the society.[82] As a result, the Burghers lost Hamilton, who became an Independent in 1803, and John Gibson of Richill, while Thomas Campbell left the Antiburghers to emigrate to America.[83] Over the next twenty years, however, resistance to evangelical currents weakened. In 1811 the Scottish Seceders approved a proposal to open correspondence with other religious denominations holding evangelical sentiments in Scotland, Ireland, and England. Contacts were established with the London Missionary Society, whose founder, Dr Waugh of the Secession church in London, visited Scotland in 1815. Support was expressed for the activities of the British and Foreign Bible Society in 1804 and for the Indian missions which followed the renewal of the East India Company charter in 1813.[84] Five years later, the old split between the Burgher and Antiburgher wings of the Secession was finally healed, a reconciliation which owed much to the missionary societies which were drawing together Presbyterians of all shades.[85]

The correlation between evangelical commitment and loyalism is further strengthened by the fact that one of the three ministers of the Synod who joined the ESU, Thomas McKay of Brigh, County Tyrone, was the only minister of the Synod to publicly associate himself with the Orange Order at this period.[86] If we turn to the later dissensions of the 1820s, we find that Henry Cooke's declaration of war on heresy was also tangled up with political objectives. The non-subscribers claimed that the Calvinist revival was nurtured by 'the Orange faction', while Cooke identified the Arians with those who had raised the standard of rebellion in 1798. With some justice, the New Light leader Henry Montgomery attributed Cooke's extraordinary

---

[80] Joseph Thompson, 'The Evangelical Society of Ulster', *Bulletin of the Presbyterian Historical Society of Ireland*, 17 (Mar. 1988), 4–10.

[81] Martha McTier to Sarah Drennan, 27 Sept. 1801, *Drennan Letters*, 313.

[82] Thompson, 'Evangelical Society', 14–15.   [83] Ibid. 18.

[84] John McKerrow, *History of the Secession Church*, rev. and enlarged edn. (Glasgow, 1841), 575, 628, 633, 646.   [85] Hempton and Hill, *Evangelical Protestantism*, 70.

[86] In 1799 McKay published a sermon, now lost, which he had preached to the Orange lodges of Killyman, Cookstown, Pomeroy, and Coagh: Thomas Witherow (ed.), *Historical and Literary Memorials of Presbyterianism in Ireland*, 2 vols. (Belfast, 1879–80), ii. 334. It should also be noted, however, that McKay had an unusually close relationship with the local gentry: see R. S. Fisher, *'The Brigh': Worship and Service over 375 Years* (n.p., [1990]), 61.

popularity to his explosive mixture of religious orthodoxy and anti-popery.[87] The link was asserted once again when Cooke famously called for Presbyterians to unite with Anglicans on a 'platform of common Protestantism' at an anti-repeal demonstration in 1834.[88] Right from the beginning, then, the rebirth of enthusiasm was associated with Protestant solidarity against the Catholic threat—first on the frontier of south Ulster, and later throughout the whole province.

What impact did this revival have upon attitudes to Catholic emancipation, now the most pressing political question in British politics? In 1813 the General Synod had drawn up an overture approving the removal of political disabilities on account of religion, 'so far as may be consistent with the principles of the constitution', a rather more qualified expression of sympathy with the Catholics than the resolution passed twenty years before.[89] It was later claimed, however, that this declaration was pushed through a very thin house by the Arian party on the final day of the meeting.[90] On a more ominous note, that year's business also included the censure of a County Armagh congregation which had ejected its minister for signing a petition in favour of emancipation.[91] Growing concern for the safety of the Protestant constitution was stimulated by the schism of the 1820s. As moderator in 1824–5, Cooke had been invited to give evidence to a select committee of the House of Lords investigating Irish affairs. When asked for his views on the furious debate over emancipation he declared himself in favour of the concession, with the proviso that important public offices should be reserved for Protestants, but he suggested that the 'less informed' Presbyterians were almost entirely hostile to the measure, an assertion which the Liberal *Northern Whig* was forced to concede.[92]

During the 1820s the Church made no public pronouncements on the subject. Despite pressure from the *Belfast News-Letter* and other quarters, the Synod refused to come out in defence of the Protestant constitution, and the Presbytery of Ballymena was the only one to call for a petition against further concessions. Even Cooke, whose evidence to the select committee had guaranteed his popularity among advocates of no-popery, did not come out in public opposition until a late stage. Nevertheless, his personal connections with Ascendancy gentlemen and the Second Reformation movement identified him with the most strident anti-Catholic voices in Ireland. Other active opponents of emancipation—Alexander Carson, Robert Stewart, and Robert Magill—also tended to be prominent evangelicals, while those ministers who associated themselves with the Catholic cause were declared Arians.[93] The polarization of theological opinion in the 1820s thus had the effect of clarifying the relationship between heterodoxy and pro-Catholic politics.

The new conversionist theology served to refuel the ideology of anti-popery, while dissolving the denominational boundaries which divided the Protestant Churches.

---

[87] Holmes, 'Controversy and Schism', 125–7.
[88] Hempton and Hill, *Evangelical Protestantism*, 98.
[89] *RGSU*, iii. 397; for 1793, see ibid. 157.   [90] Holmes, *Henry Cooke*, 65.
[91] *RGSU*, iii. 397. Eighty-one members of his congregation had defected to the Seceders and continued to exclude him from the meeting-house.
[92] Hempton and Hill, *Evangelical Protestantism*, 72; Holmes, *Henry Cooke*, 64.
[93] Holmes, *Henry Cooke*, 64–5.

In the transition from radical republicanism to conservative unionism, vital religion had further contributions to make. First, as David Hempton and Myrtle Hill have shown, Victorian evangelicalism reinforced the equation between Protestantism and material progress, contributing to ethnic stereotypes which still persist. Secondly, missionary endeavour united Ulster Presbyterians with other British and imperial organizations in the drive for overseas expansion, encouraging the tendency to invest parochial battles with global significance. Anti-Catholicism was thus blended with a sense of moral and economic superiority, faith in the civilizing mission of the British Empire, and an increasing awareness of Ulster's divergent history and culture, to create a distinctive provincial consciousness which underpinned resistance to home rule. Even today, it has been argued, evangelicalism continues to equip Ulster Protestants with the central beliefs, values, and symbols of what they take to be 'the British way of life'.[94]

In the political sphere, then, Catholic emancipation can be identified as the point of no return for Ulster Presbyterians. Eighteenth-century radicalism had proceeded upon the assumption that Protestants would demonstrate their liberality, and Catholics would respond with appropriate expressions of gratitude. What this view did not allow for was Catholic self-organization, particularly when such political autonomy was perceived to be clerically directed.[95] O'Connell represented more than the demand for emancipation: he pioneered a kind of Catholic communalism, a mass mobilization which involved a whole range of popular grievances. It was perhaps inevitable, then, that Protestants should come to regard the creation of a domestic legislature as not just an economic threat, but also a vehicle for Roman Catholic ascendancy.[96] In the face of an increasingly ultramontane, politically powerful hierarchy, examples of interdenominational co-operation in politics were destined to be short-lived, fragile, and restricted to specific issues.

This is not to say that the reformist and radical impulses in Ulster Presbyterianism had been entirely extinguished. With the benefit of hindsight, the surprising feature of the Victorian era is the survival of Presbyterianism as an independent political force. Although Cooke's enormous personal prestige earned him the nickname of 'Presbyterian Pope', he was in fact a marginal figure in Ulster politics for the greatest part of his career—vulnerable when the question of the validity of Presbyterian marriages was reopened in 1840, isolated during the tenant right protests of 1848–52, and in a clear minority in his opposition to the disestablishment of the Anglican Church.[97] The fissures which emerged over the national education system, the privileges of the Established Church, and, above all, the land question, reflected the persistence of political and social inequalities among Protestants. Since the greater part of the land (and consequently control of parliamentary seats) remained

[94] Steve Bruce, *God Save Ulster: The Religion and Politics of Paisleyism* (Oxford, 1986), esp. ch. 9.
[95] Frank Wright, *Two Lands on One Soil: Ulster Politics before Home Rule* (Dublin, 1996) 17–20.
[96] *The Repealer Repulsed! A Correct Narrative of the Rise and Progress of the Repeal Invasion of Ulster* (Belfast, 1841), 4.
[97] For the land question, see Paul Bew and Frank Wright, 'The Agrarian Opposition in Ulster Politics, 1848–87', in Samuel Clark and J. S. Donnelly, jun. (eds.), *Irish Peasants: Violence and Political Unrest 1780–1914* (Madison, Wis., 1983), 192–229.

in Episcopalian hands, landlordism could still be regarded as synonymous with the Anglican establishment, and Presbyterians were still drastically under-represented in both national and local government. As late as 1898, a convention attended by 1,438 delegates met in the Ulster Hall to launch the Presbyterian Unionist Voters' Association, designed to increase representation in the House of Commons, the recently established district and county councils, and other elective boards, and to secure a fair share of public appointments.[98]

Presbyterian politics before 1886 hesitated between the pan-Protestant policy announced by Cooke and a Liberal, or at least autonomous, programme rooted in denominational interests. By the close of the century, however, the social gap between Church and Dissent was narrowing, while the distance between Protestants and the Roman Catholic Church was growing. Since the political baptism of the Catholic masses under O'Connell, the fundamental relationship in Irish politics had been between the British State and those political elites which could deliver the majority of the population; this shift in the balance of power left little room for Presbyterian Liberalism. As long as land remained a key issue in Ulster elections there was some basis for an oppositional politics, as the Liberal gains of 1874 and 1880 demonstrated; the historical literature on the period wistfully reminds us that things might have turned out differently.[99] But Liberal vitality also relied upon the absence of serious agitation over constitutional issues or Catholic questions (such as clerical influence over education). After the reform acts of 1884–5, which brought the electorate into line with demographic realities, these fundamental issues could no longer be avoided.

Ulster unionists and Irish nationalism

The nationalism of the United Irishmen originated in the exclusively Protestant conception of the Irish people embodied in the revolution of 1782, and broadened by later reformers who hoped for the gradual incorporation of at least part of the Catholic population. It grew out of a mentality which instinctively coupled liberty with Protestantism and defined Roman Catholicism as superstitious, authoritarian, and unfree. A century later, in contrast, Irish nationalism had already come to represent explicitly Catholic grievances and aspirations. Its emotive power derived from the compelling story of an indigenous people, dispossessed of their land, persecuted for their religion, but destined to rise again. This core narrative, whose origins lay ultimately in the Gaelic response to conquest and colonization, connected the *ancien régime* ideology of the Jacobites with Defenderism and O'Connellism, and would reach its apogee in the imagery of the martyred nation deployed by the 1916 generation. In an age of mass politics, Roman Catholicism inevitably supplied the most obvious badge of Irish ethnicity, and O'Connell, Parnell, and Redmond all found it necessary to make a concordat with the Church. By the early years of

[98] Richard McMinn, 'Presbyterianism and Politics in Ulster, 1871–1906', *Studia Hibernica*, 21 (1981), 142.
[99] B. M. Walker, *Ulster Politics: The Formative Years, 1868–86* (Belfast, 1989), pp. xiv, 46.

the twentieth century it was possible to assert openly that Ireland was '*de facto* a Catholic nation'.[100]

During the long nineteenth century which ran from 1801 to 1922, the United Irishmen were subsumed into this unified, continuous narrative of nationality, sometimes by portraying them as honorary Catholics.[101] An elaborate hagiography was developed in which Tone rubbed shoulders with St Patrick while, in left-wing versions, James Hope played Connolly to Henry Joy McCracken's Pearse. In retrospect the significance of the United Irish movement seems to lie in the civic, secular vocabulary which it inserted into an otherwise ethnic, mystical ideology. But latter-day republicans drew other lessons from the 1790s, usually on the basis of a reductive reading of Tone's effervescent autobiography: that the blame for Ireland's problems could be laid at Britain's door; that sectarianism was an artificial product of divide-and-rule imperialism; and that the means of redemption lay in armed struggle.[102] To the advocates of physical force, 1798 presented an example of the declamatory violence which each generation had offered as testimony to the survival of the national spirit. Those Presbyterians who were admitted to the nationalist canon were often valued less for their rich contributions to republican thought than for their token significance as Protestants who had gone over to the other side.

When the home rule issue first erupted in 1886, it appeared that the major stumbling block on the road to self-government was not so much the Protestant democracy of the north as the aristocracy of the south, hence the Gladstonian obsession with Grattan's parliament.[103] As organized resistance to home rule became focused on the north-east, however, the moment when Ulster joined Ireland assumed its modern function in nationalist propaganda, its importance later confirmed by the partition of the island. The obvious attractions of the United Irishmen for irredentists were demonstrated in Aodh de Blácam's *The Black North* (1938), which set out to prove the underlying Irishness of the fourth green field and the essential place of Ulster Protestants in 'the national tradition'.[104] His idealized picture of the Protestant heartland was conveniently summed up in chapter headings such as 'Down: Betsy Gray's County', 'Antrim: Glensmen and United Men', and 'Old Belfast: A Patriotic Record'. The usefulness of Presbyterian radicalism to the case against partition was underlined in a foreword written by Eamon de Valera, in which the architect of the republic declared that Ulster, 'the land . . . of Henry Monroe, of William Orr and Henry Joy McCracken', was his favourite province.[105] Here was an ideological challenge which could not be ignored by those unionist intellectuals who refused to disown their own radical forebears.

---

[100] D. P. Moran, 1901, quoted in D. G. Boyce, *Nationalism in Ireland*, 2nd edn. (London, 1991), 243.

[101] For a recent example see Eamonn McCann, *War and an Irish Town*, 3rd edn. (London, 1993), 174.

[102] For 1798 in nationalist consciousness see Elliott, *Partners in Revolution*, 365–72; ead., *Wolfe Tone: Prophet of Irish Independence* (New Haven, 1989), 411–19; Whelan, ' "'98 after '98" '. On the revolutionary generation see Tom Garvin, *Nationalist Revolutionaries in Ireland 1858–1928* (Oxford, 1987).

[103] Paul Bew, *Ideology and the Irish Question: Ulster Unionism and Irish Nationalism 1912–1916* (Oxford, 1994), 2.

[104] Aodh de Blácam, *The Black North: An Account of the Six Counties of Unrecovered Ireland* (Dublin, 1938), 287.   [105] Ibid., p. ix.

Not all Ulster Protestants, of course, rejected nationalism. A handful of Presbyterian clergymen, among whom the best known was J. B. Armour, came out in support of self-government, arguing as their United Irish forefathers had that the influence of the priesthood would be diminished in a democratic Ireland.[106] For the vast majority, however, home rule was translated as Rome rule. In this conviction, of course, they stood shoulder to shoulder with their erstwhile enemies in the Anglican church. 'Ulster Day', 28 September 1912, marked the final consummation of Cooke's policy of Protestant union: at the elaborately staged signing of the Solemn League and Covenant in Belfast City Hall, the names of Edward Carson and Lord Londonderry were closely followed by the Moderator of the General Assembly and the Anglican Bishop of Down. On the previous evening, at a religious service held in the Ulster Hall, the former moderator William McKean had delivered a political sermon which neatly recapitulated the chief themes of the unionist position: the identification of liberty with the reformed religion, the conception of the seventeenth-century plantation as a contract with the Crown, the sacrifices made at Derry and Enniskillen, and the subsequent transformation of a barren province into a beautiful and prosperous land. Above all, there was the familiar assertion that self-rule meant Catholic supremacy: 'The Irish question is at bottom a war against Protestantism; it is an attempt to establish a Roman Catholic ascendancy in Ireland to begin the disintegration of the Empire.'[107]

Ulster unionism rested on a mixture of anti-Catholicism, economic self-interest, and an emerging sense of historical and cultural apartness.[108] The tradition of scripture politics, increasingly anomalous in the English-speaking world, was now stripped down to a bare, negative no-popery. Whereas many eighteenth-century radicals, from New Lights to Covenanters, had generated utopian visions of a reformed society, Victorian evangelicalism had turned inwards to concentrate on individual piety. A reading of providential history which focused on specific human communities—nations, kingdoms, and empires—and located the dynamics of change in wars and revolutions, was replaced by a preoccupation with spiritual revival. During the same period, of course, the last vestiges of the Protestant constitution were giving way before the growth of a modern, secular state which had taken over many of the social functions once performed by the Church in the realms of crime, welfare, and—most controversially—education. Although evangelicalism formed the bedrock of unionist mentality it could not therefore sustain the sort of political theology which had defined the positions of New Lights, Old Lights, Seceders, and Covenanters in the previous century. The negative image of the Roman Church as

---

[106] Hempton and Hill, *Evangelical Protestantism*, 185.

[107] *BNL*, 30 Sept. 1912. For a general account of Presbyterian opposition to home rule see R. F. G. Holmes, ' "Ulster will Fight and Ulster will be Right": The Protestant Churches and Ulster's Resistance to Home Rule, 1912–14', in W. F. Sheils (ed.), *Studies in Church History*, xx, *The Church at War* (Oxford, 1983), 321–35.

[108] From an extensive literature see D. W. Miller, *Queen's Rebels: Ulster Loyalism in Historical Perspective* (Dublin, 1978), esp. ch. 3; Alvin Jackson, *The Ulster Party: Irish Unionists in the House of Commons, 1884–1911* (Oxford, 1989), esp. ch. 1; Jennifer Todd, 'Unionist Political Thought', in D. G. Boyce, R. Eccleshall, and V. Geoghegan (eds.), *Political Thought in Ireland since the Seventeenth Century* (London, 1993), 190–211.

an authoritarian system remained a stock feature of Protestant polemic, but the war of religion once fought out on the battlefields of Europe was now confined to the working-class ghettos of Belfast, Glasgow, and Liverpool.[109]

The contrast between Presbyterian politics in 1798 and 1912 would appear to be complete. This was certainly the opinion of those nationalists who reduced unionism to an alliance of aristocratic privilege and Orange tribalism. It cannot be denied that the roots of Ulster unionism lie primarily in a long tradition of conservative political mobilization—in the defence of the Church of Ireland and landlordism, in the plebeian sectarianism of the Orange Order, and the no-popery preaching of the evangelicals.[110] But unionism was a more heterogeneous movement than its enemies cared to admit; even the sectarian demagogue Hugh Hanna was anxious to point out that he was neither an Orangeman nor a Tory.[111] As with nationalist ideology, so too the case for the Union came in both ethnic and civic varieties, the latter drawing on the long-standing, provincial brand of Liberalism, which gave the unionists an ideological respectability in Britain which they could not otherwise have attained.[112] The Liberal defenders of legislative union spoke of the British connection not as a guarantee for Protestant advantage, but as a constitutional framework within which the liberty and prosperity of all denominations could be secured. While acknowledging that British rule had been oppressive in the past, they pointed to the positive benefits—land reform, increased wealth, the disestablishment and disendowment of the Church of Ireland, and the extension of education—which had been granted since 1801.[113] 'The days of privilege and exclusion are at an end', declared Thomas Witherow, 'so far as it is in the power of law and government to end them.'[114] A professor of church history at Magee College, and sometime editor of the Liberal *Londonderry Standard*, Witherow was typical of the progressive unionism that expressed an unshakeable faith in the superiority of British political institutions and regarded imperialism as an instrument for the promotion of freedom, religion, and civilization around the globe. 'Our island now is not a colony or dependency', he boasted, 'but a constituent portion of a great empire, whose subjects reside in every clime, and whose flag waves on every sea.'[115]

Unionism, its Liberal exponents tirelessly insisted, was not the ideological alibi for Protestant Ascendancy; on the contrary, it represented the defence of civil and religious equality against the threat posed by sectarian intolerance. In 1886 the

---

[109] Frank Wright, 'Protestant Ideology and Politics in Ulster', *European Journal of Sociology*, 14 (1973), 213–80. This is not to deny the basic continuity in the idioms and paradigms of Presbyterian politics. One can find many echoes of the Covenanting tradition in Ian Paisley's anti-Catholicism, his Biblical fundamentalism, his language of resistance, and even in his apocalyptic denunciations of the European Community. It is interesting to note that while Paisley's father was an evangelical Baptist, his mother was a Scottish Covenanter. [110] For a summary see Jackson, *Ulster Party*, 17–21.

[111] Hugh Hanna, *Scotland, Ulster, and Home Rule for Ireland* (Dublin, 1888), 5.

[112] Bew, *Ideology and the Irish Question*, ch. 2.

[113] R. J. Lynd, *The Present Crisis in Ireland* (Belfast, 1886); [Anon.], *From Liberal Ulster to England* [London, 1886]; Robert MacGeogh, *Ulster's Apology for Being Loyal* (Belfast, 1888); J. MacDermott, *Grattan's Parliament, and 90 Years of Union* (Belfast, 1892), 18–19; J. B. Woodburn, *The Ulster Scot: His History and Religion* (London, 1914), 370–1.

[114] Thomas Witherow, *Derry and Enniskillen in the Year 1689* (Belfast, 1873), 323.

[115] Ibid. 322.

General Assembly pronounced that the creation of a separate legislature would lead inevitably to 'the ascendancy of one class and creed in matters pertaining to religion, education and civil administration', in which the rights of minorities would be set at nought.[116] Another special meeting convened to protest against the second home rule bill recognized the reality of agrarian grievances, put forward the solution of peasant proprietorship, but argued that the establishment of an Irish Parliament would be 'a cure far worse than the disease'.[117] Finally, in 1912, a Presbyterian anti-home rule convention of up to 50,000 members opened with a declaration that unionism was activated by 'no spirit of sectarian exclusiveness'. The Ulster Presbyterians, it was stressed, had shared in the struggle for ecclesiastical and land reform, and would continue to co-operate with Irishmen of every creed in the advancement of the social, moral, and material prosperity of their country. Their only demand, they concluded, was 'the undisturbed continuance of our present place in the constitution under which our Church and our country have so signally prospered'.[118]

The rejection of Irish nationalism thus implied no repudiation of Liberal values, and a number of unionists went so far as to portray themselves as the legitimate heirs of Presbyterian radicalism. Where republicans stressed the physical-force, separatist aspects of the United Irish movement, however, Liberal unionists generally identified with the more moderate, reformist elements, though many took a certain pride in the 'turn-out' at Antrim and Ballynahinch. A good example is James Shaw, formerly professor of political economy in the University of Dublin, addressing his fellow Liberals:

You are not, nor am I, ashamed of the fact that our ancestors were United Irishmen. We do not fear to speak of '98. Had we lived in '98 we should probably have been rebels ourselves, just as our rebellious forefathers, were they now alive, would be contented and loyal subjects of the empire.[119]

The aims of the United Irishmen, he insisted, had now been obtained. The confessional state had been dismantled and all civil and religious disabilities swept away, while restrictions on commerce and industry had been removed. It was not the imperial Parliament that their grandfathers had opposed in arms, protested the Liberals, but the corrupt, sectarian Dublin assembly which nationalists were now trying to reinstate in reverse form. As they had struggled against the Protestant Ascendancy in the eighteenth century, so they vowed to fight against the threatened Catholic Ascendancy of the nineteenth. This comparison, dubious to the historian but typical

---

[116] Hempton and Hill, *Evangelical Protestantism*, 172.

[117] McMinn, 'Presbyterianism and Politics', 142, 145–6.

[118] Graham Walker, *Intimate Strangers: Political and Cultural Interaction between Scotland and Ulster in Modern Times* (Edinburgh, 1995), ch. 2; quotations from pp. 38–9.

[119] J. J. Shaw, *Mr Gladstone's Two Irish Policies: 1868 and 1886. A Letter to an Ulster Liberal Elector* (London, 1888), 9. For other examples of continuing pride in the United Irishmen see Thomas McKnight, *Ulster as It Is; or Twenty-Eight Years' Experience as an Irish Editor*, 2 vols. (London, 1896), vol. i, ch. 2; MacGeogh, *Ulster's Apology*, 1; W. T. Latimer, *Ulster Biographies Relating Chiefly to the Rebellion of 1798* (Belfast, 1897), preface; Woodburn, *Ulster Scot*, chs. 22–4.

of the self-centred, persecuted note struck by Presbyterian writers, allowed the resistance to home rule to be reconciled with the revolutionary politics of 1798. 'If our
forefathers rebelled against Grattan's Parliament', demanded Shaw, 'will their descendants be happy and contented under Mr Parnell's?'[120]

The blind spots in Liberal unionism are all too obvious. Their reading of post-
union politics ignored the unevenness of the progress which had undoubtedly been
made since 1801. An inquiry into local government in 1877 discovered that while
Catholics formed nearly a third of Belfast's population, they supplied just two out
of the city's forty councillors, while in Derry, where they outnumbered the Protestants, the figure was two out of twenty-four.[121] Such disparities, of course, were
only the most public examples of the social gulf which still separated Protestant
from Catholic. Liberal apologists also overlooked the fact that all concessions to
Roman Catholics, from emancipation onwards, had been imposed by the British
government in opposition to public opinion in the northern province. In general,
they simply refused to recognize the existence of a distinct sense of Irish nationality
which demanded institutional expression in some form of political autonomy. While
they too clung to the common name of Irishman, this national identification was
qualified both by their loyalty to a wider British community and by a growing appreciation of the distinctive cultural inheritance of the 'Ulsterman'. The population of
Ireland did not form a single nation, they argued, but two separate, antagonistic
communities, and if one had the right to self-government, then so too did the other.[122]

The willingness of Ulster Liberals to ignore the profound inequalities between
denominations casts doubt on their professed commitment to a plural, inclusive society. They adhered to a sense of historical progress which identified the Roman Church
with the forces of oppression and reaction, rather like the radicals of one hundred
years before. Their political philosophy, however, was narrower and more provincial. Although the Ulster Liberals had consistently taken a principled stand against
Orangeism, they tended to define their Liberalism by reference to the Church and
land questions, the two issues where Presbyterian sectional interests were paramount.
During the home rule era, the remedy of social grievances, as we have seen, had
taken second place to the desire 'to remain undisturbed'. Finally, and fatally, the
Liberals spoke for a minority within a unionist coalition which was tainted by
supremacist attitudes, and as resistance to nationalism became more militant and
populist, their influence inevitably waned. In the upheavals which led to partition
the Liberals lost their distinctive identity, and in the new Northern Ireland which
emerged after 1922 the old Dissenting voice was seldom heard.

While the legacy of the United Irishmen had been narrowed down to physical-
force separatism on the one hand, it was thus reduced to a residual faith in the benign
workings of the British constitution on the other. Neither of these ideological positions was equipped to account for the depth and tenacity of religious and ethnic antagonisms on the island of Ireland. Republicanism, which in theory embraced Irish

---

[120] Shaw, *Gladstone's Two Irish Policies*, 9, 31.   [121] Walker, *Ulster Politics*, 25.
[122] Holmes, 'Ulster Will Fight', 330–1.

people of all cultures and creeds, relied in practice upon Gaelic and Catholic sentiment. All too often, the myth of the moment when Ulster joined Ireland was employed as a substitute for creative thinking on how unionist and nationalist aspirations might be reconciled. Among the Ulster Liberals, meanwhile, the generous radical conscience of the 1790s had dwindled to the articulation of specific, localized grievances.

In the nineteenth century, as I have tried to show in this chapter, unforeseen political and social transformations thus enabled revitalized sectarian identities to triumph over the pluralist vision of the United Irishmen. In retrospect, of course, it is possible to discern the germs of these later developments within the republican movement even at the moment of its inception. By locating late eighteenth-century Jacobinism in the longer trajectory of Presbyterian social and intellectual development, this book has demonstrated the continuity of the underlying confessional loyalties and religious habits of thought which circumscribed United Irish political thinking. The different ideological strains within eighteenth-century Presbyterianism had all been nourished within the confines of anti-Catholicism, and it was only the apparent disintegration of the Roman Church that permitted the brief but spectacular fruition of this tradition in the age of the American and French Revolutions. Even as Tom Paine led the assault on the dead generations who governed from beyond the grave, the United Irishmen were discovering that they were not free to wipe the historical slate clean. Those who mourn the extinction of the pre-lapsarian Presbyterianism which supposedly prevailed before Cooke—enlightened in religion and republican in politics—would do well to recall its fragile and conditional nature.

Was the United Irish project bound to fail? The short answer must be yes. With hindsight it is possible to see that the sectarian warfare of Armagh rather than the reformism of Antrim and Down would set the pattern for Ulster politics. More damning, perhaps, is the evidence of confessional tensions within the United Irish system itself. Of course, all revolutionary movements are based on unstable coalitions, and in the end it was military force rather than internal divisions that defeated the United Irishmen. Nevertheless, it is ominous that the nationalist historian Richard Madden, who interviewed the surviving United Irishmen in the 1840s, should have concluded that 'even had they united in successful rebellion, the exasperating passions called into action by civil war, would have prevented them from uniting in forming a settled government'.[123]

From the beginning it was clear that the northern and southern insurrections were fundamentally different in character. Viscount Castlereagh contrasted the 'heated bigotry' of the Wexford rebels with the 'cold, reasoning disaffection of the northern Presbyterians'.[124] Wolfe Tone had made a similar distinction between the nationalism of the Dissenters, which was based on 'reason and reflection', and that of the

---

[123] R. R. Madden, *The United Irishmen, their Lives and Times*, 3 ser., 7 vols. (London, 1842–6), 1st ser., i. 31.   [124] Castlereagh to Portland, 3 June 1799, *Castlereagh Correspondence*, ii. 325–6.

Catholics, which stemmed from 'hatred to the English name'.[125] In fact, the gulf which separated east Ulster from Wexford was greater still, for neither Castlereagh nor Tone were aware of the Covenanter undercurrents in the Antrim and Down risings. Presbyterian radicalism bore the stamp of its religious origins, particularly in its millenarian manifestations. Only the New Lights subscribed to the enlightened vision of a non-confessional polity in which all civil distinctions founded on religious differences would be abolished, and even then it was assumed that the Catholic Church had been relegated to the dustbin of history.

Such hard considerations militate against the construction of the neoromantic versions of 1798 whose outlines can already be discerned among 'post-revisionist' historians.[126] A genuinely secular nationalism has never struck deep roots in Irish society, not even among the 'sincere and enlightened republicans' who so impressed Wolfe Tone in Belfast. And yet, to the extent that political debate in Ireland continues to revolve around the relationship between Ulster Protestants and Irish nationalism, it is easy to see why the first 'year of liberty' has lost none of its fascination. It is, perhaps, the very intractability of Presbyterian radicalism, its refusal to yield to the presuppositions of either nationalists or unionists, which makes it such an attractive subject for historical study. Nationalists of every generation have naturally turned to the unfulfilled promise of the first republic, and they must continue to do so as long as they pursue the ideal of an inclusive, democratic nation-state. But Ulster Protestantism too, if it is to find the creative capacity to renew itself, must engage critically with its own past, including the alternative cultural strands and political philosophies which came to the surface in the 1790s. It is for these reasons, two hundred years later, that we find ourselves still spellbound by the United Irishmen.

[125] *Life of Theobald Wolfe Tone*, ed. W. T. W. Tone, 2 vols. (Washington, 1826), i. 278. See also William Parnell, *An Enquiry into the Causes of Popular Discontents in Ireland by an Irish Country Gentleman* (London, 1805), 29.

[126] Note e.g. the frankly nationalist and teleological perspective adopted by one of the outstanding scholars currently working on the eighteenth century: Whelan, *Tree of Liberty*, preface; id., 'Reinterpreting the 1798 Rebellion in County Wexford', in Keogh and Furlong, *Mighty Wave*, 9–36.

APPENDIX: PRESBYTERIAN MINISTERS AND PROBATIONERS SUSPECTED OF INVOLVEMENT IN THE 1798 REBELLION[1]

PRESBYTERY OF ANTRIM

1. Revd Arthur MacMahon of Holywood (New Light).[2]
2. Revd Futt Marshall of Ballyclare (New Light).[3]
3. Revd William Sinclair of First Newtownards (New Light).[4]
4. Revd James Worrall of First Larne (New Light).[5]

GENERAL SYNOD OF ULSTER

Presbytery of Armagh

5. Revd Boyle Moody of Newry (New Light).[6]
6. Revd William Neilson of Dundalk (New Light).
7. Mr William Hamilton Drummond (New Light).[7]

Presbytery of Ballymena

8. Revd Henry Henry of Connor (Old Light).
9. Mr John McNish of Clough (New Light?).[8]

---

[1] The basic sources are James and Samuel McConnell, *Fasti of the Irish Presbyterian Church, 1613–1840*, ed. David Stewart, 2 vols. (Belfast, 1935–51); *RGSU*; the *DNB*; J. S. Reid, *History of the Presbyterian Church in Ireland*, ed. W. D. Killen, 3rd edn., 3 vols. (Belfast, 1867); Thomas Witherow (ed.), *Historical and Literary Memorials of Presbyterianism in Ireland*, 2 vols. (1879–80); W. I. Addison, *The Matriculation Albums of the University of Glasgow from 1728 to 1858* (Glasgow, 1913). Additional information can be found in the footnotes below.

[2] 'Arthur MacMahon's Petition to the Most Noble the Marchioness of Downshire', 20 Feb. 1810, PRONI, Downshire Papers, D607/C/12/53; W. A. Maguire, 'Arthur MacMahon, United Irishman and French Soldier', *Irish Sword*, 9 (1969–70), 207–15.

[3] William McMillan, 'The Subscription Controversy in Irish Presbyterianism from the Plantation of Ulster to the Present Day: With Special Reference to Political Implications in the Late Eighteenth Century', MA thesis (Manchester University, 1959), 346–7.

[4] MS notebook on the history of First Newtownards by Revd Hugh Moore, *c*.1887, PRONI, CR4/7/C1/1–8.

[5] McMillan, 'Subscription Controversy', 347–9; Alexander Haliday to Castlereagh, 26 Aug. 1798, NAI, Rebellion Papers, 620/4/29/29.

[6] William Campbell, 'Sketches', PHSI, Campbell MSS, 124; John Pollock to Downshire, [21 Mar. 1797], PRONI, Downshire Papers, D607/E/214.

[7] See his *Hibernia: A Poem* and *The Man of Age*, both published by the *Northern Star* office in 1797.

[8] John Caldwell, 'Particulars of a North County Irish Family', PRONI, Caldwell Papers, T3541/5/3, p. 128; Edward Cooke to Major General George Nugent, 12 Aug. 1798, PRONI, McCance Collection, D272/40. This name was also spelt Mineese and Miniss; the modern equivalent, presumably, is McNeice.

Presbytery of Bangor

10. Revd James Porter of Greyabbey (New Light).[9]
11. Revd Robert Gowdie of Dunover.[10]
12. Mr James Hull (New Light).
13. Mr John Miles (New Light?).[11]
14. Mr David Bailie Warden (New Light).[12]

Presbytery of Belfast

15. Revd Thomas Ledlie Birch of Saintfield (Old Light).[13]
16. Revd Alexander Henry of Castlereagh (Old Light?).[14]
17. Revd Sinclair Kelburn of Third Belfast (Old Light).
18. Revd James Simpson of Second Newtownards (Old Light).
19. Mr Archibald Warwick (Old Light?).[15]

Presbytery of Clogher

20. Revd James Davidson of Aughnacloy and Ballygawley.[16]

Presbytery of Derry

21. Revd Robert Steel of Scriggan (Dungiven) (Old Light).
22. Mr John Pinkerton.
23. Mr Reuben Rogers (Old Light?).

Presbytery of Dromore

24. Revd Samuel Barber of Rathfriland (New Light).[17]
25. Revd Alexander Patterson of Drumbanagher (Old Light?).[18]
26. Revd John Sherrard of Tullylish (Old Light?).[19]

---

[9] W. T. Latimer, *A History of the Irish Presbyterians* (Belfast, [1893]), 62–74.
[10] Hugh McComb to John Catherwood, [29 or 30 July 1798], PRONI, D3579/1; *BNL*, 26 June 1798.   [11] 'Black Book', PRONI, McCance Collection, D272/1.
[12] Ibid. The most complete biography of Warden is W. T. Latimer, 'David Bailie Warden, Patriot 1798', *UJA*, 2nd ser., 13 (1907), 29–33.
[13] Aiken McClelland, 'Thomas Ledlie Birch, United Irishman', *Proceedings and Reports of the Belfast Natural History and Philosophical Society*, 2nd ser., 7 (1965), 24–35.   [14] Ibid. 33.
[15] 'Black Book', PRONI, McCance Collection, D272/1; Charles Dickson, *Revolt in the North: Antrim and Down in 1798* (Dublin, 1960), 146, 202–3; Richard Musgrave, *Memoirs of the Different Rebellions in Ireland* (Dublin, 1801), 557.
[16] 'Black Book', PRONI, McCance Collection, D272/1; List of members of United Irish committees, NAI, Rebellion Papers, 620/4/42/3.
[17] W. D. Bailie, 'The Revd Samuel Barber 1738–1811: National Volunteer and United Irishman', in J. L. M. Haire (ed.), *Challenge and Conflict: Essays in Irish Presbyterian History and Doctrine* (Antrim, 1981), 72–95.
[18] Thomas Kennedy to 'McCabe', 29 Aug. 1796, PRONI, Downshire Papers, D607/D/136.
[19] Examination of Edward Gorman, 15 June 1797, BL, Pelham Papers, Add. MS 33104, fos. 225–6.

27. Revd Samuel Watson of Killinchy (New Light).[20]
28. Mr William Adair.[21]

Presbytery of Killyleagh

29. Revd William Steel Dickson of Portaferry (New Light).[22]
30. Revd Joseph Jackson of Creggan and Newtownhamilton.[23]
31. Revd Robert Porter of Clough (New Light).[24]

Presbytery of Letterkenny

32. Revd Francis Dill of Ray (Old Light).[25]

Presbytery of Monaghan

33. Revd John Arnold of Ballybay (Old Light?).[26]
34. Revd Robert Montgomery of First Bailieborough (Corglass).[27]
35. Revd William Moore of Ervey and Carrickmaklin (Corvalley).[28]
36. Revd Thomas Stewart of Cootehill.[29]

Presbytery of Route

37. Revd John Glendy of Maghera (Old Light?).
38. Revd Robert Scott of Duneane (New Light).[30]
39. Revd John Smyth of First Kilrea (Old Light?).[31]
40. Mr Benjamin Mitchell.

Presbytery of Strabane

41. Revd William Dunlop of Badoney (New Light).[32]

[20] Watson was one of six names supplied to David Miller by Mr Aiken McClelland of the Ulster Folk Museum (since deceased) when he was researching his 'Presbyterianism and "Modernisation"' article. I have independent sources for three of these—the other two were Moses and Robert Hogg—but I am forced to accept the last three on trust. See D. W. Miller, 'Presbyterianism and "Modernization" in Ulster', *Past and Present*, 80 (Aug. 1978), 77 n. 31.

[21] 'Black Book', PRONI, McCance Collection, D272/1. See also Alexander Marsden to General Nugent, 21 Aug. 1798, ibid., D272/39.

[22] Ibid., D272/1; W. D. Bailie, 'William Steel Dickson, D.D.', *Bulletin of the Presbyterian Historical Society of Ireland*, 6 (May 1976).

[23] *Memoirs of Miles Byrne*, ed. by his widow, 3 vols. (New York, 1863), i. 245.

[24] R. M. Young, *Ulster in '98: Episodes and Anecdotes* (Belfast, 1893), 67.

[25] A. G. Lecky, *The Laggan and its Presbyterianism* (Belfast, 1905), 68–9; J. R. Dill, *The Dill Worthies* (Belfast, 1888), 57.

[26] *UJA*, 2nd ser., 14 (1908), 32, has an article by D. C. Rushe on 'William Arnold, Minister of Ballybay, First Presbyterian Congregation, Country Monaghan' which is obviously about the same individual.

[27] L. T. Brown, 'The Presbyterians of Cavan and Monaghan: An Immigrant Community in South Ulster over Three Centuries', Ph.D. thesis (QUB, 1986), 708, 712.   [28] Ibid. 709.

[29] H. Clements to unknown, 20 Apr. 1797, NAI, Rebellion Papers, 620/29/289.

[30] J. L. Porter, *The Life and Times of Henry Cooke* (London, 1871), 26.

[31] J. W. Kernohan, *The Parishes of Kilrea and Tamlaght O'Crilly: A Sketch of their History, with an Account of Boveedy Congregation* (Coleraine, 1912), 39–40, 60; Samuel McSkimmin, *Annals of Ulster* (Belfast, 1849), 56.

[32] A. A. Campbell, *Notes on the Literary History of Strabane* (Omagh, 1902), 67–70.

Presbytery of Templepatrick

42. Revd Robert Acheson of Glenarm (New Light).[33]
43. Revd Thomas Alexander of Cairncastle.[34]
44. Revd Robert Campbell of Templepatrick (New Light).[35]
45. Revd Adam Hill of Ballynure (New Light).[36]
46. Revd John Lawson of Cairncastle.[37]

Presbytery of Tyrone

47. Revd Moses Hogg of Loughgall.
48. Mr Robert Hogg (New Light).[38]
49. Mr Charles Wallace.

SECEDERS[39]

50. Revd James Harper of Knockloughrim (Old Light) (Burgher).
51. Revd Thomas Smith of Ahoghill and Randalstown (Old Light) (Burgher).[40]
52. Revd Josias Wilson of Donegore (Old Light) (Burgher).[41]

REFORMED PRESBYTERY[42]

53. Revd William Stavely of Knockbracken (Old Light).[43]
54. Revd William Gibson (Old Light).
55. Revd Joseph Orr (Old Light).
56. Mr John Black (Old Light).
57. Mr Samuel Brown Wylie (Old Light).

OTHERS

58. Mr James Connell of Garvagh.[44]
59. Revd George Potts.[45]
60. Revd — Thompson.[46]

---

[33] Musgrave, *Rebellions*, 181.   [34] Young, *Ulster in '98*, 66.
[35] McMillan, 'The Subscription Controversy in Irish Presbyterianism', MA thesis (Manchester University, 1959), 365.   [36] Ibid. 368–9.
[37] Young, *Ulster in '98*, 20.
[38] For the two Hoggs, see n. 20. For Robert Hogg's theological views see 'Substance of a conversation with the Revd Mr Hogg, Presbyterian Minister of Loughgall, 12 Jan. 1828', PRONI, D172/11.   [39] See David Stewart, *The Seceders in Ireland* (Belfast, 1950), 271, 331.
[40] W. D. Bailie *et al.*, *A History of Congregations in the Presbyterian Church in Ireland 1610–1982* (Belfast, 1982), 7.   [41] *NS*, 20 June 1796.
[42] For the Covenanting clergy and the rebellion, see Adam Loughridge, *The Covenanters in Ireland* (Belfast, 1984), 44–9; Samuel Brown Wylie, *Memoir of Alexander McCleod, D.D.* (New York, 1855), 29–30.   [43] McSkimmin, *Annals*, 18; 'Black Book', PRONI, McCance Collection, D272/1.
[44] Young, *Ulster in '98*, 67.
[45] George Hill to Edward Cooke, 12 Sept. 1797, NAI, Rebellion Papers, 620/32/114. He was licensed by the Presbytery of Monaghan in 1795 but does not seem to have found a congregation.
[46] *BNL*, 26 June 1798.

61. Mr James Townsend of Greyabbey.[47]
62. Mr John Wardlow.[48]
63. Revd William Warnock of County Down.[49]

[47] George Stephenson to Downshire, 27–8 June 1798, PRONI, Downshire Papers, D607/F/28; 'Black Book', PRONI, McCance Collection, D272/1; Cooke to Nugent, 12 Aug. 1798, ibid., D272/40.

[48] 'Black Book', PRONI, McCance Collection, D272/1; list of members of United Irish committees, NAI, Rebellion Papers, 620/4/42/3.

[49] *BNL*, 7 Sept. 1798; Edward Cooke to Nugent, 12 Aug. 1798, PRONI, D272/40.

SELECT BIBLIOGRAPHY

PRIMARY SOURCES

Manuscripts

Belfast

Linenhall Library

Joy MSS

Presbyterian Historical Society of Ireland

Barber MSS
Campbell MSS
Stavely MSS

Public Record Office of Northern Ireland

D162 Dobbs Papers
D272 McCance Collection
D456 Additional Drennan Papers
D531 Drennan Notebooks
D553 Drennan–Bruce Papers
D561 John Galt's Diary
D562 Foster–Massareene Papers
D572 Macartney Papers
D607 Downshire Papers
D638 Downshire Papers
D668 Hezlett Papers
D714 Cleland Papers
D729 Drennan–Duffin Papers
D856 Sharman Crawford Papers
D1140 Weir Papers
D1606 Gosford Papers
D1748 Tennent Papers
D1759 D. Stewart Papers
D1857 Belfast Chamber of Commerce Records
D2092 Castleward Papers
D2673 Bruce Papers (uncatalogued)
D2966 McClelland Collection
D3030 Castlereagh Papers
D3077 Hart Papers
D3167 Stewart of Killymoon Papers
D3579 Notes on Revd James Porter
D3696 Morrow Papers
T765 Drennan Papers
T780 Crossle Papers
T965 Drennan MSS

T1053 Minutes of Presbytery of Antrim
T1101 Immigrants to New York, 1802–18
T1210 McCracken Papers
T1336 Dunlap Papers
T1815 Emigrant Letters to Robert Simms
T2541 Abercorn Papers
T2822 McSkimmin MSS
T2873 Ellison–Macartney Papers
T3030 Redesdale Papers
T3041 Bruce Papers
T3048 McPeake Papers
T3202/1A Minute Book of the First Newry Volunteers
T3229 Sneyd Papers
T3541 Caldwell Papers
T3578 Johnston Papers
T3649 Fitzwilliam/Grattan Papers
CR3/46/1 Minutes of Secession (Burgher) Synod, 1779–1814
CR4/7/C1 Hugh Moore, MS notebooks on the history of Newtownards First Presbyterian
    Church
CR5/9A/1 Minutes of the Reformed Session of Antrim
MIC 361 Down Election Pamphlets 1789–90

Queen's University of Belfast

James Bryson, MS Sermons (13 vols.)
Journal of a tour from Dublin to the north, 4 July 1781, Miscellaneous MSS (uncatalogued),
    Box 1 (1), acc. 58360

Derry

Magee College, University of Ulster

Steward Correspondence

Dublin

National Archives of Ireland

Rebellion Papers

Edinburgh

National Library of Scotland

Wodrow MSS

London

British Library

Add. MSS 38716 Northington Letterbook
Add. MSS 33100–1 Pelham Papers

Public Record Office

HO, 100 Home Office, Ireland
PRO30/8/329 Chatham Papers

Printed Collections of Documents

ADDISON, W. I., *A Roll of Graduates of the University of Glasgow, 1727–1897* (Glasgow, 1898).

—— *The Matriculation Albums of the University of Glasgow from 1728 to 1858* (Glasgow, 1913).

BARTLETT, THOMAS, 'Select Documents XXXVIII: Defenders and Defenderism in 1795', *IHS* 24 (1985), 373–94.

The Correspondence of Edmund Burke, ed. T. W. Copeland *et al.*, 10 vols. (Cambridge, 1958–78).

BURNS, ROBERT, 'The Holy Fair', in *The Poems and Songs of Robert Burns*, ed. James Kinsley, 3 vols. (Oxford, 1968), i. 128–37.

The Manuscripts and Correspondence of James, First Earl of Charlemont, 2 vols., HMC, 12th report, app. pt. 10 (1891), 13th report, app. pt. 8 (1894).

CHART, D. A. (ed.), *The Drennan Letters, 1776–1819* (Belfast, 1931).

[ANON.], 'Autobiographical Sketch of Andrew Craig 1754–1833', *UJA*, 2nd ser., 14 (1908), 10–15, 51–5.

CRAWFORD, W. H. (ed.), *Letters from an Ulster Land Agent 1774–85 (The Letter-Books of John Moore of Clough, County Down)* (Belfast, 1976).

—— and TRAINOR, BRIAN (eds.), *Aspects of Irish Social History 1750–1800* (Belfast, 1969).

FISK, W. L., 'The Diary of John Cuthbertson, Missionary to the Covenanters in Colonial Pennsylvania', *Pennsylvania Magazine of History and Biography*, 73 (1949), 441–58.

Records of the General Synod of Ulster from 1691 to 1820, 3 vols. (Belfast, 1890–9).

GILLESPIE, RAYMOND (ed.), *Settlement and Survival on an Ulster Estate: The Brownlow Leasebook 1667–1711* (Belfast, 1988).

GREEN, E. R. R., 'The "Strange Humours" that Drove the Scotch-Irish to America, 1729', *WMQ*, 3rd ser., 12 (1955), 113–23.

The Letters of David Hume, ed. J. Y. T. Grieg, 2 vols. (Oxford, 1932).

KELLY, JAMES, 'Select Documents XLVIII: A Secret Return of the Volunteers of Ireland in 1784', *IHS* 26 (1989), 268–92.

'Additional Manuscripts of Captain H. V. Knox', HMC, *Report on MSS in Various Collections*, vi (1909).

Macartney in Ireland 1768–72: A Calendar of the Chief Secretaryship Papers of Sir George Macartney, ed. Thomas Bartlett (Belfast, 1978).

McCONNELL, JAMES, and McCONNELL, SAMUEL, *Fasti of the Irish Presbyterian Church, 1613–1840*, ed. David Stewart, 2 vols. (Belfast, 1935–51).

McDOWELL, R. B., 'Select Documents II: United Irish Plans of Parliamentary Reform in 1793', *IHS* 3 (1942), 49–51.

MILLER, D. W. (ed.), *Peep O'Day Boys and Defenders: Selected Documents on the County Armagh Disturbances, 1784–96* (Belfast, 1990).

'Manuscripts of M. L. S. Clements, Esq. Preserved at Ashfield Lodge, Cootehill, County Cavan' [Molesworth Letters], HMC, *Report on Manuscripts in Various Collections*, viii (1913).

MURE, ELIZABETH, 'Some Remarks on the Change of Manners in My Own Time', in *Selections from the Family Papers Preserved at Caldwell*, ed. William Mure for the Maitland Club, 3 vols. (Glasgow, 1853–4), i. 259–72.

Pembroke Papers (1780–1794): Letters and Diaries of Henry, Tenth Earl of Pembroke and his Circle, ed. Lord Herbert, 2 vols. (London, 1950).

Correspondence Between the Rt. Hon. William Pitt and Charles, Duke of Rutland, 1781–1787 (London, 1842).

The Correspondence of Richard Price, ed. D. O. Thomas, 2 vols. to date (Cardiff, 1983–).

The Manuscripts of His Grace the Duke of Rutland, K.G. Preserved at Belvoir Castle, iii. HMC, 14th report, app. pt. 1 (1894).

[ROBERT STEWART, VISCOUNT CASTLEREAGH], *Memoirs and Correspondence of Viscount Castlereagh*, ed. Charles Vane, 3rd Marquis of Londonderry, 12 vols. (London, 1848–54).

The Letters of Lord Chief Baron Edward Willes to the Earl of Warwick 1757–62: An Account of Ireland in the Mid-Eighteenth Century, ed. James Kelly (Aberystwyth, 1990).

YOUNG, R. M. (ed.), 'News from Ireland: Being the Examination and Confession of William Kelso, &c., 1679', *UJA*, 2nd ser., 2 (1896), 274–9.

Parliamentary Proceedings and Reports

The Journals of the House of Commons of the Kingdom of Ireland, 19 vols. (Dublin, 1796–1800), ix–x, xv–xvii.

First Report of the Commissioners of Education in Ireland, HC (1825), xii.

First Report of the Commissioners of Public Instruction in Ireland, HC (1835), xxxiii.

Newspapers and Periodicals

Belfast Mercury
Belfast Monthly Magazine
Belfast News-Letter
Northern Star

Other Contemporary Works

ABERNETHY, JOHN, *The People's Choice, the Lord's Anointed: A Thanksgiving Sermon for his Most Excellent Majesty King George his Happy Accession to the Throne, his Arrival and Coronation. Preach'd at Antrim, October, 27, 1714* (Belfast, 1714).

—— *A Sermon Recommending the Study of Scripture-Prophecie, as an Important Duty, and a Great Means of Reviving Decay'd Piety and Charity: Preach'd in Belfast, June 19. 1716. Before the Presbyterian ministers of the North of Ireland, Met in their Annual Assembly* (Belfast, 1716).

—— *Religious Obedience Founded on Personal Persuasion. A Sermon Preach'd at Belfast, the 9th of December. 1719* (Belfast, 1720).

—— *Persecution Contrary to Christianity: A Sermon Preached in Wood-Street, Dublin, on the 23 of Oct, 1735, Being the Anniversary of the Irish Rebellion* (Dublin, 1735).

—— *A Letter from the Presbytery of Antrim, to the Congregations under their Care: Occasion'd by the Uncharitable Breach of Synodical Communion, Made by the General-Synod at Dungannon, June 25th, 1726* (Belfast, 1726).

—— *Sermons on Various Subjects*, 4 vols. (London, 1748–51).

—— *Scarce and Valuable Tracts and Sermons* (London, 1751).

ABERNETHY, JOHN [OF TEMPLEPATRICK], *Philalethes, or, Revelation Consistent with Reason: An Attempt to Answer the Objections and Arguments against it in Mr Paine's Book, Entitled, Age of Reason* (Belfast, 1795).

An Address to the Freeholders of the County of Antrim, Respecting the Choice of Representatives, to Serve in the Ensuing Parliament. By an Irishman (Belfast[?], 1789).

Advice to the Patriot Club, of the County of Antrim, on the Present State of Affairs in Ireland, and Some Late Changes in the Administration of that Kingdom (Dublin, 1756).

ALEXANDER, ANDREW, *The Advantages of a General Knowledge of the Use of Arms. A Sermon Preached before the Strabane, Finwater, and Urney Volunteers and Strabane Rangers in the Meeting-House of Urney, Oct. 1779* (Strabane, 1779).

[ANON.], *From Liberal Ulster to England* [London, 1886].

ANTRIM, PRESBYTERY OF, *A Narrative of the Proceedings of Seven General Synods of the Northern Presbyterians in Ireland, with Relation to their Differences in Judgement and Practice, from the Year 1720 to the Year 1726 in which they Issu'd in a Synodical Breach* (Belfast, 1727).

APPRICHARD, RICHARD, *Narrative of the Proceedings of the General Synod, which Met at Dungannon, 1739; Relating to Some Scruples, Against Subscribing the Westminster Confession of Faith, Referr'd to their Consideration* (Belfast, 1739).

ARMSTRONG, JAMES, *Observations on the State of Education in Belfast* (Belfast, 1807).

ASSOCIATE PRESBYTERY, *Act, Declaration and Testimony for the Doctrine, Worship, Discipline and Government of the Church of Scotland; Agreeable to the Word of God, the Confession of Faith, the National Covenant, and the Solemn League and Covenant of the Three Nations: and against Several Steps of Defection from the Same, Both in Former and Present Times* (Edinburgh, 1737).

—— *Address by the Associate Presbytery, to Reasons of Dissent, Given in to the Said Presbytery, at Stirling, Dec. 23. 1742; as Also, the Representation and Petition Dictated to their Clerk, and Reasons of Dissent and Secession Given in to them at Edinburgh, Feb. 3 1743; by the Reverend Mr Thomas Nairn, Minister of the Gospel at Abbotshall. Together with a Declaration and Defence of the Associate Presbytery's Principles Anent the Present Civil Government* (Edinburgh, 1744).

ASSOCIATE SYNOD, *A Testimony by the Associate Synod, against the Legal Encouragement Lately Given to Popery* (Edinburgh, 1778).

—— *A Warning against Popery. Drawn up, and Published, by Order of the Associate Synod, at their Meeting on the 2d of September 1778. To which are Subjoined, Observations on the Nature of the Laws now in Force against Popery; and on the Danger and Impropriety of Repealing Them* (Edinburgh, 1779).

BARBER, SAMUEL, *Remarks on a Pamphlet, Entitled The Present State of the Church of Ireland, by Richard, Lord Bishop of Cloyne* (Dublin, 1787).

—— *Reply to the Reverend Mr Burrowes and the Reverend Mr Ryan's Remarks Etc.* (Dublin, 1787).

BIRCH, THOMAS LEDLIE, *The Obligations upon Christians and Especially Ministers to be Exemplary in their Lives, Particularly at this Important Period when the Prophecies are Seemingly about to be Fulfilled in the Fall of Antichrist, as an Introduction to the Flowing in of Jew and Gentile into the Christian Church. A Sermon Preached before the very Reverend, the General Synod of Ulster, at Lurgan, June 26th, 1793* (Belfast, 1794).

—— *Physicians Languishing Under Disease. An Address to the Seceding, or Associate Synod of Ireland, upon Certain Tenets and Practices, Alledged to be in Enmity with all Religious Reformation* (Belfast, 1796).

—— *A Letter from an Irish Emigrant to his Friend in the United States Giving an Account of the Rise and Progress of the Commotions in Ireland of the United Irishmen and Orange Societies and of Several Battles and Military Executions* (Philadelphia, 1799).

—— *Seemingly Experimental Religion, Instructors Unexperienced [sic]—Converters Unconverted —Revivals Killing Religion—Missionaries in Need of Teaching—or, War against the Gospel by its Friends. Being the Examination of Thomas Ledlie Birch, a Foreign Ordained Minister by the Rev. Presbytery of Ohio, under the Very Rev. General Assembly's Alien Act* (Washington, Pa., 1806).

BLACK, ROBERT, *Substance of Two Speeches, Delivered in the General Synod of Ulster at its Annual Meeting in 1812. . . . With an Abstract of the Proceedings of the Synod Relative to the Rev. Doctor Dickson* (Dublin, 1812).

[BLACKBURNE, FRANCIS], *Memoirs of Thomas Hollis Esq.* (London, 1780).

BOYLE, FRANCIS, *Miscellaneous Poems* (Belfast, 1811).

[BRUCE, ARCHIBALD], *A Serious View of the Remarkable Providences of the Times: and a Warning as to the Public Sins, Dangers and Duty of British Protestants* (Glasgow, 1795).

BRUCE, MICHAEL, *The Rattling of the Dry Bones: or, A Sermon Preached in the Night Time at Chapel-Yard in the Parish of Carluke. Clydesdale 1672* (n.p., [1672]).

[BRUCE, WILLIAM (the bookseller)], *Some Facts and Observations Relative to the Fate of the Late Linen Bill, Last Session of Parliament in this Kingdom* (Dublin, 1753).

—— *Remarks on a Pamphlet Intitled Considerations on the Late Bill for Paying the National Debt etc*, 4 pts. (Dublin, 1754).

[BRUCE, REVD WILLIAM], *The History of the Last Session of Parliament, Addressed to the Rt. Hon. the Earl of Charlemont*, signed Gracchus (Dublin, 1784).

—— *The Christian Soldier. A Sermon Preached before the Belfast Merchants' Infantry, September 25, 1803* (Belfast, 1803).

—— 'The Progress of Non-Subscription to Creeds', *Christian Moderator*, 1–2 (1826–8).

[—— and JOY, HENRY (eds.)], *Belfast Politics; or, A Collection of the Debates, Resolutions and other Proceedings of that Town, in the years M,DCC,XCII, and M,DCC,XCIII. With Strictures on the Test of Certain of the Societies of United Irishmen: Also, Thoughts on the British Constitution* (Belfast, 1794).

BRYCE, JAMES, *A Narrative of the Proceedings of the Associate (Antiburgher) Synods, in Ireland and Scotland, in the Affair of the Royal Bounty. With Remarks on Ordination* (Belfast, 1816).

BURDY, SAMUEL, *The Life of the Rev. Philip Skelton* (Dublin, 1792).

BURGH, JAMES, *Political Disquisitions: or, An Enquiry into Public Errors, Defects and Abuses*, 3 vols. (London, 1774–5).

Memoirs of Miles Byrne, Chef de Bataillon in the Service of France, Officer of the Legion of Honour, Knight of Saint-Louis, etc., ed. by his widow, 3 vols. (New York, 1863).

CAMPBELL, WILLIAM, *The Presence of Christ with his Church in every Age and Period of it, Explained and Improved. A Discourse Delivered at Antrim, June 28, 1774. At a General Synod of the Protestant Dissenting Minsters of the Presbyterian Persuasion in Ulster* (Belfast, 1774).

—— *A Vindication of the Principles and Character of the Presbyterians in Ireland; Addressed to the Bishop of Cloyne, in Answer to his Book Entitled the Present State of the Church of Ireland* (Dublin, 1787).

—— *An Examination of the Bishop of Cloyne's Defence of his Principles; with Observations on Some His Lordship's Apologists, Particularly the Rev. Dr Stock: Containing an Inquiry into the Constitution and Effects of our Ecclesiastical Establishment; and also, an Historical Review of the Political Principles and Conduct of Presbyterians and Episcopals in Great Britain and Ireland* (Belfast, 1788).

A Candid and Impartial Account of the Disturbances in the County of Meath in the Years 1792, 1793, and 1794. By a County Meath Freeholder (Dublin, 1794).

CARLISLE, JOHN, *The Nature of Religious Zeal. A Sermon on Phil. 3: 6. Preached at a General Synod held in Antrim, June the Eighteenth, 1745* (Belfast, 1745).

CATHOLIC COMMITTEE, *Declaration of the General Committee of the Catholics* (Dublin, 1792).

Christ in Triumph, Coming to Judgement! As Recorded in the Most Holy Sacred Scriptures, by the Holy Prophets and Evangelists, by 'Revd A- B-' (Strabane, n.d.). A copy of this pamphlet can be found in NAI, Rebellion Papers, 620/29/8.

A Citizen of Londonderry, *A Test of Roman Catholic Liberality, Submitted to the Consideration of both Roman Catholicks and Protestants* (Londonderry, 1792).

A Citizen of the World, *Paine's Age of Reason, with Remarks, Containing a Vindication of the Doctrine of Christianity from the Aspersions of that Author* (Belfast, 1794).

CLARK, THOMAS, *New Light Set in a Clear Light* (Dublin, 1755).

—— *Pastoral Letter to the Associate Congregation of Presbyterians in Ballybay New Erection* (Monaghan, 1807). A copy of this pamphlet can be found in PRONI, T3549.

CLERK, MATTHEW, *A Letter from the Belfast Society. To the Reverend Mr Matthew Clerk, &c. with an Answer to the Society's Remarks on a Pamphlet lately Publish'd, Entitled, A Letter from the Country, to a Friend in Belfast, &c.* (Belfast[?], 1723).

A Cloud of Witnesses, for the Royal Prerogatives of Jesus Christ or, The Last Speeches and Testimonies of those who have Suffered for the Truth in Scotland since the Year 1680, 5th edn. (Glasgow, 1751).

A Collection of All the Authenticated Public Addresses, Resolutions, and Advertisements, Relative to the Late Election of Knights of the Shire for the County of Antrim: Together with a Correct List of the Poll, Alphabetically Arranged, Shewing at One View how and when Each Elector Voted. By a Member of the Independent Committee (Belfast, 1790).

A Collection of the Letters which Have been Addressed to the Volunteers of Ireland, on the Subject of a Parliamentary Reform (London, 1783).

COLVILLE, ALEXANDER, *The Persecuting, Disloyal and Absurd Tenets of those who Affect to Call themselves Seceders Laid Open and Refuted, in a Letter Addressed to the People under the Care of the Presbytery of Antrim* (Belfast, 1749).

—— *Some Important Queries Humbly and Earnestly Recommended to the Serious Consideration of the Protestant Dissenters in the North of Ireland, Belonging to the Synodical Association* (Belfast, 1773).

[CONWAY, FRANCIS I. S., VISCOUNT BEAUCHAMP], *A Letter to the First Belfast Company of Volunteers, in the Province of Ulster. By a Member of the British Parliament* (London, 1783).

COOPER, WILLIAM, *The Flying Angel: A Sermon, Delivered in the New Meeting House Armagh, Ireland, before the Committee of the Evangelical Society of Ulster, on Monday, the 27th of May, 1799* (London, 1799).

[COOTE, CHARLES, EARL OF BELLAMONT], *A Letter to Viscount Beauchamp, upon the Subject of his Letter to the First Belfast Company of Volunteers, in the Province of Ulster* (London, 1783).

CRAWFORD, WILLIAM, *Remarks on the Late Earl of Chesterfield's Letters to his Son* (London, 1776).

—— *The Connection betwixt Courage and the Moral Virtues Considered, in A Sermon Preached before the Volunteer Company of Strabane Rangers, on Sunday the Twelfth of September, 1779* (Strabane, 1779).

—— *A History of Ireland. From the Earliest Period, to the Present Time. In a Series of Letters, Addressed to William Hamilton, Esq.*, 2 vols. (Strabane, 1783).

—— *Regulations of the Strabane Academy, and an Address to the Students in General, on Opening that Seminary* (Strabane, 1785).

CROMBIE, JAMES, *A Sermon on the Love of Country. Preached before the First Company of Belfast Volunteers, Sunday 19th July 1778* (Belfast, 1778).

—— *The Expedience and Utility of Volunteer Associations for National Defence and Security in the Present Critical Situation of Public Affairs Considered, in a Sermon Preached before the United Companies of the Belfast Volunteers on Sunday, the first of August, 1779, in the Old Dissenting Meeting House* (Belfast, 1779).

—— *The Propriety of Setting apart a Portion of the Sabbath for the Purpose of Acquiring the Knowledge and Use of Arms in Times of Public Danger Illustrated. A Sermon Preached before the Belfast Volunteer Company 4 March 1781 in the Old Dissenting Meeting House* (Belfast, 1781).

DE BLÁCAM, AODH, *The Black North: An Account of the Six Counties of Unrecovered Ireland: Their People, Their Treasures, and Their History* (Dublin, 1938).

Declaration of the General Committee of the Catholics (Dublin, 1792).

The Declaration, Protestation and Testimony of a Poor Wasted, Desolate, Misrepresented and Re- proached Remnant of the Suffering Anti-Popish, Anti-Prelatick, Anti-Erastian, Anti-Sectarian, True Presbyterian Church of Christ in Scotland, United Together in Truth and Duty. Published against the Proclamation, Accession and Establishment of George D.[uke] of Hanover to be King in these Lands, and All his Abettors and Supporters, in Aprile 1715 (n.p., [1715]).

DELAP, HUGH, *An Inquiry Whether, and How Far, Magistracy is of a Divine Appointment, and of the Subjection Due Thereunto. A Sermon Preached in the Old-Bridge Meeting-House near Omagh, the 14th of Nov. 1779 before the Omagh and Cappagh Volunteers* (Strabane, 1779).

DICKSON, WILLIAM STEEL, *Sermons on the Following Subjects: (I) On the Advantages of National Repentance, Preached to the Protestant Dissenting Congregation of Ballyhalbert, December 13th, 1776, (II) On the Ruinous Effects of Civil War, Preached before the Protestant Dissenting Congregation of Ballyhalbert, February 27th, 1778, Being a Day Appointed by Government as a General Fast, (III) On the Coming of the Son of Man, Preached before the Particular Synod of Belfast, at their Annual Meeting, November 4th 1777, and Printed at their Request, (IV) On the Hope of Meeting, Knowing, and Rejoicing with Virtuous Friends, in a Future World* (Belfast, 1778).

—— *A Sermon on the Propriety and Advantages of Acquiring the Knowledge and Use of Firearms in Times of Danger. Preached before the Echlinville Volunteers on Sunday the 28th of March 1779* (Belfast, 1779).

—— *Three Sermons on the Subject of Scripture Politics* (Belfast, 1793).

—— *A Narrative of the Confinement and Exile of William Steel Dickson, D.D.* (Dublin, 1812).

—— *Retractions; or, A Review of, and Reply to, a Pamphlet, Entitled, Substance of Two Speeches, Delivered in the General Synod of Ulster, at its Annual Meeting, in 1812, by the Rev. Robert Black, D.D.* (Belfast, 1813).

DOBBS, FRANCIS, *A History of Irish Affairs, from the 12th of October, 1779, to the 15th of September, 1782, the Day of Lord Temple's Arrival* (Dublin, 1782).

DONALDSON, JOHN, *A Historical and Statistical Account of the Barony of the Upper Fews in the County of Armagh 1838* (Dundalk, 1923).

Drawcansir: or, The Mock Reform. An Heroic Poem (Dublin, 1784).

DRENNAN, WILLIAM, *A Letter to Edmund Burke Esq; by Birth an Irishman, by Adoption an Englishman. Containing Some Reflections on Patriotism, Party-spirit, and the Union of Free Nations. With Observations upon the Means on which Ireland Relies for Obtaining Political Independence* (Dublin, 1780).

—— *An Address to the Volunteers of Ireland, by the Author of A Letter to Edmund Burke Esq., Containing Reflections on Patriotism, Party Spirit, and the Union of Free Nations* (Dublin, 1781).

—— *Letters of Orellana, an Irish Helot, to the Seven Northern Counties not Represented in the National Assembly of Delegates, held at Dublin, October, 1784, for Obtaining a more Equal Representation of the People in the Parliament of Ireland* (Dublin, 1785).

—— 'The Volunteers of Ireland', in William Guthrie (ed.), *An Improved System of Modern Geography*, Royal Irish Academy edn. (Dublin, 1789), 495–512.

—— 'Intended Defence, on a Trial for Sedition, in the Year 1794', reprinted in John Larkin (ed.), *The Trial of William Drennan* (Dublin, 1991), 121–39.

—— *A Philosophical Essay on the Moral and Political State of Ireland in a Letter to his Excellency Earl Fitzwilliam* (Dublin, 1795).

—— *A Letter to the Right Honourable William Pitt* (Dublin, 1799).

—— *A Second Letter to the Right Honourable William Pitt* (Dublin, 1799).

—— *A Protest against an Union* (Dublin, 1800).

—— *A Letter to the Right Honourable Charles James Fox*, 2nd edn. (Dublin, 1806).

DRUMMOND, W. H., *The Man of Age. A Poem* (Belfast, 1797).

—— *Hibernia. A Poem* (Belfast, 1797).

—— *Posthumous Sermons*, ed. J. S. Porter (Dublin, 1867).

DUCHAL, JAMES, *A Sermon on Occasion of the Much Lamented Death of the Late Reverend Mr John Abernethy* (Belfast, 1741).

'An Elder', *Analytical Review of a Pamphlet Lately Published by a Person Styling Himself the Rev. Robert Black, D.D. In a Series of Letters* (Belfast, 1813).

EMMET, THOMAS ADDIS, 'Part of an Essay towards the History of Ireland', in W. J. MacNeven, *Pieces of Irish History* (New York, 1807), 1–114.

FLEMING, ROBERT, *A Discourse on the Rise and Fall of Antichrist; Wherein the Revolution in France, and the Downfall of Monarchy in that Kingdom are Distinctly Pointed Out. Delivered at London, in the Year 1701*, with a preface by William Stavely (Belfast, 1795). A copy of this pamphlet can be found in NAI, Rebellion Papers, 620/22/63.

[FLETCHER, WILLIAM], *The Scripture-Loyalist: Containing a Vindication of Obedience to the Present Civil British Government in Things Lawful* (Glasgow, 1784).

—— *The Scripture-Loyalist Defended, from Unfair and False Reasoning: with a Refutation of False Glosses Imposed on Several Passages of the Holy Scriptures* (Falkirk, 1795).

[ANON.], *A Letter to Henry Flood, Esq. on the Present State of Representation in Ireland* (Belfast, 1783).

Fragment of a Letter to a Friend, relative to the repeal of the Test (Dublin, 1780).

From Liberal Ulster to England [London, 1886].

GAMBLE, JOHN, *Sketches of History, Politics and Manners Taken in Dublin, and the North of Ireland, in the Autumn of 1810* (London, 1811).

—— *A View of Society and Manners in the North of Ireland in the Summer and Autumn of 1812* (London, 1813).

—— *Views of Society and Manners in the North of Ireland, in a Series of Letters Written in the Year 1818* (London, 1819).

GIB, ADAM, *A Warning against Countenancing the Ministrations of Mr George Whitfield, Published in the New Church at Bristow, upon Sabbath, June 6, 1742* (Edinburgh, 1742).

[GRACE, GEORGE], *Presbyterio-Catholicon: or A Refutation of the Modern Catholic Doctrines, Propagated by Several Societies of Catholic Presbyterians, and Presbyterian Catholics, in a Letter to the Real Roman Catholics of Ireland* (Dublin, 1792).

HALIDAY, SAMUEL, *Reasons Against the Imposition of Subscription to the Westminster Confession of Faith; or, Any Such Human Tests of Orthodoxy* (Belfast, 1724).

—— *A Letter to the Reverend Gilbert Kennedy; Occasion'd by Some Personal Reflections, Contain'd in his Answer to Mr Haliday's Reasons against the Imposition of Subscription to the Westminster-Confession, or Any Such Human Tests of Orthodoxy* (Belfast, 1725).

HANNA, HUGH, *Scotland, Ulster, and Home Rule for Ireland: A Letter Addressed to a Friend in Scotland* (Dublin, 1888).

[HENRY, HENRY], *An Address to the People of Connor, Containing a Clear and Full Vindication of the Synod of Ulster: From the Aspersions of the People called Covenanters. Written in the Name of Sanders Donald: Late Sexton of Connor* (Belfast[?], 1794).

—— 'Presbyter', *An Illustrative of the Present Critical State of the Synod of Ulster in Three Letters* (n.p., 1802).

[ANON.], *An Historical Account of the Late Election of Knights of the Shire for the County of Down. Together with the Petition to Parliament Complaining of an Undue Election and Return for the Said County; and the Proceedings thereon. And also, the several addresses, songs, squibs &c. which were published before and during the election* (n.p., 1784).

—— *History of the Proceedings and Debates of the Volunteer Delegates of Ireland on the Subject of a Parliamentary Reform* (Dublin, 1784).

HOUSTON, THOMAS, *The Covenanter's Plea and Narrative* (Belfast, 1841).

HULL, JAMES, *Religion Founded upon Knowledge, and Productive of Forbearance, Moderation, and Peace. A Sermon Preached before a General Synod, of Protestant Dissenting Ministers; at their Annual Meeting in Dungannon, June 26th, 1770* (Belfast, 1770).

HUME, DAVID, *Essays Moral, Political and Literary*, ed. E. F. Miller, rev. edn. (Indianapolis, 1987).

[HUTCHESON, FRANCIS], *Considerations on Patronage. Addressed to the Gentlemen of Scotland* (London, 1735).

JAMES, WILLIAM, *Homesius Enervatus. A Letter, Addressed to Mr John Holmes; Containing, Ist. An Essay Church Communion. IId. The Terms of Church Communion Held by the Reformed-Presbytery, Vindicated. IIId. Grounds of Separation from the Synod of Ireland. And, IVthly, Animadversions upon a Pamphlet, Intitled, a Testimony, &c, Written by Mr Holmes, Minister at Glendermond* (Londonderry, 1772).

JONES, WILLIAM TODD, *A Letter to the Electors of the Borough of Lisburn* (Dublin, 1784).

—— *A Letter to the Societies of United Irishmen of the Town of Belfast, upon the Subject of Certain Apprehensions which have Arisen from a Proposed Restoration of Catholic Rights* (Dublin, 1792).

—— *Reply to an Anonymous Writer from Belfast, Signed Portia* (Dublin, 1792).

[JOY, HENRY (ed.)], *Historical Collections Relative to the Town of Belfast, from the Earliest Period to the Union with Great Britain* (Belfast, 1817).

KELBURN, SINCLAIR, *The Morality of the Sabbath Defended. A Sermon, Preached in the Third Meeting-House in Belfast* (Belfast, 1781).

KENNEDY, GILBERT, *A Defence of the Principles and Conduct of the Reverend General Synod of Ulster* (Belfast, 1724).

KENNEDY, GILBERT, JUN., *The Wicked Ruler; or, The Mischiefs of Absolute Arbitrary Power. A Sermon Preached at Belfast, December 18th, 1745, Being the Day of the General Fast Appointed by the Government* (Belfast, 1745).

—— *The Great Blessing of Peace and Truth in Our Days. A Sermon Preach'd at Belfast on Tuesday, April 25th, 1749. Being the Day of Public Thanksgiving for the Peace* (Belfast, 1749).

—— *The Ambitious Designs of Wicked Men, under the Restraint of Divine Providence, and Made Subservient to Wise and Good Ends. A Sermon Preached at Belfast, on Thursday, November 29, 1759. Being the Day of Public Thanksgiving Appointed by Authority, for the Success of the Preceding Campaign* (Belfast, 1759).

KING, JOHN, *Remarks on the Reverend S. M. Stephenson's Declaration of Faith. And his Reasons for not Subscribing the Westminster Confession of Faith. To which are Annexed, Reasons of Dissent, of Some of the Members of the Old Presbytery of Bangor, now Members of the Presbytery of Belfast, Respecting Mr Stephenson's Ordination* (Belfast, 1774).

[KIRKPATRICK, JAMES], *An Historical Essay Upon the Loyalty of Presbyterians in Great Britain and Ireland from the Reformation to this Present Year 1713. Wherein Their Steady Adherence to the Protestant Interest, our Happy Civil Constitution, the Succession of Protestant Princes, the Just Prerogatives of the Crown, and the Liberties of the People is Demonstrated from Public Records, the Best Approv'd Histories, the Confession of their Adversaries, and Divers Valuable*

Original Papers Well Attested, and Never Before Published. And an ANSWER Given to the Calumnies of their Accusers, and Particularly to Two Late Pamphlets, viz 1. A Sample of True Blue Presbyterian Loyalty &c. 2. The Conduct of the Dissenters of Ireland &c. (Belfast[?], 1713).

——— *A Vindication of the Presbyterians in the North of Ireland* (Belfast, 1724). This pamphlet was published under the name of Dr Victor Ferguson, an elder in the Second Belfast Congregation.

KNOWLES, JAMES, *An Appeal to the Dignified Visitors and the Noblemen and Gentlemen, Proprietors of the Belfast Acadical Institution* (Belfast, 1817).

LAWLESS, JOHN, *The Belfast Politics, Enlarged; Being a Compendium of the Political History of Ireland for the Last Forty Years* (Belfast, 1818).

A Layman's Sermon, Preach'd at the Patriot Club of the County of Armagh, which Met at Armagh, the 3rd of September, 1755 (Dublin, 1755).

LELAND, THOMAS, *A Sermon Preached in the Church of St. Anne's, Dublin, on Wednesday the 10th of February, 1779; being the Day Appointed by Authority for a General Fast and Humiliation* (Dublin, 1779).

A Letter from a Blacksmith, to the Ministers and Elders of the Church of Scotland. In which the Manner of Public Worship in that Church is Considered; and its Inconveniences and Defects Pointed Out; and Methods for Removing them Humbly Proposed, signed A. T. Blacksmith (London, 1759). Attributed, almost certainly falsely, to John Witherspoon by the British Library.

A Letter to the People of Ireland, on the Subject of Tythes. By a Friend to the Constitution (Dublin, 1758).

Letters Addressed to the Electors of the County of Antrim. By a Freeholder (Belfast, 1776).

LYND, R. J., *The Present Crisis in Ireland* (Belfast, 1886).

[McBRIDE, JOHN], *A Sample of Jet-Black Prelatick Calumny. In Answer to a Pamphlet, Called, Treu-Bleu Presbyterian Loyalty* (Glasgow, 1713).

MACDERMOTT, J., *Grattan's Parliament, and 90 Years of Union* (Belfast, 1892).

MACGEOGH, ROBERT, *Ulster's Apology for Being Loyal* (Belfast, 1888).

MACKAY, JAMES, *The Happiness of the Righteous in a Future State, Explained and Improved. A Sermon Preached in the Old Meeting-House in Belfast, February 28th, 1768. On Occasion of the Death of the Late Reverend Mr Thomas Drennan, Pastor of that Congregation, who Departed this Life, February 14, 1768* (Belfast, 1768).

McKINNEY, JAMES, 'A View of the Rights of God and Man', extracted in *The Covenanter*, 1 (1831). This pamphlet was originally published in 1793 but there are no surviving copies.

MACLAINE, ALEXANDER, *A Sermon Preached at Antrim, December 18, 1745. Being the National Fast* (Dublin, 1746).

MACNEVEN, WILLIAM JAMES, *Pieces of Irish History, Illustrative of the Condition of the Origin and Progress of the Political System of the United Irishmen; and of their Transactions with the Anglo-Irish Government* (New York, 1807).

McSKIMMIN, SAMUEL, *Annals of Ulster: or Ireland Fifty Years Ago* (Belfast, 1849).

MOLYNEUX, WILLIAM, *The Case of Ireland's Being Bound by Acts of Parliament in England Stated* (Dublin, 1698; repr. Belfast, 1776).

MOODY, JAMES, *A Sermon Occasion'd by the Present Rebellion in Scotland, Preached at Newry, October the 6th 1745* (Belfast, 1745).

——— *A Sermon Preached at Donoughmore, on Thursday October the Ninth, 1746. Being the General Thanksgiving for the Suppression of the Late Rebellion. Published at the Desire of Captain Johnston's Independent Company of Militia, to whom it was Preached* (Belfast, 1746).

MUSGRAVE, RICHARD, *Memoirs of the Different Rebellions in Ireland, from the Arrival of the English: with a Particular Detail of that which Broke Out the XXIIID of May, MDCCXCVIII; the History of the Conspiracy which Preceded it; and the Characters of the Principal Actors in it* (Dublin, 1801).

NEITHERSIDE, TOM, *A Candid Review of the Merits of the Present Candidates, for the Representation of the County of Antrim: Containing a Short History of the Contested Elections for the County, for a Century Past* (n.p., 1790).

NEVIN, WILLIAM, *The Nature and Evidence of an Over-Ruling Providence Considered. A Sermon, Preached before the Downe Volunteers, and Fuzileers [sic], on the 5th of September, 1779* (Belfast, 1779).

New Light [Dublin, 1725], anonymous broadside in the British Library.

A New Song Called the Beautiful Phoenix, Together with the Battle of Bunker's Hill (Belfast, [1776]).

NICHOLSON, JOHN, *A Lecture and Sermon: Preached at Belfast* (Belfast, 1799).

The Patriot Soldier; or, Irish Volunteer. A Poem. By a Member of the First Belfast Company (Belfast, 1789).

PATTERSON, JAMES, *The Rights of Kings, and the Duties of Subjects, Explained and Enforced from Sacred Scripture: in A Sermon Preached to the Presbyterian Congregation of Ballee* (Belfast, 1793).

[ANON.], *A Plain Statement of Facts in Answer to Certain Charges, Adduced by Francis Plowden, Esq. in his History of Ireland, against the Rev. Philip Johnson* (Lisburn, 1905; first pub. Dublin, 1814).

POCOCKE, RICHARD, *Pococke's Tour in Ireland in 1752*, ed. G. T. Stokes (Dublin, 1891).

POLLOCK, JOHN ('OWEN ROE O'NIAL'), 'Letters to the Men of Ireland' (first pub. Dublin, 1779; repr. in J. Lawless (ed.), *The Belfast Politics, Enlarged* (Belfast, 1818), 111–54).

—— *Letter to the Inhabitants of the Town and Lordship of Newry* (Dublin, 1793).

[PORTER, JAMES], 'Billy Bluff and Squire Firebrand', *Northern Star*, 18 July 1796 (repr. Belfast, 1868).

—— *Wind and Weather. A Sermon on the Late Providential Storm which Dispersed the French Fleet off Botany Bay. Preached to the Congregation of Gray-Abbey, on Thursday the 16th February, Being the Day Appointed by Government for Thanksgiving* (Belfast, 1797).

PRICE, RICHARD, *A Discourse on the Love of Our Country, Delivered on Nov. 4, 1789, at the Meeting-House in the Old Jewry, to the Society for Commemorating the Revolution in Great Britain* (London, 1789).

PRINGLE, FRANCIS, *The Gospel Ministry, an Ordinance of Christ; and the Duty of Ministers and People: A Sermon, at the Opening of the Associate Synod of Ireland, in Belfast—July 12, 1796* (Belfast[?], 1796).

REFORMED PRESBYTERY, *Act, Declaration, and Testimony, for the Whole of our Covenanted Reformation, as Attained to, and Established in Britain and Ireland; Particularly, betwixt the Years of 1638 and 1649, Inclusive: as Also, against all the Steps of Defection from Said Reformation, whether in Former or Later Times, since the Overthrow of that Glorious Work, Down to this Present Day*, 3rd edn. (Edinburgh, 1777).

—— *Testimony and Warning against the Blasphemies and Idolatry of Popery; the Evil and Danger of Every Encouragement Given to it. And more Particularly, of that Toleration Granted by the Legislature in the Revocation of the Penal Statutes against Papists in England and Ireland. Addressed to all Professors of the Protestant Religion* (Edinburgh, 1779).

—— *Act of the Reformed Presbytery for a Public Fast, with a Summary of the Causes Thereof* (Glasgow, 1795).

REID, JAMES SEATON, *The History of the Presbyterian Church, Briefly Reviewed and Practically Improved* (Belfast, 1828).

REID, JOHN, *Truth No Enemy to Peace. Animadversions on the Rev. Mr Fletcher's Defence of his Scripture-Loyalist* (Falkirk, 1799).

Remarks on a Late Pamphlet Entitled, Advice to the Patriot Club of the County of Antrim in a Letter from a Member of that Club to his Friend in Dublin (Dublin, 1756).

The Repealer Repulsed! A Correct Narrative of the Rise and Progress of the Repeal Invasion of Ulster (Belfast, 1841).

ROGERS, JOHN, *A Sermon Preached at Lisnavein, Otherwise Ballybay New Erection, on Saturday, June 10, 1780. To the Lisnavein Independent Rangers, Trough Volunteers, Lisluney Volunteers, and Monaghan Rangers* (Edinburgh, 1780).

Autobiography of Archibald Hamilton Rowan, Esq., ed. W. H. Drummond (Dublin, 1840).

[SAMPSON, GEORGE VAUGHAN], *Remarks on the State of the Catholic Question in Ireland.* . . . *By a Clergyman of the Church of England, Member of the Royal Irish Academy, and a Citizen of London-Derry* (Belfast, 1793).

[SAMPSON, WILLIAM], *Advice to the Rich: In a Series of Letters, Originally Published in the Northern Star: by an Independent Country Gentleman* (Belfast, 1796).

A Second Letter to the People of Ireland, on the Subject of Tythes. With a Particular Address to the Dissenters. To which is Added, a State of the Case of the Inhabitants of the Province of Ulster, in Relation to the Demands of the Clergy. By a Friend to the Constitution (Dublin, 1758).

SHERRARD, JOHN, *A Few Observations on the Nature and Tendency of the Changes Lately Proposed to be Made in the Constitution of the Protestant Dissenting Church, shewing how far these Changes, if Adopted, are Likely to Affect the Honour, Peace, and Prosperity of that Church, and the Only Constitutional Way of Preventing these Bad Effects Pointed Out* (Belfast, 1803).

SINCLAIR, ROBERT, *Fortitude Explained and Recommended. A Sermon, Delivered before the Larne Volunteers, the First of August, 1779* (Belfast, 1779).

STAVELY, WILLIAM, *War Proclaimed, and Victory Ensured; or, The Lamb's Conquests Illustrated* (Belfast, 1795).

—— *Appeal to Light; or, The Tenets of Deists Examined and Disapproved; and the Authority of the Holy Scriptures Asserted and Vindicated* (Belfast, 1796).

STEVEN, WILLIAM, *Answers to Twelve Queries, Proposed to the Serious Consideration of the Reformed Presbytery and their Followers* (n.p., 1794).

—— *Letter Second to the Reverend William Fletcher* (Glasgow, 1798).

TEELING, CHARLES HAMILTON, *Personal Narrative of the 'Irish Rebellion' of 1798* (London, 1828).

THORBURN, JOHN, *Vindiciae Magistratus: or, The Divine Institution and Right of the Civil Magistrate Vindicated . . . against the Truly Factious and Immoral Doctrine of John Thomson (Burgher Associate) Minister of the Gospel at Donaghcloney in Ireland, now at Kirkintilloch near Glasgow, Maintained in his Pretended Confutation of the Principles of the Reformed Presbytery, in a pamphlet intituled The Presbyterian Covenanter Displayed in his Political Principles, and the Impostor Detected* (Edinburgh, 1773).

[TISDALL, WILLIAM], *A Sample of Treu-Blew Presbyterian Loyalty, in all Changes and Turns of Government* (Dublin, 1709).

—— *The Conduct of the Dissenters of Ireland, with Respect to Church and State* (Dublin, 1712).

—— *The Nature and Tendency of Popular Phrases in General. With a Particular Enquiry into those Two which are Calculated to Exasperate the Protestant Dissenters of Ireland, Against the Church and Legislature, viz. Persecution of Protestants. And, Ranking the Dissenters in the Same Class with the Irish Papists* (Dublin, 1714[?]).

TONE, THEOBALD WOLFE, *An Argument on Behalf of the Catholics of Ireland* (Dublin, 1791).

The Life of Theobald Wolfe Tone, ed. W. T. W. Tone, 2 vols. (Washington, 1826).

Town Meeting. A Handbill, Lately Circulated from the Belfast Post-Office, and Cool Strictures Thereon. By a Townsman (Belfast, 1797).

WAKEFIELD, EDWARD, *An Account of Ireland, Statistical and Political*, 2 vols. (London, 1812).

[WITHERSPOON, JOHN], *Ecclesiastical Characteristics; or, the Arcana of Church Policy. Being an Humble Attempt to Open up the Mystery of Moderation* (Glasgow, 1753).

WODROW, ROBERT, *Analecta: or, Materials for a History of Remarkable Providences: Mostly Relating to Scotch Ministers and Christians*, ed. Matthew Leishman for the Maitland Club, 4 vols. (Glasgow, 1842–3).

WOODWARD, RICHARD, *The Present State of the Church of Ireland: Containing a Description of its Precarious Situation; and the Consequent Danger to the Public. Recommended to the Serious Consideration of the Friends of the Protestant Interest. To which are Subjoined, Some Reflections on the Impracticability of a Proper Commutations for Tithes; and A General Account of the Origin and Progress of the Insurrection in Munster* (Dublin, 1787).

WYLIE, SAMUEL BROWN, *The Two Sons of Oil; or The Faithful Witness for Magistracy and Ministry upon a Scriptural Basis. Also, A Sermon on Covenanting* (Greensburg, Pa., 1803).

—— *Memoir of Alexander McLeod, D.D.* (New York, 1855).

SECONDARY SOURCES

Nineteenth Century

ANDERSON, JOHN, *History of the Belfast Library and Society for Promoting Knowledge, Commonly Known as the Linenhall Library* (Belfast, 1888).

ARMSTRONG, J., *History of the Presbyterian Churches in the City of Dublin* (Dublin, 1829).

BENN, GEORGE, *A History of the Town of Belfast from Earliest Times to the Close of the Eighteenth Century* (London, 1877).

DILL, J. R., *The Dill Worthies* (Belfast, 1888).

FERGUSON, SAMUEL, *Brief Biographical Sketches of Some Irish Covenanting Ministers who Laboured During the Late Half of the Eighteenth Century* (Londonderry, 1897).

[GORDON, ALEXANDER, and SMITH, G. K.], *Historic Memorials of the First Presbyterian Church of Belfast* (Belfast, 1887).

HARDY, FRANCIS, *Memoirs of the Political and Private Life of James Caulfeild, Earl of Charlemont* (London, 1810).

HINCKS, T. D., 'Notices of William Bruce, and of his Contemporaries and Friends, Hutcheson, Abernethy, Duchal, and others', *Christian Teacher*, NS 5 (1843), 72–92.

HUTCHISON, MATTHEW, *The Reformed Presbyterian Church in Scotland: Its Origin and History 1680–1876* (Paisley, 1893).

IRWIN, C. H., *History of Presbyterianism in Dublin and the South and West of Ireland* (London, 1890).

LATIMER, W. T., *A History of the Irish Presbyterians* (Belfast, [1893]).

—— *Ulster Biographies, Relating Chiefly to the Rebellion of 1798* (Belfast, 1897).

LECKY, W. E. H., *A History of Ireland in the Eighteenth Century*, 5 vols. (London, 1913; first pub. 1892).

MCKERROW, JOHN, *History of the Secession Church*, rev. and enlarged edn. (Glasgow, 1841).

MCKNIGHT, THOMAS, *Ulster as It Is; or Twenty-Eight Years' Experience as an Irish Editor*, 2 vols. (London, 1896).

MADDEN, R. R., *The United Irishmen, their Lives and Times*, 3 ser., 7 vols. (London, 1842–6).

MANT, RICHARD, *History of the Church of Ireland*, 2 vols. (London, 1840).

MILLER, J. P. (ed.), *Biographical Sketches and Sermons of Some of the First Ministers of the Associate Church in America* (Albany, 1839).

MONTGOMERY, HENRY, 'Outlines of the History of Presbyterianism in Ireland', *Irish Unitarian and Bible Christian*, 2 (1847).

PARNELL, WILLIAM, *An Enquiry into the Causes of Popular Discontents in Ireland by an Irish Country Gentleman* (London, 1805).

PORTER, J. L., *The Life and Times of Henry Cooke* (London, 1871).

[ANON.], 'Biographical Sketch of the Reverend Francis Pringle', in J. P. Miller (ed.), *Biographical Sketches and Sermons, of Some of the First Ministers of the Associate Church in America* (Albany, [NY], 1839).

REID, J. S., *History of the Presbyterian Church in Ireland*, ed. W. D. Killen, 3rd edn., 3 vols. (Belfast, 1867).

SCOTT, DAVID, *Annals and Statistics of the Original Secession Church: Till its Disruption and Union with the Free Church of Scotland in 1852* (Edinburgh, 1886).

SHAW, J. J., *Mr Gladstone's Two Irish Policies: 1868 and 1896. A Letter to an Ulster Liberal Elector* (London, 1888).

SPRAGUE, W. B., *Annals of the American Pulpit*, 7 vols. (New York, 1857–61).

WITHEROW, THOMAS, *Derry and Enniskillen in the Year 1689: The Story of Some Famous Battlefields in Ulster* (Belfast, 1873).

—— (ed.), *Historical and Literary Memorials of Presbyterianism in Ireland*, 2 vols. (Belfast, 1879–80).

YOUNG, R. M., *Ulster in '98: Episodes and Anecdotes* (Belfast, [1893]).

Twentieth Century

ADAMS, J. R. R., 'Reading Societies in Ulster', *Ulster Folklife*, 26 (1980), 55–64.

—— *The Printed Word and the Common Man: Popular Culture in Ulster 1700–1900* (Belfast, 1987).

ALLEN, ROBERT, *James Seaton Reid: A Centenary Biography* (Belfast, 1951).

APPLEBY, JOYCE, 'Republicanism and Ideology', *American Quarterly*, 37 (1985), 461–73.

BAILIE, W. D., *Edengrove Presbyterian Church 1774–1974* (Newcastle, Co. Down, 1974).

—— 'William Steel Dickson, D.D.', *Bulletin of the Presbyterian Historical Society of Ireland*, 6 (May 1976).

—— 'The Revd Samuel Barber 1738–1811: National Volunteer and United Irishman', in J. L. M. Haire *et al.*, *Challenge and Conflict* (Antrim, 1981), 72–95.

—— (ed.), *A History of Congregations in the Presbyterian Church in Ireland 1610–1982* (Belfast, 1982).

BAILYN, BERNARD, *The Ideological Origins of the American Revolution* (Cambridge, Mass., 1967).

BAKER, S. E., 'Orange and Green: Belfast, 1832–1912', in H. J. Dyos and M. Wolff (eds.), *The Victorian City: Images and Realities*, 2 vols. (London, 1973), ii. 789–814.

BARDON, JONATHAN, *A History of Ulster* (Belfast, 1992).

BARKLEY, J. M., *The Westminster Formularies in Irish Presbyterianism* (Belfast, 1956[?]).

—— *A Short History of the Presbyterian Church in Ireland* (Belfast, 1959).

—— *The Eldership in Irish Presbyterianism* (Belfast, 1963).

—— 'The Arian Schism in Ireland, 1830', in Derek Baker (ed.), *Studies in Church History*, ix, *Schism, Heresy and Religious Protest* (Oxford, 1972), 323–39.

BARKLEY, J. M., 'The Presbyterian Minister in Eighteenth-Century Ireland', in J. L. M. Haire *et al.*, *Challenge and Conflict* (Antrim, 1981), 46–71.

BARLOW, R. B., *Citizenship and Conscience: A Study in the Theory and Practice of Religious Toleration in England During the Eighteenth Century* (Philadelphia, 1962).

—— 'The Career of John Abernethy (1680–1740), Father of Nonsubscription in Ireland and Defender of Religious Liberty', *Harvard Theological Review*, 78 (1985), 399–419.

BARNARD, T. C., 'The Uses of 23 October and Irish Protestant Celebrations', *English Historical Review*, 106 (1991), 889–920.

—— 'Reforming Irish Manners: The Religious Societies in Dublin during the 1690s', *Historical Journal*, 35 (1992), 805–38.

—— 'Protestants and the Irish Language, *c.*1675–1725', *Journal of Ecclesiastical History*, 44 (1993), 243–72.

—— 'Identities, Ethnicity and Tradition among Irish Dissenters, *c.*1650–1760', in Kevin Herlihy (ed.), *The Irish Dissenting Tradition 1650–1750* (Blackrock, Co. Dublin, 1995), 29–48.

—— 'Improving Clergymen, 1660–1760', in Alan Ford, James McGuire, and Kenneth Milne (eds.), *As by Law Established: The Church of Ireland since the Reformation* (Dublin, 1995), 136–51.

BARTLETT, THOMAS, 'An End to Moral Economy: the Irish Militia Disturbances of 1793', *Past & Present*, 99 (1983), 41–64.

—— 'Review Article: A New History of Ireland', *Past & Present*, 116 (1987), 206–17.

—— '"A People Made Rather for Copies than Originals": The Anglo-Irish, 1760–1800', *International History Review*, 12/1 (February 1990), 11–25.

—— *The Fall and Rise of the Irish Nation: The Catholic Question 1690–1830* (Dublin, 1992).

—— and HAYTON, D. W. (eds.), *Penal Era and Golden Age: Essays in Irish History, 1690–1800* (Belfast, 1979).

BECKETT, J. C., 'William King's Administration of the Diocese of Derry, 1691–1703', *IHS* 4 (1994).

—— *Protestant Dissent in Ireland 1687–1780* (London, 1948).

—— 'Swift: The Priest in Politics', in id., *Confrontations: Studies in Irish History* (London, 1972), 111–22.

BEW, PAUL, *Ideology and the Irish Question: Ulster Unionism and Irish Nationalism 1912–1916* (Oxford, 1994).

—— and WRIGHT, FRANK, 'The Agrarian Opposition in Ulster Politics, 1848–87', in S. Clark and J. S. Donnelly, jun. (eds.), *Irish Peasants: Violence and Political Unrest, 1780–1914* (Madison, Wis., 1983).

[BIGGER, F. J.], 'Alexander Peden, the "Prophet"', *UJA*, 2nd ser., 9 (1903), 116–27.

BLOCH, R. H., *Visionary Republic: Millennial Themes in American Thought, 1756–1800* (Cambridge, 1985).

BOLAM, C. G. (ed.), *The English Presbyterians from Elizabethan Puritanism to Modern Unitarianism* (London, 1968).

BONOMI, PATRICIA, *Under the Cope of Heaven: Religion, Society and Politics in Colonial America* (Oxford, 1986).

BONWICK, COLIN, *English Radicals and the American Revolution* (Chapel Hill, 1977).

BOYCE, D. G., *Nationalism in Ireland*, 2nd edn. (London, 1991).

—— and O' DAY, ALAN (eds.), *The Making of Modern Irish History: Revisionism and Revisionist Controversy* (London, 1996).

—— ECCLESHALL, ROBERT, and GEOGHEGAN, VINCENT (eds.), *Political Thought in Ireland since the Seventeenth Century* (London, 1993).

BRADLEY, J. E., 'Whigs and Nonconformists: "Slumbering Radicalism" in English Politics, 1739–1789', *Eighteenth-Century Studies*, 9 (1975–6), 1–27.

—— 'The Anglican Pulpit, the Social Order, and the Resurgence of Toryism during the American Revolution', *Albion*, 21 (1989), 361–88.

—— *Religion, Revolution and English Radicalism: Nonconformity in Eighteenth-Century Politics and Society* (Cambridge, 1990).

BRADSHAW, BRENDAN, 'Nationalism and Historical Scholarship in Modern Ireland', *IHS* 26 (1989), 347–8.

BRADY, CIARAN, *Interpreting Irish History: The Debate on Historical Revisionism, 1938–1994* (Dublin, 1994).

BRAIDWOOD, JOHN, 'Ulster and Elizabethan English', in Ulster Folk Museum, *Ulster Dialects: An Introductory Symposium* (Holywood, 1964), 5–45.

BREWER, JOHN, *Party Ideology and Popular Politics at the Accession of George III* (Cambridge, 1976).

BRIC, M. J., 'Priests, Parsons and Politics: The Rightboy Protest in County Cork, 1785–1788', in C. H. E. Philpin (ed.), *Nationalism and Popular Protest in Ireland* (Cambridge, 1987), 163–90.

BRIDENBAUGH, CARL, *Mitre and Sceptre: Transatlantic Faiths, Ideas, Personalities, and Politics, 1689–1775* (New York, 1962).

BRIMS, JOHN, 'The Covenanting Tradition and Scottish Radicalism in the 1790s', in Terry Brotherstone (ed.), *Covenant, Charter, and Party: Traditions of Revolt and Protest in Modern Scottish History* (Aberdeen, 1989), 50–62.

BROOKE, PETER, *Ulster Presbyterianism: The Historical Perspective, 1610–1970* (Dublin, 1987).

BROWN, A. W. G., 'A Theological Interpretation of the First Subscription Controversy (1719–1728)', in J. L. M. Haire *et al.*, *Challenge and Conflict* (Antrim, 1981), 28–43.

BROWN, T. M., 'The Image of the Beast: Anti-Papal Rhetoric in Colonial America', in R. O. Curry and T. M. Brown (eds.), *Conspiracy: The Fear of Subversion in American History* (New York, 1972), 1–20.

BRUCE, STEVE, *God Save Ulster: The Religion and Politics of Paisleyism* (Oxford, 1986).

BURNS, R. E., 'The Belfast Letters, the Irish Volunteers and the Catholics, 1778–9', *Review of Politics*, 21 (1959), 678–91.

—— 'The Catholic Relief Act in Ireland, 1778', *Church History*, 32 (1963), 181–206.

BURRELL, S. A., 'The Apocalyptic Vision of the Early Covenanters', *Scottish Historical Review*, 43 (1964), 1–24.

CAMPBELL, A. A., *Notes on the Literary History of Strabane* (Omagh, 1902).

CAMPBELL, JOHN, *Short History of the Non-Subscribing Presbyterian Church of Ireland* (Belfast, 1914).

CLAEYS, GREGORY, *Thomas Paine: Social and Political Thought* (Boston, 1989).

—— 'The French Revolution Debate and British Political Thought', *History of Political Thought*, 2 (1990), 59–80.

CLARK, I. D. L., 'From Protest to Reaction: The Moderate Regime in the Church of Scotland, 1752–1805', in N. T. Phillipson and Rosalind Mitchell (eds.), *Scotland in the Age of Improvement* (Edinburgh, 1970), 200–24.

CLARK, J. C. D., *English Society 1688–1832: Ideology, Social Structure and Political Practice During the Ancien Regime* (Cambridge, 1985).

—— 'On Hitting the Buffers: The Historiography of England's Ancien Regime: A Response', *Past & Present*, 117 (November 1987), 194–207.

—— 'England's *Ancien Regime* as a Confessional State', *Albion*, 21 (1989), 450–74.

CLARK, J. C. D., *The Language of Liberty 1660–1832: Political Discourse and Social Dynamics in the Anglo-American World* (Cambridge, 1994).

CLARK, W. S., *The Irish Stage in the County Towns 1720–1800* (Oxford, 1965).

CLARKSON, L. A., 'Armagh 1770: Portrait of an Urban Community', in D. W. Harkness and Mary O'Dowd (eds.), *The Town in Ireland*, Historical Studies no. 18 (Belfast, 1981), 81–102.

CONNOLLY, S. J., 'Violence and Order in the Eighteenth Century', in T. P. O'Flanagan, P. Ferguson, and Kevin Whelan (eds.), *Rural Ireland: Modernisation and Change* (Cork, 1987), 42–61.

—— *Religion, Law, and Power: The Making of Protestant Ireland 1660–1760* (Oxford, 1992).

—— 'Eighteenth-Century Ireland: Colony or *ancien régime*?', in D. G. Boyce and Alan O'Day (eds.), *The Making of Modern Irish History: Revisionism and the Revisionist Controversy* (London, 1996), 15–33.

CONWAY, STEPHEN, *The War of American Independence 1775–1783* (London, 1995), ch. 8.

COWAN, I. B., *The Scottish Covenanters 1660–1688* (London, 1976).

—— *The Scottish Reformation: Church and Society in Sixteenth-Century Scotland* (London, 1982).

CRAWFORD, W. H., 'Change in Ulster in the Late Eighteenth Century', in T. Bartlett and D. W. Hayton (eds.), *Penal Era and Golden Age* (Belfast, 1979), 186–203.

—— 'The Belfast Middle Classes in the Late Eighteenth Century', in D. Dickson, D. Keogh, and K. Whelan (eds.), *The United Irishmen* (Dublin, 1993), 62–73.

CULLEN, L. M., 'Population Trends in Seventeenth-Century Ireland', *Economic and Social Review*, 6 (1975), 149–65.

—— *The Emergence of Modern Ireland 1600–1900* (London, 1981).

—— 'The 1798 Rebellion in its Eighteenth-Century Context', in P. J. Corish (ed.), *Radicals, Rebels and Establishments*, Historical Studies no. 16 (Belfast, 1985), 91–113.

—— 'Catholics Under the Penal Laws', *Eighteenth-Century Ireland*, 1 (1986), 23–36.

—— 'The 1798 Rebellion in Wexford: United Irishman Organization, Membership, Leadership', in Kevin Whelan (ed.), *Wexford: History and Society* (Dublin, 1987), 248–95.

—— 'The Political Structures of the Defenders', in David Dickson and Hugh Gough (eds.), *Ireland and the French Revolution* (Dublin, 1990).

—— 'The Internal Politics of the United Irishmen', in David Dickson, Dáire Keogh, and Kevin Whelan (eds.), *The United Irishmen: Republicanism, Radicalism and Rebellion* (Dublin, 1993).

—— 'Politics and Rebellion: Wicklow in the 1790s', in Kenttannigan and Kevin Nolan (eds.), *Wicklow History and Society: Interdisciplinary Essays on the History of an Irish County* (Dublin, 1994).

—— 'The Political Troubles of County Armagh: A Comment', *IESH* 23 (1996), 18–23.

CURTIN, N. J., 'The Transformation of the United Irishmen into a Mass-Based Revolutionary Organization, 1794–6', *IHS* 24 (1985), 463–92.

—— 'The United Irish Organization in Ulster: 1795–8', in D. Dickson, D. Keogh, and K. Whelan (eds.), *The United Irishmen* (Dublin, 1993), 209–21.

—— *The United Irishmen: Popular Politics in Ulster and Dublin, 1791–98* (Oxford, 1994).

DAVIES, SIMON, 'The *Northern Star* and the Propagation of Enlightened Ideas', *Eighteenth-Century Ireland*, 5 (1990), 143–52.

DICKINSON, H. T., 'The Eighteenth-Century Debate on the Glorious Revolution', *History*, 61 (1976), 28–45.

—— *Liberty and Property: Political Ideology in Eighteenth-Century Britain* (London, 1977).

DICKSON, CHARLES, *Revolt in the North: Antrim and Down in 1798* (Dublin, 1960).

DICKSON, DAVID, 'Catholics and Trade in Eighteenth-Century Ireland: An Old Debate Revisited', in T. P. Power and Kevin Whelan (eds.), *Endurance and Emergence: Catholics in Ireland in the Eighteenth Century* (Dublin, 1990), 85–100.

—— and GOUGH, HUGH (eds.), *Ireland and the French Revolution* (Dublin, 1990).

—— KEOGH, DÁIRE, and WHELAN, KEVIN (eds.), *The United Irishmen: Republicanism, Radicalism and Rebellion* (Dublin, 1993).

DICKSON, R. J., *Ulster Emigration to Colonial America 1718–1775*, 2nd edn., with a new introduction by G. E. Kirkham (Omagh, 1988).

DONALDSON, G., *The Scottish Reformation* (Cambridge, 1960).

DONNELLY, J. S., JUN., 'The Rightboy Movement, 1785–8', *Studia Hibernica*, 17–18 (1977–8).

—— 'The Whiteboy Movement 1761–5', *IHS* 21 (1978).

—— 'Propagating the Cause of the United Irishmen', *Studies: An Irish Quarterly Review*, 69 (1980), 5–23.

—— 'Hearts of Oak, Hearts of Steel', *Studia Hibernica*, 21 (1981), 7–73.

—— 'Irish Agrarian Rebellion: The Whiteboys of 1769–76', *PRIA* 83C, no. 12 (1983).

DONOVAN, R. K., 'The Military Origins of the Roman Catholic Relief Programme of 1778', *Historical Journal*, 28 (1985), 79–102.

—— 'The Popular Party of the Church of Scotland and the American Revolution', in R. B. Sher and J. R. Smitten (eds.), *Scotland and America in the Age of Enlightenment* (Edinburgh, 1990), 81–99.

DOYLE, D. N., *Ireland, Irishmen and Revolutionary America, 1760–1820* (Dublin, 1981).

DUNN, JOHN, 'The Politics of Locke in England and America in the Eighteenth Century', in J. W. Yolton (ed.), *John Locke: Problems and Perspectives* (Cambridge, 1969), 45–80.

ECCLESHALL, ROBERT, 'Anglican Political Thought in the Century after the Revolution of 1688', in D. G. Boyce, R. Eccleshall, and V. Geoghegan (eds.), *Political Thought in Ireland* (London, 1993), 36–72.

ELLIOTT, MARIANNE, *Partners in Revolution: The United Irishmen and France* (New Haven, 1982).

—— *Watchmen in Sion: The Protestant Idea of Liberty* (Derry, 1985).

—— *Wolfe Tone: Prophet of Irish Independence* (New Haven, 1989).

FAGERSTROM, D. I., 'Scottish Opinion and the American Revolution', *WMQ*, 3rd ser., 11 (1954), 252–75.

FISHER, J. R., and ROBB, J. H., *Royal Belfast Academical Institution: Centenary Volume 1810–1910* (Belfast, 1913).

FISHER, R. S., '*The Brigh': Worship and Service over 375 Years* (n.p., [1990]).

FISK, W. L., 'The Diary of John Cuthbertson, Missionary to the Covenanters in Colonial Pennsylvania', *Pennsylvania Magazine of History and Biography*, 73 (1949), 441–58.

FITZPATRICK, MARTIN, 'Toleration and Truth', *Enlightenment and Dissent*, 1 (1982), 3–31.

—— 'Heretical Religion and Radical Political Ideas in Late Eighteenth-Century England', in E. Hellmuth (ed.), *Transformation of Political Culture* (Oxford, 1990), 338–72.

FORBES, DUNCAN, *Hume's Philosophical Politics* (Cambridge, 1975).

—— 'Sceptical Whiggism, Commerce and Liberty', in A. S. Skinner and T. Wilson (eds.), *Essays on Adam Smith* (Oxford, 1975), 179–201.

FORD, ALAN, McGUIRE, JAMES, and MILNE, KENNETH (eds.), *As by Law Established: The Church of Ireland since the Reformation* (Dublin, 1995).

FOSTER, R. F., *Modern Ireland 1600–1972* (London, 1988).

FRUCHTMAN, JACK, JUN., 'The Apocalyptic Politics of Richard Price and Joseph Priestley: A Study in Late Eighteenth-Century Millennialism', *Transactions of the American Philosophical Society*, 73/4 (1983).

GAILEY, ALAN, 'The Scots Element in North Irish Popular Culture', *Ethnologia Europaea*, 8 (1975), 2–22.

GARRETT, CLARK, *Respectable Folly: Millenarians and the French Revolution in France and England* (Baltimore, 1975).

GIBBONS, LUKE, 'Identity without a Centre: Allegory, History and Irish Nationalism', in id., *Transformations in Irish Culture* (Cork, 1996), 134–47.

GILLESPIE, RAYMOND, *Colonial Ulster: The Settlement of East Ulster, 1600–1641* (Cork, 1985).

—— and O'SULLIVAN, HAROLD (eds.), *The Borderlands: Essays on the History of the Ulster–Leinster Border* (Belfast, 1989).

—— 'The Presbyterian Revolution in Ulster, 1660–1690', in W. J. Sheils and Diana Wood (eds.), *Studies in Church History*, xxv, *The Churches, Ireland and the Irish* (Oxford, 1989), 159–70.

GOLDIE, MARK, 'The Civil Religion of James Harrington', in Anthony Pagden (ed.), *The Languages of Political Theory in Early-Modern Europe* (Cambridge, 1987), 197–222.

GOOD, J. W., *Ulster and Ireland* (Dublin, 1919).

GREEN, E. R. R., 'The Scotch-Irish and The Coming of the Revolution in North Carolina', *IHS* 7/26 (September 1950), 77–86.

—— *Essays in Scotch-Irish History* (London, 1969).

GREENE, JACK, *Peripheries and Center: Constitutional Development in the Extended Polities of the British Empire and the United States, 1606–1788* (Athens, Ga., 1986).

HAAKONSSEN, KNUD, *Enlightenment and Religion: Rational Dissent in Eighteenth-Century Britain* (Cambridge, 1996).

HAIRE, J. L. M. (ed.), *Challenge and Conflict: Essays in Irish Presbyterian History and Doctrine* (Antrim, 1981).

HANNIGAN, KEN, and NOLAN, WILLIAM (eds.), *Wicklow History and Society: Interdisciplinary Essays on the History of an Irish County* (Dublin, 1994).

HARRISON, J. F. C., *The Second Coming: Popular Millenarianism 1780–1850* (London, 1979).

HATCH, N. O., *The Sacred Cause of Liberty: Republican Thought and the Millennium in Revolutionary New England* (New Haven, 1977).

HAYTON, D. W., 'The Beginnings of the "Undertaker System"', in T. Bartlett and D. W. Hayton, *Penal Era and Golden Age* (Belfast, 1979), 32–54.

—— 'Anglo-Irish Attitudes: Changing Perceptions of National Identity among the Protestant Ascendancy in Ireland, *c*.1690–1750', *Studies in Eighteenth-Century Culture*, 17 (1987), 145–57.

—— 'The Williamite Revolution in Ireland, 1688–91', in Jonathan Israel (ed.), *The Anglo-Dutch Moment: Essays on the Glorious Revolution and its World Impact* (Cambridge, 1991), 185–213.

—— 'Exclusion, Conformity and Parliamentary Representation: The Impact of the Sacramental Test on Irish Dissenting Politics', in K. Herlihy (ed.), *The Politics of Irish Dissent* (Dublin, 1997).

HELLMUTH, ECKHART (ed.), *The Transformation of Political Culture: England and Germany in the Late Eighteenth Century* (Oxford, 1990).

HEMPTON, DAVID, 'Religion in British Society 1740–1790', in Jeremy Black (ed.), *British Politics and Society from Walpole to Pitt 1742–1789* (London, 1990), 201–21.

—— and HILL, MYRTLE, *Evangelical Protestantism in Ulster Society 1740–1890* (London, 1992).

HERBISON, IVAN, 'Oor Ain Native Tung', in *Talking Scots*, a supplement published with *Fortnight: An Independent Review of Politics and the Arts*, 318 (June 1993).

HERLIHY, KEVIN (ed.), *The Irish Dissenting Tradition, 1650–1750* (Blackrock, Co. Dublin, 1995),

—— (ed.), *The Politics of Irish Dissent, 1650–1800* (Dublin, 1997).

HILL, JACQUELINE, 'Ireland without Union: Molyneux and his Legacy', in John Robertson (ed.), *A Union for Empire: Political Thought and the British Union of 1707* (Cambridge, 1995), 271–96.

HOLMES, R. F. G., 'Controversy and Schism in the Synod of Ulster in the 1820s', in J. L. M. Haire (ed.), *Challenge and Conflict: Essays in Irish Presbyterian History and Doctrine* (Antrim, 1981).

—— *Henry Cooke* (Belfast, 1981).

—— '"Ulster will Fight and Ulster will be Right": The Protestant Churches and Ulster's Resistance to Home Rule, 1912–14', in W. F. Sheils (ed.), *Studies in Church History*, xx, *The Church at War* (Oxford, 1983), 321–35.

—— *Our Irish Presbyterian Heritage* ([Belfast], 1985).

—— 'United Irishmen and Unionists: Irish Presbyterians, 1791 and 1886', in W. J. Sheils and Diana Wood (eds.), *Studies in Church History*, xxv, *The Churches, Ireland and the Irish* (Oxford, 1989), 171–89.

HOOK, ANDREW, and SHER, R. B. (eds.), *The Glasgow Enlightenment* (East Lothian, 1995).

HUTCHINSON, W. R., *Tyrone Precinct: A History of the Plantation Settlement of Dungannon and Mountjoy to Modern Times* (Belfast, 1951).

INNES, JOANNA, 'Review Article: Jonathan Clark, Social History and England's "Ancien Regime"', *Past & Present*, 115 (1987), 165–200.

JACKSON, ALVIN, *The Ulster Party: Irish Unionists in the House of Commons, 1884–1911* (Oxford, 1989).

JACOB, ROSAMUND, *The Rise of the United Irishmen, 1791–94* (London, 1937).

JOHNSTON, E. M., *Great Britain and Ireland 1760–1800: A Study in Political Administration* (Edinburgh, 1963).

—— 'Members of the Irish Parliament, 1784–7', *PRIA* 71C, no. 5 (1971).

JONES, M. A., 'The Scotch-Irish in British America', in Bernard Bailyn and P. D. Morgan (eds.), *Strangers within the Realm: Cultural Margins of the First British Empire* (Chapel Hill, NC, 1991), 284–313.

JUPP, PETER, 'County Down Elections 1783–1831', *IHS* 18 (1972), 177–206.

KELLY, JAMES, 'Inter-Denominational Relations and Religious Toleration in Late Eighteenth-Century Ireland: The "Paper War" of 1786–88', *Eighteenth-Century Ireland*, 3 (1988), 39–57.

—— 'The Parliamentary Reform Movement of the 1780s and the Catholic Question', *Archivium Hibernicum*, 43 (1988), 95–117.

—— 'The Genesis of "Protestant Ascendancy": The Rightboy Disturbances of the 1780s and their Impact upon Protestant Opinion', in G. O'Brien (ed.), *Parliament, Politics and People* (Dublin, 1989), 93–127.

—— 'Relations between the Protestant Church of Ireland and the Presbyterian Church in Late Eighteenth-Century Ireland', *Eire-Ireland*, 23 (1988), 38–56.

—— 'Eighteenth-Century Ascendancy: A Commentary', *Eighteenth-Century Ireland*, 5 (1990).

KELLY, JAMES, *Prelude to Union: Anglo-Irish Politics in the 1780s* (Cork, 1992).

—— '1780 Revisited: The Politics of the Repeal of the Sacramental Test', in K. Herlihy (ed.), *The Politics of Irish Dissent* (Dublin, 1997), 74–92.

—— 'William Molyneux and the Spirit of Liberty in Eighteenth-Century Ireland', *Eighteenth-Century Ireland*, 3 (1988), 133–48.

KELLY, PATRICK, 'Perceptions of Locke in Eighteenth-Century Ireland', *PRIA* 89C, no. 2 (1989), 17–35.

—— 'Ireland and the Glorious Revolution: From Kingdom to Colony', in Robert Beddard (ed.), *The Revolutions of 1688* (Oxford, 1991), 163–90.

KENYON, J. P., *Revolution Principles: The Politics of Party, 1689–1720* (Cambridge, 1977).

KEOGH, DÁIRE, *'The French Disease': The Catholic Church and Radicalism in Ireland 1790–1800* (Dublin, 1993).

—— and FURLONG, NICHOLAS (eds.), *The Mighty Wave: The 1798 Rebellion in Wexford* (Blackrock, Co. Dublin, 1996).

KERNOHAN, J. W., *The Parishes of Kilrea and Tamlaght O'Crilly: A Sketch of their History, with an Account of Boveedy Congregation* (Coleraine, 1912).

—— *The County of Londonderry in Three Centuries* (Belfast, 1921).

KILLEN, JOHN, *A History of the Linenhall Library 1788–1988* (Belfast, 1990).

KRAMNICK, IZAAC, 'Republican Revisionism Revisited', *American Historical Review*, 87 (1982), 629–64.

LAKE, PETER, 'Anti-Popery: The Structure of a Prejudice', in Richard Cust and Ann Hughes (eds.), *Conflict in Early Stuart England: Studies in Religion and Politics* (London, 1989), 72–106.

LANDSMAN, NED, *Scotland and its First American Colony, 1683–1765* (Princeton, 1985).

—— 'Evangelists and their Hearers: Popular Interpretation of Revivalist Preaching in Eighteenth-Century Scotland', *Journal of British Studies*, 28 (1989), 120–49.

LANGFORD, PAUL, 'The English Clergy and the American Revolution', in E. Hellmuth (ed.), *The Transformation of Political Culture* (Oxford, 1990), 338–72.

LATIMER, W. T., 'David Bailie Warden, Patriot 1978', *Ulster Journal of Archaeology*, 2nd ser., 13 (1907), 29–38.

LATOCNAYE, CHEVALIER DE [JACQUES LOUIS BOUGRENET], *A Frenchman's Walk through Ireland*, trans. John Stevenson (Belfast, 1917).

LECKY, A. G., *The Laggan and its Presbyterianism* (Belfast, 1905).

LEERSEN, J. T., 'Anglo-Irish Patriotism and its European Context: Notes Towards a Reassessment', *Eighteenth-Century Ireland*, 3 (1988), 7–24.

LEHMANN, W. C., *John Millar of Glasgow 1735–1801: His Life and Thought and His Contributions to Sociological Analysis* (Cambridge, 1960).

LEIGHTON, C. D. A., *Catholics in a Protestant Kingdom: A Study of the Irish Ancien Régime* (Basingstoke, 1994).

LEPPER, J. H., and CROSSLE, PHILIP, *History of the Grand Lodge of Free and Accepted Masons of Ireland*, 2 vols. (Dublin, 1925).

LOUGHRIDGE, ADAM, *The Covenanters in Ireland* (Belfast, 1984).

MACAFFEE, W., and MORGAN, V., 'Population in Ulster, 1660–1760', in Peter Roebuck (ed.), *Plantation to Partition: Essays in Ulster History in Honour of J. L. McCracken* (Belfast, 1981), 46–63.

McALLISTER, J. L., JUN., 'Francis Alison and John Witherspoon: Political Philosophers and Revolutionaries', *Journal of the Presbyterian Historical Society*, 54 (1976), 33–60.

McBride, Ian, 'William Drennan and the Dissenting Tradition', in D. Dickson, D. Keogh, and K. Whelan, *The United Irishmen* (Dublin, 1993), 49–61.

—— '"The School of Virtue": Francis Hutcheson, Irish Presbyterians and the Scottish Enlightenment', in D. G. Boyce, R. Eccleshall, and V. Geoghegan (eds.), *Political Thought in Ireland* (London, 1993), 73–99.

—— 'Presbyterians in the Penal Era', *Bullán: An Irish Studies Journal*, 1/2 (Autumn 1994), 73–86.

McCabe, Leo, *Wolfe Tone and the United Irishmen: For or Against Christ?* (London, 1937).

McCalman, Iain, 'New Jerusalems: Prophecy, Dissent and Radical Culture in England, 1786–1830', in Knud Haakonssen, *Enlightenment and Religion* (Cambridge, 1996), 312–35.

McCann, Eamonn, *War and an Irish Town*, 3rd edn. (London, 1993).

McClelland, Aiken, 'Thomas Ledlie Birch, United Irishman', *Proceedings and Reports of the Belfast Natural History and Philosophy Society*, 2nd ser., 7 (1965), 24–35.

MacDermot, Frank, *Theobald Wolfe Tone: A Biographical Study* (London, 1939).

MacDonagh, Michael, *The Viceroy's Post-Bag: Correspondence Hitherto Unpublished of the Earl of Hardwicke First Lord Lieutenant of Ireland after the Union* (London, 1904).

MacDonagh, Oliver, *O'Connell: The Life of Daniel O'Connell 1775–1847* (London, 1991).

McDowell, R. B., 'The Personnel of the Dublin Society of United Irishmen, 1791–4', *IHS* 2 (1940), 12–53.

—— *Irish Public Opinion, 1750–1800* (London, 1944).

—— *Public Opinion and Government Policy in Ireland, 1801–1846* (London, 1952).

—— *Ireland in the Age of Imperialism and Revolution* (Oxford, 1979).

McEvoy, Brendan, 'The United Irishmen in County Tyrone', *Seanchas Ardmhacha*, 3 (1959), 283–314 (part 1); 4 (1960–1), 1–32 (part 2); 6 (1969), 37–65 (part 3).

McFarland, E. W., *Ireland and Scotland in the Age of Revolution: Planting the Green Bough* (Edinburgh, 1994).

McFarland, S. S., *Presbyterianism in Maghera: A Social and Congregational History* (Maghera, 1985).

McGuire, J. L., 'The Irish Parliament of 1692', in T. Bartlett and D. W. Hayton, *Penal Era and Golden Age* (Belfast, 1979), 1–31.

McMinn, J. R. B., 'Presbyterianism and Politics in Ulster, 1871–1906', *Studia Hibernica*, 21 (1981), 127–46.

McNeill, Mary, *The Life and Times of Mary Ann McCracken, 1770–1866: A Belfast Panorama*, 2nd edn. (Belfast, 1988).

Mac Poilin, Aodan, 'The Most "Expressive and Polished" Language', *Fortnight: An Independent Review of Politics and the Arts*, 287 (September 1990), 29.

Maguire, W. A., 'Arthur MacMahon, United Irishman and French Soldier', *Irish Sword*, 9 (1969–70), 207–15.

—— 'Lord Donegall and the Hearts of Steel', *IHS* 21 (1979), 351–76.

Malcomson, A. P. W., 'Election Politics in the Borough of Antrim, 1750–1800', *IHS* 27 (1970), 32–57.

—— *John Foster: The Politics of the Anglo-Irish Ascendancy* (Oxford, 1978).

Mant, Richard, *History of the Church of Ireland*, 3 vols. (London, 1840).

Miller, D. W., 'Presbyterianism and "Modernization" in Ulster', *Past & Present*, 80 (1978), 66–90.

—— *Queen's Rebels: Ulster Loyalism in Historical Perspective* (Dublin, 1978).

MILLER, D. W., 'Politicisation in Revolutionary Ireland: The Case of the Armagh Troubles', *IESH* 23 (1996), 1–17.

MILLER, K. A., *Emigrants and Exiles: Ireland and the Irish Exodus to North America* (New York, 1985).

MILLIN, S. S., *History of the Second Congregation of Protestant Dissenters in Belfast*, new edn. (Belfast, 1930).

MOODY, T. W., and VAUGHAN, W. E. (eds.), *A New History of Ireland*, iv, *Eighteenth-Century Ireland 1690–1800* (Oxford, 1986).

MOORE, JAMES, and SILVERTHORNE, MICHAEL, 'Gershom Carmichael and the Natural Jurisprudence Tradition in Eighteenth-Century Scotland', in Istvan Hont and Michael Ignatieff (eds.), *Wealth and Virtue: The Shaping of Political Economy in the Scottish Enlightenment* (Cambridge, 1983), 73–87.

MORROW, ANDREW, 'The Revd Samuel Barber, A. M., and the Rathfriland Volunteers', *UJA*, 2nd ser., 24 (1908).

MURPHY, DESMOND, *Derry, Donegal and Modern Ulster 1790–1921* (Londonderry, 1981).

MURRAY, DAVID, *Memories of the Old College of Glasgow* (Glasgow, 1927).

NORTON, D. F., 'Francis Hutcheson in America', *SVEC* 114 (1976), 1553–5.

O'BRIEN, GERARD (ed.), *Parliament, Politics and People: Essays in Eighteenth-Century Irish History* (Dublin, 1989).

O'BRIEN, SUSAN, 'A Transatlantic Community of Saints: The Great Awakening and the First Evangelical Network, 1735–1755', *American Historical Review*, 91 (1986), 811–32.

Ó BUACHALLA, BREANDÁN, 'Irish Jacobitism and Irish Nationalism: the Literary Evidence', in Michael O'Dea and Kevin Whelan (eds.), *Nations and Nationalisms: France, Britain, Ireland and the Eighteenth-Century Context* (Oxford, 1995), 103–16.

O'DONOVAN, DECLAN, 'The Money Bill Dispute of 1753', in T. Bartlett and D. W. Hayton, *Penal Era and Golden Age* (Belfast, 1979), 55–87.

O'GORMAN, FRANK, *Voters, Patrons, and Parties: The Unreformed Electoral System of Hanoverian England 1734–1832* (Oxford, 1989).

OLIVER, W. H., *Prophets and Millennialists: The Uses of Biblical Prophecy in England from the 1790s to the 1840s* (Auckland, 1978).

OLLERENSHAW, PHILIP, 'Businessmen in Northern Ireland and the Imperial Connection, 1886–1939', in Keith Jeffrey (ed.), *'An Irish Empire'? Aspects of Ireland and the British Empire* (Manchester, 1996), 169–90.

PAKENHAM, THOMAS, *The Year of Liberty: The Story of the Great Rebellion of 1798* (London, 1982).

PARSSINEN, T. M., 'Association, Convention and Anti-Parliament in British Radical Politics, 1771–1848', *English Historical Review*, 88 (1973), 504–33.

PATTERSON, T. G. F., 'The County Armagh Volunteers of 1778–1793', in *UJA*, 3rd ser., 4–7 (1941–4).

—— 'The Volunteer Companies of Ulster, 1778–1793', *Irish Sword*, 7 (1965–6), 91–116, 204–30, 308–12, and 8 (1967–8), 23–32, 92–7, 210–17.

PHILP, MARK, 'Rational Religion and Political Radicalism', *Enlightenment and Dissent*, 4 (1985), 35–46.

POCOCK, J. G. A., 'Machiavelli, Harrington, and English Political Ideologies in the Eighteenth Century', *WMQ*, 3rd ser., 22 (1965), 556–7.

—— 'The Revolution against Parliament', in id. (ed.), *Three British Revolutions: 1641, 1688, 1776* (Princeton, 1980), 265–88.

—— 'Cambridge Paradigms and Scotch Philosophers: A Study of the Relations between the Civic Humanist and the Civil Jurisprudential Interpretation of Eighteenth-Century Political Social Thought', in I. Hont and M. Ignatieff, *Wealth and Virtue* (Cambridge, 1983), 235–52.

—— *Virtue, Commerce and History: Essays on Political Thought and History, Chiefly in the Eighteenth Century* (Cambridge, 1985).

—— 'Between Gog and Magog: The Republican Thesis and the Ideologia *Americana*', *Journal of the History of Ideas*, 48 (1987), 325–46.

—— 'Within the Margins: The Definitions of Orthodoxy', in Roger D. Lund (ed.), *The Margins of Orthodoxy: Heterodox Writing and Cultural Response, 1660–1750* (Cambridge, 1995), 33–53.

POWER, T. P., and WHELAN, KEVIN (eds.), *Endurance and Emergence: Catholics in Ireland in the Eighteenth Century* (Dublin, 1990).

RICHEY, R. E., 'The Origins of British Radicalism: The Changing Rationale for Dissent', *Eighteenth-Century Studies*, 7 (1973–4), 179–92.

ROBBINS, CAROLINE, ' "When it is that Colonies May Turn Independent": An Analysis of the Environment and Politics of Francis Hutcheson (1694–1746)', *WMQ*, 3rd ser., 11 (1954), 214–51.

ROBERTSON, JOHN, *The Scottish Enlightenment and the Militia Issue* (Edinburgh, 1985).

ROBINSON, P. S., *The Plantation of Ulster: British Settlement in an Irish Landscape* (Dublin, 1984).

ROGERS, PATRICK, *The Irish Volunteers and Catholic Emancipation (1778–1793)* (London, 1934).

RUSHE, D. C., 'William Arnold, Minister of Ballybay, First Presbyterian Congregation, County Monaghan', *UJA*, 2nd ser., 14 (1908), 32.

SAYLES, G. O., 'Contemporary Sketches of the Members of the Irish Parliament in 1782', *PRIA* 56C, no. 3 (1954).

SCHMIDT, L. E., *Holy Fairs: Scottish Communions and American Revivals in the Early Modern Period* (Princeton, 1989).

SEED, JOHN, 'Gentlemen Dissenters: The Social and Political Meanings of Rational Dissent in the 1770s and 1780s', *Historical Journal*, 28 (1985), 299–325.

SENIOR, HEREWARD, *Orangeism in Ireland and Britain, 1795–1836* (London, 1966).

SHEILS, W. J., and WOOD, D. (eds.), *Studies in Church History*, xv, *The Church, Ireland and the Irish* (Oxford, 1989).

SHER, R. B., *Church and University in the Scottish Enlightenment: The Moderate Literati of Edinburgh* (Princeton, 1985).

—— 'Professors of Virtue: The Social History of the Edinburgh Moral Philosophy Chair in the Eighteenth Century', in M. A. Stewart, *Studies in the Philosophy of the Scottish Enlightenment* (Oxford, 1990), 87–126.

—— '1688 and 1788: William Robertson on Revolution in Britain and France', in Paul Dukes and John Dunkley (eds.), *Culture and Revolution* (London, 1990), 98–109.

SIMMS, J. G., 'The Making of a Penal Law (2 Anne, C. 6), 1703–4', *IHS* 12 (1960), 105–18.

SMART, I. M., 'The Political Ideas of the Scottish Covenanters 1638–88', *History of Political Thought*, 1 (1980), 167–93.

SMITH, GEORGE, *Belfast Literary Society 1801–1901: Historical Sketch* (Belfast, 1902).

SMOUT, T. C., LANDSMAN, N. C., and DEVINE, T. M., 'Scottish Emigration in the Seventeenth and Eighteenth Centuries', in Nicholas Canny (ed.), *Europeans on the Move: Studies on European Migration, 1500–1800* (Oxford, 1994), 76–112.

SMYTH, JIM, *The Men of No Property: Irish Radicals and Popular Politics in the Late Eighteenth Century* (London, 1992).

SMYTH, PETER, ' "Our Cloud Cap't Grenadiers": The Volunteers as a Military Force', *Irish Sword*, 13 (1978–9), 185–207.

—— 'The Volunteers and Parliament', in T. Bartlett and D. W. Hayton (eds.), *Penal Era and Golden Age* (Belfast, 1979), 115–36.

STEVENSON, DAVID, *The Scottish Revolution, 1637–44: The Triumph of the Covenanters* (Newton Abbot, 1973).

STEVENSON, JOHN, *Two Centuries of Life in Down, 1600–1800* (Belfast, 1990; first pub. 1920).

STEWART, A. T. Q., ' "A Stable Unseen Power": Dr William Drennan and the Origins of the United Irishmen', in John Bossy and Peter Jupp (eds.), *Essays Presented to Michael Roberts* (Belfast, 1976), 80–92.

—— *The Narrow Ground: Aspects of Ulster 1609–1969* (London, 1977).

—— *A Deeper Silence: The Hidden Origins of the United Irishmen* (London, 1993).

—— *The Summer Soldiers: The 1798 Rebellion in Antrim and Down* (Belfast, 1995).

STEWART, DAVID, *The Seceders in Ireland with Annals of their Congregations* (Belfast, 1950).

STEWART, M. A., 'Rational Dissent in Early Eighteenth-Century Ireland', in Knud Haakonssen (ed.), *Enlightenment and Religion: Rational Dissent in Eighteenth-Century Britain* (Cambridge, 1996), 42–63.

—— (ed.), *Studies in the Philosophy of the Scottish Enlightenment* (Oxford, 1990).

STRAIN, R. W. M., *Belfast and its Charitable Society: A Story of Urban Social Development* (London, 1961).

THOMPSON, E. P., *The Making of the English Working Class*, 3rd edn. (London, 1988; first pub. 1963).

—— *Customs in Common* (London, 1991).

THOMSON, JOSEPH, 'The Evangelical Society of Ulster', *Bulletin of the Presbyterian Historical Society of Ireland*, 17 (March 1988).

THUENTE, M. H., *The Harp Restrung: The United Irishmen and the Rise of Irish Literary Nationalism* (Syracuse, NY, 1994).

TRINTERUD, L. J., *The Forming of an American Tradition: A Re-examination of Colonial Presbyterianism* (Philadelphia, 1949).

TULLY, JAMES, *An Approach to Political Philosophy: Locke in Contexts* (Cambridge, 1993).

—— 'Placing the "Two Treatises" ', in Nicholas Phillipson and Quentin Skinner (eds.), *Political Discourse in Early Modern Britain* (Cambridge, 1993), 253–80.

VICTORY, ISOLDE, 'The Making of the 1720 Declaratory Act', in G. O'Brien (ed.), *Parliament, Politics and People* (Dublin, 1989), 9–29.

VINCENT, EMMA, 'The Responses of Scottish Churchmen to the French Revolution, 1789–1802', *Scottish Historical Review*, 73 (1994), 191–215

WALKER, B. M., *Ulster Politics: The Formative Years 1868–86* (Belfast, 1989).

WALKER, GRAHAM, *Intimate Strangers: Political and Cultural Interaction between Scotland and Ulster in Modern Times* (Edinburgh, 1995).

WALL, MAUREEN, *Catholic Ireland in the Eighteenth Century: Collected Essays of Maureen Wall*, ed. Gerard O'Brien (Dublin, 1989).

—— 'The United Irish Movement', *Historical Studies*, 5 (1965), 122–40.

WESTERKAMP, M. J., *Triumph of the Laity: Scots-Irish Piety and the Great Awakening, 1625–1760* (Oxford, 1988).

WHELAN, KEVIN, 'The Religious Factor in the 1798 Rebellion in County Wexford', in Patrick O'Flanagan *et al.* (eds.), *Rural Ireland 1600–1900: Modernization and Change* (Cork, 1987).

—— 'Politicization in County Wexford and the Origins of the 1798 Rebellion', in David Dickson and Hugh Gough (eds.), *Ireland and the French Revolution* (Dublin, 1990).

—— 'Reinterpreting the 1798 Rebellion in County Wexford', in Dáire Keogh and Nicholas Furlong (eds.), *The Mighty Wave* (Blackrock, Co. Dublin, 1996).

—— *The Tree of Liberty: Radicalism, Catholicism and the Construction of Irish Idenity 1760–1830* (Cork, 1996).

WHYTE, JOHN, *Interpreting Northern Ireland* (Oxford, 1991).

WINCH, DONALD, *Adam Smith's Politics: An Essay in Historiographic Revision* (Cambridge, 1978).

WOODBURN, J. B., *The Ulster Scot: His History and Religion* (London, 1914).

WRIGHT, FRANK, 'Protestant Ideology and Politics in Ulster', *European Journal of Sociology*, 14 (1973), 213–80.

—— *Two Lands on One Soil: Ulster Politics before Home Rule* (Dublin, 1996).

Theses

BARRETT, R. J., 'A Comparative Study of Imperial Constitutional Theory in Ireland and America in the Age of the American Revolution', Ph.D. thesis (Trinity College Dublin, 1958).

BLACKSTOCK, A. F., 'The Origin and Development of the Irish Yeomanry, 1796–*c*.1807', Ph.D. thesis (QUB, 1993).

BROOKE, PETER, 'Controversies in Ulster Presbyterianism, 1790–1836', Ph.D. thesis (Cambridge, 1980).

BROWN, A. W. G., 'Irish Presbyterian Theology in the Early Eighteenth Century', Ph.D. thesis (QUB, 1977).

BROWN, L. T., 'The Presbyterians of Cavan and Monaghan: An Immigrant Community in South Ulster over Three Generations', Ph.D. thesis (QUB, 1986).

CANAVAN, ANTHONY, 'The Hearts of Steel: Agrarian Protest in Ulster 1769–1773', MA thesis (QUB, 1982).

CRAWFORD, W. H., 'Ulster Economy and Society in the Eighteenth Century', Ph.D. thesis (QUB, 1983).

GAMBLE, N. E., 'The Business Community and Trade of Belfast 1767–1800', Ph.D. thesis (University of Dublin, 1978).

HILL, C. P., 'William Drennan and the Radical Movement for Irish Reform 1779–94', M.Litt. thesis, 2 vols. (University of Dublin, 1967).

KELLY, JAMES, 'The Irish Parliamentary Reform Movement: The Administration and Popular Politics, 1783–5', MA thesis (UCD, 1981).

MCMILLAN, WILLIAM, 'The Subscription Controversy in Irish Presbyterianism from the Plantation of Ulster to the Present Day: With Special Reference to Political Implications in the Late Eighteenth Century', MA thesis (Manchester University, 1959).

SMYTH, P. D. H., 'The Volunteer Movement in Ulster: Background and Development 1745–85', Ph.D. thesis (QUB, 1974).

STEWART, A. T. Q., 'The Transformation of Presbyterian Radicalism in the North of Ireland, 1792–1825', MA thesis (QUB, 1956).

VICTORY, ISOLDE, 'Colonial Nationalism in Ireland 1692–1725: From Common Law to Natural Right', Ph.D. thesis (University of Dublin, 1984).

INDEX